THE BBC: Public Institution and Private World

LIBRARIES NI
WITHDRAWN FROM STOCK

EDINBURGH STUDIES IN SOCIOLOGY

General Editors: TOM BURNS, TOM MCGLEW, GIANFRANCO POGGI

In the same series

Published

John Orr: TRAGIC REALISM AND MODERN SOCIETY: STUDIES IN THE SOCIOLOGY OF THE MODERN NOVEL

Forthcoming titles

Anthony P. M. Coxon and Charles L. Jones: THE IMAGES OF OCCUPATIONAL PRESTIGE

Anthony P. M. Coxon and Charles L. Jones: SOCIAL MEANINGS OF OCCUPATIONS

Anthony P. M. Coxon and Charles L. Jones: TECHNIQUES AND METHODS IN OCCUPATIONAL COGNITION

THE BBC

Public Institution and Private World

TOM BURNS

© Tom Burns 1977

All rights reserved. No part of this publication may be reproduced or transmitted, in any form of by any means, without permission

First published 1977 by
THE MACMILLAN PRESS LTD
London and Basingstoke

Associated companies in Delhi Dublin Hong Kong Johannesburg Lagos Melbourne New York Singapore Tokyo

Printed in Great Britain by
REDWOOD BURN LIMITED
Trowbridge & Esher

British Library Cataloguing in Publication Data

Burns, Tom, b. 1913
The BBC: – (Edinburgh studies in sociology)
1. British Broadcasting Corporation
2. Broadcasting – Social aspects – Great Britain
I. Title II. Series
301.16′1 HE8689.9.G7

ISBN 0–333–19720–8

This book is sold subject to the standard conditions of the Net Book Agreement

Contents

Acknowledgements vii

Preface ix

1 *PAST AND PRESENT* 1
The Creation of a Social-industrial Complex – The Westminster Connection – Control and Consensus – The Governors and the Public Interest

2 *FROM PUBLIC SERVICE TO PROFESSIONALISM* 34
The Power of Broadcasting – The Idea of Public Service in Broadcasting – The Reithian Ethos – From Monopoly to Competition – Industrial Relations

3 *SETTINGS* 78
Physical Setting – Social Settings – Grading – Social Distinctions – Commitment and Career – The Appointments System and Boardmanship

4 *A PRIVATE WORLD* 122
Professionalism as a Moral Order – Against the Image of Public Service – Cryptomicrocosmos – BBC Policy and Internal Politics

5 *PRESS FREEDOM AND BROADCASTING LIBERTIES* 155
The National Interest and the Public Good – Into Politics – The Pride and Terror of Broadcasting – Divisions and Dimensions – The Fourth Estate – From News Bulletins to 'Yesterday's Men'

6 *THE SERVANT OF TWO MASTERS* 186
The Politics of Accommodation – Eyes, ravenous and half-shut; Mirrors, ugly and in corners; the Manufacture of Bad News from Nowhere, etc. etc. – Technical Constraints –

Organisational Controls – The Rhetoric and the Grammar of Broadcast Journalism – The Corporate Idea – The Adversary Stance – Beating the Clock – 'Viewability'

7 *MANAGING THE BBC* 211
The Industrialisation of the BBC – A Segmented Organisation – Financial Pressures – The 'McKinsey Reorganisation' – The Planning Cycle – Under New Management

8 *MANAGEMENT STRUCTURE AND ORGANISATIONAL PROCESS* 252
The New Managerialism – The Expropriation of Commitment – The Common Interests of Common Resources – The Conditions of Engagement as a Human Resource – Social Interaction, Skilled and Unskilled – Organisational Processes within Management – The BBC as Unfinished Business

Notes 298

Index 309

Acknowledgements

Both Mr Oliver Whitley, who did so much to make it possible for me to begin this whole study, and Sir Charles Curran, who not only permitted but encouraged me to finish it, knew well enough that the result would be critical of many aspects of BBC policy and organisation. They are both entitled to a good deal more credit than the bare acknowledgement of my own indebtedness affords them. In similar, though more limited ways, I am indebted to trade union officials and, of course, to the three hundred or so members of the BBC who were prepared to let me interrupt their work and to describe, show, explain and discuss the work of the BBC and their place in it.

Earlier drafts have been seen by a number of members and ex-members of the BBC – including, of course, Oliver Whitley and Sir Charles Curran. These comments brought to light one or two errors of fact which I have corrected. The Director General and one or two present members of staff have, naturally, disagreed strongly with my interpretations of some of the situations I have described but have also, in every case, fully acknowledged my right to adhere to my own views.

I have also to thank Lord Annan, Stuart Hood, Antony Jay, Dipak Nandy, John Tusa, Donald Schon, Everett Hughes and Benson Snyder, all of whom have seen the book in penultimate draft and sent comments which were, at so late a stage, especially helpful and encouraging.

My wife, Elizabeth Burns, has done her best to deliver the reader from the more tortuous or obscure passages of writing, to meet unending demands for help in sorting out my ideas and to supply courage for my convictions.

The knowledge that I could depend on Violet Laidlaw to translate successive drafts, badly written and worse typed, into a readable, presentable, manuscript has been of the greatest value, and I am glad to have this opportunity for acknowledging the high competence she has displayed in this, as in so much else, and for recording my thanks.

Earlier versions of some parts of chapters have been included in articles published at intervals since the first 'working report' was completed – all, I should make it clear, with the consent of the BBC.

They are:

'Des fins et des moyens dans la direction des entreprises', *Sociologie du Travail*, Vol. 3, 1962.

'Public Service and Private World', in P. Halmos (ed.), *The Sociology of Mass Communications*, Sociological Review Monograph 13, 1969, reprinted in J. Tunstall (ed.), *Media Sociology* (Constable, 1970).

'Commitment and Career in the BBC', in D. McQuail (ed.), *Sociology of Mass Communications* (Penguin Books, 1972).

'The Organisation of Public Opinion', in M. Gurevitch (ed.), *Mass Communication and Society*, (Arnold, 1977).

The author and publisher wish to thank the editors of the *Sociological Review* and Edward Arnold (Publishers) Ltd for permission to use previously published material.

T.B.

February 1977

Preface

This book is for the most part based on tape recordings and notes I took during some fifteen weeks spent in the BBC in 1963 and on a second period of study in 1973. It is about the BBC as I have got to know it as a working community and an occupational milieu, about the changes which have taken place during the ten years' interval between the two series of interviews, and about the continuities observable over the same period. It is about the BBC as a public institution, and as an organisation. In all these respects, the BBC is a rather special place, perhaps unique.

Yet just as the 'BBC manner', distinctive as it used to be, is nevertheless an assemblage of elements of conduct styles current in British society at large, so, in much the same way, the organisational structure, the codes of working behaviour, the way people fit their work situation, invest in commitments of different kinds, and try to steer their careers are all in one respect unique to the BBC; but the factors which are discernibly at work are common to many other milieux in which professionals and managers, clerical workers, technicians, and manual workers spend their lives. The distinctive political situation of the BBC and the way it affects the political, social and cultural life of the country can be seen in the same way as a constellation of elements visibly present in a wide variety of different contexts.

The whole study originated, as these things usually do, in the chance concurrence of my own research interests, as they were developing early in the 1960s, with an opportunity for exercising them in an appropriate and accessible setting. In 1960, the BBC had begun a series of management conferences, which still continue, at Uplands, a country house establishment near High Wycombe. Each conference lasted a fortnight, and was attended by twenty or more senior staff drawn from as wide a variety of departments and places as was feasible. The Uplands Conferences were planned and directed by Mr Oliver J. Whitley, then Controller, Staff Training and Appointments.

I was invited early on to contribute to these conferences as an 'outside speaker'. After performing the second time, in May 1961, I was asked if I would be prepared to spend a week at the next conference in October, attending all the lectures and such other meetings as I saw fit, but especially mixing in the extra-curricular proceedings of the conference. The suggestion was attractive, but I made it clear that I had no experience of participant activities of this kind, and, in accepting the invitation, I asked for an opportunity to gain some slight acquaintance with the Corporation in its own setting. This was agreed, and I spent a week or so in September interviewing some twenty people, mostly in senior positions, in a variety of departments in Broadcasting House and Television Centre. At the end of my week at the Uplands conference in October, I delivered myself of some critical observations about the conference and about the Corporation at large which were received courteously, and I think, appreciatively, but were taken no further in discussion.

The episode ended there, but left me in the unsatisfactory position, as a student of occupations and organisations, of having glimpsed some extremely interesting situations bearing closely on my current interests but having far too little evidence on which to do more than speculate. Accordingly, some months later, I wrote to Oliver Whitley asking for permission to prosecute enquiries of the kind I had broached in the preliminary set of interviews at greater length and in more organised fashion. This appeal was received sympathetically. In April 1962, I met the Director of Administration and discussed my proposal, and my interest, with him. In August, I was told that permission for the enquiry was granted, and I arranged to carry it out during the first four months of the following year.

During the early months of 1963, I interviewed about two hundred people. They were confined to members of the staff of four sections of the Corporation, chosen to give a fairly wide array of people and functions: Technical Operations and Maintenance (Engineering), in Television Centre; Schools Broadcasting (Sound and Television); Staff Administration (including Central Establishment Office); and Light Entertainment (Television).

While these departments differ greatly from each other in many respects, they are not, of course, a representative sample of the Corporation's activities or staff. So that while, to avoid the annoyance of perpetual qualification or periphrasis, I shall speak of 'the Corporation', or aspects of it, or of 'staff', or categories of staff, I hope it will be borne in mind that the reference is always to the Corporation as it appears in, or to, those departments I know and the three hundred or so members of the Corporation I met then and later.

I should perhaps say, of the interviews themselves, that the term may be a little misleading; they followed neither the method of the professional journalist (whether accoucheur or wrestler) nor the standardised procedures familiar in social surveys. Although I tried, by the end of a conversation, to see that I had obtained comments or facts on the points I thought relevant or interesting, I used no standard sequence or form of questions; and my ideas of what was interesting or relevant information tended to change, too. The procedure has much more in common, perhaps, with that followed by social anthropologists than with any of the research methods currently practised in sociology. What each interview, or conversation, had in common was a lengthy prefatory statement about my interests and objectives in making the enquiry. These interests and objectives can be summarised as the study of:

> the different commitments in which the individual becomes involved and the ways in which he tries to meet each of them and to reconcile them,

and, secondly,

> the different social systems which are built up out of these commitments – systems such as the working organisation (out of his commitment to his employer), the system of internal politics (out of commitments to fellow members of a department, to people of the same rank, to leaders or dependent followers, to fellow-professionals) and the career system (out of commitment to his own present standing and future prospects).'

There is, then, a double perspective, one individual, the other social. The same material of observation is related both to the individual's own array of commitments and to the social systems existing within the working community of the Corporation. Such systems are defined by their explicit or implicit set of purposes.

Further, I was interested in:

> The interaction of these systems, i.e. the working organisation with the political system, the career system and so forth.

All this had, in fact, been a major focus of interest in a previous study of the electronics industry, in which I had tried to ascertain the factors which seemed to facilitate, or hinder, the capacity of firms to operate effectively in conditions of rapid market and technological change.[1] But I wanted to pursue these matters further, and in the context of rather hazy notions about the widespread tendency to 'professionalise' jobs (particularly evident, I thought, in the Corporation, but observable in most occupational milieux).

The interviews which followed this rather lengthy introduction lasted anywhere from one to three hours. In fact, as I have said, 'conversation' or 'discussion' are less misleading terms than 'interview' for what went on. Having begun by declaring my interests fairly fully at the outset, I often followed this up by interjecting attempts at articulating half-formed impressions or interpretations which had already occurred to me, usually illustrating them at some length from previous research or other experience. In general, therefore, I followed the procedure natural to ordinary discourse, which means that the whole study was conducted in and through these interviews; almost all the interpretative and explanatory ideas put forward in this book occurred – or, often, were suggested – to me in interview, and none of them has not been discussed, developed, or amended during interviews or subsequently in talking with people who were or had been members of the Corporation.

There is no question, therefore, of the interviews – or rather, the records and transcripts made of them – serving as 'data', to be subjected to analysis and interpretation at a later stage. The later stages, after finishing the study, were taken up with repeated reading of my notes and playback of the recording tapes, reconciling and arranging the relevant contents, and composing all I wanted to say in a reasonably coherent and comprehensible way without losing anything of consequence and without misrepresenting it. How successful the procedure turns out to be depends, in the first place, of course, on the competence and experience of the enquirer – and of this all I can say is that I had by then carried out studies, some on similar and others on quite different lines, in some thirty industrial and non-industrial organisations. More especially, any success depends on how non-threatening and intrinsically interesting the researcher can make his enquiries appear to the people he meets. It amounts, in short, to a matter of engaging the people interviewed as willing cooperators in his enquiries – of involving them in the furtherance of the study. Hence, the constant need to make clear what I was up to, and what I was making of the information I had gathered thus far.

Some fifty or sixty of the lengthier interviews in 1963 (and all sixty in 1973) were recorded. I was also able to attend a number of meetings and outside rehearsals, and to spend some time in television studios and control rooms. The method of enquiry, in short, follows much the same lines as those of my earlier studies in industry,[2] except that I was able to record a much higher proportion of interviews. Yet the time I spent in the BBC in 1963 was a quite different personal experience, and not merely because I was met everywhere with civility and consideration, for this is as unfailingly present in industry as in the BBC. Most of the difference lies in the fact that people in the BBC conduct their everyday business, as well as incidental conversations and the more intense discussions of the minutiae of production and design and editing, in an articulate, intelligent and civilised way. There is an urbanity about the Corporation which may be at its polished and uniform best among those who deal with the outside world but which permeates much of the organisation at large.

It seemed to be the prevalence, persistence and consistency of this styling of conduct rather than any distinctive features which lie behind the frequent reference to the 'BBC manner' and even the 'BBC type'; in other words, the reference was to a normative system composed of specific elements – of language, bearing, lines of talk, and social skills – which are severally present in modern British society but which in the Corporation were combined to form an organised code of conduct and values. The code allowed for sizeable differences in attitude, opinion and aspiration: indeed these differences, and the conflicts they engender, formed much of the content of the Corporation's internal business and social life. The manner, in fact, was a way of defining the 'rules of the game' according to which the internal and external business of the Corporation and all the manifold social intercourse to which this business gives rise should be conducted. The most dangerous conflicts, consequently, were those which were expressed, in almost ritualistic terms, by a deliberate departure from the BBC manner, signifying, as they did, a challenge to the 'rules of the game' themselves.

All this had a good deal of effect on the way in which the study developed in terms both of the kind of information which interviews and observation yielded and of the formulation which eventually imposed itself on the information. To begin with, I found the interviews more immediately rewarding and enjoyable than any series I had previously undertaken; but this was not merely a matter of degree – of getting more information and of quicker and better understanding of the point of the enquiry. There was a qualitative difference in the emphasis given to different factors in the organisation itself, at one extreme, and in the occupational situation of its individual members, at the other. The span of considerations seen as relevant to the topics I raised was much wider. It was as if one had moved from the world, say, of C. P. Snow's novels into that of Anthony Powell's.

So that, in the second place, the variety of loosely related interests I had begun with assumed coherence as parts of a general study of the cultural ambience of the Corporation. The BBC 'manner', that is, was the expressive aspect of a normative system, peculiar to the BBC, of behaviour and values which were not. The study therefore developed into an attempt to describe this social and cultural artefact and to explain it in terms of the organisation which sustained it and which it sustained, and in terms of the individuals who consciously or compliantly, self-interestedly or unwillingly, became immersed in the culture of the BBC.

For convenience, I arranged the programme of interviews and observation so as to stay wholly within one department until I had heard and seen enough – i.e., until interviews began to show that little would be added to what I had already learned in that area. In each department the first interviews would be with the senior members, and thereafter I arranged meetings with the rest of the staff as they became free until I had talked with at least half of them. As soon as possible afterwards I composed notes on which I could base a general appreciation of what I had learned, and 'reported back' to the head of department and as many of his juniors as he chose – or I could persuade him – to invite. Meetings with Technical Operations and Maintenance, Television (Engineering) and with Schools Broadcasting (Television and Radio) took place while the study was still in progress; what I had to say was usually well received, and they proved to be extremely useful occasions in which I was able to corroborate and often amend or correct facts and inferences.

Thereafter, I composed a lengthy 'working report' on the whole study. This went to the BBC late in 1964. By that time Oliver Whitley, who had throughout been sympathetic and extremely helpful, had been appointed Chief Assistant to the Director General, and all subsequent dealings were with the Director of Administration and his immediate subordinates. It was quickly made clear to me that their sole interest in the report was in preventing its publication. In this they were able to rely, as they were entitled to do, on the undertaking I had given not to publish anything based on the study without the consent (which did not necessarily mean the approval) of the Corporation. Not only so, but the Administration Division went to what seemed to me at the time insulting lengths in trying to prevent what I am sure they would have called 'leakages', asking that I should guarantee that none of my 'personal' professional colleagues to whom I might show the report would allow the report 'in whole or in part [to] get out, be published or pass beyond these people other than in their private professional capacities' – and this, I may add, at the same time as commending the report itself:

> '. . . . speaking for myself, and I think for those who have also read it, it is certainly interesting and, more than interesting, fascinating. It is also reasonable and balanced, but within its own restricted confines only and provided that you do not take these words as meaning agreement with everything in it. . . . . .'

The one reason advanced for refusing consent was that the BBC was receiving hostile treatment from 'certain newspapers', and that the report could be used as 'a stick to beat it with'.

The whole business remains a puzzle. And the later developments which led not only to a removal of the embargo but to a complete reversal of attitudes, to the point of inviting me to return and, exactly ten years later, to repeat the study, increases the mystery rather than lessens it; because, for the life of me, I am still unable to see anything in that working report which, however ingeniously and maliciously quotations from it were stitched together by some enterprising journalist, could have been half as damaging as, say, the 'disclosures' sold to the press by a Director immediately on his retiring, or the perennial flow of innuendos and hearsay reports which appear in gossip columns and are even printed as news about the internal affairs of the BBC.

'Corporation paranoia', the phrase which has occurred most frequently in the few discussions I've been drawn into about the episode, explains nothing. It is, indeed, meaningless. Nor is it helpful, though perhaps it is a little reassuring, to know that the experience I had fits a common, even international, tradition. Over a quarter of a century ago, Paul Lazarsfeld, the first social scientist of any note to interest himself in broadcasting as a subject of study, wrote:

> 'If there is any one institutional disease to which the media of mass communications seem particularly subject, it is a nervous reaction to criticism. As a student of mass media I have been continually struck and occasionally puzzled by this reaction, for it is the media themselves which so vigorously defend principles guaranteeing the right to criticize.'[3]

Lazarsfeld offered no explanation of this state of affairs beyond the suggestion that one part of the explanation might be that this kind of criticism had not achieved any formal standing as a legitimate field of academic or any other sort of enquiry. There is perhaps some substance in this. The situation is very different now, but at that time I did experience extraordinary difficulty in making clear to officials in Administration who were not the subject of interviews, and had either to be told of what I was doing or be shown the results, just what the purpose and point of it all was. The provenance and purpose of the study were well known, of course, to Oliver Whitley, who did fully understand what I was about and was sympathetic to the undertaking, believing as he did that public corporations like the BBC had public obligations, one of which was certainly to permit, and possibly encourage, investigation into their organisational structure and operating procedures, and into the assumptions, beliefs and values of the people who worked in them and who controlled them.

All this is much in accordance with a tradition which used to be thought of as centrally important in British public affairs, and was held in high regard in Europe. Perhaps the best testimony to this, having regard to the time (1917), the nationality (German), and the weight of authority now carried by his writings, is a passage from one of a series of articles Max Weber wrote for the *Frankfurter Zeitung* on the governmental problems which would face his country after the war:

> 'The integrity of British officialdom and the public's high level of political sophistication are founded on . . . the parliamentary right of enquiry, the mere existence of which will force the administrative chiefs to account for their actions in such a way as to make its use unnecessary . . . This maturity is reflected not in votes of no-confidence, indictments of ministers and similar spectacles of French-Italian unorganised parliamentarism, but in the fact that the nation keeps itself informed about the conduct of its affairs by the bureaucracy.'[5]

Even when they were being written, the words were being disproved by developments which diluted and dissipated this particular accountability and information system almost into nothingness; but Weber's final point was that 'ultimately the bureaucracy can only gain by such a development', and it is this belief that Oliver Whitley shared.

On the other hand, of course, criticism and accountability on these lines and at this level are matters of parliamentary right – whether the right is exercised or not – and it is nowadays improbable that any government department or public corporation created by Parliament which might be (and sometimes, even now, actually is) held answerable in some comparable fashion to Parliament would accept, let alone invite, critical investigation by other agencies or individuals – unless the gain to itself was visible.

I suspect that neither Oliver Whitley's beliefs nor his understanding of the object of the study were shared by his immediate colleagues and superiors. More than once I had to try to make it clear to them that I was not acting as a voluntary and unpaid industrial consultant, which, to revert to Paul Lazarsfeld's remarks, had by then become an understandable and acceptable role; but I was not sure that I had succeeded. And brief as they were, some of the comments on the report, which came exclusively from senior officials in the Administration Directorate who were responsible for 'personnel' matters, reflected some polite puzzlement about the usefulness I thought the work could have for the Corporation's management. If there was no identifiable slot between unpaid consultant and remote (and therefore, presumably, ineffectual) don into which they could fit me, and if, as seemed evident from the report, I was not concerned with making recommendations, giving advice, or even providing the kind of information which management could use to mend whatever needed mending, what the hell was I doing in the BBC? And if the only answer was that I, like any other busybody, was merely satisfying my own curiosity, I suppose it could have seemed positively irresponsible actually to sanction publication of the report (or something based on it), knowing that it could certainly do the BBC no good and might just possibly do it harm. Since I had been good enough to provide a gag for myself by undertaking not to publish without 'the consent, which did not necessarily mean approval', of the BBC, the correct administrative decision was obvious.

After 1970 the situation changed. The entire Board of Management had been replaced by 1973 and it is quite possible to attribute the very different attitude I encountered in 1972 to the ability of the Director General and others, with nobody on the premises having to defend the previous decision, to take an entirely fresh look, and to see that perhaps too much fuss had been made of a relatively unimportant matter. The whole climate had changed, too, in that a sizeable volume of writings had been published on broadcasting and the press, many by broadcasters and journalists, which had commanded widespread and serious attention. At all events, when, in 1972, I had occasion to write to the Director General, I reopened the question of using the material I had collected in 1963 in writing a rather more general essay on the BBC. Not only was assent forthcoming to this proposal but with it came an invitation from the Director General to spend some time again in the Corporation so that I could 'brief' myself on recent developments. This was totally unexpected, and despite the underlying changes in the situation which I have remarked on, and which I believe contributed to the turnaround, was rather handsome. There was, after all, no new and positive reason why the repeated refusals of earlier years should have been reversed; it was easier, in fact, merely to uphold those decisions. There must be few chief executives, and none that I know, who would have done so without any compelling reason other than what must be construed as fairmindedness.

Clearing sufficient time meant a further delay, but eventually, almost exactly ten years after the end of the 1963 study, I spent six or seven weeks interviewing about sixty people, more than half of them senior BBC officials, and collecting other material.

I have thought it proper to relate, as briefly as I could, the history of this piece of writing largely because too many people know part of that history for me to ignore it completely. So I have had to run the risk of parading what were, after all, rather slight frustrations and difficulties partly to explain how what began as a short piece of research, and is still a minor one, took over ten years to see the light of day, and partly to forestall some misconstructions which might otherwise be put on the behaviour of officials, past and present, in the BBC.

Over and above all this, what remains true now, as it was ten years earlier, is my indebtedness to all the BBC people I interviewed. This is meant as more than the usual polite gesture of acknowledgement. Without saddling them with responsibility for the ideas contained in this essay, or for its arrangement and presentation, I have nevertheless to make it clear that their part in this study is much more considerable than is usual in such affairs. The liberal use of quotations in most chapters makes this even clearer. Furthermore, earlier versions both of the first working report and of this essay have been read by and discussed with senior members of the departments in which the earlier study was, for the most part, carried out, and with senior officials more recently. Their comments and criticisms have of course been of the greatest value. In no case have I been asked to remove or dilute passages which seemed to them hostile or unjust, although where I have thought what I had written was wrong, I have corrected it.

I have, throughout, refrained from using the names of present members of the BBC and have tried to ensure that when I have used quotations from recordings of what they said, neither they or anybody they may have mentioned is identifiable – or, that, if they are, they have no objection. Ensuring this has meant that I have sent copies of their quoted utterances to everybody whose words I have used (with one or two exceptions in the case of people of whose names I have no record, because they were interviewed more or less by chance). Consent was readily given in all cases of the 1963 interviews and in all but two or three of the 1973 series; in these few instances, the quotation has been deleted, or reduced to a remark incorporated in my own text.

1 Past and Present

The BBC has always been one of the more self-conscious of British institutions, and the circumstances of its origins and history are better recorded and more widely known than most. Latterly, however, the mixture of reverence for its founders, of affectionate nostalgia for the golden period of its first twenty-five years, and of the general esteem which had become habitual, seems to have thinned. More, the continued existence of the BBC in the form in which it has made itself familiar is being put to the question. For these reasons alone, there is some point in examining some of the history which can be said to have formed the BBC, or at least to have left an indelible mark on it.

So, while there is no point in offering yet one more outline history of the BBC, it is important at the outset of a book which purports to give an account of the BBC as an organisation and as a public institution to recall certain episodes of that history, and to particularise certain decisions and presumptions which have gone to make it what it now is.

THE CREATION OF A SOCIAL-INDUSTRIAL COMPLEX

The British Broadcasting Corporation was founded on 31 December 1926. It was the direct successor of the British Broadcasting Company which had been formed at the end of 1922, inheriting the Company's broadcasting monopoly, its plant, its staff, and its Managing Director, John Reith.

The first thing that has to be said about the British Broadcasting Company is that it was a consortium of manufacturers of domestic wireless receiving sets. Their purpose in financing and organising radio broadcasts was to provide regular transmissions of programmes which people who bought domestic receivers from them could listen to. During the war, wireless telegraphy had been superseded in many respects by wireless telephony; after 1918, messages in common speech were broadcast by the armed services, ships, public authorities commercial concerns, and amateurs, licensed and unlicensed, for anyone with a suitable receiving set to hear. Listening to these messages had become an immensely popular hobby before 1920, and selling receivers a very profitable business.

Technically, broadcasting owed its birth to the accident of wireless messages being openly transmitted in all directions, even though they were intended for specific receivers. There was no 'Gutenberg revolution'. So far as the Post Office, with its monopoly of civil telecommunications, was concerned, broadcasting was a nuisance.

After 1920, the first wave of enthusiasm for the instruments themselves was dying down. Amateur transmitters were few, for each single transmission had to be licensed. The Post Office exercised its powers with a strictness which had the enthusiastic backing of the armed services. The attitude of the Navy, especially, was hostile to any erosion of the monopoly it had enjoyed during the war; it was also concerned about the dangers of interference, the possible intrusion of specific communications and – even more alarming – the ever-present danger of the transmission of joke messages to ships and aircraft of the kind which had achieved some notoriety in the United States.

There was a further complication, of rather long standing. The Marconi Company owned most of the relevant patent rights, both in Britain and in the United States. This is not necessarily a deterrent to the exploitation of innovations for military or civil purposes. But the Marconi Company had been tight-fisted almost to the point of suicide about licensing the manufacture and even sale of transmitters and receivers; for the first part of the century, for example, merchant ships could not buy any of their apparatus, but only lease it, and hire from Marconi an authorised wireless telegraphy operator who continued to be an employee of the company: he was, in fact, familiarly known as 'the Marconi man' on board ship. With naval vessels, of course, the situation was different, and it was the power of the Navy, especially, which led not only to the commandeering of the products of the Marconi Company, but to the taking over of all its British production capacity by the Admiralty for the duration of the war and for some time after it. The long tale of abrasive and difficult relationships between the Post Office and the Marconi Company, after the honeymoon period when the Post Office had sponsored Marconi's first efforts, and memories of the very embarrassing episode of the Marconi scandal, can but have deterred the Government from even permitting far less encouraging, the major expansion of the Marconi Company's interests in telecommunications which a venture into broadcasting would have brought about.

As late as April 1922, Isaacs, the Managing Director of the Marconi Company, issued a public statement arguing for the establishment of a wireless service in a similar form to that which its subordinate company,

Marconi Marine, operated for ships' wireless telegraphy. Marconi's would 'supply instruments to the householder on hire', with transmitters erected in different parts of the country broadcasting on particular wavelengths which would be received only on the sets supplied by the company.

Without admitting some such factor as the dominant position of Marconi's, it becomes difficult to account for the extraordinary diffidence shown by the British Government about the development of what was an obviously popular, apparently innocuous, and certainly commercially profitable venture, in which Britain, at the end of the First World War, held a technically commanding position.

Whatever lead, in technical and production terms, Britain had had in 1918 had certainly been lost to America four years later. The 'experimental' broadcasts by the Marconi Company from Writtle were closed down towards the end of 1920. The only broadcast programmes to be heard between that time and the reopening of the Marconi station at Writtle in 1922 were those from the Eiffel Tower and the Hague. Virtually a fresh start had to be made towards the creation of a British system. The 'American Boom' continued unchecked, and its success (and failures) rightly figures as a major influence on the creation of the BBC.[1]

In America, as in Britain, public broadcasting was begun in order to promote sales of receivers, and the form taken by the first major organisation was, in principle, not very different. But the differences which did exist are instructive.

Again, the entry of the United States into the war in 1917 had meant the suspension of the Marconi monopoly. The U.S. Navy took over all transmitting facilities. There, too, Marconi was an unpopular name, this time as a foreign interest in virtual control of a technology of proven vital importance for military operations. The civil war in Ireland and the disenchantment of the President and the Executive with the British after the long, wearing, embittered altercations at Versailles made British interests especially unpopular.

So, in the post-war years, the American scene was set for engineering a takeover of Marconi interests. This was done swiftly and adeptly by General Electric, which formed the Radio Corporation of America in 1919, with American Marconi 'invited' to transfer its assets and operations to it. 'For the Marconi interests there was virtually no alternative but to accept the entire plan. Almost all land stations of American Marconi were still in Government hands. The attitude of the Navy Department – with apparent Presidential backing – seemed to make it clear that they would not be returned to a British dominated company.'[2]

The creation of the Radio Corporation of America, which was intended to be virtually a commercial monopoly in American domestic radio production (both transmitters and receivers), took two years. It was, it must be said, initiated by a major tactical error by Marconi's, who, in 1919, in their eagerness to acquire exclusive use of a new alternator developed and owned by General Electric, offered to buy General Electric-built complete transmitters for world-wide use, at a price of over four million dollars, with an agreement to buy additional alternators; in return, Marconi would have exclusive rights in the use of the product. It was a simple matter then, as now, to marshal an industrial, military, and personal lobby in aid of a counter-move. By 1921, G.E. had not only floated R.C.A. but had successfully involved Westinghouse, together with their patent rights, A.T. & T., and a fourth concern, whose possession of certain specific patents made it useful, but which also, for outsiders, gives the new creation a certain rich, all-American, flavour: it was the United Fruit Company. Also, 'to no-one's surprise, Rear-Admiral W. H. G. Bullard' [who had been the operative figure in the counter-attack mounted by General Electric in 1919, beginning with a letter to the Acting Secretary of the Navy – Franklin D. Roosevelt] 'was named the Government representative who was to sit with the Board.'[3]

Even a company as big as R.C.A. could not keep up with the boom in sales. The constituent companies, legally, had monopoly control of the more expensive components for receivers, but of the 60 million dollars spent on equipment in 1922, R.C.A.'s share was only 11 million. Most of the valves sold that year 'were finding their way, through one channel or another, into sets assembled for sale by the two hundred companies' making and selling receivers.[4] In fact, the boom could not have occurred without the free-for-all in setting up transmitting stations which were just as cavalier as the two hundred manufacturers in their disregard of monopoly rights; in May 1922 alone, 99 new stations were started. By the end of July 1923 there were 460 stations broadcasting – all on the same wavelength (360 metres).[5] In 1923, sales of radio sets and parts more than doubled at $135 million.

Any attempt by the Federal Government (in the person of Mr Secretary Hoover) to control the ensuing muddle was hopeless. The conference which was assembled in Washington to discuss the situation and produce some rational solution seems merely to have given new impetus to the boom. Even technical control in terms of geographical location, strength, and operating wavelength of stations proved impossible. There was no workable Federal machinery or supporting legislation to control the multiplication of transmitters comparable to the licensing power exercised by the British Postmaster General. Moreover, General Electric, the major enterprise in the field in America, had close and well-lubricated connections with highly-placed officials in the Executive and with Navy officers.

The sales boom had begun almost immediately after the war, and broadcasting stations were already operating in 1921. But the 'chaos' to which lack of control over broadcasting transmissions had led, was certainly well known in Britain[6] a year earlier than the official memorandum published as an appendix to the Sykes Committee Report:

> 'Broadcasting as a means of entertainment had its birth in the United States between one and two years before it was adopted in Europe. It is still carried on there on a much larger scale than in any other country, although the Committee is informed that technically this country is now equally advanced. A licence is required for the operation of a transmitting station in the United States, but no licence is required for any type of broadcast receiving set. Transmitting licences can be obtained without much difficulty, and there are at present between 500 and 600 broadcasting stations in operation. The number of receiving sets in use is unknown but it is certainly very large, one authority estimating it at about three millions. Most of the licences for broadcast transmissions are held by Electrical Companies, Department Stores, Newspapers and Wireless Societies. . . .
>
> 'At one time the numerous broadcasting stations all used the same wave-length, with the result that they were constantly "jamming" one another's signals. A wide band of wave-lengths has, however, recently been allocated by the United States Government to broadcasting; different wave-lengths are allotted to different stations; and the interference due to "jamming" has been much reduced, although according to some accounts, is still troublesome.'

The monopoly sought by R.C.A. was subverted early on in the game, local stations and manufacturers of transmitters and receivers finding it not too difficult to maintain virtually a free trade in distributing and assembling components bought from R.C.A. and its member companies, supplemented by sizeable imports. So, not surprisingly, the sales achieved by R.C.A., enormous as they were, did not satisfy the member companies. The in-fighting continued for many years, with intervals for seeing off enterprising newcomers, and it was only in 1927 that the eventual stand-off was arrived at between the National Broadcasting Company (the creature of R.C.A.) and the Columbia Broadcasting System (which eventually emerged as the leading challenger, having the backing of the biggest gramophone record company in the U.S.) with the Federal Government attempting some kind of closure with a new Bill which set up a Federal Radio Commission empowered to issue licences to broadcast transmitting stations.

Long before this, broadcasting had discovered its own saleable commodity: time. WEAF, the pioneer station in New York, sold both time and 'talent' – bands, singers and speakers – to business firms who quickly found that 'sponsoring', which meant attaching brand names to a programme, was more profitable than using time for direct advertising. When WEAF developed the strategy of signing contracts with advertising agencies rather than with 'sponsors', and then paying the agencies 15 per cent commission (as newspapers did in similar circumstances) the pattern of public broadcasting in America was set. All that the 1927 Act did was to appoint a Federal Commission to allocate wavelengths, guard against too overt a trend towards monopoly, and to administer whatever controls over the content of broadcasting the Federal Government, from time to time, saw fit to draw up. By 1931, both NBC and CBS were making a profit of over \$2¼ million.

The price paid is familiar enough: the incorporation of the entire broadcasting industry into the marketing, sales and advertising sector of American business. It has filled the same role ever since.

All these events influenced the course followed in Britain in the setting up of broadcast transmission. The Marconi Company, still the majority holder of patent rights in the more important components, remained on the defensive, able to conduct only experimental transmissions, which required special permission from the Post Office for every major 'experiment'. Behind the Post Office, in which control over all wireless telegraphy had been vested since 1904, stood the Admiralty and the other armed forces, all represented in and by the Wireless Telegraph Board. The combination of suspicion and guardedness culminated, in 1920, in the ban on experimental broadcasts from the Marconi Laboratories at Chelmsford.

Remarkably, what eventually forced the hands of the Government authorities into granting a temporary licence to Marconi for a broadcast transmission of half-an-hour a week – a broadcast of 'special calibrations' – was pressure from enthusiastic amateurs, organised into 'Wireless Associations', not the efforts of Marconi's or rival companies. And it was again the associations of amateurs which forced the hand of the Post Office to grant a licence for more frequent transmissions, this time of music and talk.

In terms of sales of receivers, the 'wireless boom' was now running at the same rate in Britain as in America; the major difference in the situations of the two countries concerned the transmitting end. There were, in Britain as in the U.S., competing manufacturers interested in acquiring a stake in transmitting broadcasts, so as to secure a share in the market for receivers. But it was a special combination of circumstances, with the commercial pressures, suspect as they were, being spearheaded by public demand from wireless enthusiasts, that led to the formation of the British Broadcasting Company in 1922.

It was an enterprise governed at all points by the oversight of officials and technical experts from the Post Office and other ministries concerned, and pinned down to a limit of 7½ per cent profit on the enterprise. Besides the Marconi Company there were five other sizeable concerns with a stake in the market: Metropolitan-Vickers, Western Electric, Radio Communication Company, General Electric Company, and British Thomson-Houston, with the minor manufacturers represented by Burndept. The essential difference between this company and R.C.A. was, of course, that there was no pooling of patents, and no merging, even in formal terms, of manufacturing resources; each continued in competition for sales of receivers with the others. The BBC was founded, as was R.C.A., to transmit broadcasts in the sure hope that this would expand the market for wireless receivers manufactured by the member firms, as well, of course, as providing a market itself for all the apparatus required for transmitters. The 7½ per cent profit was to be gained from the licence fees of ten shillings collected by the Post Office, half of the proceeds from which were to be handed to the company to finance broadcast programmes. The individual companies were to benefit from a royalty to be derived from each set sold, which was to bear the stamp of the BBC.

In fact, the scheme fell victim to the same disregard of monopoly rights which was keeping R.C.A. sales to less than 20 per cent of total sales of receivers in America. Most listeners bought and assembled their own receivers, usually avoiding both royalty and licence fee. Indeed, by 1923, as the Sykes Committee pointed out, it had become impossible for the Post Office to take action against the large number of persons who were using home-made sets without a licence. For however willing such a person might be to take out a licence, the Post Office had no licence to give him, seeing that he was not fulfilling the conditions of a broadcast receiving licence (i.e. did not own a BBC set) and was not entitled to an experimental licence.[8]

The Sykes Committee did recommend a blanket licence fee of ten shillings (which remained unchanged for nearly thirty years) for all receivers, whether 'amateur' or 'experimental', but did nothing to ensure that the member companies of the British Broadcasting Company would receive their royalties on all sales of receivers and parts.

So the distinction between broadcasting and the radio industry in terms both of economic interest and of public interest made itself apparent very early on. Again, the Marconi Company may well have played a critical role in the final division of interests between public service broadcasting and commercial manufacture and sale of receivers. There was all too clear a correspondence between its endeavours to create a monopoly in broadcasting and its persistence in trying to recover a monopoly position in British international wireless telegraphy services. Marconi's pursuit of a monopoly in a long-range wireless service covering the whole British Empire, begun in 1910, had partially succeeded in 1912, when the company built, for the Government, six high-power stations in England, Africa, India and Singapore. Its endeavours were renewed after the interruption of the war, with what the Donald Committee called 'lamentable consequences' in delaying the setting up of a British Empire system.[9]

Not surprisingly, the Postmaster General voiced strong disapproval of monopoly in his outline of the negotiating procedure to be followed in setting up a first broadcasting system.

> 'The same word had been hurled like a brickbat during the protracted negotiations between the various interests, big and small, and the Marconi Company was the obvious target. For the small manufacturers feared the potentially excessive influence of this firm with its established expertise, its numerous patents, its capital wealth, and its high international reputation; and so, for that matter, did two or three of the bigger and better placed concerns, jealous of the unequal power of Marconi in doing down its rivals.'[10]

The reluctance of the Post Office to set up a broadcasting system which would have had to be an outright or *de facto* monopoly, and the opposition of rival firms, was reinforced by the fears of the press. The restricted range then available for broadcasting transmission pointed to regional or local systems, as it had in America, rather than to one national system. And, in contrast to the U.S. Federal Government, the British Government had every power it needed to licence, control and monitor transmission.

The obvious solution was to hive off the now profitable nuisance of broadcasting to commercial concerns with a direct interest in promoting it, so that they could sell receivers, with the Postmaster General or another Minister directly or indirectly responsible (as he had in any case to be) for the allocation of wavelengths and for any rules governing transmitter strength, broadcasting times, or even broadcasting content.

Yet the very fear of monopoly may well have been the operative cause of the setting up of the British Broadcasting Company and granting it monopoly rights. For it was impossible to deny Marconi's any right to participate, and if it were to be included in any distribution of licences, it must inevitably, as the largest concern, the owner of essential patents, and the only company with experience of broadcasting, take a commanding position at the outset and perhaps achieve a monopoly position in a short time. Duopoly (Marconi's *v.* the rest), which was canvassed as a possible solution, turned out to be a demonstration of the inevitability of monopoly. The models which seemed clearly relevant pointed, one to national coverage, for the press was now dominated by London publications with a national circulation; and the second, to monopoly control for the Post Office had its telecommunications monopoly. This last would in fact be strengthened by hiving off the broadcasting nuisance, and the attendant trivia of composing broadcast programmes, to a single organisation which it could control without being responsible for it. The threat of dominance by the Marconi Company in this new field could only be contained, commercially, by the establishment of a national broadcasting cartel, in which any manufacturer of receivers would be able to take shares.

So the creation of the BBC, the first of the 'Morrisonite' nationalised industries, is visible as a superb example of accommodatory politics, spreading satisfactions and dissatisfactions fairly evenly among the interest groups concerned.

It is also visible as something else. The British Broadcasting Company was brought into existence 'so that the wireless trade could profit by selling receivers'.[11] All the equipment, technicians, performers, and administrative staff needed for broadcasting were paid for by the Government, out of money paid by the public for the right to listen to broadcast programmes.

Fifty years later, when the threat of a commercial monopoly in broadcasting has been so completely obliterated (to be replaced by the fear of a monopoly, or at least oligopoly, in newspapers), it seems oddly perverse for the system as a whole to have been split between, on the one hand, a national broadcasting system maintained by a uniform charge imposed by the Government on the owners of receiving sets sold at a profit by commercial enterprises and, on the other, the enterprises themselves, which were free of any special charge or levy. Not only Marconi's, but the Post Office itself, in its telephone service, had demonstrated the practicability and the financial and technical wisdom of treating receiving sets as part and parcel of a whole communication system, charging a fee for installation and a rent for providing the service and for maintaining the equipment.

In fact, a proposal that the British Broadcasting Corporation should adopt (or, rather, revert to) this arrangement was made in a reservation to the Report signed by three of the nine signatories[12] of the Ullswater Report in 1936.

The reservation (which has been almost totally ignored ever since) reads:

> 'When a public service is established, it is, we think, necessary that the public interest should predominate throughout the whole range.

If private profit is allowed a loophole, a proportion of the advantages of the system will be lost to the community. The weak spot of broadcasting is in the provision of receiving sets by private industry. There are strong trade organisations although there is still a considerable amount of competition. Evidence has been given that there is a combination in the manufacture of valves which keeps prices unnecessarily high. There are obviously further possibilities of the formation of other associations. The position in regard to the provision of service by retailers is also unsatisfactory.

'We understand the BBC has in fact the power to manufacture and provide receiving sets which are technically receiving stations. We consider that the BBC should make an enquiry at the earliest possible moment into the possibility of either using this power itself or, perhaps preferably, coming to an arrangement with the Post Office for manufacturing receiving sets and supplying them to the public.'[13]

In 1935, most receivers were selling at between £7 and £10. During the year, output of domestic receivers was 1,850,000, which suggests that receipts from sales must have amounted to over £15 million. The BBC's net income from licences for the same year was just over £2 million.[14] Apart from its sheer financial feasibility, a new technical development cleared the way for a comprehensive broadcasting-receiving system. For the Ullswater Committee followed closely on the Selsdon Committee which had been deciding on the future of television, a development which at that time, just after the BBC had ended its contract with Baird, was being actively developed by EMI along the lines on which it was finally established. This development, one need hardly add, involved both the Post Office and the BBC intimately, and could conceivably have replicated the confrontation between the national interest and a commercial monopoly which had so bedevilled the beginnings of wireless broadcasting.

No such confrontation occurred. The symbiotic, or rather, commensal, relationship between the national broadcasting service and commercial enterprise was already too firmly established. So firmly established was it, in fact, that in 1936 the Government even rejected the committee's proposal that the BBC or the Post Office take over, or at least control the operation of, the Wireless Relay Stations, which provided wired transmission of programmes and in fact relayed rather more foreign broadcasts from commercial stations in Luxembourg and France than they did from the BBC. The Ullswater Committee had proposed that the Post Office take over the Wireless Exchanges, which by that time had almost a quarter of a million subscribers, and that the BBC be given 'executive responsibility' for their operations. Nothing could be done, despite much political activity over the years, to curtail the activities of the foreign stations themselves, which broadcast programmes in English, by British broadcasters, and were run on American lines, selling broadcasting time to advertisers in the form of sponsored programmes and spot advertising. What the Government could have done was to prohibit the relaying of the broadcasts by commercial companies in Britain; this represented a manifest invasion of the BBC's constitutional monopoly of broadcasting and an infringement of the principles of public service broadcasting. All that the Government did, however, was to rule that one BBC programme should be made available to listeners by any Wireless Exchange Station capable of relaying two services.

The alternative view to that of the creation of the BBC as a shining example of British political pragmatism, then, is that it was the most convenient and acceptable device for promoting radio broadcasting without burdening either the Government with the responsibility for the composition of programmes, or commercial undertakings with the cost of developing or maintaining a service without benefit of income from advertising, which had been ruled out as early as April 1922.[15] The formation of the BBC, twenty years before the more considerable measures of 'Morrisonite' nationalisation, is a blueprint for State financing of products and services which are either essential for, or favourable towards, profitable ventures by private enterprise. In fact, the creation of the BBC is almost contemporary with the setting up of Government organisations to promote research and development in weapons and defence, a move which converted the Government's role from that of customer of armaments manufacturers to that of inventing, designing, provisioning and contracting for new weapons, tanks, ships and aircraft, and so laid the foundations of what is now familiar as the 'military-industrial complex'. The creation of the BBC may be seen as marking an equally significant step in the rise of what James O'Connor calls the 'social-industrial complex', by which an increasing proportion of the capital and overhead costs of industry is siphoned off into State-financed ventures and enterprises.[16]

THE WESTMINSTER CONNECTION

The formal terms of the relationship between the BBC and Government were laid down explicitly by the Ullswater Committee, and have never been challenged or amended:

> '49. The relation in which the BBC should stand to His Majesty's Government has more than once been discussed in Parliament.

When the establishment and financing of the Corporation was first brought before the House of Commons on 15th of November 1926 the Postmaster General (Sir William Mitchell-Thomson, now Lord Selsdon) said:—

> "While I am prepared to take the responsibility for broad issues of policy, on minor issues and measures of domestic policy and matters of day to day control, I want to leave things to the free judgement of the Corporation."

'50. This policy was reaffirmed on 22nd February 1933 when the House of Commons resolved, after debate—

> "That this House, being satisfied that the British Broadcasting Corporation maintains in general a high standard of service, is of opinion that it would be contrary to the public interest to subject the Corporation to any control by Government or by Parliament other than the control already provided for in the Charter and the Licence of the Corporation; that controversial matter is rightly not excluded from broadcast programmes, but that the governors should ensure the effective expression of all important opinion relating thereto; and that only by the exercise of the greatest care in the selection of speakers and subjects can the function of the Corporation be fulfilled and the high quality of the British broadcasting service be maintained."

'51. The position of the Corporation is thus one of independence in the day-to-day management of its business, and of ultimate control by His Majesty's Government. We find that this line of demarcation has been observed in practice, and we are convinced that no better can be found. We agree with those who in recent years have examined the question that the constitutional independence of the BBC brings advantages to the general public and to listeners which could not otherwise be secured. Our proposals under this heading are designed to make both sides of this two-fold position simpler and more evident.

'52. It is inevitable that the State, in establishing a sole broadcasting authority, should reserve to itself those powers of ultimate control; but we have no reason to suppose that, in practice, divergent views of the lines of public interest have been held by the Corporation and by Government departments, or that the Corporation has suffered under any sense of constraint or undue interference. Where the interests of the State appear to be at all closely involved, it is open to the Corporation to consult a Minister or Department informally and of its own accord. This method leaves decision and discretion in the hands of the Corporation and is consistent with the independent status which was formulated ten years ago as the desirable objective.'[17]

Nevertheless, the BBC's relationships with Government, Parliament and political parties, and its handling of current political affairs have confronted it with a perpetual and unresolvable dilemma. From time to time, the terms in which the dilemma manifests itself have changed. In its contemporary form the BBC has come to be regarded as occupying a position of political power, while it sees itself as the politically neutral custodian of the nation's interests in the uses to which broadcasting, as an instrument for the exercise of political power, may be put. It is probably nearer the truth to regard the BBC's position as one of responsibility without power.

The contemporary dilemma is revealed fairly clearly in two quotations, one from the report of the Select Committee on Nationalised Industries (Sub-Committee B) published in 1972:

> 'There has been a shift of emphasis from considering the broadcasting media solely in terms of the programmes they produce to one in which the BBC and the Authority are seen as powerful institutions in their own right, whose whole style of decision making and action profoundly affects the community.'[18]

The other is taken from an article in *The Listener* (6 June 1974) by Oliver Whitley, formerly Assistant to the Director General of the BBC:

> 'Neither the broadcasting organisations nor the public in this country really know what the objectives of the broadcasting organisations are supposed to be, because these objectives have never been properly and officially defined. . . . If you reflect that broadcasting is the medium which everyone nowadays seems to regard as chief public-impression former, is it not very strange, indeed rather alarming, that Parliament, which decides who should provide these uniquely influential services, apparently has nothing of practical significance to say about their main purposes?'

Parliament, he went on to say, was 'particularly inept in its handling of broadcasting'. A reading of parliamentary debates over the years since the early twenties suggests that, while this is not an altogether fair judgement, it is true that, for the most part, leading politicians have treated broadcasting very much as I have suggested the Post Office did at the outset – as a nuisance. On the other hand, the kind of interest which leading politicians like Churchill in the 1920s, Kingsley Wood in the 1930s, Wedgwood Benn in the 1960s have occasionally taken in broadcasting has not been altogether welcome to the BBC.

Not surprisingly, therefore, the BBC's relationships with national politics, political parties and politicians, uneasy at the beginning, have been more and more difficult and troubled. Throughout, BBC programmes have become at times increasingly circumspect, at other times increasingly adventurous, its pronouncements increasingly simple-minded and increasingly devious, and its handling of individual politicians and groups increasingly clumsy and increasingly finicky.

There is a world of difference between the picture of Reith editing and polishing the script of Baldwin's 'Message to the Nation' during the General Strike, broadcast from Reith's home, or 'titivating' Baldwin's election broadcast in 1929[19] and that of the anxious trimming of the course of balance and impartiality by constant consultation with Party Whips. On the other hand, the decision to risk presenting programmes like 'The Question of Ulster'[20] and 'Yesterday's Men'[21] is even farther removed from the time, in 1930, when Churchill could be denied the opportunity of airing his views on the Conservative Party's India policy, or when Chamberlain, as Chancellor of the Exchequer, could see to it that there was no Opposition reply to his broadcast talk on the 1933 Budget.

In the 1950s, the 'fourteen day rule' forbade any broadcast discussion of matters which were to be the subject of Parliamentary debate at any time within the next two weeks, an embargo which seems improbably crude and arbitrary compared with the gentlemanly provision recommended by the Crawford Committee in 1926, which was that 'a moderate amount of controversial matter should be broadcast, provided that the material is of high quality and distributed with scrupulous fairness, and that the discretion of the Commissioners [i.e. Governors of the BBC] in this connection should be upheld'.

Yet again, the crude stopwatch conception of 'scrupulous fairness' that operates nowadays is accompanied by a quite extraordinary acceptance of the notion that 'when politicians or any public figures have access to the powerful platform of television, they should be open to questioning of a critical and challenging nature'[22] – by 'television journalists' or by 'invited audiences', themselves selected, and their interventions stage-managed, by broadcasting producers or by the television journalists themselves.

Every year seems to reveal more depths and more versions of the basic dilemma. Reporting on the television coverage of the February 1974 election, Jay Blumler wrote that much of the effort

'was channelled into the main evening T.V. news programmes.

> Fully merging its news and current affairs staffs, the BBC devoted the second half-hour of each edition of the nine o'clock news to the Election, and often presented campaign items in the more topical first half as well. . . . But the disturbing consequence of the campaign role of television news was a tendency for news events to dictate much of the flow of the subsequent argument.'

He goes on to detect an even more indefinable and unmanageable source of bias:

> 'The British communication media are apparently so organised that the Conservatives may count on the entirety of their message, whatever it may be, receiving a thorough airing. In so far as Labour is a Party for egalitarian redistribution and radical social change, it cannot rely on the same treatment. . . . The bulk of the mass media tended to present the Election issues in middle class terms.'[23]

It is variously argued that this fundamental dilemma is inescapable, given the nature of broadcasting itself, given the fact that broadcasting was a monopoly, or alternatively, that it is now dominated by competition between the BBC and Independent Television for numbers of viewers; that, being so powerful a means of influencing opinion, it must be subject to governmental control; or, that being so important to the functioning of a democracy, it should be free from government control; that being so expensive, its programmes must be such as to appeal to the majority most of the time, or, at the very least, not offend the majority, or, being so important a medium of communication, it must make room for the expression of minority views and dissenting opinion.

Politics in the twentieth century, at least in Western democracies, has resolved itself into a cliff-hanging affair. The eleventh hour is the very earliest that one can expect a decision to be made. Yet the decisions which were written into the original constitution of the BBC have been hailed as a masterpiece of foresight and characteristically British political wisdom. At this distance, it seems a masterpiece of calculated imprecision.

It was the work of Mitchell-Thomson, then Postmaster General in Baldwin's Government. He followed, in the main, the recommendations of the Crawford Committee, which reported in April 1926, but made one or two notable changes. The Crawford Report envisaged the new broadcasting organisation operating, as previously, very much as an ordinary private firm under the provision of the Companies Act, but consisting of a number of Commissioners, 'persons of judgement and independence, free of commitments, with business acumen and experience in affairs', who would act corporately as trustees for the national interest. An alternative arrangement, also canvassed by the Crawford Committee, was that the 'British Broadcasting Commission' should be set up by Act of Parliament. Mitchell-Thomson rejected both these proposals, the first because 'it would lack a certain amount of status and dignity' and the second because the Corporation might be invested 'in the mind of the public with the idea that in some way it is a creature of Parliament and connected with political activity'.[24]

Having argued the case for giving the new Corporation a privileged position, and at least the appearance, in the mind of the public, of *not* being a creature of Parliament, the Postmaster General provided himself with overriding rights over transmission (including the wavelengths to be used, the location and the power of transmitters) and powers over the content of broadcasting; indeed, even before the Corporation came into being on the last day of 1926, the Postmaster General had instructed it not to broadcast on matters of political, industrial or religious controversy; nor was it to broadcast any opinion of its own on matters of public policy.

These instructions, which rejected the Crawford Committee's recommendations, were a belated affirmation, in explicit terms, of the control exercised over the British Broadcasting Company by the Government a few months previously at the time of the General Strike. In fact, they were no more than an insurance – a stick held well behind the back of the Government – and used very rarely. A broadcast by Ramsay MacDonald during the General Strike had been forbidden, even though his general line fully supported the Government's stand; five years later, with a Labour Government in power, Winston Churchill was denied the right to broadcast his own views of the Conservative Party line on India, his violent opposition to which had led to his resigning from the Shadow Cabinet. (It was the Secretary of State for India, and not the P.M.G., who applied the veto – which it was, although Reith's own words for it were 'a request emphatically made by the Minister responsible'.)

'Control', then, becomes an inapposite word. The powers assumed by the Postmaster General have never been exercised publicly and officially. It was, in fact, hardly necessary to do so. The kind of arrangement arrived at between the Government and the BBC at the time of the General Strike provided the mould for the kind of compromise solution and understanding which has prevailed since then.

In 1926, Reith made it quite clear, in a memorandum to Baldwin, that the BBC could be relied on to support the Government:

'Assuming the BBC is for the people and that the Government is for the people, it follows that the BBC must be for the Government in this crisis too.'[25]

An *obiter dictum* inserted by a High Court Judge on a case which came before him towards the very end of the General Strike, to the effect that the 'so-called General Strike was illegal', gave Reith an opportunity to assert to his senior staff that 'we were unable to permit anything which was contrary to the spirit of that judgement, which might have prolonged or sought to justify the Strike'.[26] But on their side, the trade unions saw the picture differently, and, according to their lights, much more clearly; at the start of the General Strike, the T.U.C. warned its members against believing the BBC, 'because radio would be just another tool in the hands of the Government', and Beatrice Webb noted that 'directly the news began, it was clear that the BBC had been commandeered by the Government and the main purpose was to recruit blacklegs'.[27]

It took seven years, which included two years of a Labour Government, for the situation to ease sufficiently for the Parliamentary Opposition to be given the chance to respond to 'political' (as against 'ministerial') broadcasts by the Government. Almost certainly, it was the exaggerated fears of the 'power of broadcasting' which prevailed at the time which led to this development, since every time the Government used it for blatantly political purposes (as for example Churchill did in his broadcast on his 1928 Budget) there were counterblasts from the Opposition in Parliament and in the press; the BBC felt able 'not to invite' Churchill to repeat the performance in 1929. At times of crisis, of course, the BBC could prove as reliable as it had in 1926; during the critical months of 1931, after the National Coalition Government had been formed in August, but before the election campaign opened in October, no Labour speaker broadcast, (although in the three weeks of the election campaign itself, time was doled out between the contending parties, fractured as they were). After the election, Attlee raised the first demand for 'equal time', a demand which was laughed out then, but eventually became the principle which governed 'access' by major political parties to broadcast time.

On the other hand, political altercation about 'fair play' between Government and Opposition seems, if anything, to have strengthened Government control, both direct – and, more effectively – indirect, over the broadcasting of anything controversial. Throughout the 1930s, the BBC was ridden with a tight rein. Mild as the incursions by commentators into foreign politics and genteel as discussions between political figures were, there were frequent occasions on which objections were raised in the House and in the press to what were labelled errors in editorial judgement or lapses in taste. Such occasions reinforced the propensity of the chief officials of the BBC to prove themselves even more 'reliable'; and, as ever, self-censorship proved to be the most effective form of censorship. As Andrew Boyle remarks, 'BBC controllers and producers were not encouraged to flaunt their consciences or to demonstrate their powers of initiative. The most sensible course, especially for newcomers in the early 30's, was to dispense outright with such luxuries.' Of the transgressions he instances, one met with a warning from the Director General never again to commit so serious an 'error of judgement' as to allow hunger marchers to vent their opinions in broadcast interviews; the other, the summary banning of an allegorical play in verse by D. G. Bridson by the Programme Controller, is more comic than outrageous and ended in T. S. Eliot's publishing the text in his 'highly conservative' literary journal, *The Criterion*.

In the light of such developments, documented both by Andrew Boyle, and, rather less incisively, by Asa Briggs, and in the light, too, of one's memories of those days, it is quite extraordinary to read in Briggs' *History*,[28] that two directors of 'General Talks' were charged with 'left-wing bias', and resigned. Even so, in 1936, the Ullswater Committee felt it necessary to reaffirm once again the ban on 'editorialising' and to extend it to publications as well as to programmes – a cautionary move which, in the years when public controversy in the press, especially the weekly press, about national and international policies were becoming more and more inflamed, was a good deal more significant than Briggs' comment suggests.[29]

Reith left the BBC just twelve years after the General Strike. It was during those years that the basic organisational structure of the Corporation took shape, that the principles of public service broadcasting in this country were developed, to serve as a normative pattern for the next generation, and that the fundamental dilemma in relationships between Broadcasting House and Westminster was fully articulated, to remain as a perpetual problem thereafter.

By 1933, Parliament (not the BBC) had argued out and established the principle that political broadcasting was not to be wholly at the disposal of Government, but was to be shared, so far as major parliamentary issues and elections were concerned, (equally) between the major parties. Outside this circumscribed area, the use of broadcasting to inform the public about national and international affairs, economic and social as well as political, was limited in terms of time, circumspect in terms of the choice of speakers and commentators, usually balanced or 'neutral' in content, and perpetually liable to forcible criticism in the House of Commons, or even censorship. The very fact that such matters did come to the attention of Ministers and other politicians before the event is sufficient indication of the quite explicit and ingrained deference with which the Corporation treated Ministers and ministerial opinion.

All the troubles hatched out of these ambiguities came home to roost in the later years of the 1930s and the early years of the war – by far the most troubled period in the BBC's existence, and a period which ended not with the problems being solved, and the difficulties overcome, but by their being battened down and locked up.

So it was that the newly instituted foreign news service of the BBC was to be 'based on telling the truth' – but Foreign Office guidance would be sought on all complex issues of policy.[30] Finance for overseas broadcasting was originally provided by the BBC (then financially flourishing, even though it was still operating on the receipts of 75 per cent only of the licence fee) but in 1937 it was decided that the cost of the service would be met by a Foreign Office grant – uncovenanted, with the 'BBC's actual needs' left entirely to the Foreign Office to decide – something which probably counts as Reith's most inexcusable piece of improvidence.

> 'Unquestionably the BBC itself paid the penalty for Reith's aloof but unabashed paternalism by pulling too many punches in its staid, and often excessively cautious, approach to the unending problem of enlightening its enormous but often bewildered public. The dangerous undercurrents of international trends, speeding the drift towards the Second World War which nobody wanted, were by no means always indicated by the broadcasters.'[31]

Yet unquestionably, too, the BBC by this time had gained enormous prestige and acceptance as a public service broadcasting system. Listening had become a major pastime for the majority of people; because broadcast news, as it had been from the very beginning, consisted of selections of agency messages, which were always credited by the announcer (with the phrase 'by copyright') to the particular agency from which they originated, BBC news bulletins won the reputation, which they have never lost since, for objectivity and veracity.

More strikingly, and more assuredly, the BBC had begun – or at least, can claim the greatest share in – what amounted to a cultural transformation. What the Public Libraries Acts of the 1890s had already achieved for books was capped by the BBC in other regards. It reduced virtually to zero the marginal cost to every member of the nation of full access to an enormous cultural heritage, previously available to a privileged minority. The clearest manifestation of the sheer cultural gains achieved through broadcasting is, of course, music. Perhaps the greatest single achievement of the BBC has been to transform this country from what was musically the most barbarous nation in Europe into what has some claims to be the musical capital of the world. Its role in the development of new forms of dramatic writing, and in new dramatic genres – and thus in the wartime and, especially, post-war developments in the theatre – is less easy to assess, but is certainly very considerable.

There is a striking contrast between the sheer cultural and educational achievements of the BBC and its complete failure to wrestle free from its political swaddling clothes. This may well have been because Reith saw no point in trying to do so. He was, after all, a man of the Establishment, the more so because he was not a birthright member. And, ambitious as he was for further, higher, office, it was unthinkable that he would want to jeopardise his career and risk writing off the extraordinary success story with which his name was associated. During a period when almost every organisation of any kind, industrial and non-industrial, was sliding into the pit of the Great Depression, and fighting hard merely to survive, the BBC was growing richer, bigger, more popular, more authoritatively organised. The licence-fee system of financing, adopted and maintained as expressing the correct approach to the question of how far the BBC should be seen to be under Government control, provided a safe and generous source of money – so generous, in fact, that there was hardly a murmur of protest when the Government subverted the arrangement, and the principle it was meant to enshrine, by raiding the licence fee and handing a quarter of it to the Treasury.

Reith was a man of many contradictions, but perhaps the most important, in this context, were his limitless political ambitions and his disdain for parliamentary and party politics. He counted Baldwin and MacDonald among his friends; yet his distaste for the subordination of the BBC to so lowly a Ministry as the Post Office led him actually to intrigue with the Secretary to the Treasury and the Head of Post Office to have the BBC 'answerable not to the Postmaster General but to the Lord President of the Council, a Minister of Cabinet rank, on all questions of policy and direction'.[32] A recommendation somewhat to this effect found its way into the Ullswater Report. It was rejected. Although 'the BBC with its 4,889 employees in 1939 prided itself that it was independent of the Government of the day',[33] Reith had raised no objection to or even comment on the Ullswater Committee's recommendation that 'in serious or national emergencies . . . full Government control would be necessary'. Again, while Reith contrived to get his own nominee, Ronald Norman, to replace Whitey as Chairman, Reith himself left the BBC in 1938 'at the express behest of the Prime Minister, Neville Chamberlain'.[34] Then, as before, and since, the BBC fell an easy victim to what I have called the calculated imprecision of its relationship with the State (an imprecision itself betrayed by the ease with which the Ullswater Report could use the words State, Government, and Parliament almost interchangeably), an imprecision which the BBC has been lulled, or gulled, into believing allows it all the liberty, independence, autonomy that can be hoped for, but which has proved, time and again, to be liberty on parole – the terms of which can be altered, without notice, by the Government.

This the Government did, with disastrous effect, in September 1939. The most pronounced effect of broadcasting during the months of the 'phoney war' was to contribute to what Harold Nicolson called 'a situation in which boredom and bewilderment would be the main elements'; but the BBC had been put, immediately, under the general command of the new Ministry of Information, where it remained until the end of 1941. That the BBC can look back on the years of the war as a period of its greatest triumphs is due to the initiative, intelligence, and sheer hard work of the thousands of people who joined it in the latter years of the war to man its Home, European and Overseas services.

CONTROL AND CONSENSUS

Early in 1923, Reith appointed Rear-Admiral C. A. Carpendale as his deputy. Carpendale, a disciplinarian, or 'experienced man-manager', to use a favoured term of the time, provided the right complement to Reith, the visionary, the born leader, the living embodiment, even in the twentieth century, of the Protestant ethnic, brimming with moral certitudes and ambition. The first effect of Carpendale's appointment was to assure centralised control to London (broadcasting, it will be remembered, was and remains a local or, at most, regional service, in technical terms). And, since the sun shed its light of approval and the warmth of promotion only in Savoy Hill, by the time the Corporation was founded, in 1926, transfer to a regional station had already made its potency felt as an instrument for ensuring conformity.

The Corporation's staff doubled in size in the first seven years of its existence; the hours of broadcasting remained virtually unchanged. During that period, Reith, backed by Carpendale, fought and won the battle for supreme control against the first Chairman (Lord Clarendon) and the Board of Governors. Constitutionally, there is no question but that control, like ownership, of the British Broadcasting Corporation had been vested by the Government in the Board of Governors; this is spelled out in the original Charter. Too late in the day, the Beveridge Committee, in 1949, accepted this as meaning that

> 'The Governors in effect must themselves undertake the function of the Ministers, that of bringing outside opinion to bear upon all the activities of the permanent staff, of causing change where change is necessary, of preventing broadcasting from falling in any way whatever into the hands of a bureaucracy which is not controlled. It follows from this that the Governors, in relation to the staff, must have the position of a Minister and must not be excluded from that by the present Whitley document . . . or by anything like it. The Minister in charge of a Government Department in practice seldom interferes with the executive responsibilities of his staff, but he is entitled to do so whenever he thinks it necessary.'[35]

This kind of utterance from the Crawford Committee, twenty-three years earlier, *might* have altered things, but even that is doubtful. By 1926 Reith had already taken over command of the British Broadcasting Company from the Board of Directors – who were only too glad, on the whole, to leave it to him. The Board of Governors of the new Corporation proved more difficult, and as late as 1929 Lord Clarendon was still asserting that 'The Charter makes absolutely clear the supremacy of the Board of Governors'.[36] But in 1930 Lord Clarendon left (to govern, not New South Wales, but South Africa), to be replaced by John Whitley, who brought with him, according to Reith, 'Light, and understanding and excellent wisdom',[37] an understanding later incorporated in the so-called 'Whitley document'. This laid it down that while the Governors of the BBC might be *de iure* in supreme control, authority *de facto* belonged to the Director General. In this document, the Board renounced any executive function, and defined its role as that of acting 'primarily as Trustees to safeguard the Broadcasting Service in the national interest. . . . Their responsibilities are general and not particular.' And while 'with the Director-General they discuss and then decide upon matters of policy and finance,' the essence of the document lies in the statement that, 'They leave the execution of that policy and the general administration of the Service in all its branches to the Director-General and his competent officers.'[38]

With that matter settled, in terms which remained unchanged (despite the Beveridge Report) for more than thirty years, the Director General felt able to proceed with the design of a new administrative structure through which that command could be exercised. Significantly, in the same year, 1932, that saw the Whitley document composed, submitted to the Postmaster General and to the Prime Minister (MacDonald) and approved by them, the BBC moved to its new premises in Broadcasting House. Recruitment, which had slowed down during the years of struggle with the first Board, quickened; the staff doubled between 1931 and 1935, and doubled again between 1935 and 1938, the year Reith left the BBC.

Outside the apparatus of government, the bureaucratic form of organisation was developed, as we know it, in the last quarter of the nineteenth century and the first quarter of the twentieth. It did so because (as I have indicated elsewhere)[39] bureaucracy is the form of organisation best adapted to accommodate growth in scale. The development of the bureaucratic structure of the BBC during the thirties, then, was the product not of the genius or the whim or the sense of self-importance of its Director General, but – in so far as anything can be said to be so – of historical necessity or, perhaps more accurately, of the application of the social technology of organisations then available to a familiar problem. (The kind of new thinking about organisations which had transformed General Motors and a few other large American corporations during the twenties was well beyond the bounds of possibility for the BBC, or any other organisation in Britain, then. Whether it was appropriate to apply the 'new thinking' of the 1920s to the reorganisation of the BBC in 1968–9 is another matter.)

The organisation of the BBC in its formative years along straightforwardly bureaucratic lines may have been inevitable, simply because no other organisational model was available at the time. But the particular form of bureaucratic structure which was adopted had its own distinctive, and revealing, peculiarities. Reith's response to the growth of the BBC up to 1933 had been to insulate himself from the everyday traffic of proposals, requests, complaints and internal politics at lower levels by interposing not only Carpendale but a 'Control Board' comprised of Carpendale ('Controller') and three Assistant Controllers, meeting under the Director General, as chairman. This Control Board, with slight differences in size and name, was begun in 1923. By 1927, there were, under the Director General and the Controller, five Assistant Controllers, only one of whom was concerned with programmes. (The others were in charge of information, internal administration personnel, engineering and finance.)

Asa Briggs, basing his remarks on Reith's own description in *Into the Wind*, gives this account of the 'familiar and established pattern', as it had become by the thirties:

> 'Reith saw the pattern in simple terms. At most five or six people were directly responsible to him. This narrowed "the span of control". The five or six individuals who were in charge of major units of broadcasting constituted an executive or control board. "Here was in operation an ideal combination of cooperative management and definite leadership and direction. There was nothing

statutory about it. It might be said to have begun as a convenience to myself – a weekly meeting at which I could have the several and collective views of senior officials, and at which problems that affected them all might be discussed. It was more than that, however; I had in mind from the earliest days that it should function as a real management committee." '[40]

Immediately after this paragraph, Asa Briggs provides what might be called the punch line: 'There was never any suggestion, however, that the Control Board was settling BBC policy by democratic vote.' Reith made out that the relationship between him and the Control Board matched the relationship between the Governing Board and the Director General. This was at best disingenuous of him, seeing that most of his energies between 1927 and 1931 seem to have been spent in contesting any control which might be exercised over his activities by the Board of Governors. This contest he won, so that the Director General became the ultimate source of authority for everything that happened, or was allowed to happen, with the Corporation. For it was an often repeated principle that the Assistant Controllers (later renamed Controllers) could only exercise that authority which he, the Director General, chose to devolve on to them, and this principle was to be maintained downwards throughout the organisation.

With the reorganisation of 1933, supreme control was concentrated still further, again under Reith, in a triumvirate: himself, the Controller of Administration (Carpendale) and a newly appointed Controller of Output. It was at this point that the grand principle of the separation of administration from the production of programmes became formalised, and with it the 'article of faith' as Briggs calls it, or 'convenient fiction' as it might more correctly be called, of the administration acting as the helpmeet of the programme staff:

> 'Administrative staff will work, under their administrative chief, to the requirements of the creative staff who will be relieved of all immediate and direct responsibility in administrative matters. It is intended that the . . . administrative staff shall form something in the nature of an Output Secretariat, carrying out the smallest administrative function on behalf of the creative staff.'[41]

Output was headed by Col. Alan Dawnay, a newcomer, straight from the Army, but, as a staff officer, without even Carpendale's presumptive claim to service experience in 'man management'.

Briggs, rightly, reserves his criticism for the system. Boyle, probably drawing on his own memories of how disruptive the system could be even in the milder form in which he later experienced it, claims Dawnay to have been almost entirely responsible for the 'ossification' of BBC organisation during the 1930s.[42]

It is more likely that Dawnay saw himself as carrying out the 'policy guidelines', if not direct instructions, of Reith, and as acting in cooperation with Carpendale. Carpendale's administrative staff seems to have acted not only as a secretariat, but as a body of commissars. Even Briggs goes so far as to suggest that they 'could all too easily come to regard themselves – and even more easily come to be regarded – as the "policemen" of the system'.[43] In fact, they could not seem to be anything else if the express intention of the reorganisation was to free the 'creative staff' from all managerial responsibility – which could all too easily be construed by the programme staff themselves as an incitement to managerial irresponsibility. Once set up, such a system becomes inescapably self-perpetuating.

In simplified, but not incorrect, terms, one can say that in 1932 Reith, having seen to it that the Chairman and the Governors would 'go along with' what he wanted to do, also saw to it that ultimate control was thereafter vested in himself, and exercised it through an idiosyncratic system of bureaucracy. Immediately beneath the Director General, a dyarchy was created. Each side of it was, in effect, a system of bureaucratic control, although one was called 'Administration' and the other 'Output'. Both were, and saw themselves as, control systems for the Director General to manipulate.

It is, I believe, right to blame Reith for the internal stresses and strains which afflicted the BBC during the 1930s; after gaining his victories, he lost interest in the internal affairs of the Corporation, coming to life mainly in his dealing with the Ullswater Committee and in his attempts, through it, to gain authorisation for his own assumption of power (in which he succeeded) and to dislodge the powers retained by Government from the Postmaster General and have them transferred to a Minister of Cabinet rank, who would carry greater prestige and perhaps be more amenable (in which he failed). Still, all the outward signs were that the BBC was a great success; it was Reith's creation; he had fought several battles to obtain supreme and undisputed control of the BBC, and the bureaucratic structure he constructed in 1933 was meant to ensure that he retained it.

Yet none of this explains why the mistakes of the 1933 structure were perpetuated for a generation or more. If an administrative structure is bad or harmful, it can be improved, or changed altogether. We have to look for the reasons for its survival elsewhere.

The centralised administrative control structure instituted from the first, and fully developed within the framework of the bureaucracy of the thirties, was intended to manifest itself not in disciplined subordination or compliance but in what was called 'consensus'. For Reith and many other officials, consensus was a word in frequent use. The connection between control and consensus was put by Reith himself forcibly and lucidly. He, as Director General, devolved authority on people below him, and this process of devolution was to spread throughout the Corporation:

> 'The four Controllers can give their subordinates no more than they themselves get from above, but increasingly they too are devolving authority and responsibility on their Departmental Directors. . . . There are, therefore, a great many people party to and concerned in management at the BBC. . . . What the BBC does, therefore, is more and more not what one individual thinks, more and more, it comes from a consensus of opinion and experience.'[44]

Such consensus would naturally, it was supposed, express itself in a unitary dedication to the ideals of public service broadcasting, and in the whole style and manner – if not the content – of broadcasting. Contemplation of this *e pluribus unum* transformation led one Announcement Editor into the curiously rapturous language in which one official memorandum was composed:

> 'The BBC is one Corporation, and can only be thought of by the listener as individual. It has many voices, but one mouth. It can speak in many styles, but the variety is due to the difference of subject matter and must not betray any inconsistency of treatment.'[45]

There is another side of the matter, barely touched on by Briggs, perhaps exaggerated by Boyle. The counterscarp, so to speak, of the slope from control to consensus was the continuum which can be conceived as extending from dedication to the ideals of public service broadcasting, and upwards through devotion to the BBC to loyalty to the Director General, coupled with regard for him; and there was a third face to the pyramid, one which stretched down from submission to the Administration to fear of dismissal and thus of unemployment, a fear ever present in the thirties.

These things are not to be distinguished from each other as different interpretations of the same kinds of action: at different times and in different measure, all must have been involved in the actions of individuals and groups of people. The sense of corporate unity, bred as it may have been out of the rather special amalgam of membership of a growing organisation and necessary compliance with regulations and guidelines during the 1930s, afterwards became visible, through the curtain of muddle and absorption in the day-to-day struggle for survival of the years from 1939 to 1941, as the essential foundation of loyalty to a new corporate identity with a capacity for growth, for encouraging initiative and adventure, which was wildly different from the BBC of the thirties. A golden glow surrounded the people and the organisation which seemed to have made this possible. During the war, too, consensus was ready-made, as it was for the country as a whole, and overrode argument, disagreement, and remembrance of the thirties.

By the fifties, then, one could begin to speak of a 'BBC ethos', even of a 'BBC type', which had a living connection with the past in the persons who had survived from the thirties and were now, many of them, leading officials, and for whom, like the rest of the staff, and the public itself, the history of the BBC was one of continuous and unqualified success.

THE GOVERNORS AND THE PUBLIC INTEREST

It was the Postmaster General, Sir W. Mitchell-Thomson, who, as the Minister responsible, assumed the task of framing the Constitution of the BBC in 1926 and setting out its powers and responsibilities in the Charter and Licence. It was an entirely novel undertaking. The only Government undertakings of a comparable kind in existence up to the Second World War were boards and authorities instituted by Parliament to control (but not operate) the docks and harbours of Merseyside and London, and to superintend and coordinate the generation and distribution of electricity by the mixture of commercial and municipal undertakings which had grown up all over the country. (These few were joined, in 1933, by the London Passenger Transport Company, which, during the next six years rivalled the BBC in enterprise, and surpassed it in pace of development. But the BBC was unique.)

In immediate, practical, terms, Mitchell-Thomson's task was simple enough. The British Broadcasting Company was a going concern, and there was no question of any substantial alteration to its working organisation. As a company with limited profits as well as limited liability, no very fierce resistance to the transfer of ownership to the Government was expected, or forthcoming, from the company directors or the shareholding companies they represented. But there was a constitutional problem, and not only in defining the relationship of the new Corporation to Parliament and Government. Responsibility for the property and powers, and for the proper conduct of the Corporation had to be vested in a person, or a corporate body.

As soon as the problem is presented in this way, it is easily answered. The only feasible model, in Britain, is a Board – of commissioners, of trustees, of governors, of directors. The terminological differences, though subtle, are significant – rather more so, perhaps, than the difference Reith saw in having ministerial responsibility for the BBC lodged with a Cabinet Minister rather than the Postmaster General. A Board of Directors is clearly associated with commercial undertakings, as the BBC had been, and trustees are, conventionally, concerned with the guardianship of persons and property rather than with the proper ordering of public affairs. The Crawford Committee had used the term 'Commissioners' in reference to the people in whom responsibility for the Corporation would be vested; the term carries with it the connotation of direct appointment by Parliament and direct responsibility to Parliament. Mitchell-Thomson's preference for 'Governors' must have been deliberate, and is therefore important.

The English reliance on, and delight in, lexical niceties is of immense practical utility. It delivers legislators from the labour of enunciating principles, of designating precisely how these principles are to be applied, and defending their decisions by reasoned argument. It also keeps lawyers busy, civil servants unhampered, and drives foreigners mad; all three consequences are worthwhile bonuses. The choice of the term governors did in fact prove to be of decisive importance in subsequent attempts to define the role of the Board. Two Chairmen of the Board, Lord Simon and Lord Hill, made attempts to redefine the position of the Chairman (and with him, the Board of Governors) in relation to the Director General and the organisation and policies of the BBC, but even their perception of the latitude allowed them by the terms of the Charter and Licence in defining that role, let alone their success in doing so, was strictly limited. And, in practice, these limits have always been even narrower than the extremes which were articulated in the first place by the Government, and some thirty years later by the Beveridge Committee.

Reith's view undoubtedly stems from his experience with the British Broadcasting Company, the directors of which were content to act as trustees of the interests of their own individual companies, which they represented on the Board of Directors of the BBC. The crucial statement of this position is Reith's own, and Lord Simon cites this passage from *Into the Wind*:

> 'Having discovered what broadcasting was, reflected, giving reign to imagination, I realised to some extent at least what had been committed to me. For to me it was committed. I had thought that the Chairman, Sir William Noble, might be around a good deal, and when Noble came to see me before the first Board meeting on January 4th, 1923, I asked him about this. "Oh no", he replied, "we're leaving it all to you. You will be reporting at our monthly meetings and we'll see how you're getting on." *Leaving it all to me.*

I thought of what that "it" involved. He misunderstood my silence. "That's all right, isn't it?" Quite all right.'[46]

Reith spent three years in fashioning the Company into the instrument of public service broadcasting he wanted. In 1926, he saw his endeavours crowned by the commendation of the Crawford Committee, and by its recommendation that it be converted into a State Corporation responsible to Parliament and Government. He himself was appointed Director General by the Crown. It was humanly impossible for Reith to regard the newly appointed Board of Governors as filling any other role than the *fainéant* Board of Directors of the company, which had been content to 'leave it all to him'. The attempts by one or two of the new governors, particularly Mrs Snowdon, and by the new Chairman, Lord Clarendon, to redefine their own position and authority in terms which they thought reflected the intention of Parliament were no more than a nuisance, although a nuisance powerful enough for his very considerable achievements in creating the archetypal public service broadcasting organisation to turn sour on Reith, and goad him into successive attempts to gain an appointment elsewhere which would be elevated enough to free him altogether from such annoyances. As we have seen, the appointment of John Whitley as Chairman in 1933 put an end to conflict, and the position reverted, almost, to that which had obtained in the old days of the British Broadcasting Company.

Almost, but not quite. The Directors of the Company had seen their own function, properly enough, as representatives of the shareholders' interests, the shareholders being the companies they represented on the Board. This kind of specific limitation was hardly feasible with a Board of Governors of the Corporation, but the matter was resolved by transposing 'shareholders' interest' into 'public interest', a concept so nebulous as to offend nobody and be open to any interpretation the principals involved cared to put on it. Even in recent years, one member of the Board of Management of the BBC saw the role of the governors as closely analagous to that of the governors of a public school, 'cherishing' it, but keeping in the background, and certainly not having any say in the school curriculum or in its management.

At the other extreme, there is the Beveridge Committee view, in which the proper position of the Board of Governors is clearly regarded as equivalent to a Board of Commissioners responsible to Parliament in much the same way as a Minister is responsible:

'The Governors, who constitutionally form the Corporation, must assume and must have power to perform effectively the function of a Minister in keeping his department in touch with public opinion and subject to external criticism. The channel for informed democratic control of broadcasting must lie in the governors. . . . The Charter should place them in unfettered control of the staff and all its activities, for only if they have full authority can they feel fully responsible. The Charter should require them to have organs for receiving and considering public opinion.' (para. 552)

'From the same analogy with the Minister follows the conclusion that the governors, collectively, must be completely masters in their own house. They cannot, any more than a Minister does, themselves undertake the daily work for which they are responsible, but they must have the unquestioned right to look into every detail as a Minister has and like a Minister they must be prepared to defend or correct every detail. No Minister in answering for his department to Parliament would be allowed in the words of the Whitley document now defining the position of the BBC Governors to say that his responsibilities were "general, not particular". In dealing with this document below we recommend that it should come to an end. Any suggestion that the governors should formally be confined to matters of policy or principle and warned off the ground of practice and execution is dangerous: policy and principle have no life except in individual instances.' (para. 554)

The Pilkington Committee[47] reiterated the Beveridge Committee phrase about the role of the Governors being equivalent to that of a Minister in keeping his department in touch with public opinion and subject to external criticism and went on to make some play with the need for the Governors to 'know and interpret public opinion' and to

'keep aware of public opinion in every way open to them: through its expression in Parliament and in the Press, through the views of their Advisory Committees, through the letters the public write to the organisations, and through the results of wide and relevant audience research.'

But the Pilkington Report refrained, interestingly enough, from repeating the Beveridge Committee's prescription of the Governors' right to be 'completely masters in their own house' and to 'look into every detail'.

Beveridge, and Lord Simon, who was Chairman at the time, undoubtedly saw eye to eye in this matter. Both saw it as impracticable, and in a real sense dangerous, for the Governors to be formally 'confined to matters of policy or principle' and to have to keep their distance from operation and management. Simon himself, a man of very considerable experience in industrial management and public administration, believed, quite rightly, that it was simply not feasible to draw any line between 'policy' and 'day-to-day management'.

But Simon found it quite impossible to assert the kind of authority he thought proper over the Director General. In the book he wrote after leaving the BBC, he was clear and forthright about this, without being embittered:

> 'The Reith tradition of a powerful Director General, combined with the excellence of the BBC, must tend to make the Director General wish to keep effective power in his own hands.
>
> . . . Sir William Haley and myself . . . had together been Directors of *The Manchester Guardian*; we were agreed completely in principle as to the aims and ideals of the Corporation . . . but we differed throughout the whole of my Chairmanship both as regards the attitude of the BBC towards criticism and as regards the proper relations between the Chairman, the Governors and the Director General.
>
> . . . I set to work to learn all I could, and gradually acquired the increasingly firm conviction that it was quite wrong that any one man, whatever his ability, should be allowed to be in effect sole dictator of the BBC; and the Reith conception almost resulted in that when put into practice. . . .
>
> It is hard to find any parallel in public affairs for the position of the Director General of the BBC. A Minister of the Crown is everywhere recognised, both internally and externally, as the sole head of his department; the Permanent Head as his adviser. In local government the council and the committee are fully responsible, not the Town Clerk or the head of a department. The question does not arise in the nationalised industries, where the whole-time chairman is the single head both as regards policy and administration; there is nobody corresponding to the Director General. . . .
>
> So far as I can discover, no other chief official of any public concern has the *de facto* power comparable to that of the Director General of the BBC, and no other has the public reputation for such power with the single exception of university Vice-Chancellors. Even so, no Vice-Chancellor has power in any way comparable to that of the Director General; indeed, in all academic matters (at least in the provincial universities) the Senate is practically self-governing, although Vice-Chancellors are, I think rightly, regarded by the public as the heads of their universities.'

All this has some point, in that Simon was concerned that the BBC (this was in the early fifties) should find out as much as possible about the operating practices of American broadcasting companies and the kind of programmes they broadcast. Only after some difficulty did he persuade the Director General to get his senior people to visit the United States and see what they could *learn*; yet the reports he saw on their return 'showed little signs of their writers' having gone for the purpose of learning what U.S.A. radio did better than the BBC. 'I fear', he concluded, 'that complacency is a real danger to the BBC.'[48]

Complacency, by a predictable coincidence, was the term also used by the Beveridge Report about the seeming inability of the BBC to admit that any other broadcasting system did anything better, or that it had anything to learn from them.

The charge of complacency is an old one (it antedates the Beveridge Report) and no BBC bones are likely to be broken by its reiteration. But its seeming ineffectiveness over the years is due rather to its being misplaced, I believe, than to its age. The charge of complacency, in any case, is simply not compatible with the responsiveness and sensitivity – often amounting to anxiety – with which senior officials and programme staff relate to the world around them, especially to the noises and moves made by the larger and more powerful bodies in the immediate vicinity of the BBC. This is a matter of some complexity, which will be examined in more detail later, but what it amounts to is that the world of broadcasting seems to require its tenants to create an autistic world out of their activities and beliefs. This is partly because of the nature of broadcasting, which seems to demand a kind of commitment which is deeper and more binding and more complete than anything one encounters outside the life and death professions; it is also partly due to the need to be perpetually tensed against the pressures, or the threat of pressures, from outside the Corporation which may be generated at any time by a programme, or an incident in a programme. 'Broadcasting', as Anthony Smith has remarked, 'is always conducted with a certain degree of fear; an error or misjudgement by a producer can by damaging the public image of the BBC . . . severely endanger its essential economic or political interests.'[49]

The BBC, then, sees itself as perpetually beleagured, under pressure, being lobbied, or being compelled to lobby. The outsider tends to read this as caginess, defensiveness – or complacency. And in this regard, the Chairman and the Governors are forced into an impossible situation. If they are perceptive enough to see what is going on, it is impossible for them not to assume the protective posture which people inside the BBC obviously expect of them, or at least to retire to a comfortable arms-length distance, accepting from the Director General and the Board of Management what they 'need to know'. To assume anything approaching the role of 'trustees of the national interest' or 'quasi-ministerial responsibility' merely means that they add themselves to the pressures on the system as a whole, and on individual producers. Occasionally, the system of 'referral upwards' of awkward decisions will take individual matters as far as the Board of Governors, and they will pronounce. But in the role which the constitution, and circumstances, and the BBC tradition have thrust on them, and given the superlatively vague definition of their constitutional position, it is difficult to see how they can bring any new light, or additional wisdom. 'Yesterday's Men' was, after all, seen by some Governors before it was broadcast.

What is remarkable about Lord Hill's reflections on his years as Chairman of the BBC is his sheer insensitiveness to the implicit threats contained in his insistence on things like having separate accommodation, his own secretary, setting up a finance sub-committee of the Governors, and actually rewriting policy statements. When the present Chairman, Sir Michael Swann, in one of his earlier public statements, broke the news that 'nobody loves the BBC', what was remarkable was the implication that anybody (outside the BBC) could, or should, imaginably 'love' the BBC – any more than they 'love' Parliament, or the British Council, the Post Office or the Transport and General Workers' Union.

Yet, at bottom, the BBC needs to be loved, or at least cherished, by its Board of Governors. And for the most part, it is. If it were not, and if the Governors discharged their constitutional role as 'trustees of the public interest' it is difficult to see why there should have been any need to set up the succession of Committees of Inquiry under Major-General Sykes, Lord Crawford, Lord Ullswater, Lord Beveridge, Lord Pilkington and Lord Annan.

The Governors of the BBC are trapped in an impossibly contradictory situation. For the most part, they have accepted the compliant, consultative role the Director General, *and* the Corporation generally, needs of them and – Clarendon, Simon and Hill notwithstanding – has fitted them into. They speak, publicly at least, *for* the Corporation to Parliament and its agents, to the press and the public at large, and not as the chosen guardians of the public interest vis-à-vis the Corporation and its activities. How could it be otherwise? For the true situation is represented by a simple adaptation of Reith's fatal remark in his letter to Baldwin at the time of the General Strike:

> 'Assuming that the BBC is for the public interest, and the Governors are appointed to serve the public interest, it follows that the Governors must serve the BBC too.'

2 From Public Service to Professionalism

THE POWER OF BROADCASTING

From the very beginning, public controversy about broadcasting has been dominated by the strong and almost universally held belief about its immense potency as a means of social, cultural and, ultimately, political influence and power. It is this belief which lies behind the unceasing watchfulness of government, Parliament and party politicians over the BBC's news and discussions programmes, and has made for recurrent outbursts of criticism of BBC policy, allegations of political bias and a continuous mumbling undertone of disquiet, suspicion or downright animosity.

Belief about the power of broadcasting rests on a single and manifest truth: broadcasting makes it possible for one man to address an audience of millions – nowadays, indeed, of hundreds of millions. For the first two or three decades the power of broadcasting was seen as vested in its potentiality as an instrument of propaganda. Indeed, the very first use of broadcasting made by Britain was the foreign broadcasts operated directly by the Foreign Office immediately after the end of the 1914–18 war. Twenty years later, the BBC's European services were begun so as to counter the foreign broadcasting services mounted by Germany, Italy and Russia. But after the Second World War, claims about the propaganda power of broadcasting, both political and commercial, tended to become more modest. It was persuasive, an instrument of influence rather than power. The Pilkington Committee, which reported in 1962, shared this view, although rather guardedly: 'Unless and until there is unmistakable proof to the contrary, the presumption must be that television is and will be a main factor in influencing the values and moral standards of our society.'[1] Even so, it was the fact of the sheer pervasiveness of broadcasting that carried with it the belief that it is powerful *because* it is pervasive, and a corresponding fear of the ways in which, and the groups by whom, that power might be exercised.

More recently still, fear even of the persuasive influence of broadcasting over 'the masses' has tended to slacken, much in the way that the fear of broadcasting as propaganda faded earlier on. Neither fear, though, has entirely disappeared, and it is revived from time to time by claims still being made by interested parties about the effects of propaganda and persuasion through broadcasting.

Yet if one looks for evidence to support such beliefs in the researches which have been conducted during the past thirty-five years, there is none – or precious little. 'In retrospect,' concludes Denis McQuail, 'it seems that the expectation of great persuasive power from the new media has been largely misplaced.'[2] And he is not alone in reaching that conclusion. But all this does, apparently, is to render the propositions which the belief subtends less specific. McQuail, three pages earlier in the same essay, asserts that the 'media' 'are largely responsible for the creation of public opinion'. The Langs, equally short of supporting evidence for the political persuasiveness of television, nevertheless conclude that 'The media also structure a very real political environment which people can know about only through the media. Information about this environment is hard to escape. It filters through and affects even persons who are not directly exposed to the news.'[3]

We are dealing, in fact, with a set of beliefs much older than broadcasting. During its own formative years (which extended from the beginning of the eighteenth century until well into the nineteenth), the press was regarded with even greater alarm and suspicion. Windham, says Aspinall, laid most of the blame for the mutinies at Spithead and the Nore at the doors of the press, and Burke saw in it 'the grand instrument of the subversion of order, morals, religion, and human society itself'.[4]

At the outset, of course, the power of broadcasting over public opinion and the life of the nation could only be regarded as potential. Nevertheless, the Sykes Committee regarded its 'social and political possibilities as great as any technical attainment of our generation', and recommended that, because of this, control over it must lie in the hands of the State. The State would, of course, see to it that it was used as an instrument for the public's good.

THE IDEA OF PUBLIC SERVICE IN BROADCASTING

The State, in fact, considered that it had discharged this particular responsibility by creating the British Broadcasting Corporation. As the Pilkington Committee pointed out, forty years later, it is impossible to legislate for good broadcasting 'Good broadcasting is a practice, not a prescription.'

Legislation is a necessary condition, however, for good broadcasting to be practised. The State had made what contribution it could by creating the British Broadcasting Corporation. Thereafter, it was for the BBC to formulate the practice. It did so, and it is the BBC's code of practice which has governed the conception of public service broadcasting in this country and, indeed, throughout the world.

The shaping of public service broadcasting as an institution, and the acceptance by society at large of the form it assumed in Britain is almost entirely the work of John Reith. This is clear enough from Reith's own words in *Broadcast over Britain*, written in 1924 and published as a manifesto, to which he himself adhered, and saw that the BBC adhered until he left. Reith's own words have been echoed and paraphrased by committee after committee. In Asa Briggs' rendering.

> 'Reith's theory of public service began with the conception of the public. Without such a conception the conception of public service itself becomes bleak and arid . . . The "publics" are treated with respect not as nameless aggregates with statistically measurable preferences, "targets" for a programme sponsor, but as living audiences capable of growth and development. The BBC, in brief, was to be dedicated to the "maintenance of high standards, the provision of the best and the rejection of the hurtful". Reith had no sympathy with the view that it is the task of the broadcaster to give the customer what he wants. "It is occasionally indicated to us that we are apparently setting out to give the public what we think they need – and not what they want – but few know what they want and very few what they need. . . . In any case it is better to overestimate the mentality of the public than to underestimate it." '[5]

The BBC, during the inter-war years, was undoubtedly instinct with the kind of moral and cultural zeal which was Reith's own personal endowment to broadcasting. The apparatus of *conventions* which thereafter came to mark it as a model public broadcasting service was developed by the people who were brought into the BBC then and who knew that, in whatever other ways they differed from the Director General, or smarted under Carpendale and Dawnay, he was at one with them in this. This is revealed very clearly in one of the earliest treatments of broadcasting, a testimony all the more valuable because it comes from Hilda Matheson, who had resigned in 1931 from the post of Director of Talks after, and as the result of, a lengthy and difficult period of argument and recrimination about the definition of her powers and duties:

> 'It is easy to write sentimentally and superficially about broadcasting – its elevating effects, its shortcuts to culture, its universal message, its vast audience thrilled by one simultaneous emotion. It is not necessarily an advantage that the humble crofter in his

lone sheiling may hear sounds generated in Paris, Vienna or New York if these sounds are silly, or vulgar, or false. The ripples started by silly noises spread further and pollute more widely – that is all. Broadcasting may spread the worst features of our age as effectively as the best; it is only stimulating, constructive and valuable in so far as it can stiffen individuality and inoculate those who listen with a capacity to think, feel, and understand. . .'[6]

The way in which Hilda Matheson poses the alternatives, without admitting of any compromise or mixture, has a familiar ring. They are not Reith's words, but they are certainly his sentiments. They do not reflect his missionary zeal or his dogmatism, but the commitment is as clear.

The lead given by Reith in this development is undeniable; he wrote down the principles which should govern a public broadcasting service, reiterated them constantly to his staff, and kept unceasing watch to see that they were followed. He was, as we have seen, less sure of himself, less purposeful, in defining and upholding the path of political rectitude, but he had less personal assurance about these matters; the devils he knew from personal experience were sloth, incompetence, inefficiency, immorality, paganism and vulgarity. And these were enemies enough.

Yet the 'pull' of leadership, authoritarian or charismatic, is of itself insufficient to explain how it came to colour the attitude of all his subordinates to their individual tasks, and, moreover, why it was that the conception of public service broadcasting established itself firmly enough in the BBC to be reasserted after the calamitous years (as they were, comparatively speaking) of 1939–42 and to be sustained so triumphantly during the latter years of the war, and for ten or more years after it.

The complementary 'push' of external circumstances was supplied by the condition of the two other, and, at the time overwhelmingly 'powerful' media (in the sense of being even more pervasive than broadcasting): the press and films.

Film, interestingly, had begun to shape itself in a form which during the present century has reversed the historical path followed by the press. For the most part unashamedly commercial, film makers set out to make films which would attract audiences of millions. In the first twenty years of the industry's existence, production and distribution companies and property developers had built up an enormous, complicated international network which made it possible for the whole population of every city in North America and Western Europe, and of most small towns, to see films a few minutes' walk, or a short bus-ride at most, from their homes, and at prices which were a quarter or less of the cheapest seats in theatres or music-halls. They did this by exploiting what were by now a well-established apparatus and body of expert knowledge concerned with capital funding, with entrepreneurship, with recruiting and training an appropriate labour force, with marketing and with product development. America provided the biggest national market. Southern California provided the climate needed for the strong and reliable lighting necessary for filming; fixed cameras and outdoor filming prescribed the need for large, outdoor action space; the briefest acquaintance with popular tastes in theatre and fiction made it easy enough to design the three brands of product – the action pack, the romance pack, and the laugh pack. They were made to provide entertainment for the largest audiences possible, entertainment which, in terms of price, was better value than anything else. In these rigorously commercial terms, the industry by the early twenties was proving itself extravagantly successful and profitable. And in the view of people like Reith (and Hilda Matheson), and the Conservative Party politicians and civil servants who made the decision, the products of the industry represented the consequences of 'giving the public what it wants' and were consequently silly and vulgar and false. Broadcasting, if they were to have anything to do with it, had somehow to be developed in the completely opposite direction.

The historical origins of the press are altogether different, but by the twenties the popular press had begun to show many signs of going in the same direction as films. Indeed, suspicion of the malign influence of the popular press on public opinion and, especially, on 'public taste' had been voiced more than thirty years before by no less a person than Lord Bryce. His observations were concerned with American newspapers, but these were made at the very moment when Harmsworth's *Daily Mail*, taking the American popular press as its model, had begun to sweep the board in England:

> 'Towards the middle of the last [i.e. nineteenth] century an enterprising man of unrefined taste created a new type of "live" newspaper, which made a rapid success by its smartness, copiousness, and variety, by addressing itself entirely to the multitude. Other papers were almost forced to shape themselves on the same lines, because the class which desired something more choice was still relatively small; and now the journals of the chief cities become such vast commercial concerns that they still think first of the mass and are controlled by its tastes, which they have themselves done so much to create.'[7]

Mass-circulation newspapers, popular weeklies, children's comics, and pulp fiction had, by the 1920s, subverted the role of the printed word as an instrument of religious, cultural, social and political enlightenment; they had become elements in, and chief supporters of, the structure of economic and political power which it had been the task of the press to expose, discuss, and criticise. The 'freedom of the press', like other freedoms since, was beginning to shed its quality of absoluteness, and 'freedom for what?' became an increasingly pertinent question.

'Freedom of the press' is historically no more than a natural extension of the concept of freedom of speech, and the traditional and legal authority on which it rests (from Milton onwards) refers both freedoms to the freedom of the individual citizen. But, by the time the BBC was founded, mass circulation newspapers had begun to put fairly obvious constraints on what constituted news, so far as the vast majority of newspaper readers was concerned. The twenties saw the reopening of the old question of the problematical role of the press, particularly its political role, which had been so ambiguous in its formative period before the Reform Bill. Was it the voice of public opinion or the instrument by which public opinion was 'regulated', organised, even formed, by the politically and economically powerful?[8]

The astonishing thing about the power of the press in the 1920s was the unabashed arrogance with which it was exercised – and claimed to be exercised – by its proprietors. A. J. P. Taylor in his *Beaverbrook*[9] quotes a remark made by Rothermere to Beaverbrook about what he could do for Bonar Law; 'If Bonar places himself in my hands I will hand him down to posterity at the end of three years as one of the most successful prime ministers in history, and if there is a general election, I will get him returned again. This may sound boastful but I know exactly how it can be done.'

The notion that the press, in addition to being free, should be responsible, has been slow in gaining acceptance (it was first formally and officially endorsed by the Royal Commission on the Press, 1947–9) and even slower in achieving practical application. But in the 1920s, what was chiefly impressive about the popular press was its power and its irresponsibility – a point which Baldwin made tellingly in his 1931 Queen's Hall speech.[10]

Films and the popular press together form the backcloth, the negative reasons, which have to be added to the positive reason of Reith's missionary zeal, his energy and his ability, to understand that, in undertaking the task of ensuring that broadcasting would not go the same way – as it already was going in America – he had the backing of the powerful, from Baldwin, Prime Minister at the time of the founding of the BBC, down, as well as of the good and the godly. More importantly, younger people, of much the same social class, and with the same sort of outlook, were available for recruiting into a public broadcasting service and ready to accept the principles he had formulated – if they did not already have them.

THE REITHIAN ETHOS

The form of words by which public service broadcasting is defined by Parliament in the BBC's Licence and Charter (as the operation of a broadcasting service as a means of information, education, and entertainment), has remained virtually unchanged since the Crawford Committee Report and the Postmaster General's Licence of 1925. Yet the definition is really no more than a discretionary formula, essential perhaps, but no more so than the injunction laid on a commercial company by its shareholders that it should make a profit, or on the State itself that it should promote the welfare of its citizens and protect them and their interests. The prescription of itself poses a number of questions about the nature of the information, education and entertainment to be provided, about the quantity and the quality of each element, and about the proportion of total broadcasting output which should be allocated to each, as well as about what will promote and what will prevent their successful presentation. Indeed, these questions have formed the matter of national debates inside and outside Parliament and a major concern of the six Committees of Inquiry on Broadcasting which have been constituted since public broadcasting began in 1922.

By 1960 public service broadcasting had begun to attract question marks – much as the 'freedom of the press' had in the 1920s, though for different reasons and with different connotations. It is a mark of the transition from the clear lines of definition and demarcation which the concept of 'social institution' denotes to the more ambient, autonomous and debatable rule of 'convention'. The first official recognition of the change came with the charge raised by the Pilkington Committee of 'trivialisation', which it went so far as to designate as the 'natural vice' of television. By this they seem to have meant an unconditional surrender of critical faculties, unthinking conformism, fear of the erosion of differences in aesthetic tastes, differences in cultural values, differences in moral standards, and thus of the vulgarisation of everything and everybody. The emergence of such feelings is not unlike the growth, over the past decade or two, of the conventional distaste by the well-heeled and well-concerned for the vulgarisation of European travel by tourism.

Perhaps the fear not of trivialisation but of vulgarisation (or what some Americans have called 'massification') has sounder foundations than have so far been articulated in official reports and public discussion. Because we are all creatures in society, we are the creatures of society. But we are also individuals, partly in the familiar sense of each of us representing a unique combination of inherited genetic elements, family circumstances, and life experience, but also in the sense that each of us combines the elements of culture that we derive from society in an individual manner. Particular interests, occupational, moral, religious, political, cultural and sociable, may affiliate us with different social groups which, so to speak, objectify that interest; but the individual retains his individuality because his *pattern* of participation is unique to itself – an observation first made by Georg Simmel some seventy years ago. But if the average number of viewing and listening hours per person amounts to almost three a day in this country, and rather more in America, this means that about one-third of every man, woman and child's disposable, or leisure, time is spent as an affiliate of the viewing or listening audience of broadcasting. So, in a very real sense, broadcasting has reduced the range of feasible 'patterns of social individuality' merely by filling a sizeable amount of the time available.

If one has to think of broadcasting in terms of costs and benefits: cultural, social political, and moral: then undoubtedly vulgarisation of the kind that has caused so much hand-wringing, from Matthew Arnold to Richard Hoggart, has to be regarded as perhaps the biggest item on the debit side. But it is important to make clear what exactly the loss consists in. It is not the particular cultural or intellectual level of 'Coronation Street' or 'Panorama' or the 'Come Alive with Pepsi' commercial – or, for that matter, the curious mutations by which the author of *War and Peace* seemed to become John Galsworthy, and Trollope's 'political' novels as if written by Georgette Heyer. It is the homogenising effect of making programmes for audiences which are counted in millions which is at the root of the matter. If so large a slice of everybody's time is spent watching or listening to the one Stentor, it does matter very much whether he is 'presenting' Max Beerbohm or Max Miller, Hitler or Churchill, and whether he is relaying Beethoven or the Bay City Rollers, but it also matters that the choice is made by a few people in the light of what they regard as consonant with the nation's central, political, cultural and moral values or a desirable and tolerable departure from them. (Thus, for example, it is both encouraging and dismaying that the audiences for 'That Was the Week That Was' rose to 8 or 9 millions.)

Even so, the debits are indissociable from what undoubtedly have to be counted as benefits. What the Public Libraries Acts of the 1890s had already achieved for reading was capped by the BBC; it reduced virtually to zero the marginal cost to every member of the nation of full access to an enormous cultural heritage, previously available to a privileged minority.

The clearest manifestation of the sheer cultural gains achieved through broadcasting is, of course, music. Britain, fifty years ago, was a musically barbarous nation. By the 1960s, London had some claim to be the musical capital of the world. Even if the BBC cannot claim the whole credit for this achievement, it was certainly the prime mover in it (*pace* A. J. P. Taylor[11]). Its role in the development of new forms of dramatic writing, and in new dramatic genres – and thus in the wartime and, especially, post-war developments in the theatre – is less easy to assess, but was certainly very considerable.

The great merit of the Reithian conception of the role of broadcasting was that he had a clear view of a task for broadcasting, even if his interpretation of that task was a restricted one. If we take the view that broadcasting (along with the press, publishing, and the interchanges which form public opinion out of events) is an extension of the personal equipment each one of us has for interpreting our environment and our situation in it, and for coming to best terms with it (just as bureaucratic and other organisational forms have taken us beyond the limits of face-to-face power and authority, competition and working cooperation), then the job that Reith chose for the BBC to carry out was that of maintaining a pilot navigation service for the individual in a world extended for him by communications technology. To shift the line of vision a little, the BBC was developed under Reith into a kind of domestic diplomatic service, representing the British – or what he saw as the best of the British – to the British. BBC culture, like BBC standard English, was not peculiar to itself but an intellectual ambience composed out of the values, standards and beliefs of the professional middle class, especially that part educated at Oxford and Cambridge. Sports, popular music and entertainment which appealed to the lower classes were included in large measure in the programmes, but the manner in which they were purveyed, the context and the presentation, remained indomitably upper middle class; and there was, too, the point that they were only there on the menu as ground bait.

Reith, in short, knew what he was doing. More than twenty years after Reith left the BBC, the Pilkington Committee regarded the role of broadcasting as normative, just as Reith had. But the Reithian ethos, the final product of the system of control and consensus established in the thirties, began to break up in the later fifties. Television, and then commercial television, broke the unity of the link between broadcasting and the nation. Broadcasting was no longer *sui generis*. The cinema, television's model as well as rival, had its own conventions, its own standards, its own mythology, and, more important, an entirely different relationship with its audience – it put an entirely different construction on the task of charting the social, economic and political world and of providing the individual with a navigational service for piloting him through it. Commercial television, when it came, destroyed not only the monopoly of the BBC in the economic and political sense but also its special relationship with the nation. Competition meant the intrusion of other renderings of Britishness and of right-mindedness, and the consequent shrinking of BBC values to something sectional and questionable. While the social function of commercial television was, as before, to provide interpretations and models with the greatest acceptability (but this time obviously and admittedly to provide groundbait for a very different kind of fishing), one considerable side-effect was to put the whole BBC operation into the framework of 'brand image' making.

It is also arguable, of course, that changes in Britain's social structure which occurred, or became manifest, between 1945 and 1960 brought into question the authority of the whole hierarchy of values on which the Reithian system of control, consensus and ethos itself depended. But arguments of this global sort quickly become circular; after all, the breaking of the BBC monopoly, and the disintegration of the BBC ethos played no small part in the change in orientation of British society.

Of course, there had been plenty of criticism and complaint about the BBC during the 1930s – about bureaucratic control, unadventurous programmes, high-mindedness and uplift, banality and timidity. These complaints had come from within the BBC (though very rarely directed upwards, where they might have been heard) as well as from outside it. But the main parameters of the conception of public service broadcasting, as it had developed within the BBC, remained unchallenged; the most serious problems, then, had been how to deal with the broadcasting invasion from Luxembourg and Fécamp.

Naturally enough, the sense of corporate identity, the striving for consensus to support it, and the belief in the BBC's normative role in the cultural, moral and political life of the country survived longest in Administration, especially the higher reaches of it. Outside it, there was apparent among a large number of people – perhaps the majority whom I met in 1963 – a feeling that a distinction had to be drawn between the Corporation as it was and some platonic idea of the BBC, which showed itself in depreciatory references to 'the way the BBC does things', 'Broadcasting-House-mindedness', and 'the kind of line being taken by the people on top now', by the same people who saw 'what the BBC stands for' and 'the public service idea in broadcasting' as altogether admirable. There was another dimension of the same feeling in the distinction drawn by engineers between the communication system the Engineering Division had created and now maintained – the best there was – and the vulgar or tedious uses to which some of them said it was being put.

The solidary consensus which had been achieved in previous decades, and, which, by the early sixties, was still referred to as the 'Reithian ethos', had been fractured. Dedication to 'public service broadcasting' was distinguishable from 'loyalty to the BBC'. But, since the system of selection and promotion was in the hands of the Administration, there still existed a 'BBC type'. In 1963, this was acknowledged as a fact, though a surprising one, by a number of people, but it was the relative newcomers with whom I talked in 1963 who saw this most clearly:

People outside the Corporation have a notion of there being a BBC type. They used to have a notion of there being a BBC culture. This has been lost a bit, now, but there exists an image – a myth, if you like – about people inside the Corporation. Have you found any truth in this? Is there something the Corporation tends to imprint on the people in it?

I think you see it in the older members of the Corporation. You do notice a kind of sameness in looking at things, but you would expect to find this in a number of people who had been together for a number of years. It seems to be a kind of – I don't know – 'liberal reactionism' – or something. I mean they are perfectly prepared to eat up new ways of doing things, but they wouldn't like to be associated with them – or be thought of as opposing them.

Among younger people, there is a certain type, which is generally speaking a kind of Oxbridge graduate who is generally taken on the General Trainee course because it's really selective and they are generally the ones to be chosen: charming, very well dressed, very cultured, very clever, very refined – all of these things, and what else? – perhaps rather narrow, because they have not travelled very much, or never been hungry, or whatever it may be. . . .

They are – civilised. . . . Everyone is on christian name terms – which you don't meet outside the Corporation nearly so much. And there is the informality, and yet a kind of gentlemanly informality, with which you deal with people – all this, I think. And this allied with a kind of campness as well. . . .

You don't find any other definable type?

No. I have now been placed myself. I met someone at a party and he said 'there are three BBC people here, and you're one,

> and he's one, and he's one', and he was absolutely right. So it seems as if there is, but I couldn't tell it.
>
> *How did you react?*
>
> With horror – not that I had been classed as a BBC type, but that I had been classed at all.

The view of those people in Administration who themselves did the selecting was totally opposed to this:

> Our central belief, if we've got a central belief at all in this department, is that if you are recruiting for an organisation that sets out to reflect the community, then to a very large extent you have got to have a staff that reflects the community, too. And you've got to get people from as many sources, as many different backgrounds, forms of education, and so on that you can.

These remarks were echoed in other interviews which touched on the same topic:

> There is no such thing as a Corporation type, as far as we are concerned. We're dead against this concept, and don't practice it, that there is a Corporation type –
>
> *– in the outside world waiting for you to pick up?*
>
> Waiting for us to pick up, yes. If the Corporation makes people into a certain type, well, I'm not saying it's a good thing, but it's not in our control.

Yet another General Trainee, this time from Oxford, remarked:

> Periodically, John Ambleside gives parties for trainees, and – this didn't happen at the last one, but the one before – I suddenly thought 'My God, aren't all the trainees alike!'

The 'BBC type', in fact, was, like BBC pronunciation and what used to be called BBC culture, a tacitly agreed amalgam of styles of conduct and deportment which was seen by the perceptive and socially skilled graduate trainee and other entrants as demonstrating to seniors their possession of the more appropriate talents and qualities. It was a 'front' – a managed impression of oneself.

What began as a centralised bureaucratic control system of a very manifest kind, developed through a series of mutations, thirty years later, into a latent system of approved conduct and demeanour. Such conduct and demeanour was by no means uniform, but it was always consonant with the prevailing code by which individuals (*inter pares*) were selected and gained approval and promotion.

This is how bureaucratic structures are translated, imperceptibly, into career systems, which become self-sustaining – because it is as career systems that they come to be seen, always, by the people who work in them.

FROM MONOPOLY TO COMPETITION

Unquestionably, the BBC ended the fifties in better shape than when they began. In 1950, the BBC had been under severe criticism from a number of quarters, not least from the fourth of the Committees on Broadcasting, whose Chairman was Lord Beveridge;[12] and four years earlier the campaign against the BBC monopoly had been opened by no less a person than Ogilvie, Reith's successor as Director General. But by 1960, the broadcasting monopoly had ceased, even though the BBC had grown in staff numbers from just under 12,000 to 17,000; its income had risen from under £11 millions to over £32 millions (excluding the grant-in-aid for External Services); it had just produced its first 'comprehensive round-the-clock' coverage of results of the General Election; 'Panorama', 'Tonight', 'Monitor' and 'Face-to-Face' were all new-style television programmes which had begun to attract very sizeable audiences (a quarter of television output in the year ending March 1960 consisted of talks, discussions, documentary and current affairs programmes). Even Light Entertainment had begun its come-back with 'Dixon of Dock Green' and the BBC's own discovery, Tony Hancock. Everything was set for the new Director General who succeeded Sir Ian Jacob in 1961, the very first Director General to attain that position from within the BBC, to 'open the windows', as he put it, and make it the mirror of the age.

Any account of the transformation wrought by television during the 1950s would be hopelessly distorted without some reference to the very distinctive character of the decade in which it happened. The 1950s had an apocalyptic quality. So, of course, had the decades of the two World Wars, the twenties and the thirties. But the nature of the changes which affected people during the fifties was categorically different from these and other decades of revolution. They were the years of the Bomb, of the computer, of the exploration of outer space and, of course, of television. All of these things were products of advanced technology, all were spectacular achievements of the twinned development of science and industry, and it was to science and industry that Western civilisation had become increasingly dedicated, as central to its values and its welfare. But each of them carried its own menace – of universal holocaust, of subjection to a new technocracy of immeasurable consequences, of the immersion of the variety of mental and cultural attributes of everyday life in an all-embracing sameness. There was, of course, no immediate threat – everything was immanent; but if the qualification for a decade's achieving distinction in terms of social history lies in the universal recognition of a single descriptive tag, then the Frightened Fifties would probably serve.

Well, we survived. And merely to survive, after the thirties, and then the forties, seemed like becoming a supreme individual, and national, ambition. Institutional, as well as individual, survival was on its way to becoming, for Britain, a central article of faith. The BBC, as a public institution, not only survived, but survived triumphantly. Survival, however, was a matter of coping – of finding some immediate and adequate response to demands, threats and challenges. And survival under these conditions tended to be bought at the inevitable, though unwitting, expense of its special role in the life of the nation and its special character as an institution.

Three principal factors contributed to the change – or governed the 'coping' responses of the Corporation: the disaggregation of the national audience for sound broadcasting; the advent of television as a national service; and the breaking of the BBC monopoly with the inauguration of commercial television. Different as the three factors were, their effects were cumulative and decisive.

The solidary, virtually monolithic, pattern of sound broadcasting (the Home Service, with the Regional Service as supplementary, but still centrally controlled, programmes) was broken up. The Light Programme perpetuated the Forces programme which had been developed during the war to entertain servicemen and women stationed at home and overseas, and which had consisted of light, popular music, variety, and news. With the inauguration of the Third Programme, a couple of years later, diversification of radio was taken as far as technical limitations allowed.

Of course, the conception of the radio audience as homogeneous had become largely fictional, even during the 1930s. Everybody in possession of a wireless set, and able to operate it, may have listened to Melba in the early twenties, but by the end of the thirties it had to be assumed that the listening audience had become selective. Nevertheless, although the range of style and content of programmes had broadened, every item was designed to fit into a single, planned, sequence. As the hours of broadcasting increased to a point at which it was impossible to expect all listeners to listen to every item, there was inevitably an increasing obligation to provide something for everybody. 'Balancing the programme' acquired increasing importance, over and above the attainment of a high standard of individual broadcast programmes, but the balance was something which it was for the BBC to achieve in its own terms, and within the limits of its own resources, or the resources which its own production staff knew of and could draw on. And balance, what is more, was achieved in respect of an entirely notional assemblage of tastes, needs, and preferences existing among the population of the country. The idea of attempting to ascertain what those tastes, needs and preferences were at first hand was something which gained acceptance only very late in the day, and reluctantly.

The very act of disaggregating the national audience after the war, and of providing different kinds of programmes for different kinds of audience (distinguished from each other somewhat invidiously, as the Pilkington Committee later remarked, by 'height of brow'), brought with it intimations of a break-up of the homogeneity imposed by control and consensus inside the BBC. Internal competition was explicitly adopted as one of the cardinal principles of broadcasting policy. The three services – Home, Light, and Third – as now constituted were to compete with each other for the attention of the listening audience. Imbued thus with a spirit of healthy rivalry, the services were expected to strive for higher standards of quality, and for new and more vigorous ideas for programmes; from this competition, listeners would be attracted in greater numbers, or for longer periods of time, or both, to *all* three services, presumably, and derive greater satisfaction and profit. Nevertheless, the same reorganisation stipulated that while the services might cater for all kinds of different interests, they should also aim at audiences of different levels of culture and capable of different degrees of sustained interest or intellectual effort. Thirdly, all services were to use the same orchestras, the same studios, and the same departments responsible for mounting programmes – Talks, Music, Drama, News, Documentary Features and the rest. Supply represented the various departments (Talks, Music, Drama, etc.) responsible for devising and producing individual programmes; Output consisted of programme planners, who built up the broadcasting schedule put out by each of the three channels from the programmes which were produced by Supply departments, to whom producers and their aides were attached.

Circumscribed in this way, the healthy rivalry between the three Output services was reduced to competition for the names and events with the greatest ready-made popular appeal. As one man put it: 'That kind of competition had no teeth. You'd get a programmer saying "We've got Toscanini. So the best of luck to you, old boy!" and that was all there was to it.'

More fully dentured competition, however, did enter into the relationship between Supply and Output. Programme planners in

Output and heads of Supply departments were designated equal in rank. 'Supply', I was told, 'doesn't "work to" Output. We all "work to" the Director of Radio.'

What happened was that the structure designed to promote healthy rivalry between Home, Light and Third programmes resulted in increase in rivalry – of indeterminate hygienic value – between Supply departments for time, and for favourable positions in the programmes which the Output programme planners composed. As one programme planner put it, 'Output people have editorial responsibility for the composition of what goes out from the channels. We decide what we're going to offer – and whether to make any changes.'

Power to exercise this editorial control lay manifestly in the control of expenditure on programmes, which was in the hands of programme planners. Thus, despite the equality of rank between planners and production departments, their joint subordination to the Director, and the convention that differences of view between them had to be settled by discussion and persuasion or by arbitration by the Director of Sound Broadcasting, Output came out on top: 'Because planning is an editorial job and conditions what goes before the public, and has control of the spending on programmes, this has come to be regarded as the senior job.'

Seniority, in fact, was simply a function of the greater power possessed by the programme planners. The competition between Supply departments for transmission time and for money inevitably extended to much more than the display of their wares. In order to advance or defend the interests of their own departments and get their programmes accepted by planners, heads of Supply departments and individual producers, as one informant put it, found themselves driven to 'cajole, persuade, lobby, and even try to bully the Output side on occasion'.

Thus the relationship between programme planners and production departments was eventually realised in terms of conduct characteristic of a client relationship. The superior power of the Output side developed to the point of it being possible for programme planners to claim that the source of new 'bright ideas' for programmes lay in Output, and not in the Supply departments – 'at least, the successful ones come from the programme planners'. There was a rationale for this: producers in Supply departments, I was told, tended to live in worlds created by a successful programme idea, and were therefore unlikely to 'dream up something new'; they also became committed to teams of performers and writers, and found these links difficult to break; consequently, they tended inevitably to think in terms of the variants of previous programmes. 'Revolutionary ideas', on the other hand, 'came from thinking about the whole output of a channel.'

The system had been designed, originally, to inject vitality into the three services by building in competitiveness. During the fifties, it became obvious that the attempt had failed – or rather, had exhausted any beneficial effects it might have had, and had produced a different situation from that which its creators had envisaged. The buyer and seller relationship intended for Output and Supply developed into a *de facto* subordinate relationship which was superimposed on the *de iure* equality of the two. The monopsony position enjoyed by the consumer (Output) of the products of Supply departments enabled the former not only to exercise effective control over the choice of programmes, but to lay claim to the greater part of the ultimate value in broadcasting – 'creativity' – in the development of new programmes.

This particular consequence outlasted the system which brought it into being and has now become an integral part of the organisational process of Radio. It was made very clear in 1973 that network controllers in Radio saw themselves as the 'creative innovators' – in marked contrast to Television, where new, 'creative', ideas were still supposed to emanate from within programme departments. One man made the historical connection himself, and reiterated the notion of an inherent tendency of programme departments towards conservatism:

> The planning function and the editorial function used to be so handled that predominance was given to the departmental function. . . . Editorially, that was tied to a situation where no change was envisaged. The moment you began thinking of change, of doing away with this department because its function no longer existed, and creating that department because we ought to be concerned with a different kind of broadcasting – the moment you look at the kind of talks I've put into Current Affairs, for example, and decided that instead of the straight talk, or the talks magazine, or the news bulletin, instead of that you had a sequence, and you began reshaping your departments – the emphasis almost inevitably, editorially, moves over to that of the network controller.
>
> *Why not the head of department, though?*
>
> Because the head of department tends to be conservative. He tends to be a man who is more concerned with the wellbeing of his department than the requirements of broadcasting as a whole. He's concerned with securing employment for the members of his staff and ensuring that what he was doing last year he's going to do next year as well. The old system was conservative.

There were other consequences. The system had been designed in the fifties to promote 'healthy rivalry' between the three services. This had become translated into competition between the production departments in Supply. Competition, in turn, had become overlaid by attempts to manipulate a favourable decision by tactics quite unrelated to the operational problems of the three services, which could be said to consist in providing conditions under which producers would be stimulated to invent and develop the best programme ideas and in selecting the best programmes. Much of the task of production departments converted itself over the years into the diplomatic struggle among a number of dependencies for the attention and favour of the dominant authority.

There were, by the early 1960s, two further consequences apparent in the later phases of this development. In some instances, or in some senses, the competitive struggle had been seen by the contenders for what it was – an artificially contrived race track designed to keep them fit. Once people involved in such a situation are able – as was the case by this time – to speak quite freely about the structure of the competitive system and its purpose, and about the illegitimate tactics which at times predominated, the invidiousness of their position, particularly vis-à-vis the spectators and judges who were nominally their equals in rank, became keenly and unbearably obvious. They ceased, effectively, to compete. Alternatively, or even perhaps concurrently, the stresses imposed by the situation became oppressive rather than stimulating, and suspicions about unfairness and illegitimate manoeuvres mounted far beyond any feasible actuality. The personal insecurity generated in this way turned preoccupation away from endeavours to improve performance and into worry – an unsatisfiable need for reassurance and applause.

By the end of the fifties, it was television, of course, which had made the much more manifest changes in the BBC. Commercial television, when it came, not only broke the BBC monopoly. It was also disruptive for the Corporation internally, since, when it did start, the only source of production staff, engineering and technical staff, and studio services was the BBC. The new companies had, of necessity, to tempt BBC staff away with more money and with the offer of more 'freedom'.

Competition between the BBC and commercial television was not confined to competition for audiences, although this did most to change the content of BBC programmes in the scramble to recover at least an equal share of the television audience from the depths of the 30 per cent or so to which it had been driven in the first three or four years. Television broadcasting staff – engineers, technicians, and production staff – now had a market to play, instead of competing for rewards within the one organisation. And the response of the BBC, though natural enough, was possibly even more damaging in that it demonstrated in the clearest possible way to its own staff the significance and value to them of the advent of commercial competition. During the months before ITV stations opened, the BBC television offered short-term contracts at almost double salary to thirty or so key people, who thereafter, of course, saw to it that the people who worked with themselves, whom *they* regarded as key people, were offered similar reinforcement to their loyalty.

Gerald Beadle, Director of Television at the time, later wrote:

> 'The onslaught had a disturbing effect on the staff who remained. Morale went down. Many newspapers, especially those involved in commercial television, did their best to exacerbate the position by hammering the BBC and trying to represent it as an effete organisation which would collapse at the first breath of competition from big business, and Norman Collins who had been Head of BBC Television until his rather over-dramatised resignation in 1950, and was now the leading public proponent of commercial television, publicly said that BBC Television would soon grind to a halt.'[13]

Twenty years later, the agonising that went on in the BBC about the loss of 'its' audience seems a little bewildering. The figures of ITV's share of the audience as rising quickly to 70 per cent, with which so much play was made, refer to a proportion of those with television licences who had sets capable of receiving both BBC and ITV channels. It is reasonable to suppose that only those people who positively wanted ITV programmes would have gone to the length of purchasing another, and more expensive, set. Equally significant, though quite ignored, is the fact that the inauguration of ITV had little or no effect on the growth of the television audience.

Growth of Television Audiences, 1950–60

	No. of new licence-holders, sound and TV combined	*Percentage increase on previous year*
1950–51*	420,059	122
1951–52	685,319	90
1952–53	693,192	48
1953–54	1,110,439	52
1954–55	1,254,874	39
1955–56	1,235,827	27
1956–57	1,226,663	21
1957–58	1,123,747	16
1958–59	1,165,419	14
1959–60	1,214,331	13

* i.e. year ending 31 March   Source: *BBC Handbook, 1961*

The one hiccup in an otherwise fairly smooth curve of increase in TV licence-holders during the fifties occurred in the year before the Television Act; in that year, 1953, the Coronation raised the percentage increase in television licences higher than the preceding year.

As the number of single-channel receivers declined, so did the discrepancy between the 'average' BBC and ITV audiences.[14]

So the correlation between the comparative popularity, or acceptability, of ITV as against the BBC, which so agitated people at the time, is at best a partial correlation, or, rather, a correlation skewed in favour of ITV for the first half-dozen, and crucial, years. (The average life of a television set is usually reckoned to be seven years.) But the BBC was undoubtedly thrown into agitation, especially by the roaring success achieved by the give-away shows, and imported American drama series. 'They had never seen anyone earn pound notes for correctly distinguishing his left foot from his right, or a wife win a refrigerator for white-washing her husband in 30 seconds starting from NOW.'[15]

Towards the end of 1956 the ITV network was running nineteen series and serials a week, five of them on Saturdays, the one day on which BBC was still able to claim a majority audience.

A growing body of criticism and some embarrassing incidents, rounded off by the Pilkington Committee's general charge of 'trivialisation', effectively reduced the amount of programme time devoted to quiz shows and similar fairground booby shows, which had for Independent Television Companies the overwhelming attraction of being both vastly popular and very cheap.

The BBC refused to fight ITV on the same terms. It was only slowly that senior officials in the BBC shed their distrust of television, and their distaste for it. (Sir William Haley, Director General until 1952, when he saw a demonstration of television at E.M.I. in 1944 'commented to its then Managing Director in my presence that he wouldn't have a television set in his home'.[16]) Sir Ian Jacob and Gerald Beadle, then Director of Television, both claimed that the BBC could, if it would, regain a majority audience if it did fight ITV at its own game, but devoted themselves instead to what they saw would be a lengthy campaign of holding at least 30 per cent of the audience (which became something of a magic figure, with the widespread belief that if the BBC's audience share fell below that, the BBC would be faced with a revolt against the licence fee) with the possibility, over the years, of climbing back to parity. This in fact was done, but largely by a continually grudged, and unspoken, acknowledgement of the original, and still fundamental, function of broadcasting – to provide entertainment. The BBC's climb back to parity was achieved by 1962, when more than 95 per cent of viewers possessed two-channel receivers.

It was regarded by the BBC as accomplished by expanding the range of entertainments ('Steptoe and Son', 'Z Cars', 'Maigret', 'TW3' and so forth) and by the 'new look' of news and current affairs.

> 'In my view, BBC-TV's new management achieved the same end by the more subtle means of infusing new life into its output, so that, still clearly distinguishable from the output of ITV, it was in its own distinct way just as entertaining.'[17]

All the same, it has to be remembered that the biggest regular audiences commanded by the BBC during the early sixties were for the 'Billy Cotton Bandshow' and the 'Black and White Minstrel Show'. And entertainment, recognised as the big audience-puller, was undisguisedly regarded and used as groundbait which was the term used to describe their own contribution by Light Entertainment producers in the BBC during the sixties. By Independent Television Companies it was very clearly regarded as groundbait for advertisers; in the BBC it was regarded as groundbait for audiences who might be induced to continue watching programmes of a more informative, or intellectually stimulating but less entertaining kind. In terms of the ethos which had been cultivated within the BBC during the fifties, Light Entertainment remained an unfortunate necessity, its marginal character inescapably perpetuated in the adjective tagged on to its very title.[18] So, even in 1963, the producer of 'Steptoe and Son' could say:

> 'It is very difficult, no matter what prestige one attains in a good Light Entertainment show, to realise that prestige in comparison to other parts of the BBC output. The cachet is not there.'

But, however shamefacedly, the BBC had been driven back to first principles. Broadcasting was, first and foremost, a means of entertainment. Even news came second, and still does. By 1960, most people in the BBC had been made aware that, whatever else it did, it had to deliver programmes which were entertaining. Only if it showed itself able to broadcast enough, good enough, and varied enough programmes of entertainment would it be able to survive, let alone exploit its entertainment in the way in which sound broadcasting had done, as a carrier of information and enlightenment.

The competitive relationship which now exists between the BBC and ITV becomes increasingly difficult to describe and to evaluate, not only for outsiders but also, it seems for officials within the Authorities themselves. There are areas of direct competition, and areas of cooperation, but these are overlaid by layer after layer of convenient fictions, 'traditional' public images, and labels fixed by each on the other. (Patronising terms like 'Auntie BBC' and 'the Beeb', so current now, were not in use during the fifties, and are a fairly obvious counter to the hauteur with which the BBC treated its 'commercial' rivals in the early years when it was losing almost two-thirds of the television audience to Independent Television.)

The problem of dealing with 'the competition' has resolved itself into matching like with like. Huw Wheldon, in his apologia, 'Competition in Television', shows how much this simplified life:

> 'During the sixties, it became clear, after a good deal of research [sic], that the BBC Television audience as a whole was suffering between 8 and 11 o'clock at night because the ITA Companies at that time were running *Coronation Street* and *Emergency Ward 10* at 7.30, thus winning the audience in the early evening. The audience then tended to stay with that network for the rest of the evening, come what may. This again was simply the inheritance factor at work. We, therefore, went to great lengths to put a group of programmes on at the same time – popular comedy shows, in fact, Monday through Friday – and by so doing were eventually able, with popular competing against popular, to claim half the audience available at 7.30 and, in consequence (and it is this that matters) half the audience available for the whole range of programmes which followed during the evening as a whole.
>
> Gradually, and ineluctably, what was emerging was that, given competition – and a competition, incidentally, that was not of the BBC's seeking – we were driven, in some degree, to fight like with like; film against film, Current Affairs against Current Affairs . . .
>
> In theory it would indeed seem very sensible that if *Panorama* was at 8 o'clock, as it has been since what, in Television terms, is time immemorial, *World in Action* should be placed elsewhere so that the audience could exercise a choice, and, furthermore, if they wished, see both. In practice, *World in Action* has in fact been transmitted at 10.30 on Mondays, 10'clock on Tuesday, 10'clock on Friday and 10'clock on Mondays, and since 1968 where it is at present, at 8 o'clock on Mondays. . . . The simple fact [is] that *World in Action* drew a better audience in its present setting than elsewhere. Certainly, this can be said: that if *Panorama* ran opposite a movie on ITV, and if *World in Action* ran opposite a comedy show on BBC1, the audience of *both* Current Affairs programmes would drop steeply.[19]

The people who run the BBC and ITV are at least as intelligent as their critics. If people like Huw Wheldon and his colleagues really believe that this is the way to handle a competitive situation, there must be reasons other than those advanced in his lecture, although those same reasons may have been honestly held.

Competition now seems to be accepted as a fact of life for both BBC and ITV, and is defended by both. There is one obvious reason for this; it makes life easier for them. Whatever may have been the case in the first ten years, what we now have is the BBC and the ITV pacing each other rather than competing with each other. This is less mentally taxing, makes scheduling easier, is some kind of insurance against being driven into extravagance, and provides a very simple criterion for comparison in ratings. The principal field in which competition, rather than pacing, prevails is in sport; 'matching' does not occur to anything like the same extent so far as British sports are concerned, and the BBC and the ITV are competitive in a slightly more rewarding way than they are in other regards. When it comes to big international events, competition of a straightforward matching kind occurs and leads to quite pointless extravagance.

The benefits of duopoly are not confined to controllers and planners. They are certainly shared by producers, broadcasters, and technicians, who have developed some special expertise in the kind of programmes matched in this way. With the kind of closure of the labour market imposed by the three principal unions involved (NUJ, ACTT, ABS), the financial benefits are fairly considerable, especially, as we shall see later in this chapter, for technical operations staff.

INDUSTRIAL RELATIONS

The title, *Reluctant Militants*, which Professor Roberts and his colleagues at the London School of Economics chose for their book[20] on the growth of trade unionism among technicians and 'white-collar' workers is not one that would commend itself to the leaders of such unions, or to many of their members, nowadays. Yet it is an apt enough description of the history of the spread of trade unionism among workers of higher occupational status or with higher educational or training qualifications than skilled manual workers, who used to form the 'aristocracy of labour' in earlier generations.

Since the changed pattern of industrial relations in the BBC is in part the consequence of a national – indeed, international – trend, it seems proper to give some indication of the size and significance of this general trend by way of preface to what can be said about industrial relations within the Corporation.

Nationally, the numbers of white-collar and technical workers together grew by 166 per cent between 1911 and 1966. Manual workers' numbers grew by only 5 per cent during the fifty-five-year period; in the later years, moreover, the numbers of manual workers actually fell – although the trend was slightly reversed after 1961.

Most of the growth of white-collar workers and technicians occurred after 1945, and at an accelerating pace.

Membership of trade unions among this section of the workforce has increased even more rapidly – again especially in more recent years; between 1964 and 1970, the membership of 'white-collar' members of trade unions went up from 2,623,000 to 3,531,000, an increase of 35 per cent. And there is plenty of room for further growth, since trade union members in 1970 accounted for only 38 per cent of the white-collar labour force, as against the 53 per cent of manual workers who belonged to trade unions.

While the absolute and relative growth of the white-collar and technical labour force has been universal among Western industrialised countries, the growth of trade unionism among them on the British scale is not. In the United States, for example, the white-collar membership of unions actually fell, and would have fallen much more had not the Kennedy administration given the all-clear for government employees to join unions. In France, Italy and other European countries, while there may have been a growth in trade union membership among white-collar workers, especially technicians, junior managers and supervisors and lower professional workers, they seem to have joined existing trade unions – which in any case are much fewer in number and tend to be 'industrial' unions – i.e., they draw their membership from workers in single or closely related industries rather than from occupational groups. Nevertheless, the underlying factors which have led to the emergence of white-collar unionism in Britain obtain in these other countries too; what is different is the variety of strategies adopted by the occupational groups concerned, strategies seemingly determined by the existing pattern and the prevailing climate of industrial relations, trade unionism, and the historical circumstances which had produced it. In America, for example, it seems like that similar and even more strongly marked changes in the industrial structure and the occupational system – changes which have led to white-collar workers actually outnumbering manual workers – have produced a strategy of 'professionalisation' – a tendency to define rights, pay and conditions in terms of educational and technical qualifications, a tendency facilitated by the much higher rate of change of jobs characteristic of American office-workers, technicians, lower professionals, and managers. In France, one of the most distinctive features of the political scene in the sixties was the formation of loosely associated but militant groups among *les cadres*, often highly politicised; May 68 in France was not unconnected with this development, but in fact seems to have succeeded in smothering it – at least as a distinctive movement, at least temporarily.

The reasons for the sheer growth in numbers of the technical and white-collar labour force are familiar enough: the enlargement of civil service and governmental agencies, national and local; the acceleration in the growth of social and educational services; the expansion of industries based on new technological advances; and the accelerated rate at which more sophisticated manufacturing, handling, and control machinery replaced manual labour in established industry. But this does not explain the increased attractiveness of trade unionism for people in occupations which had traditionally regarded the trade union movement as at least irrelevant to their work situation and career prospects, and, in most cases, inconsistent with their political affiliations and social status.

The explanation is perhaps clearer if one resorts to the terminology of the French for distinguishing the separate sections of the industrial and occupational system: the *patronat*, the owners and controllers of enterprises and organisations; the *cadre*, the block of line managers and ancillary staff, office workers, technicians, salesmen and others which forms the framework (*cadre*) of the organisation, serving the *patronat* as the instrument of organising planning, and controlling productive activity (Galbraith's 'technostructure' is a somewhat dramatised term for the same concept); and the *contingent*, the people who man the productive plant, or whose work consists in serving customers or providing services to users. Traditionally – i.e., during the long period of what is now called 'mature industrialism' – the *patronat* was of course identified with the organisation as the owners or the representative of the owners; the *cadre* provided the essential instrument of management and acted as the carriers of the special knowledge and experience needed to conduct the enterprise: they had career hopes, if not career prospects, which might conceivably gain them entry to the *patronat*; the *contingent* was the 'labour force', essential, of course, but a force which could be expanded or contracted as market and other circumstances dictated, with their movement in and out of employment regulated by the familiar machinery – often state-operated by employment exchanges – of the labour market, and facilitated by the provisions of the welfare state.

What the figures quoted earlier demonstrate is the immense growth of the *cadres*, as against the *patronat* and the *contingent*, a growth which was the direct consequence of their much greater significance to the operation of enterprises, industrial and non-industrial alike. At the same time, the numerical stability of the *patronat* meant – very clearly – that the odds against ever ascending that far were much smaller than they had previously seemed to be. More importantly, the growth of specialisation – which had itself contributed to the increased numbers recruited into the *cadres* – lowered the ceiling of promotion and shrunk the space for movement between jobs within the organisation. Most important of all, perhaps, the long period of near-full employment which followed the war was used by organised trade unions in all countries to negotiate higher earnings for their members. (By 1968, average manual workers' earnings in Britain were 2½ times – in real terms – what they had been in the twenties.) B. C. Roberts and his co-authors quote a passage from the evidence given by the General Secretary of the Draughtsmen and Allied Trades Union to the Donovan Commission which reflects the feelings of his membership about what they saw as the unfair and absurdly anomalous situation they had been forced into:

> 'If [the draughtsman] had chosen to remain in the workshops in a manual craft capacity – not having to accept the higher demands for technical education, performance or responsibility – then at the age of twenty-one years he would enjoy earnings several pounds more per week than had he accepted "promotion" or "creaming off" into the design office.'[21]

Draughtsmen, who are recruited from the ranks of craft apprentices, may be a special case, but the same sentiments were present throughout many, if not most, of the occupational groups who staffed the *cadres*. In 1970, I interviewed lecturers in university engineering departments who, with good professional qualifications and useful industrial experience, had applied for academic posts because the salaries (£2500–£3000) then, were so much higher than they had received or could expect, in industry. Technicians who did not possess qualifications of this kind were, of course, much worse off not only in terms of their existing work situation and salary, but of their prospects – because the influx of 'graduates' had introduced a virtually impenetrable ceiling to their own advancement.[22]

These tendencies, felt throughout the occupational structure, of shrinkage of career prospects, increased distance from the *patronat* (in any case increasingly concerned with policy planning and considerations external to the enterprise itself, and devolving concern with all their employees to personnel officers, management development schemes, 'training courses', and the like),[23] relative deprivation in terms of earnings, and growing awareness of being boxed in by their own specialism – all these, I believe, led to the dissolution during, the sixties of the *cadre* as an entity, as a set of occupational groups enjoying a privileged position in common, willingly accepting their dependence on their betters and adopting conformity with their tastes and beliefs. They had indeed constituted a *Dienstklasse*, a 'service class', the term Ralf Dahrendorf took from Karl Renner to designate the class which provides a bridge between rulers and ruled:

> 'More than any other social category, the service class is committed to the ruling norms which it administers without having made them; more than others the members of this class tend to be "conformist" (if this pseudo-sociological expression is permitted here). The member of this class has no choice but to be "other-directed". He has to take his cues from elsewhere – that is, to be more precise, from "above".'[24]

The description was out of date by the time, 1964, it was printed.

The path followed by industrial relations in the BBC over the past thirty years is almost a paradigm of the historical process I have sketched. The control-consensus period of the thirties was marred by only one episode – the quite ludicrous business of the talking mongoose.[25] 'What Reith was anxious to secure above all else', writes Briggs, of Reith's attitude towards his staff, 'was a feeling of loyalty. Given this, he felt that everything else would follow.'[26] What 'everything else' was, in this connection, transpired in 1935, at the time of the Ullswater Committee, when the question was raised of the desirability of forming a Staff Association. The question was put to the vote of the entire staff. Eighty per cent were opposed to the idea.

Two years later, however, the newly-appointed Director of Staff Administration, W. St J. Pym, while accepting the verdict of the referendum, went on to point out that 'it probably represented not so much a straight vote on the general principle as a vote of confidence in the present management', and concluded that it was advisable to provide for a Staff Association, on the grounds that 'The Corporation will no doubt continue to be exposed to hostile criticism, so long as no form of staff representation exists. Such criticism, however ill-founded, is bound to have an irritant effect on the public and on the staff.'[27]

It is hardly surprising that, although some preliminary moves were made, it took the outbreak of war, and the unsettling period of the BBC's delivery into the hands of the Ministry of Information, to get things moving. Then, not one, but two associations were formed – the engineers setting up their own. They were amalgamated shortly after V.E. Day in 1945 into the BBC Staff Association.

The first breeze of the wind of post-war change came with the Beveridge Committee, which reported in 1951. The renewed Charter of 1946 had for the very first time contained a provision for staff representation, but left it for the Corporation to 'seek consultation' only where it was not 'satisfied that adequate machinery exists for achieving' what it saw as the purpose of the provision laid down by the Charter. And the Corporation, having itself a Staff Association before the Charter had enjoined it to do so, thereafter had declined to recognise any other organisation as a body with which they were prepared to negotiate on staff questions. (Of course, when it came to performers, the Corporation had to negotiate with performers' unions: Equity, the Variety Artistes' Federation and – toughest of all – the Musicians' Union.) The Beveridge Committee commented:

> 'This attitude has been criticised on more than one occasion in Parliament. It has been challenged before us by both individual unions such as the National Union of Journalists and the Association of Cinematograph and Allied Technicians, and by the Trades Union Congress. . . . In brief, the case put by the external unions is that the attitude of the BBC is a denial of the citizen right of being represented in collective bargaining by the association of his own choice. The view was expressed also that the Staff Association is not really independent of the Corporation and further that the failure of the Association to enlist as much as half of the total staff of the Corporation is an indication of lack of faith in it by the staff.'[28]

There is a nice irony about the last allegation; fourteen years earlier, the same fact had been interpreted as a sign of the trust of the vast majority of the staff in the justice and equity which prevailed in the Corporation's treatment of its staff, and of the loyalty of the staff to the BBC. But later developments give another twist of historical irony to the BBC's response to the unions' charges; they invoked the newly instituted grading system:

> 'The Corporation's rates of pay and conditions of service, while having due regard to outside standards, are closely integrated. The Corporation has its own system of job evaluation by which it equates rates of pay throughout the Corporation among the different categories of staff in accordance with their responsibilities and other factors, and this can best be achieved if all rates are negotiated with a single trade union which understands the peculiar problems of broadcasting and is fully informed as to the nature of the duties carried out by the staff as a whole. In the Corporation's opinion, such co-ordination of rates and conditions of service, carried out in the interests of fairness to staff, could not be obtained if negotiations were conducted with a number of craft [sic] unions, even through the medium of a joint council whose composition would inevitably reflect different interests.'[29]

No one seems to have noticed that the very last phrase in that particular paragraph shot large holes in the argument the Corporation was presenting, an argument which the Staff Association fully supported in its own evidence. But the Beveridge Committee, having read and listened to an unprecedentedly large amount of evidence on the matter, left things more or less where they were, recommending only that the BBC should 'recognise' any union which could claim a membership of more than 40 per cent of employees in the relevant occupational class, but that if there were more than one union accorded recognition, the unions would have to 'work together'.[30]

The Beveridge Committee left the situation unchanged; but it had provided an opportunity for trade unions and the BBC to stake out the disputable territory. The Staff Association took sides with the BBC in the importance it attached to the conception of public service broadcasting as demanding a degree of integrity among staff and trust between management and staff beyond anything which could be contractually prescribed. Its evidence clearly reflects the 'control and consensus' concept of organisation which had been developed in the pre-war years. The memorandum is a lengthy document, but a few excerpts from some of its sections are sufficient to convey the general tenor. The brief paragraph on 'The Functions of Broadcasting' reaffirms the principles of public service broadcasting established and accepted from the very beginning:

> '22. Internal and external broadcasting in the United Kingdom must have common standards of moral responsibility and impartiality and, therefore, some form of central direction to lay them down. Any departure from the singleness or unity of the service (e.g. creation of a separate propaganda medium) would impair the effectiveness and authority of British broadcasting. It would also adversely affect the spirit of service which permeates staff. . . .'

A suggestion that rates of pay in the BBC fell short of 'the best standards' in private and public industry is prefaced by a reaffirmation of faith in the foundation of the quality of BBC staff on BBC tradition:

> '29. *Staffing*. A tradition of enterprise and adventure, a sense of service and responsibility, no less than technical responsibility, have produced the high quality of staff now in broadcasting. . . .'

Lastly, several paragraphs are devoted to the difficulties which conventional trade union organisation faced in organising BBC staff, and to the advantages over 'conventional' trade unions offered by the Staff Association.

> '31. Many of the individuals employed in broadcasting are extremely difficult to organise, and unless there exists an association of staff which caters for broadcasting as an industry, it is likely, even if there were appropriate trade unions for them, that many of them would not be recruitable at all. . . .

34. The formation of the Association provided an answer to the organisational problem, not only because it was capable of surveying the internal field as a whole, but because it contained the cohesive principle of singleness of purpose deriving from common employment. It inspired confidence because on the one hand it had no preoccupations with any other industry or service, and on the other its constitution, hammered out by the members themselves, secured for the complete democratic control of their own affairs. Finally, it was able to demonstrate that an instrument could exist completely subservient to the interests of broadcasting and its staff, and at the same time completely independent of the Management.

35. The charge has sometimes been made against the Association that it is a "yellow" union. This is completely refuted by the facts. The Association, and the bodies from which it amalgamated, have always conducted their negotiations on sound trade union lines. They have never at any time been instruments of the Management or in any way restricted in the content or manner of presentation of their cases.

Frankness in negotiation

36. It would be true to say that a degree of frankness exists between the Corporation and the Association which many trade unions and employers' organisations would have difficulty in achieving, but would gain from imitating. Subjects discussed, due to knowledge shared by members of the Association and the Management, have not infrequently been on a policy level much higher than any but the most experienced trade unions could hope to reach.'

This last paragraph (36) quoted from the memorandum, like the first (22), founded the Staff Association's claim to remain the sole organisation representing staff interests on community of purpose and interest which, in the last resort, existed between the BBC and its staff as the foundation of Reith's conception of a public service broadcasting system. His word had been 'loyalty' – from which all else followed. Yet the rest of the memorandum reveals the Staff Association itself accepting the basic premise of trade unionism, which is that no such community of purpose and interest can exist; it is an acknowledgement that the incorporation of its staff within the BBC had been succeeded by accommodation between staff and management.

The accommodation lasted no longer than the BBC monopoly of broadcasting. The Independent Television Companies, in their hurry to put into use their 'licence to print money', as Lord Thomson so embarrassingly called it a few years later, had to outbid the BBC for trained producers and technicians, and were in no mood to haggle over union recognition. The Association of Cinematograph Television and Allied Technicians (ACTT), still denied recognition by the BBC, stepped in quickly and assumed the role in commercial television which the Staff Association had in the BBC. And it negotiated agreements which went beyond anything the Staff Association had dreamed of. 'This Week', the oldest Current Affairs programme in Independent Television, to take one example, accepted an agreement with ACTT which was based on the union's experience and success in negotiating contracts for its members engaged for 'short' documentary films – which provided, usually, even shorter-length contracts and assured employment than did feature films, the whole British film industry, then as now, being characteristically run on 'casual' labour, with the casual labourers themselves, from actors to property men, seeking through their union some compensation for the inevitable periods of unemployment (of unpredictable length) by high rates of pay, allowances, and all the 'extras' which working on location, at odd hours, for extravagantly long hours – and for the times when filming was impossible – demanded of them. The 'shorts' agreement was the only precedent for the kind of work which was envisaged; the new television companies were venturing into new territory which might conceivably prove risky, so that it was hardly possible to guarantee the security of employment characteristic of work for BBC television. The 'shorts' agreement incorporated such elements as the 'four, four and four' composition of teams – four cameramen, four sound technicians, and four 'production' staff, including the producer. This kind of agreement had been fought for and won over a period of many years from British film managements which were, as they still are, suicidally opportunistic and irresponsible. Nobody knew which model – BBC or film industry – the independent television industry would follow. As it happened, the situation in television followed the BBC model, with the industry providing a structure within which people could follow a career, hold down jobs for as long as they wished (provided their competence stayed with them), and have pensionable employment. Also, over the next ten years, the industry provided more work and offered more jobs than there were people qualified to be able to fill them; even up to 1975, the ACTT kept entry open to most categories of qualified staff. Later programmes were manned according to less extravagent agreements, but 'This Week' still operated under the old 'shorts' agreement, even including provision for first-class travel for the whole team.

One of the most contentious areas of all this is the 'buying in' of material. One of the reasons why there is very little independent production in this country is that the union (ACTT) acts in total

> concert with the management over the question of 'outside material'. In the ACTT-ITCA agreement there is a clause about 'unique material'. The interpretation of that clause is extremely rigorous . . . If somebody had managed to film, say, Fidel Castro in the early sixties, that would be 'unique material', but basically there is complete hostility to the importation of 'outside' material; there's a very close watch kept on where material comes from, who shoots it. It very rarely happens, but for that reason there is the absolute sanction of 'blacking' the material; and managements tread very carefully in that sort of area.

The changes which the coming of Independent Television wrought on the BBC's situation were more immediately apparent in the pattern of industrial relations than on programme policy. In one regard, the Corporation stood firm; it refused recognition to the ACTT – even though many BBC producers and technicians joined the union so as to gain access to a labour market which provided, for the first time, employment options. The BBC Staff Association changed its name to the Association of Broadcasting Staff, the better to recruit members of the Independent Television Authority and the Independent Television companies – many of whom, of course, were departed members of BBC staff. After 1954 there was a three-year struggle between the ABS and the ACTT for recruits in independent television; the ABS lost out to the rival union so far as the companies were concerned, but gained a foothold in the Independent Television Authority itself and in the end became the sole union recognised by the Authority for its 1000 staff. A further move to broaden out from its 'house union' status by affiliating to the T.U.C. was voted down by the T.U.C.; but in 1963, when it tried again, it was successful.

On the other hand, 'outside' unions quickly got a foothold inside the BBC. The first, the National Union of Journalists, gained recognition early in 1955, though, following the recommendation of the Beveridge Committee, it had to join forces with the Staff Association in negotiations concerning particular categories of staff. A few months later, the Electrical Trades Union, which had had a sizeable membership among engineering craftsmen in the BBC, also gained recognition, largely because it was showing signs of becoming the dominant engineering union in independent television (later it changed its name to the Electrical Electronic Telecommunications Union, and then amalgamated with the Plumbing Trades Union). Lastly, the National Association of Theatrical, Television and Kine Employees (NATTKE), which had begun as an industrial union for all non-performers in the entertainment industry, was recognised by the BBC in 1958, again after it had established itself in Independent Television as the representative of the wide range of craftsmen, semi-skilled operatives and clerical workers employed in television.

In the space of five years, the BBC had become 'unionised'. It had happened largely because of the advent of independent television, and again it was a change which reduced the unique institutional quality of the BBC as well as its monopoly of broadcasting services – a unique institutional quality which consisted largely in the way in which the staff as a whole were incorporated in the BBC. In the days when Reith could speak of 'what the BBC does' as coming not from what one individual thinks but more and more 'from a consensus of opinion and experience', and when an administrative official could declare that 'the BBC is one Corporation, and can only be thought of by the listener as one individual', differences of opinion, disputes and negotiation between management and staff had been a matter of dealing with individual dissatisfactions and grievances.

In the 'control and consensus' regime established under Reith, which lasted until the creation of commercial television, loyalty could indeed be expected, and everything did follow from that. The establishment of the Staff Association after the war did recognise the possibility of divergences of interest between the 'Corporation' (i.e. management) and staff, but, as the Staff Association's memorandum to the Beveridge Committee had made clear, it was at one with the Corporation in the purposes and values to which it subscribed, and served to 'make representations' to senior management about such discontents and grievances as existed among its individual members. Trade unions, however, are founded on the assumption of ultimately conflicting interests between management and staff, and exist for the clearly stated purpose of defending or improving their members' pay and conditions of work. And the open conflict between the ABS and ACTT for recognition as the sole representative of staff interests in all broadcasting organisations could only be waged in terms of each demonstrating its ability to achieve that stated purpose more quickly and more effectively than its rival. In fact, with the ABS retaining 'recognition' in the BBC and ITA, and ACTT gaining 'recognition' in the commercial television companies, large numbers of BBC staff found it useful to join both unions; indeed, since the commercial companies were virtually fully unionised from the beginning, BBC programme staff and technicians might well become members of ACTT as an insurance policy against the time they might want to move, while staying out of the ABS. Either circumstance constituted a further incentive to the ABS to prove itself as militant as its rival.

The immediate consequence of the recognition by the BBC of the NUJ, ETU and NATTKE, alongside the ABS, as unions with which management would be prepared to negotiate on matters affecting the pay and working conditions of the members each union represented was what was called, by one union official, the 'industrialisation' of people in the lower grades of the Managerial, Production and Editorial (MP) grading structure and a definitive shift of technicians and manual workers into regarding 'working for the BBC' as something completely undifferentiated from working for any other employer, something, in fact, which was covered appropriately by the institutional framework of collective bargaining which prevailed throughout industry. Some of the older hands in the Personnel Division were all too conscious of this:

> Can I go back to one other thing you mentioned? – this 'dedication' among engineers. This is still present [in 1973], but possibly not to the degree it was. I think there is still a very healthy pride in BBC engineering; they're very much inclined to believe, though they might be quite so ready to say so in these days, that the system is the best in the world, second to none in techniques and everything else. *But*, ten years ago we still had a lot of the pioneering sense; even some of the really early boys were still with us. I think broadcasting has become to some people – some of the younger chaps – just another job in the technical field. I wouldn't want to overstress this, but, in a way, it's bound up with the increased unionisation of the BBC. The union position has changed markedly over the past ten years. We've got a great deal more union problems than we used to have. Strangely, when you were here before [1963] it was only the ETU that gave any real trouble. The ABS – which used to be just a staff association – were relatively non-militant; still fairly cosy, rather house-union. They've developed quite a lot since then; their shock troops have tended to be the technical operators in television. And there are a lot more hard-minded union members among the engineering fraternity than there used to be.
>
> *Why is this?*
>
> I honestly believe – yes, I think it's a national trend. We live in an age when doctors are active in trade unions, when airline pilots go on strike, teachers march past here in great columns shouting and handing out leaflets – it's the 'in' thing. We had a very light time with the unions for a very long time, really, and we're just catching up with what it's like in the big world outside.

For him, and for many others in senior management, 'unionisation' had lessened the 'sense of dedication' which had characterised BBC engineering. But for technicians and craftsmen as old as he in the game, it was 'managerialism' – what they called, of course, 'red tape', or 'using the proper channels' – which had punctured enthusiasm. This came out in one episode of a lengthy interview with a cameraman and a 'show working' supervisor (the equivalent of a chief stage hand).

O.K., now let me bring up the major question: How have things changed? If somebody – completely outside this situation we're in now – asked you what you thought had really changed in this place over the past ten years, what would you say?

Cmn: Well, what I think has changed is – it's in the studio, really. When I first came here, people were more enthusiastic – That's it in a nutshell.

Would you agree?

SWS: Enthusiasm, willingness to help – it all comes to the same thing.

Cmn: There was more of a pioneering feeling about it; now it's getting more like – I don't know – a 'corporation', you know?

Do you think it's the glamour which has worn off? Because there was glamour around ten years ago.

Cmn: Not really glamour.

SWS: No. You're still in there, you're one of the key people on the actual making of the thing. You can go home – and Jack there can see it in a couple of months' time. In *my* work, you can go home and the same night you can see your actual work on the box. And that's nice – I mean, you've actually been there.

Cmn: In retrospect, now, from the day I started – all the people I started with – the enthusiasm I had! And those same people and myself, now, somehow they're all a bit – war-weary. Your enthusiasm is curbed.

SWS: It's been kicked out of you.

Cmn: In a way – because you keep coming up against brick walls. It's not your job to be all that enthusiastic; you're overstepping a line, or the people you're working with might think that you're patronising them. You have to remain in a safe spot because you might upset your colleagues, or the producer, or –

Let's go at it another way. One of the things that's astonished me, and I've asked this question about how things have changed to top people and people at middle level, and so on, and they always give the same stock answer: 'everything's so much bigger now'. And this is nonsense: you've got what, 30 per cent? 40 per cent growth? That's nothing, over ten years. . . . What I think has obviously happened is that things are much more complicated for them now. So they're slower. Things are more complicated, much more elaborate. Do you think the Corporation is, in a sense, getting a bit muscle-bound so far as its organisation is concerned?

SWS: Office-staff-wise, yes.

Cmn: There's too many governors – you don't know who your governor is. In the end, I mean, it seems such a waste of time having to go through one channel and then have to go through another. You see, your whole job is based on spontaneous decisions right? and it frustrates you that they – they're there to decide! – have to go through this channel, you know, in short hops, when you're geared to a direct decision all the time. They want to deliberate, and you can't, not when you're on the floor [of the studio].

People working at this level, who knew and usually respected the producers and editors they worked for – and with – saw the 'management' at higher levels, or, rather, the system of management through which directors and production assistants had to work in order to meet emergencies or resolve dilemmas, as a bureaucratic maze, or as a kind of smog, which lowered morale and reduced people's effectiveness. And the union organisation comes to be seen as a way of short circuiting 'procedure' – of penetrating the smog.

If there's a problem on the floor, the proper channels, the paperwork, seeing all the different people before you can get a yea or nay – it all takes time. People get very frustrated. Before I relinquished the post of union representative I could get on the phone straight away to the Head of Studios and say 'This isn't on, this is against the rule book', and the thing would be done there and then. But for the normal man on the floor to try to get to him. . . ! It's a feat if you can even get inside his door. . . . The only way of stating a problem is through your Establishment Officer, who will look at you, you know, understandingly, and then say, 'I'll have a word'. Which is no satisfaction, you know. Before you came in we were talking – the things which amaze me about this vast Corporation! After all, if you're interested in your job and you ask for a tool which you feel is – relevant, it's only because you're interested in your job that you realise the tool is relevant. So you put the suggestion forward – but by the time it's come to fruition, it might be years.

What do you mean, exactly, by a tool relevant to the job?

Well, say, if I wanted a pair of stepladders – I mean, this is bringing it down to basics, and eventually I thought it ridiculous. We really do need stepladders. You tell your immediate superior, and then you wait, and wait, and wait. So in the end you can only go to your shop steward to represent you and make a louder voice. Because, after all, he is the Union, not just one man.

In this way, the industrial relations machinery in the Corporation has become lumbered with business which is properly the concern of management. Often enough, the consequence is that anxieties in senior management about the trade unions are heightened. Comparatively new to the BBC as unionisation is, its management falls easy victim to the traditional 'self-confidence trick' which the usual run of industrial management plays on itself, and comes to see trouble and dissatisfaction as generated entirely – and unpredictably – from below. Yet in many ways, craftsmen and technicians are often enough prepared to bend the rules negotiated for conditions of work – unless it happens too often, or seems unreasonable. And, with unionisation, and the new grading system, there will be different sets of rules for members of a studio team or film unit:

It has been said that the film people down here at Ealing are really more union-minded than most – that that's where all the tough-minded unionism really is. Is this so?

No. There is only one tough spot, and that is with the sparks – but that is only, again, because of the animosity that's been created against them. It all comes back to personalities. On the majority of shows I've operated, it's all been very happy – the P.A. will come up to the gaffer and say, 'Look, we want to go on a bit. Will you ask your chaps?' And he'll say, 'Yes, all right, I'll ask around' – and says, you know, either 'We're overshot a bit', or 'we're behind because of the weather'. They understand it's not the director's fault, it's the weather again, or something. Fair enough. But when you come back to base, they're union-minded in that the stages operate from nine o'clock to half-past five, right? The reason why they're union-minded there is that you are on flat money, you're not earning anything over the top. It's a hard day in the studio; you're locked in there, the lights are on the floor, on the ceiling, there's no windows, no air, and and at half-five they've had enough. They're not offered overtime – it's always asked as a favour. In the end they get fed up with favours, and they say 'No. Look, it's nine to half-five', and pull the breaker. Because otherwise you could go on to six o'clock, and then it's 'We'll just have a few more minutes', and really, nothing gets done in that time, so everyone gets shuffling – they've had enough, they want to go home anyway, because it's a hard day.

In the minds of at least some senior managers, the problems of industrial relations which had come with unionisation – and which, moreover, were regarded as entirely the consequence of increased union militancy which, they were persuaded, was a nation-wide trend – were, albeit tedious, exasperating, and, in the long run, expensive, less of a threat to the Corporation than the presence of what was always called 'a small minority' of politically left-wing people, many of them very talented, among production and editorial staff and among the upper levels of technical staff. These senior managers were particularly upset by the 'underground' press established within the Corporation – very much a spin-off from the underground press and the student movement of the late sixties – which mixed information 'confidential' to senior management with scathing, and often scatological, criticisms of individual managers, and with challenges to the constitutional legitimacy of the bureaucratic structure of the Corporation. The very combination of these very different kinds of anti-establishment tactics adopted in the BBC underground press tended to confuse – perhaps intentionally – the negotiable with what was, for the BBC, non-negotiable:

Pay and conditions is obviously one area, but that comes from the general economic climate. . . . Some of them, and it would be very difficult to generalise, some of them are much more concerned with having a say in the type of programme, about being consulted over that sort of thing.

How does this manifest itself?

Last year we were going to film a series called 'The Lotus Eaters' in Crete. We had a threat to black it – 'It was quite wrong that we should film anything in Greece.' . . . It manifests itself, in so far as it does manifest itself, in the underground press, in letters to trade union journals, in our own staff journal, saying 'we need a greater say in this, that and the other'. . . But at this stage – it's only a rumble, of course – we're saying quite unequivocally, 'Sorry. Editorial content and everything is solely a matter for management, and we're not prepared to discuss it. Certainly you can discuss the quality of the filming and this sort of thing, but not the editorial content – this is just indissoluble –

purely a managerial argument with the Government. You've got no say in it at all.'

The broadening of the area of trade union concern into what are traditionally the preserves of management is complementary to the tendency to resort to trade union representation as a quicker and more effective way of getting simple operational requirements met (like getting a stepladder for the job). This expansion of interest is sometimes recognised and accepted, but is also often difficult to disentangle from more familiar problems:

It's a general development of interest in organisation, you know. People are taking more interest in the running of organisations than they used to. Way back in '46, people used to do as they were told without actually realising that they were doing as they were told. Well, these days you can't do that with people; you've got to keep them in the picture and take them along with you.

. . . So, knowing more about it – or feeling they know more about it, at any rate – and having something to contribute, they feel they ought to be consulted. . . . It can't be written off as 'union militancy'. So how do you cope with a thing like this?

It's very difficult these days, because a lot of people in the Corporation are spending a lot of their time on union matters trying to do things they want to do but are prevented from doing by the unions wanting to do it some other way. It's almost impossible at times to get on with our work because of this. They recently installed a link from London to Birmingham to carry stereo programmes and the staff are refusing to operate that system. So, as a result, Birmingham aren't getting stereo on the radio programmes. The reason is very hard for us to fathom, but there's some demarcation dispute within the unions on whether the communications staff should run this or if the transmitter staff should run it. The fact is that it's quite ridiculous for the communications staff to run it because the installations are on the transmitter premises, with engineers present all the time. If that piece of equipment breaks down on the transmitter, you'd have to pick up the phone and ring up some communications man in Birmingham and ask them to come out and mend it. . . . It's just a fear with people about the future, they fear they are going to lose their jobs. But there won't be any redundancies because of this. . . .

Is it possible you've invented this difficulty for yourselves by creating specialist divisions between communications and transmitter engineers?

> It's different work, it's difficult to circulate people around, and I'm not sure that people want to do it, anyway.

The spontaneous shift of topic from 'interest in organisations' to 'demarcation dispute' and on to 'fear of the future' has to be regarded as significant because, one has to presume, they have become in practice indistinguishably involved one with the other. It is not, of course, only engineers who, in trying 'to do things the way they want to', find themselves 'spending a lot of time on union matters'. Embedded in their own professional concerns and committed to their own programme as they are, producers are understandably impatient of what must seem to them sheer obstruction or interference, and are very ready to defend their independence. Senior management, having 'made the grade' in programme production, as all of them, outside Engineering, Finance and Personnel, have, tend to sympathise with the producers' reaction, and to go further and harbour dark thoughts about a new wave of syndicalism.

> Broadcasting is not just for the broadcasters, broadcasting is for society, and why on earth should decisions be taken absolutely by a small commune of broadcasters who are not, certainly at the moment, and probably never will be – never can be – representative of society? Decisions about broadcasting have to be taken as a trustee for society, and if you're going to take decisions about broadcasting from a position of trusteeship of society, then the right means for taking them is not necessarily a commune of the workers in it.
>
> A fortiori, *it's not necessarily a Controller. What you might be arguing is for more power for the Board of Governors as against the Board of Management.*
>
> Oh yes, but this is the way I feel – well, the Board of Governors, the Board of Management are very important, but I mean this is the way I operate. I never take an important decision without feeling that I'm taking it as a trustee for society. . . . I think I am much more conscious of the public interest in the decisions I take than any committee of producers would be, and this simply for the reason that I have worked my way to this position through a variety of jobs.

This, I suppose, could be said to be the true voice of bureaucratic authority, in its quite specific, Weberian, sense; authority drawing its legitimacy and support from the judgement of superiors (the appointments board) that he was better fitted for the post than any other candidate according to rational criteria applied to their assessment of the necessary, and desirable, qualifications for it. However, the case is somewhat altered since Weber,[31] and the judgmental authority of superiors is now, it seems, regarded as questionable – especially in 'professional' working organisations. The confrontation which can occur between two very different views of how the process of selection should operate (and hence of the nature of the authority involved) is illustrated by the contrast between two accounts, which occurred quite spontaneously in interviews, of the preliminaries to the appointment of one senior manager in Television Centre.

The first account is from the point of view of a member of the professional staff of the department:

> Just occasionally, one hears from the Head of Department that such-and-such was said at that meeting [Weekly Programme Review], but it doesn't filter all the way down, no. I mean, if you're too far down the line, it doesn't get through, and the changes at the top that effect us really are terribly noticeable, I mean in this department. The change of head of department affected us very directly; we were all very concerned in who was going to take over, and we wished to have some part in that decision-making process.
>
> *Were you consulted?*
>
> No, we were not consulted, so we therefore went and made our views felt.
>
> *Oh, did you?*
>
> Yes.
>
> *To whom?*
>
> Well, what happened was – initially, I think, as I understand the position it was going to be a straightforward appointment. A----, who had been doing the job, was promoted to B---'s position, and his successor was going to be appointed by him. He, I think, decided that this would cause a certain amount of ill-feeling in the department, and that therefore he would 'board' it – he would have the position filled [through the 'Appointments Board' procedure]; he wouldn't make a straight appointment. That therefore threw it open to a number of candidates. But we all knew, in the department, who – if you like – the 'official' management candidate for the job was. You know he's being groomed – you can tell.
> At that point in time, a large number of us didn't feel that that person was necessarily – at that time – the right one for that position. So what we did was, we got together, we left out

senior people, because they were eligible – once the position was 'boarded', they were eligible to apply; we left out assistants because they are in vulnerable positions – a lot of them are on short-term contracts. Se we limited the number, but everybody was involved, knew what was going on.

How did you manage all this? Where did you meet?

In the largest room in the department. What we did, actually, was that we got together and discussed in great detail what we, as people working in this department, required from our head of department. We analysed the job, what we, as professionals, wanted, not what management wanted, not what anyone else wanted, but what we wanted from our head of department.

Which is. . .?

We wanted, basically, professional integrity – a complete understanding of the way we, as professionals, function. We do a very difficult job. We wanted somebody there who would fight for us – whom we could go to and who would understand, who would have the expertise to be able to express these views, but, first and foremost – a selfish thing: complete interest in us. Also someone who had nothing to lose in that he was not interested in the promotion stakes and who would not have to play it safe.

There followed a fairly lengthy account of the meetings, the nominees, the ballot – which produced three names of people with whom 'an enormous number of people would be satisfied'. A letter was then composed enumerating all the qualifications the staff wanted from a Head of Department, the whole procedure which the staff had followed, and – after a third vote – including the names of the three 'departmental' nominees.

We decided that this letter would only go to management if we got 95 per cent support. In fact we got 98 per cent solidarity. . . . There was absolutely no pressure involved. It was very impressive the way it was done; those who didn't want to sign, their views were absolutely respected. We all signed the letter and delivered it to six points in the management structure. . . . In fact, our appointment was one of the names on that letter.

Did you take into account the fact that the chap would also be part of the managerial system, and had to be – not persona grata *– but somebody who really knew about the machinery of management in the BBC?*

Yes, we took that very much into account. It is very difficult to find somebody of that calibre – because our job, by its very nature – your ethic, your whole way of thinking and functioning is to a certain extent alien from that particular sort of highly political management. This is why this department gets beaten in the political game. In other departments higher up the management scale you have people in positions of authority whose . . . working experience has been built and developed on this sort of political astuteness

And who also happen to be numerate. Your lot aren't, always.

Absolutely – so one does feel in a very vulnerable position. . . . If we are vulnerable and we can't do much about that vulnerability, then we want someone who cared about us, anyway. . . .

What is immediately striking about this narrative is that it represents in a simplified way the confrontation that ordinarily occurs more obscurely and less explicitly between the world of professional values and that of traditional administration. But equally impressive are, first, the turmoil that seemingly accompanied what – in any other context – would be a perfectly reasonable and rational course of action for grown-up people to follow and, secondly, the entirely flexible, tolerant, way in which the action was accommodated by 'the management' – which the procedure had been designed to challenge. Yet, flexible and tolerant as the management may have appeared, it is clear that the episode was treated as *sui generis* – as a special case, much as 'industrial disputes' are:

They're not asking for participation in the sense of being on the Board of Management; they are asking for the right to access to information on which they can base representations.

It sounds a terrible imposition on management time, but in fact, if you can organise it, it means less than constantly trying to deal with people who are trying to pressure you.

Oh, but we shall. We're not saying 'you can't'. We are saying 'here is the information' – I mean, we must.

So what do they do with it, then?

Well, this is just starting, you see. I think this is the first year in which they formally asked for full information about the load of work, by week, on each servicing department, for example, and we shall provide that. We are in the process of providing it now, and we shall see what happens.

They haven't got to the point – there hasn't been a notion that these people should be elected?

I don't know much about the moves within other departments in that direction. There was some kind of meeting, I think, in– – – when the last head left – saying, you know, 'We'd like to elect our head of department'. Here's an example from closer at hand. The head of one department was promoted, and it was known that the likely field of candidates was about ten senior people. The others – not the candidates themselves – did a round-robin which they sent to me and they said, 'This is just to say we hope you will feel able to appoint one of the following who would have our confidence', and they listed about four people. Now in a curious way – I mean, it might be *more* difficult to appoint one of those four people. But we did, because they were right. And then they did it again, they overstepped themselves, they did another one about the man who was appointed. He was 58 or thereabouts, and they knew that his retirement at 60 or extension was being considered, so they did another round-robin saying 'You jolly well extend it, we like him!'. And it was absolutely maddening, because this came to my desk on the day that we had actually decided to do just that! And I said, 'Look, stop it, because the next time you do that, we'll have to take the reverse decision!' But that's the only example I know of in my area.

Perhaps the one safe conclusion to be drawn from this tendency, and from the response of management to it, is that 'industrial relations' have now ramified in a number of different directions and are involved directly in wider issues of management and policy. In the BBC, as elsewhere, there is just a possibility that industrial relations may come to be seen for what they are – an integral part of the proper concern of general management, and not of a specialist section of it.

3 Settings

PHYSICAL SETTING

There is a various, shifting, but necessary relationship between ourselves in their different aspects and locations, and the scenes, furnishings and costumes which equip the events through which we move. The relationship is emblematic. Just as speech and dress are used to place a person socially, intellectually and culturally, so are furniture, house and even district used as map references for the present position and compass direction of a social career. We persuade ourselves that we can read in streets and frontages, and in the interiors deliberately, cunningly or rudely offered for view, the incomes, the social standing and the pretensions of the dwellers within, attaching the correct social weighting to looped window curtains as against straight hanging ones, or none, to figurines as against posters from the twenties, to an assortment of lamps on walls and furniture as against a central light.

It has to be said that there is a significance beyond that of the games people play attaching to the business of finding the right place to live, of matching one's home, furniture, pictures, records, wallpaper and books and friends to each other and to one's own personal identity and values. To write it off as conformism, 'other-directedness' or status-seeking is to reduce sociological explanation to market research. People do not receive their social identities from advertisers, neither are they formed in a social matrix, with the appropriate glossary distributed free to the smart, the 'with-it', the well-informed. Of course there are uniformities; it is a necessary consequence of there being a finite number of styles. There is display; it is a necessary consequence of having to declare to others the sort of reaction one looks for, or of laying claim to one place in the social order rather than others. But the teenager whose designation is written out so explicitly in his shoes, jeans, T-shirt and haircut has himself chosen that designation and its marks. The young couples who spend their Saturday afternoons searching through albums of wallpaper patterns are looking not for something that will match the Joneses', or even go one better, but for something that will 'suit' – that is, will fit the style into which they want to organise their lives.

So scene and situation are, when we can contrive it, composed to fit each other and the actions, words and demeanour with which we fill them. From this very practice, it follows that when we cannot do so, and find ourselves in settings already composed by others, we compose our behaviour, and even our purposes and feelings, to be in compliance with the settings enclosing us or in revolt against them, but in any case in some meaningful and designed relationship to them.

It is the easiest thing in the world to find the social exchange value of the buildings and furnishings which form the context of working activities in the Corporation. The people I met were either in Television Centre and the buildings (Lime Grove, Kensington House, and Ealing Studios) associated with it, or Broadcasting House with its Portland Place annexes. The contrast between the architectural manner of Broadcasting House and Television Centre, between the heavy fortress shape and 'Head Office' treatment of Broadcasting House, and the 'technological' design and exhibition styling of Television Centre is not confined to the difference in dates – the 'datedness' of sound broadcasting and the novelty of television. The sentiment expressed by the man who said that Reith lived on in Broadcasting House and not at Television Centre could be read, without being too fanciful, into the peculiarly appropriate siting of the two buildings: Broadcasting House forced into the most inconvenient of sites but standing guard at the south-eastern approaches – from Whitehall, Parliament, and the West End – to the solid professional upper crust of British society located in the district between Liberty's and Lords; Television Centre finding a location which will above all allow it to grow, but in a district which derived its strongest flavour from exhibitions, dog racing, and the film industry. And the different balance of emphasis between central authority and organisation structure on the one hand, and programme-centred activities on the other is demonstrated by the reversal of basic design in the two buildings – the sound studios enclosed by the carapace of offices at Broadcasting House, and the erruption of studios, design shops and engineering sections outwards from the hollow, office-ringed, drum in the middle of Television Centre.

The symbolic references, both intentional and unintended, are hackneyed enough, but none the less real, taking realism in this case to stand for a fairly wide consensus about them. But the references are not, of course, one-way. Work in television differs from the sound broadcasting side partly because of the difference between Television Centre and Broadcasting House. So, because the two buildings have caught so much of the sense of their time and social function, because they represent so clearly the polarities of the Corporation's self-conception, the imprint of each contrast is made deeper and more distinct.

The contrast is rooted to some extent in the nature of each medium. There is size. Studio 3 in Television Centre is almost three times as big as the Concert Hall in Broadcasting House, and the ordinary sound studio has a cosy domesticity in comparison with the ordinary television studio. Television has its enormous and baffling array of lighting equipment and scenery sets, cameras and microphones mounted on trucks and mobile cranes, all contributing to the sense of occasion and momentous technicality. And this sense is almost, as they used to say, palpable in the studio gallery overlooking the studios, the loft from which producers direct programmes with the aid of producer's assistant (to check the script and time action), a vision mixer (to switch the sequence of scenes fed into monitor screens from the half-dozen or so cameras and prepared film sequences into the single output channel), a technical operations manager, responsible for the functioning of the crew on the studio floor, and lighting and sound supervisors in the next-door rooms. It is here, in darkness which is punctuated by the monitor screens, illuminated control panels or desk lamps, and which terminates in the window overlooking the studio, that the union occurs of large-scale technical and human resources, of the social, intellectual, political and cultural processes involved in television, and the awareness of an immediate but unknown audience of millions. It is too much to say that all this is caught in the design of the producer's gallery, but every physical appurtenance, from the noiseless floor-covering to the arc of the control desk skewed across the room (and facing not the window overlooking the studio, but the double rank of monitoring screens) realises and reinforces it. It is an intensely dramatic place, dramatic not only in the obvious sense of the felt presence of an unseen audience, or of the manipulation of unseen performers and technicians, but in the immediate experience of the excitement and desperations which are enacted in it day after day as the final studio rehearsals move towards performance in front of 'live' cameras. This highly charged mental and moral environment is caught, reflected and magnified in the whole design and styling of the room. Instead of being dominated by the technical apparatus it really belongs to, the management and design of the gallery smooths and fits the complexities of the control panels and communication links into harmonious or compliant relationship with the one task. One feels the 'cockpit' sense. This rendering in visual, sensitive terms of the television combination of technology, dramatic performance and mass communications, each carrying the highest and most 'contemporary' of esteem, makes the production gallery the most glamorous of work settings, where the term 'the coal face', applied so often to the task of producing television programmes, becomes understandable in its metaphorical rightness and ludicrous inappropriateness.

The offices are offices. But even when their occupants are functionally remote from the studios, the circular form of the inner space of Television Centre and of the corridor which runs around every floor is a perpetual reminder of the singular purpose of the building, no less concrete than the traffic of dozens and sometimes hundreds of performers, studio crews, and production team members through the restaurant and cafeteria. One can almost forget the existence of the studios and the technical apparatus of broadcasting in the Langham Hotel and in the offices of Broadcasting House, which overlook streets and overhear the traffic of the everyday world outside the Corporation. The distinctness of television, so far as the Corporation is concerned, lies as much in the totality of the occupational milieu created by it and for it as in its presentational range, its comparative youth and its greater audience appeal.

The relationship between the members of the Corporation staff and the environment in which they work takes on ecological aspects which are rather more clearly apparent than in most occupational settings. Idiosyncrasy can be displayed more easily at Portland Place, and makes itself felt in the disposition of furniture, in prints and photographs on the walls. Television Centre Offices are less domesticated: the coloured holiday postcards are on the wall behind the secretary, but they are fewer, and usually from remote or exotic places; there are the token bookcases in the more highly placed executive offices and occasional joke notices in others, but the main visual representation of the occupant of an office is the particular kind of paper cluttering the desks and tables. And one significant indication of the relationship between Television Centre and the people who worked in it seemed to me, in 1963, to lie in the fact that many people, even those who had worked there from its opening, confess to losing their way in the building, the circulation space of which is designed on the simplest of plans.

What we have so far considered is, of course, the crude data from which occupational settings are composed, rather than the settings themselves. The physical surroundings, the buildings and their component rooms within which a single person lives out his working day, are resolved into a more or less diffuse network of working spaces connected by communicating passages, stairs, lifts, streets, telephones and vehicles. One individual's working life is in fact spent in one of the many networks built out of the total physical structure of all the buildings owned and operated by the Corporation and the interconnecting routes and recognised meeting places outside. This conception is again more familiar when it is applied to a whole urban society, which organises itself into social systems within the fabric of the city. Such systems are either physically segregated, like the 'worlds' of Fleet Street, of the law, of medical consultancy, of Wardour Street or of merchant banks, or are notionally – but just as clearly – segregated into networks, with what lies around each cell or cluster of the network relegated to clutter, noise, background, and intervening distance between associates. Such milieux as the worlds of advertising, gambling, scientific research, music, trade union affairs, and 'show business' are as well-defined for their inmates as if they were physically segregated.

Within the Corporation, analogous 'worlds' are built out of the whole system of buildings and traffic between them, worlds which may in large measure be physically adjacent, even largely congruent (and organisationally closely allied), but which are in actual – social – fact quite distinct. So it was only momentarily surprising for a man in Schools Broadcasting (Sound), to be able to say '[Schools] people in Television Centre and here never meet on any occasion. It was once suggested we should get in a bus once a year and go down there and have a tea-party!.'

SOCIAL SETTINGS

The fuller force of the distinctness of the individual networks begins to come home when a manager, asked if he 'was able to get round the studios', where the crews for whom he was managerially responsible worked, replied, 'Not as much as I would like. . . . I am, of course, very interested in studio work, but I have to make a distinct change of gear. I've got to say to myself, "Well I'm going down today to have a look into studios." When I get into studios I don't want to come into the office, and vice versa, you see.'

This isolation of the producer from his fellow producers, and his willing absorption in the production 'team' is something which has already been remarked upon, but the same is true of other specialist members of the team.

> Being a floor manager, I can't really speak about floor managers in general. That's a thing you might note, that floor managers don't know other floor managers terribly well.
>
> *This is true all through, it seems. People in the same department on the programme side don't know their colleagues.*

> Yes, we simply meet them socially – at odd times.

But even here, the segmentation and, more important, the feeling of separation, works itself out in the development of even smaller systems.

> Different people – classes – in the studio, technical people, are very inclined to stay as a group – in the canteen and between rehearsals. They don't mix. . . . The same is true of scenery staff. You usually get five or six allocated, and they stay together. It's something which is – traditional. You know, they eat together and so on . . . It's one of the things I found a bit off-putting when I came into television. At the lunch breaks, dinner breaks, unless I had an assistant, I'd be entirely on my own, because the scene shifters had gone off together, the technical crew would put two or three tables together and eat together, the producer and secretary – probably through sheer pressure – have a sandwich and beer somewhere – and one would find oneself on one's own. In the studio itself, there's not much of a barrier between sections. . . . As for producers being isolated from each other, they can after all see each other's shows. I should think there's less isolation between producers than there is between producers and the rest of the production staff.

It was therefore not eventually surprising, though at first and at times thereafter disconcerting, to find that, moving as I did from department to department, and even from group to group within departments, I was also shifting from one closed system of personal relationships to unconnected others, and that the people who worked in the same department, walked the same corridors, ate in the same restaurant, and followed each other occasionally in the same studio, existed in different worlds. Such worlds derived their own distinctness, necessarily, through the reduction of the other places and the other people inhabiting the same building to an anonymous background of Corporation activity.

While for the most part the networks coexist in the same physical milieu of studios, outside rehearsal rooms, workshops, conference rooms, restaurants and the BBC Club, there are certain junction points which serve to bind individuals and even groups together almost irrespective of their occupational network. Patronage of 'The George', a self-consciously preserved (rather than reconstituted) Edwardian pub and, at a rather more exalted level, membership of one or two clubs, provide for the exchange of gossip of 'shop' and other forms of social insurance familiar in the life of the British professional classes. More important in the life of the Corporation are the links established at the outset of careers in training courses or, for migrants to the London area, in a period of work in a Region: these links form part of the network of useful acquaintanceship, along with the fellow-feelings established between people in remotely different areas of the Corporation through membership of working parties and committees.

Acquaintance networks involving ordinary working relationships tend to be rather brief, or tenuous, or random, so far as the membership of the whole organisation is concerned. Yet there is, as one moves up the hierarchy, a closer interleaving of acquaintance networks and working relationships. This gives some colour to the feeling which people at the top of the Corporation – as of any other organisation – tend to have of there being under them not merely an assemblage of separate divisions and departments linked by a common technology, a common source of funds, a rationally disposed system of appointment and promotion, as well as a range of end-products similar in nature and made to specifications largely determined, or selected, by people at the top, but a large, ordered, collectivity of people at work – *their* work – infused with a moral order of its own. 'It works', said one member of the Board of Management. 'No doubt other people have used the same cliché, but it has worked and still is working on a kind of tribal wisdom.' Other people, in fact, employed other clichés, but there was little doubt that there was pervading the upper reaches of the Corporation a profound conviction that their view of what ought and what ought not to be done, of what was creditable and decent and what was not, what revealed ability, flair or brilliance and what revealed flashiness, mediocrity, insensitivity or trying to live above one's intellectual means was something generated within the Corporation and perpetuated by common purposes and common experience. After all, their own sense of the fitness of BBC things had brought them to the top. The moral order permeated all networks and all levels, but people at the top were, by definition, especially conscious of it, felt responsible for maintaining it, and, if need be, trying to correct or reorient it.

These feelings are real enough, but only in a particular sense. Read as a consensus, or a common ethos, it is usually spurious – if regarded as applying to the organisational hierarchy. If, however, the object of such feelings, is seen as a community – a working community – a specific, limited, but important significance attaches to them.

Robert Park, one of the founding fathers of community studies, overwhelmingly preoccupied with the spatial patterns of cities as he was, did say that 'ultimately the society in which we live invariably turns out to be a moral order'.[1] When E. P. Thompson, in a remarkable essay,[2] looks for some interpretation of the almost incessant series of urban disorders which occurred in English towns and cities and districts during the eighteenth and early nineteenth century, he finds it in the protest people were driven to make against the violation of what they thought of as a moral order which should govern the social relations of production, and the economic relationships of the market. Thompson, indeed, writes of a 'moral economy'. And this concept of the moral order which sustains communities runs through Norton Long's essay, 'The Local Community as an Ecology of Games'.[3]

The essay is really a criticism of the notion that a struggle for power is going on in communities in much the same way as, over the long term, a struggle for power – i.e. for sovereignty – goes on between classes and organised parties in the nation at large. But he starts from the point that, when one comes to look at local communities, there is no overall organisation which governs, or is supposed to govern, or can be appealed to, to exercise governmental control over everything that happens in a local community. 'Much of what occurs seems to just happen with accidental trends becoming cumulative over time and producing results intended by nobody.' And this kind of picture, he claims, applies to the local community whether it is seen as a political system, an economic system, or a social system.

Nevertheless, the local community stands as an order in which 'expectations are met and the functions performed'.

In trying to tease out and explain this apparent contradiction, Long suggests that we ought to envisage the local community as the field in which a very large number of games are being played – the banking game, the newspaper game, the manufacturing game, an ecclesiastical game, and so on. For each game there is an established set of rules, and a number of manifest purposes and goals to be achieved, and criteria by which success is marked. There is also a set of roles, or positions for the different players – however large a number they are – to operate in, as well as strategies and tactics learned from predecessors, from one's own experience, and 'occasionally subject to improvement and change'.

All this is familiar and acceptable enough. What Long then suggests, however, is new, and that is that the players in each game, whether it be the game of commerce, local government, of journalism, or whatever, are indeed playing a special game of their own, in which they have a prescribed part, and for which they have special training, in which they have special experience, and so on, but the game they are playing is observed, or observable, by everybody else, who may be principally concerned with playing their own game, but can also take time out to watch what is happening in other games – indeed, have to take time out to do so, for the results of other games can affect their own. So everybody, to a greater or less extent, in a local community has this double role of player and spectator. To be sure, local political leaders may be expected to be concerned with a variety of games, and have a general interest in the various games, but they have a game of their own to play, and there is a sizeable number of spectators of it, too.

But despite the absence of some overall organising institutional set-up, or set of institutions, all games have to be played under the surveillance, so to speak, of the rules of the larger, 'vaguer', set of rules which apply to all games. Try as they may to make their own particular game private, the walls which players erect may at any time prove to be embarrassingly transparent, and one of the overriding rules of the larger games is that, while it may not be possible or desirable for everybody to join in, it should be possible, and very desirable, for everybody to be able to watch.

'Working for the BBC' involves several things – a contract of employment, commitment to a job, and, beyond that, involvement in contributing to the successful accomplishment of the tasks which the group of persons of which one is a member is called upon to do. It also involves membership of a working community made up of a numerous and varied array of distinct small-scale social networks, each with its own set of 'rules of the game' for cooperating and competing with each other individually, and for cooperating and competing with other networks of persons linked by working relationships. But each game, which may be, and usually is, different for studio crews, engineers, producers, designers and so on, *and* for the production teams which they individually compose, may be, and usually is, observed by other groups, so that there have to be limits to the variation in the rules of each game. This is not to impute some kind of constant impulse to illicit moves and foul play kept under control only by the presence of spectators, but that when one speaks of a moral order prevailing in a working community as large as the BBC, what is under discussion is not some pervasive social conscience which is absorbed by recruits through some process of ethical osmosis but part of the actualities of the talk and actions which constitute work. And the essential point is that the 'management', as such, does not occupy the royal box, nor is it equipped with special penetration or scope of vision. They are indeed spectators of other games, as well as players in their own games, but they may not see any more of what is happening than others – although it is comforting, and common, for them to think so. What is true, of course, is that their own game is always much more consequential than most games – which is why it takes up much more audience time than any other game.

All of which may be illustrated by what is the most pervasive, and at times the most absorbing, of the player–spectator sports played throughout the Corporation – Grading.

GRADING

Every job in the BBC – with the exception of a small handful of top appointments – is graded for salary purposes. The system is not homologous, but consists of six 'grading structures'. These structures, reading from the highest to the lowest are:

Managerial, Production and Editorial (M.P.)
Operational (O.P.)
Administrative Services (A.S.)
Secretarial and Clerical (S.C.)
Craftsmen (Cr)
General Services (G.S.)

The grading system dates from the post-war years, and although the methods of grading have approximated more and more closely to what is generally known throughout industry as 'job evaluation', the principles and methods of the grading procedure are peculiar to the Corporation. They were developed after the war by officials in Administration Division, and, although often spoken of as obscure or couched in elaborate jargon, have been the subject of a number of expository documents. The original authors of the system have published a book on it[4] and full information about the criteria used in grading has been available to any member of the Corporation interested enough to seek it out. The essence of the BBC's grading system is the assessment of jobs – not persons – in terms of variable factors of competence, knowledge, and general ability required for them. The terms in which these criteria are couched have varied from time to time, but one rendering of them, during the sixties, was as follows:

application of specialised knowledge and experience
judgement
original thought
man management
responsibility in committing resources

Among the six 'grading structures' which are listed in descending order of seniority, responsibility, and pay, there is some overlap, especially in the last respect: pay. Some staff in the higher O.P. grades, for example, earn a good deal more in the year than some directors, partly, but by no means entirely, because of their entitlement to overtime, allowances for work which takes them away from home, and – a notable novelty – working 'unsocial' hours. Producers' Assistants, in 1975, agitated successfully for removal from the M.P. structure to O.P. grades.

The system of six separate grading structures replaced an earlier system in which there was one overall grading structure and which had lasted for some twenty years.

It is likely that the grading system provides the biggest, or at least the most widespread, source of friction and discontent in the Corporation. It was, and is, an heroic attempt to introduce order and some degree of rationality and fairness into the inordinately complex and difficult business of matching rates of pay with the value to the Corporation of a very large number of very different skills, qualifications and abilities, and to do this so as to secure people with the desired talents, to reward people with different talents but of similar value on an equitable basis, and to provide incentives for increased effort and the exercise of those talents.

Secondly, whatever may be said about the lack of precision and of objective validation of the categories used in grading, or of the criteria which distinguish grades, there has been singularly little questioning of the impartiality with which grading has been carried out by the branch of Personnel Division responsible for it. While there was much criticism of the grading system, and of its consequences, there was none of the people responsible for applying it.

Thirdly, the fact that all jobs are fitted into the grading system enforces the unity of the Corporation, and is an assurance of the intention of the Corporation that people in the background as well as in the forefront of the Corporation's activities should be paid in accordance with the demand for their job – that, as one man put it, 'poor Bush House should be equated with rich Television Centre'.

When all this is said, it remains true that the grading system has engendered a great deal of discontent. It is common enough in industry for matters of pay to act as a focus of discontent which may arise out of resentment against management generally, or against individual managers, or against conditions of work, or against boredom or the sheer pointlessness of what people are doing. Pay is the institutionalised area of conflict. But it would be unlikely that this is true of the Corporation, for two reasons. First, a great deal of evidence in interviews contradicts it, and hardly any supports it. Secondly, the level of articulate discussion in these matters, the general security of tenure which prevails among staff, and the manifest capacity of the Corporation to tolerate debate and conflict over so wide a range of its internal affairs all suggest that it is very improbable that issues of pay and grading have to serve as an interpretive medium through which grievances may be expressed which would otherwise have to remain unexpressed because of their seeming irrelevance or triviality beside the solidity and rationality of 'pay and conditions'. In the Corporation, at least, criticism of the grading system has to be taken at its face value.

Criticism is unending, and comes both from individuals and from organised groups. The secretary of one major trade union said that the BBC grading system was God's own gift to his union. It certainly enabled groups of specialists to manoeuvre themselves into higher grades by exploiting the openings presented by shifts in the technical or organisational setting, or in the grading system itself:

> I think what happened was that the Technical Operations Managers,[5] the Lighting Supervisors, Floor Managers and Designers were all at one time on grade B1. When the studio crews were formed, this was what the relativities were. So they judge everything else by what has happened to these other groups meantime. Immediately the Lighting Supervisors get worried when they discover that a particular type of Senior Designer at the next higher grade [B–] has been created and is in charge of two other Designers. And vast schemes come out which are presented to the management under the cover of, 'Don't you think the time has now come for a bit of a duality structure to be devised in lighting, in which these senior men are in charge of two juniors?' 'Wouldn't it work better if . . . ?'
> This is in fact what resulted in the up-grading of the Lighting Supervisors to B–, which happened only last year. The process is: the Lighting Supervisors make out a claim. Since they're all, if they've got to that stage, fairly intelligent, they put up a pretty good-looking claim. They pass this up to the ABS, who rewrite in in formal language, and it comes out as a claim at national level for the up-grading of Lighting Supervisors. It then gets taken over by the grading people. Naturally, management go through the motions, stalling it off as long as they can, but eventually the [section which deals with grading assessment] have got to do an investigation.

In this case, the Lighting Supervisors scored a handsome victory; indeed, their grading victory was regarded as the reason for their subsequent takeover of the leading role in studio crews from the Technical Operations Managers.

The reaction to this move illustrates precisely the way repercussions occur throughout the organisation:

> Where one naturally expected the Technical Operations Managers to object to this new arrangement, although they were given the opportunity to become Lighting Supervisors, the people who actually objected were the Sound Supervisors. You ask yourself, 'Why? The Sound Supervisors are just the same as they were before. Why are they complaining?' The answer

> was, 'We're going to be ruled by Lighting Supervisors, and they were equal to us before. There used to be this intermediate man called a Technical Operations Manager before, to whom we could both refer.' – although they spent their whole time saying they never referred to him. . . . When you suggest doing away with him, they all begin to say, 'My status is reduced. Because not only are my promotion prospects reduced but I'm also going to be under the control of my opposite number – a Lighting Supervisor.'

Carrying through a grading claim successfully could require a certain aptitude in internal politics. This particular change had been mooted a year or two earlier. When the news of the proposal began to spread, the Technical Operations Managers invoked the producers as allies. They, alarmed at the prospect of disruptive changes or, at best, a period of dispute and of disgruntlement which might seriously affect their work in the studios, came down heavily against any proposal to change the structure, and the move was blocked. It was successful at the second attempt because producers were informed and won over at the outset and, to avoid the possibility of the information leaking out and opposition being organised, meetings with staff to announce 'the Management's decision' were held before any meeting with the ABS. This procedure was later objected to by the ABS, but the Technical Operations Managers suffered a demoralising blow.

> It's been a bad year for the T.O.M.'s, especially the older ones. They don't really know what they're going to do. I suppose some of the younger ones can go on to lighting training, and some will make Supervisor eventually.

Conceived as a grid for determining the just allocation of payment for skill, judgment and effort, the grading structure manifests itself to the people who engage with it as an arena in which a complicated system of micropolitical action has developed, activated by individuals and groups looking to maximise the return on their investment in contractual engagements.

Until the last few years, there was a single grading structure, covering all staff. This eventually became extraordinarily complex, with intermediate grades interposed between every single stage in the whole ladder and, added to that, special personal allowances and, beyond these, individual merit awards. The new six-fold structure was introduced in order to reduce this complexity, but the same trend towards complication set in. By 1973 the grading structure was attracting the same kind of critical comment as it had in 1963; the only difference was that there seemed to be greater readiness to regard the anxieties, the complaints and the manoeuvering associated with grading as arising from its intrinsic defects rather than from human fallibility:

> *Are there more grades or fewer grades than there used to be* (in 1963)?
>
> There are fewer grades. We've got rid of some of the minuses, in effect.
>
> *Yes. They multiplied themselves almost year by year.*
>
> We still have quarter-grades as well as half-grades in Engineering, you know. I've always been agin this, for what it's worth, myself. We've often talked in this department about the 'salmon-ladder effect' of this. You know, you've always got the thought that you've only got to say there's a little more to a job and you can skip up another little grade level. Ideally, I'd much prefer a system where you got much more clearly defined broad bands of responsibility. The great danger now, and always has been, is that if you've got an engineer responsible for five black boxes, give him another black box and he wants a higher grade – but his function hasn't changed. So, in a way, this is one of the weaknesses of the system. We've still got it, though it's a little better; we're toying with other grading systems.

This was from a senior manager. A few days later, in 1973, a still more senior manager, discussing the selfsame weaknesses, remarked,

> Whether we can ever put this into reverse, I simply do not know. But it is very interesting that you should raise this, because when I was talking earlier about resentment towards the 'central institutions', what was in my mind was these two areas, appointments and grading – particularly the grading area.

So, while it is true to say that criticism of the grading structure was not used as a recognised and legitimate outlet for disgruntlement, it is nevertheless true that the innumerable instances of rivalry, invidious comparison, disputes about 'differentials' and so on all homed in on to the single target of the grading structure. So much so, that the placards displayed by pickets outside Television Centre after a walk-out in 1973 carried the statement 'BBC Grading = cheap labour', which was cryptic enough for insiders, and unintelligible to outsiders. A reference to it provided an appropriate starting point for an explanation by a senior official in Television of the way in which grading affected, or infected, collective bargaining and a wide sector of management–labour relations:

> *If there is an in-built constitutional or traditional system of re-grading – i.e., if you have a re-grading team going around constantly checking jobs.*

as indeed they must if the job-content of the jobs is changing – it constitutes a constant temptation to people to get bothered about other people getting rises because of what they regard as negligible differences between such jobs and their own. Do they get bothered in this way, nowadays?

No. I mean you can't stop people thinking they are under-graded in comparison with another bunch of layabouts who don't do anything like as much as we do. They might actually be right; they might not, of course. But the way they do this is to appeal; and the way this is handled is that they formulate through their union – and it's invariably done through the union – a grade claim, which is a claim for an upgrading. Now the union itself has got to accept that there is a case, a *prima facie* case, before they espouse it, and they don't always do so, by any means.

Is it always done through the union?

It is normally done through the union.

Not through you?

It depends where it comes from. Managers very often, I'm glad to say, deal with this themselves when anomalous situations have arisen, when a job content has changed, and so forth, differentials have gone wrong, and so forth, and we feel therefore that we must look at it. What I'm talking about is the chap outside with the placard, the rank-and-file man who is, by definition, I would have thought, a trade unionist, so you get stimulated a demand through the union, first from the branch, of course, and then the union head office – a claim for an upgrading. Provided the union espouses their cause, they then make a formal grade claim, and that goes to Broadcasting House. What then happens is that the grading machine is turned on to examine it. They do that in the way you'd expect. They go and look at the job, look at comparable jobs on either side, and after all that they make a grading assessment: they say either, 'We don't think the grade should be changed'; or, 'Yes, we think it should be changed and go to grade so and so'. So it's either yes or no; either there is a case for the grade to go up in their view and the BBC's view, or there isn't. If there is, then the grade goes up, and quite properly. If there is not a case for the grading to go up, in our opinion, then the union is told, 'Sorry, but for these reasons we do not think there is a case.' Now the union can do one of two things, or one of three things, now: they can either accept that and say 'O.K., well thanks awfully' and tell the branch they've had it, or they say, 'Sorry, we can't accept no for an answer, because we still think that upgrading is justified. We do not think that justice is being done. So what we propose is that this matter should be put to arbitration.' By definition, we would accept that because when there's a disagreement you go to arbitration. An arbitration tribunal is set up, the two sides present their respective cases, and the arbitration tribunal in the usual way pronounces on the claims. So, arbitration takes place, the tribunal agrees, or if they can't, there's a majority, or in the case of an even split, the chairman decides, and by tradition this is accepted by both parties.

Now there is a third alternative possibility for the union which is not to go to arbitration. Up till now, they've had, technically, or as you might say legally, no choice in the matter, because they are parties – and all our recognised unions are parties – to what is called a procedural agreement, by which, in a case of this kind, arbitration is the moral next step. The final resort, if arbitration fails, is the Department of Employment Conciliation Service. But the Association of Broadcasting Staff is now showing signs of not wanting the procedural agreement, of really wanting freedom to decide whether to go to arbitration or not as the case may be and they have given notice of the termination of the procedural agreement as it applies to them. They've put this to us very recently.

This business that's going on today here is one of the consequences of this. This was a case of grading of charge-hand fitters and two categories of semi-skilled house engineers: plant maintenance attendants and mechanical maintenance assistants, who look after the ventilation plant, the heating plant and the practicals in the studios – gas stoves, sinks and so on. . . . Anyway, the case in point is that they asked for more money – that was the way it was put. They eventually realised that they couldn't just ask for more money (this was in Stage 1, I think, of Heath's wage control programme) so you had to construe it in some way. They construed it in terms of a grade claim. That was processed in the way I have described, and the answer was a lemon. They said well, they didn't accept the lemon, and we said, 'how about arbitration?', and they said 'No, we don't want arbitration', then we said 'Well, how about going to the Department of Employment and their conciliation people?' and they said 'O.K.'. So we went down there and the answer was a lemon there, so they were in an impasse. So what they're doing now is the only thing they know, which is to withdraw their labour. The placard which says 'BBC grading = cheap labour' in a curious kind of way, you see, is not the point, because the matter is not actually grounded on a feeling that the grade is wrong, but – in a kind of double-think way – when the claim came up simply for more money, we said 'Well, come on, you can't ask for more money in the context of the present situation', and they said, 'Well, we'll convert it into a grade claim.' So we said, 'Oh, you think the grade's wrong?', and they said 'No, no, we think the grade's all right, but what else can we do?' Actually, they wanted more pay but a wage claim is out of the question – for very obvious reasons – so they went for this supposed alternative of pushing up the grade, which actually is no alternative.

So they've withdrawn their labour for 48 hours as a kind of gesture. Then they decided yesterday to make it slightly more – much more – difficult. Before they went off on nightshift this morning, they switched all the equipment off before they went. So, of course, we said, 'Well, if that's what you want to do, switch it off, do – but we'll switch it on again.' So they said, 'If you switch it on again, that'll widen the area of aggro'; they said any action by the management to switch on will be intended as provocative and will have the intended effect of widening the area of dispute.

So what is now apparently going on is a widening of the area of dispute, and where it will end, I don't know. In fact I think it will probably stop there – except that there is a disagreement between us and the union which we are trying to put to arbitration. It will make things more difficult if they don't go to arbitration, because eventually conciliation by the D. of E. is all we've got left. And in fact, it's very difficult for the D. of E. to conciliate on a grade claim; to be quite honest, it's too complicated for them.

The suggestion that the BBC grading system is too complicated for the Department of Employment Conciliation Service, of all people, could be regarded as one of the more damaging criticisms of the system that could be made. Of course, during periods of so-called 'pay restraint', wage claims in industry have often enough been converted into claims for higher grades, or reclassification of semi-skilled into skilled jobs. The existence of the BBC's grading system made the tactic of claiming for higher grades the readiest to hand; moreover, and more importantly, claims for regrading became more and more a matter which could best be operated through trade unions, so that there were reasons internal to the BBC for the growth of 'white-collar unions' as well as the several special reasons which prevailed throughout British industry for the spectacular growth of this kind of union. In Engineering Division, for example, before the 1969 reorganisation, grading claims were almost always made, as a matter of course, by trade unions. Latterly, other groups have tended more and more to use trade union machinery.

The general consequence of this constant manoeuvring is that there are always anomalies, or apparent anomalies. In 1963, a manager in charge of studio technical operations (then in Engineering Division) said:

> There are big discrepancies between internal relativities. There is no doubt about this. The biggest shake-up that ever occurred in Engineering Division was when the cameramen applied for an increased grade. This wasn't accepted. The union backed them, went to arbitration, and it was accepted. This destroyed all the relativities overnight, and since that time, under various guises, the Establishment Officers and the people responsible for grading have been trying to cover this up – in terms of individual grading assessments throughout Engineering Division. This has meant years of work. All that happened four or five years ago, and has only just come to a conclusion when . . . The relativities have slowly got back to what they were.

By contrast, of course, individuals and groups which did not exert pressure of this kind as a matter of course found themselves left behind:

> I haven't been here very long, but when I learned the grade of some of our people and how long they had been on them, I was appalled. . . . There is now a feeling of grievance against the management of this department in not having done their best by them, and seeing that their interests are furthered.
>
> *They don't want to get into this vulgar scramble themselves, but they like not to lose out?*
>
> Yes, it's grown in the last year or so, largely because financial pressures have grown, the cost of living has gone up and so on.

But financial considerations, the extra pay that goes with the higher grade, are by no means all that are involved. The special effect of the grading system is to point up and to make explicit the status system. Status, in the common usage meaning used here, is held to represent the individual's value to the organisation – and the value placed by the organisation on him – and the qualifications and talents he brings with him. There is a presumptive personal equation between an individual and his pay.

But the grading system, which applies to appointments and not persons, evaluates the resource value of a *job*, relative to other jobs. Thus there is a dual system which connects an individual's work with his pay: the grade of the job, and the salary attached to the grade.

In many instances, the system is triple, for the older, more experienced, or more skilled persons may earn a higher, personal, grade. These quite different aspects of the grading system are clearly visible to the people involved.

> *If there isn't all that much drive for promotion – in your section, is it because it is funnelled off into pressure for up-grading? There is an alternative, even on a personal basis. It could also be funnelled off into pressures for up-grading a whole group of people, such as has occurred. Is there in any sense a kind of double wages spiral about this?*
>
> Oh, undoubtedly there is. . . . But what you find is that people are devoted to their grade. If, for example, the A.B.S. negotiates a ten per cent rise, everybody gets this ten per cent rise, but they still think they're in B1, and they ought to be B—. And it's useless to say to them 'Well, you're in B2, but you're getting as much as if you'd been promoted to B— last year'. This cuts no ice at all . . . You see everybody knows what everybody else's grade is – apart from personal grades, and special awards and so on, which are always confidential. They therefore keep a very close eye on the relativities – 'Am I slightly lower or slightly higher than Jones?' is what is always in the back of their minds, rather than the actual amount of money. 'Can it be presented that my job is in fact more important than Jones' job in the end? – and can it be formulated into a claim?'

Thus, while it is true that complaints about the grading system are not an unconscious cover for complaints which would otherwise not find expression, it is also true that they represent a protest against the organisation's appraisal of the individual members and of groups in terms of the value of the work they do, an evaluation which goes beyond what is implicit in the contractual exchange of work for pay. In a sense, then, criticism of the grading system is criticism of 'the system' – the definition of people as resources.

Finally, the way in which the task of grading is discharged within the Corporation reflects the same peculiarity of organisation which is demonstrated on a larger scale by the structure which used to reproduce the division between the function of management and those of producing broadcasting output instituted in Reith's day. Grading assessment (job evaluation) is performed by a Head Office group external to the Divisions concerned with broadcasting and engineering. To say this is not to deny that central control over such matters is proper, and, indeed, necessary. But while the no less important matter of appointments to posts is operated – with even more elaboration, in fact – through a central department concerned with this particular management function, with many safeguards to ensure fairness in opportunities for promotion and justice in selection, it remains a major responsibility of the management of the sections in which appointments are made. There is criticism of the appointments system, but it has not soured management–labour relations to anything like the extent that grading has.

The grading system is the Corporation's gift of freedom of manoeuvre to trade unions, and, more than anything else, keeps them the lively and enterprising bodies they are. The integrative importance of the grading system is therefore enormous, since it incorporates the members of this highly segmented organisation for other purposes than transmitting the programme it conceives, plans and produces. It is, in short, a system for bucking the system. This hostility is institutionalised – i.e., is subject to ordinary social controls – but the controls are independent of the organisation's own control system.

Moreover, it serves not only as a directly integrative element for the staff vis-à-vis the Corporation but provides some of the operational *raison d'être* for the centralised network of administration: comparison can only be done in the light of information about comparable others, and by people who have that information.

The fact that the principles on which grading is appraised are certainly not objective, in any scientific sense of the word, or indeed reducible to any measurable terms, and amount to an original and probably unique system of either job evaluation or ranking, is irrelevant – or rather, is relevant only because it enables the principles of grading and their application to remain debatable, unaccepted by the trade unions, embarrassing to management, and yet used by both as a basis of negotiation.

Any terrain can be used as a battlefield. Any codification of differences in pay and conditions of work can provide a ready-made chessboard on which can be played out an endless game of bargaining for bigger shares of the total resources at the disposal of an organisation. The main criticism of the grading system is that in attempting to rationalise this game the BBC has succeeded in inventing an extra one. It is possible to see in it the archetypal form of the Corporation's capacity for dodging management issues and then wrestling, with endless patience and superb skill, with the consequences.

SOCIAL DISTINCTIONS

There is a division between 'careerists' and 'professionals' which has rather different connotations in different sections of the Corporation and has an important bearing on the whole structure and style of management, and is therefore best dealt with later (see pp. 106–21 and Chapter 8). Most strikingly, interestingly, and possibly fundamentally, it appears among new entrants to the Corporation as one of the major differences between people from Oxford and Cambridge and others. This was neatly enough illustrated in interviews with two 'general trainees' in 1963.

The first excerpt is from an interview with a woman from a provincial university:

> The people from Oxford and Cambridge, where there's this terrific thing about making one's mark – growing one's hair longer or one's fingernails dirtier or whatever it is . . . I must say I haven't liked them at all. Partly it's their rather immature attitude. For example, I said I admired one of the lecturers on a course very much. They'd been on a different course, and they said, 'Oh yes, we had a furious argument with him after the lecture, almost had him in tears, ha, ha, ha!' And they said we'd been arguing such and such, and I said, 'I don't agree at all', and said why. And they said, 'Oh well, you're probably right. We just thought we'd have an argument.' And they were delighted they'd upset him.
>
> *What do you think they'd scored in doing this?*
>
> In self-esteem. Here they were, just into the BBC, talking in front of a BBC audience and saying 'We're intellectually something special'. . . At a rather older level, there's a social climbing set, who know the right initials to use when you're referring to people, and drink the right drinks with the right people at the right time – it's a fairly subtle business with these older people One goes to the right parties, and jockeys for position –
>
> *Jockeys for position in front of whom? Who are the arbiters?*
>
> The people just above you, who sit on Boards, or who are going to mention your name for jobs. *The BBC is very hierarchical, you know.*

The other, a man, was from Cambridge:

> *It has been suggested by more than one person that people from Oxford and Cambridge tend to be more career-minded than the general run of people coming in.*
>
> No, I don't think so. I don't think there's any question of an Oxford and Cambridge clique.

No, that wasn't suggested. But that they come in with a rather different attitude, seeing the BBC not as an institution which will give them a good, interesting and varied job in which they can become professionally involved, but instead as a career system. There isn't much point for them in merely becoming a good and reputable producer, or administrator, or whatever. They come in because it is the BBC, a career system with a lot of entertaining and interesting work on the way to a certain number of important jobs, because it's part of a world which accepts and is acceptable to people from Oxford and Cambridge – specially.

Yes. This is certainly true. It's a very congenial atmosphere. It's congenial, too, in the sense that *it's not hierarchical, it's very democratic*. Your relationship with your head of department is the same as your relationship, say, with your tutor; you're treated very much as intellectual equals – you may be inexperienced, but you're intellectually equal.

The view of the Corporation as an Oxford and Cambridge enclave is so old that it was surprising to find it alive and vigorous. It was, of course, intimately connected with the pre-war conception of a BBC culture and a BBC type – a cultural *corps d'élite*, cementing in a very English way the worlds of gentility, government, the higher professions and the high table in a social combination of the 'well-connected'.

Things have changed, but there persists the peculiar attraction of the Corporation as granting privileged membership of this upper stratum. It was apparent in interviews that there was an almost dangerous allure about the talks producers' job. Meeting the distinguished, or the unknown to whom broadcasting would lend distinction, the producer had not only a unique editorial job to perform on what they said – he had in a real sense to edit *them*, to make them presentable, looking or sounding their best. In these encounters he acted as a competent professional, and they, whatever their ability or distinction in the outside world, as incompetent amateurs were only too willing, for the most part, to accept his advice, instruction and control.

The combination of intelligence, assurance, receptivity, and social deftness which this requires, and which must be looked for among candidates for programme departments, and candidates for promotion, may underlie the uniformity which was said to be still apparent among senior management, and for the survival of 'the BBC type', even in 1973, in Broadcasting House especially, but also in Television Centre. The reference is to the special code of manners and style of behaviour, speech and demeanour prevailing in what are regarded as the central, the most powerful, the most highly valued sectors of the Corporation's life. All members of the Corporation realise the existence of these sectors, know their boundaries, and learn how to observe, with greater or lesser degrees of skill, the rules and criteria of approved behaviour within them – the less skilled, naturally, observing them by exercising greater self-restraint.

There are other areas. There are also sub-territories within the central normative area.

> As you move around the Corporation, you find each department has its own pattern. You can drift into people's offices in one department, and you find it's just not done in another. You get a kind of crude wit in one, and a sharp, intelligent, sarcasm in another; there's a lot of comic play in a third. Once you know about this – for example, that you just can't say 'fuck' in Talks, Sound, but it's a perfectly O.K. word in Light Entertainment – once you know this, you can get in and out of departments without much trouble. Yes, you have to learn to be socially adaptable – this is very important. You find yourself working on a children's programme, or a programme like 'Compact' and everything is going immensely well, and then you find yourself in, say 'This is Your Life', and the same things making you very unpopular – being enthusiastic, impulsive, and very bright early on in the day just doesn't go down – especially when you're dealing with scriptwriters and people who've maybe been working until 3 a.m. the previous night.

Only trainees, and a few others, have had the opportunity of gaining entry to more than one or two of these sub-territories. There were, instead, frequent references to isolation. Producers claimed to see little of other producers. Floor managers thought producers must be less isolated from other producers than they were from the rest of the production team. They themselves were cut off from the gallery staff and from the technical crew, cast and scene-shifters; one commented on the fact that 'you find yourself on your own in the canteen in the meal breaks'. Technical people in the studio didn't mix.

Personal and departmental isolation clearly involves invidious distinctions, even if it is not grounded in them, but such social distinctions are not altogether related to status or prestige.

> Engineers don't like to have much to do with the production side. They don't like the producer's world, where they call each other 'darling' all the time and say something different behind their backs. They see them as terribly insincere. It's a different world, I suppose.

All occupational communities are arranged in an ordered hierarchy or rank, defined by invidious distinctions of status. In Britain, this has been attended, during the past few decades, by an increasing discomfort.

> There's certainly a highly developed consciousness about status in the Corporation – stronger or weaker in different departments, of course, and in different sections of the same department. There's a class system in the Corporation. I always regard the Corporation as a beautiful cross-section of the British way of life, right down from the Establishment to the manual workers.
>
> *But of course. It has to be. It is, after all, a very British institution. Yet you do have – superficially perhaps – a kind of mateyness which shows itself in the use of Christian names, and especially the formula of using both Christian name and surname, even with quite remote connections.*
>
> This is something peculiar to the Corporation?
>
> *It's more widely used in the Corporation than any other place I've come across.*
>
> I've certainly used it myself, and consciously, as a way of getting over this embarrassment of whether it's X, or Albert or Mr X.
>
> *Albert X is more neutral.*
>
> Yes. I'm tending to use it more and more widely with my juniors when writing to them and in reference to my superiors. But a good deal depends on how long you've known superiors, where you came across in the Corporation, what stage in your career. In memo writing you get different approaches, some your using surname, sometimes both your names, other being neutral and using the initials of your appointment. I'm interested that you find this Christian name and surname used more often in the Corporation. I've used it more often in the last two years. . . .

Nobody who has observed the unease and anxiety aroused in English people by the need to establish correct – i.e., mutually acceptable – social distance in a new relationship will dismiss this preoccupation as trivial. To use one form of address rather than another is to stake a claim or express an assumption about the social distance which exists between the speaker and the other.

Social distance has two dimensions, and it is important not only to keep these two dimensions distinct, but to be sensitive about the changes which can occur even within each of the two. Thus to call people of subordinate rank by their surnames may pass without objection in a work relationship, but may be seen as an open provocation when it is carried over into meetings in which there is a formal presumption of equality among the members, as one episode recalled by a young engineer in 1963, which now carries curiously anachronistic overtones, makes clear:

> I chaired a number of meetings with the local branch of the E.T.U. . . . We had one very delicate situation which arose because the Establishment representative always used surnames. If you happened to have known him for a long time, he used Christian names. But he was very conscious of the social order, and always used surnames with people below him and 'sir' – probably – with people above him, just as a matter of normality, nothing more and nothing less. Or he'd say 'Mister' to anyone above him and just the surname below him. This was his normal way, he'd always been like this, and he thought it was right. So then it came to meeting with the shop stewards and the clerical staff. Gradually some contention arose. Well, the new senior shop steward, towards the end of the meeting, said, 'We are a bit disturbed. We come here as the senior representatives of our colleagues to meet you. I believe we are meeting on common ground. We feel we have the justification to have the prefix "Mister" '. Not just so-and-so, you see – a surname. And the reaction to that was, 'You come here as a Corporation employee, subservient to me. I have always used surnames to juniors, chaps junior to me in the Corporation, and "Mister" to those who are senior, and I shall continue to use surnames. Surnames will go into the minutes.'

The establishment of correct *lateral* distance is just as important, especially in a large organisation; a change in the style of address marks a departure from a formal relationship, from formal requirements and expectations, not 'warmth', or friendliness. Administrative and personnel officials, whose jobs involve them constantly in working relationships for which the formally prescribed procedure, if there is one, is almost always inadequate, were most sensitive about this topic. As one man observed, it is never wise to treat the distance established during one working relationship as constant; it might be more than tactless to maintain a relationship on Christian-name terms in a committee, or in the presence of seniors.

Lastly, the vertical and lateral dimensions of social distance vary according to a fairly complicated code; to take naming again as an example, and at its simplest, managers and producers were invariably on mutual Christian-name terms with their secretaries, but disapproval attached – and was formally expressed – to any secretary who referred to her boss by his Christian name outside the immediate working group; the reverse was not, of course, held to apply.

Thus, even in this very simple respect, behaviour in the Corporation bespeaks the concurrent presence of a variety of systems of relationships, all sharing a sizeable number of common attributes but each also involving variables which could assume significance or even major importance – on occasions when they were ignored.

Social distinctions extended to a fairly clear age-grade system, with groups differentiated not so much by chronological age as by the period they joined the BBC; the differences were displayed in their attitudes towards and beliefs about people in other age grades.

Older people, on the verge of retirement, needed little or no prompting to shake their heads over the future; they couldn't, they said, think what would happen when they retired. One senior official, retiring rather early, was assured by others near his age that he was 'getting out at the right time'.

A wartime recruit said,

> I always feel that people who joined the BBC when I did – we regarded working for the BBC as a vocation. There was a tremendous aura of this during the war. Nowadays they'd just as soon be working in an ice-cream factory – if the promotion prospects and the rates of pay were the same. This is quite true. Therefore they have a different outlook from me.

There are five distinguishable age-grades: the pioneers of the nineteen twenties, now gone (one senior official, after he retired, was called 'the last of the gentlemen', by a trade union representative); a second group associated with the years of expansion and the establishment of the BBC as a nationally and internationally important institution during the thirties; the wartime group, who identified themselves with the Corporation as it was in that time of emergency and triumph; those who came in with television; and, lastly, the younger, often militantly anti-establishment entrants – generally thought of, appropriately enough, as being in 'the Current Affairs area'. Members of each group have an inescapable feeling that 'their lot has what it takes'. They also have the feeling that the others (or many of them) are, in some ineluctable but important sense, wrong-headed or not quite up to the standards which their group set – or, contrariwise, that the peculiarly different standards, qualification and values of the other groups are now more highly valued than theirs.

This interpretation was set off by the impression that the different sections of the Corporation I have encountered seem to be dominated by one or other age-grade. This is most strikingly apparent in the television service, the 'young man's world', in which the age-grading structure which prevailed in the Corporation has been dislocated. As elsewhere, the forceful rationalising which is a necessary lubricant of such changes in social structure generated a number of beliefs about age and ageing, about the 'creative years' of life, and about the finite, exhaustible nature of such qualities as inventiveness, imagination, and enterprise. The measure of the dominance of the younger age-group is the extent to which such beliefs were shared by older men.

The abnormality of the age-structure in television, where seniority in age is not related to seniority in status even within the same occupational order or career progression, adds another classificatory system to the social structure itself. Thus to be younger is to have a kind of social edge on others, even if they are senior in grade.

There was also, in 1963, a fourth kind of systematic differentiation in the cultural affinities which divide people. This is now much less in evidence but it has left traces. It derived from the implication of the whole occupational community in the world of the theatre and of social sophistication. So people were divided into professionals and amateurs, and, more significantly, into camp, butch (terms used without any hint of their nineteenth-century origins as homosexual cant) or square. Individuals could be 'camp' – i.e. act habitually with an edgy elegance or sophisticated charm – or 'play it camp' for a special occasion; groups, occasions or whole departments could be 'campish'. 'Butch', which carried an equal connotation of being sophisticated and on the inside, allowed of an alternative mode of acting – plain or coarse-spoken cynicism or directness. Both terms clearly denoted, again, not personality types but a manner and style of conduct which could be assumed, and related to traditional characters or humours in the English theatre as old as the seventeenth-century stage, in which both types are clearly discernible. To reject both, and to be square, was, in this milieu, an equally positive choice, equally a style which has to be cultivated from models and consciously maintained. These three humours cut across the other structures of economic status, rank, authority and age.

In the enclosed single space of the studio, and in the closed, concentrated world of the production, the simultaneous and coordinated interplay of all these systems creates a small, exotic, pluralistic society.

There are two material circumstances which support this peculiarly enriched social world. First, every person present – actor, vision mixer, electrician, scene-shifter, technical operations manager – contributes and represents an essential resource, or is in control of essential technical equipment. They are present as of autonomous occupational right, and there is no organisational hierarchy; the three kinds of authority – one derived from the possession of skill or information, another from the attributes of office, the third from prestige – are all clearly distinguished, are invoked on distinct occasions by producer, floor manager, or lighting supervisor, or fireman, and have well defined limits. (It is in fact the floor manager's job to see to the maintenance of these limits and to resolve any friction or problem arising from ambiguity about their definition.) The overriding authority of the producer comes, ideally, from his exercise of all three kinds of authority, but even here there are command areas defined by other people's competence and responsibilities which he must not invade or seek to amend. What exists – again, ideally – is a fully articulated organic system of cooperative action, in which the leadership role is properly that of defining problems and tasks and presenting aims, and other contributors are fully involved in working towards their realisation, within limits of feasibility which they themselves lay down.

Secondly, almost everyone is necessarily unemployed for periods of varying but unpredictable length; there may be forty or more people in the studio, and for the most part less than half a dozen may be actively engaged in rehearsal.

The mental clock in everyone present which is ticking off the minutes left before the terminal point of recording or transmission introduces the kind of multiplier into the relevance and significance of one's own and everybody else's conduct familiar in crises. On such a basis, in the sealed remoteness of the studio, people can, if they choose, free themselves from the more unsuccessful and duller aspects of their conduct and recompose models of demeanour, style of action, and level of sophistication out of a range of possibilities offered by ascriptions, age, status, membership, interests and affiliations, and ground what they affect to be in the virtually unchallengeable authority of their technical role and commitment to the production task.

The effectiveness of the total system varies. Almost universally, it is thought to vary with the effectiveness of the producer. Occasionally the complexity is dissolved into a simple relationship of command and compliance at transmission time, or, more rarely, is disrupted into a single antagonism between producer and an individual or group. But in general, a television studio at work represents an extraordinarily refined system of human and technical organisation, effective in its ability to produce what it was designed to produce, and efficient in providing a satisfying array of rewards for the people concerned in the production. To run such a system obviously requires organising, administrative, managerial, skills of the highest order. It is a curious commentary on the way in which industrial society has developed that it is firmly believed by some senior officials that good producers make poor managers and administrators. This is so, one man argued, because of the special qualities of instant decision-making and overriding authoritativeness which go to make the good, 'really professional', editor or producer. These same qualities are transformed into intolerance of suggestions, unwillingness to consult, and authoritarian command when they are carried over into positions of ordinary managerial control. This observation has some bearing on the emergence of the 'new managerialism' (discussed in a later chapter) when, at long last, the top management of the BBC consisted entirely, apart from the Directors of Engineering, Finance and Personnel, of people who had made their mark as producer or editor.

Even so far as this study has taken me, there is a much wider variety of commitments into which individuals enter than the simple trio of work, colleagues and career. There is the distinction between 'working in the BBC' and working for the Corporation as it is in reality. There is the attraction of the world of broadcasting with its own distinctive prestige and glamour and its links with the élites of every sector of sport, entertainment, art and public affairs, and the involvement in a technical or specialist job which is usually unique to broadcasting and often novel. There is the 'political' sense of loyalty to people doing the same kind of work and at the same grade, and therefore representing the same kind of human resource and sharing the same self-interest, and the devotion to 'getting the show out' and to serving the public. There is commitment to the studio, and to producers, or to others to whom one is engaged in a working relationship, and commitment to one's own career. There is affiliation with people of the same age or date of entry, and with people who share the same models of behaviour, and there is attachment to these people scattered about the Corporation who represent what is felt to be television production, or sound broadcasting, or engineering, or simply the BBC 'at its best'.

Finally, there is a balance between occupational and outside commitments, a balance which fluctuates through life (as the balance between occupational commitments fluctuates) but which is of the utmost importance to the individual to hold constant with his aspirations and his conception of what he is. It is in the disturbance of this balance, the knowledge that a balance struck has been upset by the relative devaluation of one or other of these commitments, that personal problems originate, and discrepancies arise between the needs of the individual and the needs of the organisation. To disturb the balance produces, instead of a plural society, a segmented organisation.

COMMITMENT AND CAREER

> The BBC is full of dedicated people who care more for the job than for getting on. The trouble is, they see other people around them getting on faster.

This revelatory utterance puts succinctly two of the conflicting pulls of interest which affect a great number of members of the Corporation. It shows the individual to be faced with the dilemma between the conception of public broadcasting service, to which, in very many cases, they feel their entry into and experience of the Corporation had committed them, and self-interest. It is the same dilemma with which the BBC has increasingly found itself confronted, between commitment to the vision of a public broadcasting service, which it has itself created, and the need to survive in a world which, since the advent of ITV, seemed increasingly suspicious, cynical, or sheerly hostile. Indeed, the individual's dilemma is largely consequential to the BBC's dilemma. Both the individual's and the BBC's dilemma have become more and more explicit and acute; the individual's is a moral issue, hinging, like the Corporation's, on the continued validity or the hollowness of a traditional ethos and system of beliefs; and the individual is split between rival interests, much as the Corporation is.

This division of loyalties, between self-interest, or careerism, and commitment to the aims and purposes of the organisation is familiar enough in all organisations. It is always possible for people to do their jobs and to conduct themselves in ways which do not render self-interest incompatible with the interests of the organisation. The cult of professionalism itself, as doctors, academics and lawyers have long since discovered, can merge self-interest with the interest of the organisation one works for in a very satisfactory manner. But careerism, the constant striving to win in the unending competition for advancement, increases the chances that the two will prove incompatible,[6] or, rather, it converts the compatibility which is feasible into a compatibility which is contrived, and thus is either more seeming than real or serves to bend the organisation's interests into conformity with one's own.

There was also, in 1963, a distinction frequently made between commitment to public service broadcasting and commitment to the BBC. It was possible for someone to declare that he thought it immensely worthwhile working for the Corporation and at the same time to say that he had 'no time for the kind of stuff the BBC broadcasts in sound and television'. Again, there is the familiar distinction drawn between the communications which BBC engineers have created and maintained – the best there is – and the vulgar or tedious uses to which some of them say it is put.

Remarks of this kind, and those which revealed the dilemma between careerism and 'dedication to the job' specify the array of commitments in which individual members of the Corporation become involved: commitments, loyalties, or, so to speak, investments of psycho-social capital. Most people I met seemed to feel themselves confronted with conflicting commitments, although it was only in a minority of cases that personal conflict seemed to reach serious dimensions. This second conflict of commitment, which in itself seemed to be of little consequence to senior members of the Corporation, may yet have proved to be of the most enduring significance for the Corporation at large: the widespread distinction which was made between the Corporation as it is and an ideal image of the BBC, which showed itself in depreciatory references to 'the way the BBC does things', 'Broadcasting-House-mindedness' and 'the kind of line being taken by the people on top now' by the very same people who saw 'what the BBC stands for' and 'the public service ideal in broadcasting' as altogether admirable.

There is a third pair of commitments, although this time not mutually exclusive; it is between the straightforward contractual engagement entered into by taking employment, and personal involvement in doing a job. In most concerns the distinction between the two tends to be lost in the common understanding which applies to conduct in paid employment of all kinds, which contains an element of involvement beyond contractual engagement itself ('working to rule' is, after all, now recognised as positively disruptive, and intentionally so). Involvement over and above terms of contractual employment tends to increase with rank within the same organisation, and also increases with the rate at which circumstances change in the market or in the appropriate technology. Both kinds of 'external' change present increased demands for personal involvement, because the onus of defining and redefining ultimate or mediate goals is thrust on to a larger proportion of members of the organisation.

The distinction between the public service image of the BBC and the Corporation as it actually was appeared to be simpler and more prominent among engineers in Television Centre in 1963. It was diffused much more widely in 1973, but not so sharply defined. But engineers bear no responsibility for programme content, and can therefore more easily dissociate the ideal image of the BBC from what was broadcast in its name. The distinction, in fact, could be and is, regarded as actually embodied in the contrast between the precision and reliability of the complex technical apparatus which engineers provide and maintain, and the procession of minor vicissitudes and occasional breakdowns which afflict studio programmes, and which have to be handled either by the engineers who staff the Central Control Room, where the signals generated in studios are monitored as they are 'despatched' to the transmitters.

The contrast thus established between the technical equipment of television and the material actually broadcast becomes translated into terms of moral and intellectual codes and of practical efficiency and competence. So, for engineers, professional identification may be said to *require* dissociation from what the BBC broadcasts and what the BBC actually is, and its replacement by a 'public service' image. The image needs no precise formulation, since it is composed out of dissatisfactions with actuality rather than out of some positive definition which it is possible to aspire to and work for.

These elements in the situation of the professional engineer are most clearly visible in the working style of the group of engineers in the Central Control Area in Television Centre and the Presentation Editor who works among them. It is this group which is responsible for handling the occasional disruptions and lapses in the broadcast material coming out of studios. Talk inside the room, over the multiplicity of telephone connections with the rest of the building, other stations in London and the Regions, and with transmitters is couched in a flip, offhand, joking style with a heavy loading of technical terms, jargon and initials. An intense 'insider' feeling is built up in this way. Through this interplay runs an intermittent commentary on what is appearing on the monitor screens before them. The patter both contributes to and expresses the feelings of the group's enclosure within the walls of the room, which is the communications centre of the whole of the BBC television services. It consists again of 'inside' jokes, sardonic or cynical repartee aimed at the studio performers, and highly critical discussion of the programmes. It was this particular group which was among the most outspoken of the critics of audience-catching policies. In all, the non-stop display of detached criticism might be interpretable as a kind of moral payment exacted for the engagement of their professional selves to the Corporation – much as the adversary stance of so many television journalists (see Chapter 6, pp. 203–5) is visible as a return exacted for their involvement in the necessary accommodation the BBC has to adhere to in its relationship with the political Establishment.

In contrast to this posture of critical detachment there is involvement in the goals of the organisation as it in fact is. This presumes that the individual identifies the values implicit in the organisation's ends as his own – which is, in fact, what one means by involvement of this kind. A direct and simple identification of personal and organisational goals, however, is reserved for a small minority: political leaders, owners and directors of business concerns, for example, or those whose total dedication to the social, spiritual, political or intellectual purposes of the institutions in which they have found a place shelters or absolves them from giving attention to other purposes. In the BBC, the closest approximation to complete identification with the Corporation was displayed most obviously in the higher reaches of Administration Division in 1963 and – with one or two exceptions – among top management (i.e., down to Controller level) in 1973. With this went a strong sense of solidarity with colleagues. There was hardly an interview with senior people which did not contain passages of willing admiration for superiors, in fairly marked contrast with the critical detachment apparent in other sections of the Corporation when seniors were under discussion.

The explanation for the sense of identification with the Corporation displayed by senior administrators and managers is straightforward enough. Their jobs, often enough, obliged them to speak with the voice of the Corporation. In 1963, for example, the people I met who headed up Administration Division had to appraise the deserts of individuals who applied for special consideration, concessions or assistance, to advise or influence heads of departments so as to ameliorate working arrangements, or bring them in line with customary BBC practice, and to act in certain circumstances as watchdogs of the Corporation's interests vis-à-vis the particular interests of departments or sections. Moreover, they represented the Corporation as employer in dealing with trade unions, categories of employees, or individual members of staff.

It was not surprising, therefore, to find at that time senior members of Administration appearing to assume the persona of the Corporation:

> My job is to adapt the old ethos of the Corporation to the needs of the 1960s.

And again,

> As soon as I came into the Corporation I saw the place acted as a team. I see this as a strength we must fight to keep.

All this was present, as well as an acute and perpetual awareness of the programme department staff, especially producers, as the 'business end' of the Corporation.

This degree of involvement with an organisation 'as it is' has, I believe, become increasingly rare. It was a little surprising to find it so clearly manifest among administrators in 1963. By 1973, it had become much less evident. What was evident was the more familiar attitude of stoic dedication which senior civil servants in this country have made so very much their own – a cultivated demeanour and mode of expression designed to display a determination to keep the system going at all costs, or to furthering its growth merely because to do so is better than any bearable alternative, and offers the best chance in a deplorable or actively hostile world for the survival of oneself and what one values. The shift from what I have called 'total dedication' to a 'stoic dedication' has by now occurred in so many sectors of public life, especially in those heavily populated by 'professionals' that its beginnings in the social ethic professed by the Milnerites in this country and the political ideology articulated by Ernst Jünger in Nazi Germany have become obscured and forgotten.

In the BBC, the distinction between commitment to some ideal, public-service Corporation and to the Corporation as it is emerges as a consequence of the surrender by the specialist of direct professional commitment to the individuals or groups he serves. For him to yield the direction and application of the qualities and the special competence which are as intrinsic to his make-up as those of the professional must by definition be to control by senior officials in a bureaucratic hierarchy means not only that he resigns his relationship with the public to be 'taken care of' by the organisation; it also means that the notional matching of professional performance with its full requital in client or public satisfaction or applause is never attained, or is lost in anonymous membership of the organisation. There is an inevitable discrepancy between what the professional envisages as his true relationship with the public and the uses which an organisation finds for him. Thus one finds a 'para-dedication', a commitment to the BBC as a public service, together with a critical dissociation from the Corporation as it is.

The distinction is implicit in the situation of the professional specialist. It was articulated, as I have said, in a number of interviews in which the public service image of the BBC was distinguished from the 'management', or 'the policy' or 'the way things are done' by the 'people on top'. This is not to say that active dissociation from policies as they were in practice, or depreciation of the senior members of the Corporation was widespread, but that loyalty to one's superiors, and dedication to the BBC's purposes, are not necessarily to be regarded as dedication to the purposes which they saw explicitly or implicitly pursued.

What has been discussed so far is the kind of commitments into which an individual enters, deliberately or unthinkingly, when he joins an organisation with a contractual obligation to carry out tasks. These are essentially moral commitments, although the term I have already used – 'investments of psycho-social capital' – may carry more meaning these days. For the most part, individuals deal with any conflicts between such commitments 'as they arise' – i.e., by taking them at face value as commitments arising in different situations which occur one after the other. But the variety of commitments arise from the nature of their involvement in the total system of the organisation in which they work. Work organisations in contemporary society have certain fundamental characteristics in common. Although each of these characteristics is fairly commonplace in people's working lives, the fact that they coexist and are interdependent to the point of having direct bearing on conduct in different phases of an individual's working life seems much less easy to grasp.

Organisations of the kind we are considering are cooperative systems assembled out of the usable attributes of people and are created and maintained to produce goods or services. But they are also places in which the people recruited into them compete for advancement. Thus, members of any business or non-business undertaking are at one and the same time cooperators in a common enterprise and rivals for the tangible rewards of successful competition with each other. The pyramidal hierarchy of rank and authority familiar as representing the 'structure' of organisations in fact represents both a control system and a career ladder.

Preoccupation with career, or with the standing of one's present post in relation to others, and with one's prospects of advancement, bulks larger in people's lives when the organisation is growing or changing unusually fast; preoccupation in such cases shows itself most generally as a perpetual watchfulness on developments which affect relative status and promotion criteria, but it varies from this towards a conscious abdication from the 'rat-race' on the one hand, or a troubled, self-doubting anxiety on the other. Obviously, different areas of the Corporation have very different rates of growth and change and therefore different possibilities for movement and promotion, and therefore different levels of preoccupation with career. An engineer in Television Centre saw this clearly, but as a rather puzzling aspect of life in an organisation which went to very great lengths to ensure that promotion opportunities were equally distributed throughout its entire staff.

> People are very concerned here about promotion prospects. . . . When you get changes interfering with the structure, you see, you get people thinking, well, it's up to them to put a case. You've got to look after yourself, to look sideways and see what the other chaps are doing.
>
> *Exactly, yes – and see how you're doing in relation to others.*
>
> It's a matter of keeping your end up. We've expanded so much, and people have got used to a perpetual state of expansion. . . . Even as far as our lower levels of staff are concerned it's been steady growth in the staff and now there's a great increase. Cameramen, for example, have come to see life as a succession of expansions, with upgrading and promotions and so on. And they'd be very disappointed if ever things became stable.
>
> *I don't know. These changes make themselves visible long beforehand and people can get used to the fact that life has become stable. . . .*
>
> I must say that just after the war I was at a place where stability was the order of the day. . . . As far as I know the total staff

there now is very much what it was in 1946 and the individuals are practically the same individuals.

How do they take it?

They're very happy – because they've never seen any other kind of existence.

Again one becomes conscious of the way in which changes in the external circumstances of an organisation impose organic changes on the structure and processes within it, of how these latter changes alter the life-situation of people working in the organisation, and of how, finally, the attitudes, aspirations, preoccupations and direction of effort of people are affected.

This is not a simple mechanical chain of cause and effect. The presentation of the dilemma between commitment to one's job as vocation – as *Beruf* – and as a step on a career ladder in the terms used by the man quoted in the opening sentence of this section is a gross oversimplification. The choice is not between devotion to the public interest or to artistic or professional values on the one hand, and to self-interest on the other. A man may feel that his own selfish interests impel him towards absorption in his professional role while it is the needs of his family, the social pressures exerted on him to attain a style of life commensurate with what he and his wife see as their rightful social setting, which impel him to seek promotion. He may feel guilty about *not* seeking promotion, and relieved when he finds sufficient reason for not competing. This was made evident with the utmost clarity, honesty and indeed poignancy in the course of one interview with a producer:

When you questioned what I said about careerism, what did you mean?

I don't really question it. There is a tremendous career sense in here. The trouble is, I think, that one comes into the BBC thinking there is a career here, thinking 'I'll start as a floor manager, I'll go to P.A., I'll become a producer' – that's as far as it goes.

I enjoy doing what I'm doing here and I don't see it as a career. I don't see where I'm going from here, I don't hope I'll go into pictures – I'd love to go into pictures and now and again I think 'why don't I do something about it?' but I don't think that way and I think very few producers here do, and plan for it. We're far too occupied in the here and now. . . .

I never have time. I shall have time in a month when this programme's off the air, and I shall grumble. I shall grumble for a whole month, and then I'll go for a month's holiday, and then I'll come back and say 'Come on, let's get on with this programme'. The Programme!

But you're all to conscious of all this for it to be real.

Conscious of the fact that I'm doing that? – But I suppose it must be real, mustn't it, if I think of it that way?

Well, you're very explicit about it.

Yes, you mean with the connotation, I suppose, that this has been going over in my mind, and this is why I've said it.

You've accepted the position, but consciously.

So that sub-consciously I may well be thinking of something else?

No, with a conscious abdication from something else . . . I'm not wanting to get you on the couch, mind you. But it seems to me that everybody nowadays has 'career expectations' – of going on and up even slightly, or has hopes eventually of going on and up. If this isn't so, then I think people have a sense of missing something.

I don't know. . . . Very often, I pass the notice board, and I think, 'I really should be looking at this, looking for something.' I look at the jobs. I look at the salaries, and I think 'There's something I could do, what is it, head of . . .', and I will find any reason for not doing anything about it. The last job I thought of was Head of Sport. I thought, 'I must apply for this, I must get out of the rut of this department'. I must do something to further my position. I'm forty-nine years old now; this is my last year to try something like this. I'll go for Head of Sport . . . Could I fill the job? What's it say? – oh yes, I know that, it's always been one of my interests, I know the colours of most of the teams in the Fourth Division. I could do this. I'll do something about this.' And as I'm moving away, I think 'Head of Sport. This is what Harold Opie has been brought back to do. No good my doing anything about it. Harold Opie will get it.' That afternoon I see Harold Opie in the restaurant, and I say, 'Well, I understand you'll be putting in for this Head of Sport thing.' He says, 'I'm not applying for it. Why, are you thinking of applying for it Bob? I understand Jack Rivers is going to get it.' And immediately I'm filled with relief! And Jack gets the job and when I heard I slapped Jack on the back and said, 'I'm so pleased you got it.' I really was. It took away from me that bogy of having to apply for something. . . . I'm happy to stay here. I want more money for staying here, that's all – except that next year I shall be fifty, and the year after that fifty-one; soon I shall be too old and too tired to do the thing I want to do.

Most people, of course, are more adept at finding reasons for yielding to the appeal of career interests, or are more susceptible to them. Often, indeed, careerism in the Corporation appears as a kind of reverse ambition. It appears out of anxiety or self-doubt produced by the spectacle of other people getting on, or apparently having opportunities for getting on, a little faster than oneself. Once this feeling is engendered in some sufficiently for them to seek ways of promoting their own career interests, it can pervade large sections of an organisation.

THE APPOINTMENTS SYSTEM AND BOARDMANSHIP

It is, indeed, extremely difficult to ignore this side of one's occupational existence for very long in the Corporation. The grading system and the ubiquitous notice boards thrust it, as we have seen, on the attention of the most professionally committed of people.

The Corporation has gone to great lengths to ensure that appointments and promotions are allotted according to merit, and are seen to be so. But there is a feeling among some people that the criteria which are applied, and run to be applied, by Appointments Boards are somehow less than wholly valid.

> I'm not sure that all this [preoccupation with grading and promotion] isn't a by-product of our particular appointments system. I get the feeling that people tend to adapt themselves to being acceptable to Appointments Boards, rather than to being successful in their jobs. . . . There's a disturbing sprinkling of wrong appointments. . . . There's a general feeling of despondency about the appointments system – among unsuccessful candidates.
>
> *Well, naturally!*
>
> Yes, but with some justice, I think. Because a man may be rejected time after time, by a series of Boards on one particular type of job, and never know why – and finally get it, and still not know why. And if it's straight seniority, why not say so and do away with the Boards for that job?

What manifests itself as criticism of the failings of the system is not so much the search for a perfectly just and equitable set of criteria applied by infallible Appointments Boards as the disquiet aroused by a 'success system' which is also, necessarily, a 'failure system'. A society, or an organisation, which is increasing in size, complexity and resources, needs a constantly growing supply of people with the right talents and educational qualifications to occupy the positions of control. To ensure such a supply there has to be machinery by which individuals with appropriate qualifications may climb to the positions where they are needed. But a social machinery of equal opportunity for occupational advancement is not by itself sufficient, any more than it is in education. There has also to be universal acceptance of career success – in society's terms – as one of the valuable goals in life. We seem in Western society to be increasingly adept at inculcating this necessary belief, in children as in adults. However, in the nature of things, out of the many who attempt to succeed, who seek to establish in the minds of the patrons and sponsors of the system their claim to higher status, only a few can succeed – fewer and fewer as one approaches the highest positions. So, in our society, the vast majority – one might, indeed, say everyone – is at times confronted with the fact of failure. And since, for almost all of us, or for all of us most of our lives, the fact of failure is impossible to face if we are to continue living in the situation to which we have been consigned, we have, instead of facing the fact, to alter it by seeing the criteria by which success is awarded as illegitimate, or inappropriate, the judges as ignorant, misinformed, or biased, success as overpriced or the system itself as contemptible or somehow false. We may mix the blacks and whites of both society's and our own counter-judgements as we wish, to make a tolerable grey, and half admit that we are doing so:

> If you talk to people normally in conversation, you find that most of them feel very strongly that in ninety per cent of the cases the winner has already been selected. The Board has so many people on it from the department who've already made up their minds, of people who are known to be powerful. There's undoubtedly a big element of truth in this; they can't be impartial. But what interests me in this is the fact that when you talk to people they need so much to feel that it's rigged. Because if they don't! . . . This is the reverse of the system, because instead of being kind, I think it's being desperately cruel. What it's doing is to expose absolutely the failings of the individual. You've got no outlet here. You've got to take total responsibility if you believe it's not rigged. If you fail, it's because you're a failure, and that's the hardest thing for anybody to bear.

Yet, obviously, the need remains for the organisation to select the best candidates, to offer rewards high enough for most of the possible suitable candidates to compete, and to match requirements with abilities. Obviously, too, the more effective and fair the system of selection and appointment, the better. The point is that these things have a cost, and it is paid by those who fail in the competition. The majority who fail are as much continuing members of the organisation as those who succeed. Furthermore, there is the question of whether the whole apparatus which has been developed within the Corporation to ensure both efficiency and justice in the matter of appointments and career opportunities is not too elaborate – i.e., whether the expenditure of time and thought and emotional strain which the fair-deal system generates does not make, at least in some sections of the Corporation, inordinate demands. After 1960 there was an attachments scheme, by which people who wanted to could move – at the same grade, and for a limited period – to a quite different department, to see whether they liked it better there – or were better liked. This was an innovation which actually encouraged people, and not only those who made use of it, to seek new openings for advancement through changes of location or work. Again, the system of annual reporting and interviewing, and the machinery by which adverse reports are critically reviewed and may be appealed against, not only underline the 'fair deal' aspect of the system but focus attention on the need for constant watchfulness in equating rewards with performance. Keeping everybody's capacities for promotion under review also involves keeping their aspirations constantly refreshed.

The result, therefore, is not only a career system of exemplary fairness; it is an explicit apparatus of careerism which takes up a great deal (some people say the greater part) of management time, and which invites speculation, discussion and preoccupation. Just as the attachment scheme was said by one manager to unsettle people, and to encourage shopping around for promotion, so the whole careers system can set a level of preoccupation with one's present position and future prospects which is well above anything I have encountered elsewhere.

It was a new experience to find corridor and cafeteria conversations turning most often on the membership of boards, and the performance of colleagues in front of them. At the very outset of this study, the new appointments to the highest posts in the Engineering Division were discussed largely in terms of their meaning for career prospects, and the kind of qualifications or personal qualities or Corporation experience which might be most favoured; there was no apparent concern in other kinds of policy change which the new men might institute.

It was among engineers in Television Centre also that I found the skills of boardmanship cultivated and discussed openly and seriously, although it was a familiar enough element in the lives of people elsewhere.

One of the things that's very evident in the Corporation is that the view taken of people's behaviour in front of Boards is of the utmost importance. What generally happens then is that people who are ambitious look around and see those who have been successful in front of Boards, and they go and ask them how they got the job – 'What did they ask you?' They don't get very much from this, because, certainly at the lower grades, the man who's been doing this hasn't bothered to consider his method of attack at a Board. What in fact happens is this, that the man comes to you with a direct question. 'I understand that recently questions have been asked at boards like "What would you do if Johnny came over and punched you on the nose?" or "Supposing Johnny refused to obey your instructions, what would you do?" .' They're all questions of this sort – direct – and they don't look for the reasoning behind the question. Those who've been fortunate enough to have one of the junior management courses or one of the administration courses held at the weekend are given the direct answer to this direct question, but not the philosophy behind it. They don't ask themselves, 'What does the Board really want to know when they ask these questions?'

One supervisor arranged Sunday afternoon training sessions in boardmanship which he found both popular and an excellent means of getting to know his staff and their capabilities; he found, incidentally, how different was his appreciation of capabilities in the two contexts of routine supervisory contacts and assessment in the mock Board situation.

Small bets are often placed on the outcome of Boards. This seems to be an instance of the use of betting to deplete the value of oppressively important eventualities (the bets placed before battle on chances of survival are the extreme case) by 'gaming' with them; it allows one to think of the forces controlling eventualities as systematically ordered, although irrational, as incomprehensible but assessable – in short, as providential.

Perhaps a minor, but nevertheless telling, aspect of the BBC appointments system was that it was generally supposed to replicate Civil Service procedure – indeed, one Managing Director declared that it did. In fact, as one Controller who had experience of both systems well knew, the two procedures are utterly different, both in the way they operate and in the effects they have on the organisation and on individuals in it:

You can't move around without seeing these notice boards on which there are all kinds of jobs you might be doing other than the one you're in. So every few hours, probably, one has to ask oneself the question –

– 'Should I put in for that?' That's right. I agree with you, and yet it's an essential part of the system, you see. Once you say that your only method of building the career of an individual or keeping the BBC going as an organisation is by means of free and open advertisement, it follows automatically that a good administrator, whose job it is to make sure that everybody knows about jobs, is going to put them up in every corridor – quite rightly. It follows, one from the other.

But I'd change the structure fundamentally. When I was in the Civil Service one never gave a thought to this. One just thought, 'Oh well, every couple of years my Establishment Officer will tell me what my job is for the next two years, and after five years I'll be told whether I'm to be promoted this year, or not' – and so it'll go on. You might get a little anxious as between five years and six, and you might begin to worry whether your next job will be an interesting one or not – and should you perhaps have a word with someone to make sure that he pushes you this way, but it's nothing compared with 'God! – Should I be applying?' – and the agony of going through appointments boards – and feeling you must.

Did you ever come across talk of 'boardmanship'?

Oh yes, certainly. It's a whole science within the BBC.

Nevertheless, there are people who are wholly committed to their present job – not only because of its intrinsic interest and rewards but also because of the sheer richness of the working environment – the attractions of work in places frequented by the well-known, the notable, and the powerful, the satisfactions of doing a reliable, or competent or imaginative job in a complex operation, and receiving recognition for it, the pleasurable sense of being part of a world which daily attracts the attention of millions of people, and of privileged membership of a glamour world which comprises the élites of the West End, Westminster, Fleet Street and the City, with occasional incursions from international celebrities. All this in itself can provide a large if immaterial increment to one's style of life.

Some people who have made the move out of this world into higher-paid management jobs are often filled with regrets.

It's supposed to be a step up, but you might as well be working in a cheese factory as work up here. I can't get used to working an ordinary five-day week. And you find yourself travelling at the rush-hour times. The best job in the world is on the studio floor.

> Up here, the biggest pleasure you have is being right on a personnel move – and even that's not the same as knowing you're right when it comes to making a suggestion in a production.

The fact that such moves are made, and indeed are competed for, is evidence of the strength of the pressure which the career system exerts – of the overwhelming value placed on the rewards of career advancement as against vocation. Several comments, in 1963 as in 1973, demonstrated the nature of the pressure and the judgement of self, as of others, in which it finds expression.

> You don't get many people – very few really – opting out of the rat-race, which is what it's called, and what it is. We tend to think that they're people who've reached the limits of their capacities.

> If a chap isn't career-minded, he doesn't know where he's going, he doesn't have an aim. And an aimless fellow soon runs down.

This is the negative aspect of the pressure maintained by the BBC itself on each and every member of its staff to become, and stay, 'career-minded'. To have reached the limits of one's capacities may be a judgement applied to people who, for their part, feel that they have served the Corporation best by a whole-hearted devotion to a professional or specialist job during the most productive years of their lives. Positively, it finds official expression in two ways. Appointments notice boards carry a sizeable and constantly changing array of advertisements of appointments newly vacant and for which, as part of the BBC's 'good employer' policy, any member of staff may apply:

> Some of the people on the staff side get some of these problems out of proportion, and think there's something diabolically wrong with a chap who's been working in the same job for about ten years. Also, we have this competitive appointments system. Every notice board that you look at has got advertisements for jobs: our young people, some of whom, in their mid-twenties, are now earning very good money, they'll look at something and wonder whether they should try for that. It's as though we're continually stirring the compost.

> *I've never been in a place in which vacancies were so constantly exhibited. It's a perpetual reminder, not just every week, but four or five times a day. Nobody can move around any part of the BBC without passing quite a few of these notice boards. Which means that they're constantly being silently asked, 'Are you happy in your job?'*

> Yes, and behind it the assumption that if you're happy in your job, having done as much as two years in it, then there's something wrong with you!

That particular conversation was with a Controller, but the same reaction made itself felt at junior levels. A film cameraman said,

> We now have a bigger personnel department here than we have ever had, and, again, there's a strange attitude. I sometimes wonder what backgrounds some of these people have. We had a change of personnel department people recently, and I had an initial interview with somebody who'd just taken over. One of the questions I was asked was, 'How do you see your career in the BBC developing?' And I said, 'Well, it's developed. I am where I want to be.' Then he said, 'But how do you see yourself going on?' I said, 'Becoming a better cameraman.' (Did he think I'm getting old, or what?) So he says, 'But what's your next step?' 'Well,' I said, 'my next step is most likely down there and through that gate.' I mean, there was this kind of feeling –

You're only half a man if you're content to stay where you are.

> Yes – that you ought always to be climbing up a ladder to somewhere.

The active cultivation of careerism has become implicit in another 'good employer' practice, long established in the BBC, of annual reports by managers on their subordinates:

> We have this system of annual interviews in which I see all my people, plus their deputies, actually; about forty a year at least, and a few other people as well. And, you know, the BBC ethos would really command you to say, 'Well, now you've been doing this job for 3 years, what's your long-term objective?' – And you're doing it every damned year. Why?

There is, of course, just as much competitive pushing and shoving in other places, but in the BBC there is a distinct feeling that this is not something which can be left to individuals but is to be encouraged by the Corporation. In addition, that is, to there being a general expectation that people will seek promotion, the BBC puts a positive value on careerism, on the energetic pursuit of promotion.

4 A Private World

By the 1960s, the principles of public service broadcasting had been accepted as those which should govern broadcasting in Britain, whatever organisational form it took, and from whatever source its finances came. Those principles had been eventually ratified, as much as they had first been challenged, by the creation of the Independent Television Authority and, in 1962, they were reiterated at length and fully endorsed by the Pilkington Committee. Yet public service broadcasting in the form which Reith and his disciples had given it never became fully institutionalised. Especially after the advent of television, it becomes more understandable as a set of conventions, which is rather a different matter – different, because conventions are always liable to be embellished, amended, and inverted. The distinction I want to bring out here is perhaps best illustrated by pointing to the procedure of courts of law as fully institutionalised – i.e., as following a rigorous code of practice which is the expression of a complex and fully articulated set of values and principles relating to the judicial system and encoded in court procedure. Conventions, in the sense in which the word is used here, are essentially more malleable, as they are more diffusely embodied in everyday codes of social, cultural, economic and political practice. The conventions governing the relationships of the Crown and Parliament, for example, are the latest reading given them by the head of government; and the same intrinsic malleability applies to lesser conventions constantly in use in the traffic of everyday life. The distinction is of some importance for the structure and operating principles of management, especially in establishments with a high proportion of scientists or other professional workers. Essentially, management has an inherent preference for acting through the apparatus of institutionalised relationships specific to certain business and non-business organisations; professionals, since they are constantly preoccupied with 'best practice', with innovation, and with the continuous though irregular accretion of new techniques and information which they need to recognise in others as well as acquire themselves, construct the social world of their working life in terms of conventions.

The word 'professional' had, by 1963, an extraordinarily wide currency throughout the BBC. There were times when it seemed that the word was being credited among programme staff with an almost talismanic quality, representing some absolute principle by which to judge people and achievement. Ten years later the word seemed to occur even more frequently, to have acquired a wider and more potent range of meanings and connotations, and to be used throughout all reaches of the Corporation. Among senior management in charge of television and radio it had assumed the character of some ultimate rationale:

> The more professional you become in terms of your output, the more you need professionals in Drama, Light Entertainment or on the Current Affairs side.

There are few interviews, either in 1963 or in 1973, in which the word was not brought into play to make some categorical distinction, or to deflect criticism, or to attribute importance. In trying, for example, to explain to me the importance attached by top management in the BBC to the weekly meeting of senior officials in Television, down to Heads of Department, to discuss the programmes broadcast during the previous week, a Controller in television said,

> Well, we have a weekly meeting on Wednesdays called the Weekly Programme Review which is very jealously confined to heads of departments and is essentially for the Television programme people, at which we not only discuss all the figures, R.I.s[1] and all the rest of it. We go through the *Radio Times* day by day for the past week. It's a curious occasion, because essentially it's a social occasion, really, when we all meet each other. Equally, it's a very critical occasion, because, for the record, statements are made by departments and groups that such-and-such a programme was marvellously done, and equally those jealousies that may be endemic or latent are brought into the open – and sometimes hatred, actually – and are therefore purged, in a curious sense. It's a good meeting. Actually, it's the best, because it does represent a very clear, critical, *professional* view – than which you can go no further, as it were, in professional terms. . . .

Considering the frequency of its use inside the BBC, and the heavy load of meanings which it carries, it is not surprising to find the word emerging into the light of day in the published and reported speeches which the Chairman, Director General and senior officials, present and past, are (or feel) called upon to make as part of their job of explaining or defending BBC policies. Stuart Hood, when outlining, as Controller of Television Programmes (which he then was) the BBC's intentions concerning the second television channel at a BBC 'Lunch-time

Lecture' in December 1963, commended the Chiefs of Programmes of BBC1 and BBC2 as 'young men of high intelligence and great professionalism'.

The sheer frequency of its occurrence, the variety of contexts in which it was brought into play, and the very heavy load of judgement and appraisal it was intended to carry all suggest that members of the Corporation used the word 'professional' as a kind of semantic credit card with which they could shop around a wide range of desirable ascriptions and attributes. By contrast, one hardly ever encounters this evaluative use of the word among people in those occupations which are regarded as professions in the classic, paradigmatic, sense – law and medicine. Indeed, it is rare to find lawyers or doctors using the word at all; one is either a member of the legal profession or the medical profession, or not, and that is an end of the matter. The antonym, 'unprofessional', is encountered rather more often, and its reference is not so much to lack of skill or knowledge as to infringements of the moral code by which members of the profession see themselves bound. Where the word 'professional' frequently is used is in those occupations which find a continuing need to discriminate between the attitudes, the *modus operandi*, the competence, experience, training qualifications and the quality of result which, it is claimed, can be expected from those whom one recognises as 'professionals' as against 'laymen' or 'amateurs'. In the fifties and sixties, for example, the word was fairly frequently used in this discriminatory sense among sociologists, among social workers, and among engineers.

In the BBC, also, it was often used simply to signify the opposite of 'amateurish'; i.e., good of its kind, expert, finished. Sir Michael Swann, reflecting on his first year as Chairman of the BBC,[2] spoke of 'the attitude of the professionals to the amateurs – by whom I mean the Board of Governors'.

In the context of the BBC 'professionalism' also involved 'dedication', 'commitment'. Indeed, Donald Baverstock, one of the two 'young men' to whom Stuart Hood referred, said as much to me in 1961. Among some people, though, at that time there was some suspicion that professionalism, in these senses, might be eroding or supplanting that code of broadcasting practice which had been built up in the BBC concept of public service broadcasting:

> . . . Partly because of the speed at which they have to work, there comes a certain meretriciousness, a certain slickness, a tendency to do things in their programmes which, if the press did them, they'd despise – and almost a certain degree of hypocrisy. I can give you one very good example of that. When Bennie Paret, the boxer, was killed, there was a telerecording of the fight, and the

final blows were considered so – vile – that it wasn't shown. But 'Panorama', in the course of a discussion about boxing, says, 'And now we will show you these ghastly thirty or forty seconds.' And you are shown this. And you come back, and then he says, 'Vile, disgusting, disgraceful, and now here is X, Y and Z to talk about this.'

Our stomachs have perhaps been allowed to grow a little stronger since then; but if 'commitment to the job' bulks as large as it did, and still does, in the work of producers and broadcasters, then it raises problems when the word 'professionalism' crops up in those contexts which bring in other connotations of the word, as Charles Curran recognised in a speech given to the Religious Weekly Press Group in 1970. He began by saying,

'I suppose it is inevitable that at some time a Director General of the BBC should be faced with the need to state what position he holds in the matter of broadcasting standards, and if it is my choice to make a statement of that kind first to a meeting of the Religious Press, then you will assume, and rightly, that for me the word "standards" has a significance which extends beyond that of professional judgement, and requires a discussion which is in some of its terms, at least, conditioned by considerations of morality.'

Yet, in the event, he too took his stand on 'professionalism'.

'. . . Well then, you may say, can I make a simple statement about what the BBC regards as its exemplar of correctness and of perfection? And I am bound to reply that I cannot do so except in one sense – that of defining our *professional* standard. There is only one, and it is of excellence.'[3]

The increasing salience of such preoccupations is a further, and definitive, mark of the transition of broadcasting from an occupation dominated by the ethos of public service, in which the central concern is with quality in terms of the public good, and of public betterment, to one dominated by the ethos of professionalism, in which the central concern is with quality of performance in terms of standards of appraisal by fellow professionals; in brief, a shift from treating broadcasting as a means to treating broadcasting as an end.

PROFESSIONALISM AS A MORAL ORDER

Everett Hughes, a sociologist whose teaching and writing on occupations and professions have been certainly more interesting and probably more lastingly influential than anyone else's, once remarked that in developing his own studies, 'I passed from the false question "Is this occupation a profession?" to the more fundamental one, "What are the circumstances in which people in an occupation attempt to turn it into a profession, and themselves into professional people?".'[4]

The circumstances vary. So far as the BBC is concerned, the circumstances are not unique to it, but the combination of them is. The spread of the currency of the term 'professional' throughout all the upper reaches of the Corporation and the increased frequency of its use seem to me to mark three separate, but related, trends. The first is a secular trend, affecting a large section of the occupational world, and related to the technical division of labour. The second trend is of shorter duration, but apparently cyclical, manifesting itself in the form of associations (nowadays frequently 'white-collar unions') as strategic instruments for gaining autonomy, mostly relating to power to control admission to an occupation and the reservation to members of the association of certain kinds of work, but also so as to resist 'outside' control, whether it be from management, governmental agencies, or the client public. (One such phase lasted several decades during the nineteenth century.[5]) Lastly, and most importantly, the word 'professional' is very frequently used in contexts which imply the invocation of some kind of moral order in which professional judgements, decisions, and actions are grounded. The moral order endows them with a legitimacy and authority which are regarded as distinguishable from and at times superior to contractual obligations, loyalty to the organisation, or compliance with public or other 'outside' demands or claims.

It is in this last capacity that the professionalism of the broadcaster can be regarded as having supplanted the idea of public service as it was defined and established under Reith, and as it was developed during the thirties and forties.

What is under discussion is a three-fold process of the social, technical, and moral division of labour which is a *continuing* aspect of industrial societies, at whatever stage of industrialisation they have reached. This perpetual process of fission inevitably requires the complementary development of an apparatus for coordinating, integrating, and, eventually, planning and monitoring the work of an increasingly diverse number of specialisms. Thus the 'new managerialism' (see Chapter 8) emerges as the necessary and natural complement of the new professionalism.

Broadcasting requires the combined efforts of a multiplicity of departments, groups, and individuals, each representing a specialist function. It also requires the planned utilisation of all the specialists, the coordination of their efforts and the funnelling of all their activities into a continuous output of broadcast programmes. But complementary as the two processes of differentiation and integration may be, they also represent contrary orientations and, often enough, divergent purposes.

> As I diagnose it, long before McKinsey,[6] the centrifugal tendencies in the BBC were getting stronger and stronger. . . . You have this extraordinary paradox, that you have to be the one and indivisible BBC whereas with every day that passes it is more and more clear that we are dividing, we are tending to move into separate professional camps, each of which has a distinct sense of ownership in its own professional standards, of its own professional world – the world of news, the world of children, the world of religion, the world of engineering techniques, the world of costume design. They're all in the mix, and, with growing complexity and sophistication, the mix gets richer from week to week. So we are having to accommodate, as it were, any number of heresies while still acceding to the same creed.
>
> Now this produces very odd and extreme tensions, when you look at what has happened to us managerially. . . . I guess all this stems from the fact that from its Charter position the BBC can only meet its prime obligation – which is to achieve and retain vitality – by creating a situation where, however messy it may appear, the different professional prides and the different personal prides have the maximum possible amount of liberty to run free. . . .
>
> A very good example of this is that in the studio, operational responsibilities from the very beginning of the television service were an engineering responsibility. The cameraman was recruited and trained as a Technical Operator, Engineering, because his camera was likely to burst into flames and he had to know what to do about it. In radio there was a holy war for years and years about who should own the word 'Operations'. The engineers laid claim to this because an operation is an operation – it involves hardware; it involves proper respect for circuitry and signal quality; it's got to go out through transmitters involving other engineers, and so on. But the programme side of the staff didn't feel this way; they felt the need to have somebody beside them who would be primarily in sympathy with what they were trying to do. So a kind of long-haired, sensitive-fingered kind of technician began to. First he was a 'Programme Engineer' and then, after quite a lot of argument, he struggled free of the engineering hierarchy altogether and was reborn as, first, a 'Studio Engineer' and now he's called a 'Programme Operator'. . . .
>
> I don't think that any of this arises from manoeuvring, or from sour politics, at all. I think it simply represents the strength of professionalism in a largely professional society.

There is no final answer to this particular problem, which is hardly peculiar to the BBC; certainly there is no final solution to be found in some perfectly designed bureaucratic, or management, structure. But some understanding of what is going on may help.

Specialisation, in broadcasting as anywhere else, may consist in no more than a purely *social* division of labour, by which a single task is divided among several people, often creating a succession of short operations. It has been a central article in the code of beliefs connected with industrialism that this, of itself, will increase the skill of individual workers, improve efficiency, and increase the output of a given work force. Adam Smith's treatise itself begins with the enunciation of this cardinal principle: 'The greatest improvement in the productive powers of labour, the greater part of the skill, dexterity, and judgement with which it is anywhere directed, or applied, seem to have been the effects of the division of labour.'[7]

But even by the 1770s, when Smith was completing his book, the social division of labour, which lends itself to 'improved dexterity' even in the making of pins and to the 'saving of time which is commonly lost in passing from one species of work to another' was being extended into a new dimension, the *technical* division of labour, arising from 'the invention of a great number of machines which facilitate and abridge labour, and enable one man to do the work of many.'[8]

Specialisation in both the social and technical sense multiplied and developed until, by now, the two are virtually indistinguishable. Accountancy, originally the consequence of a social division of labour, has now acquired sufficient technical specialisation for it to be regarded, at least in the upper reaches of the occupation, as a specialist profession. In the theatre, there were no directors before the 1870s. The staging of a play was a cooperative effort of the whole company (although it was a cooperative effort which was increasingly disrupted by rivalries which had to be settled by the leading actor, who was often enough the manager); nowadays, with performances for film and television having to be 'produced' rather than 'rehearsed', the single specialised role of director is itself being split into two, producer and director, with further sub-divisions in the offing.

The division of labour, social and technical, nowadays is determined largely by the differential distribution of information, experience, and technical skill which can be acquired only by a limited number of people who have chosen, or been chosen for, training or positions which will allow them to gain an adequate level of competence. Specialisation in this latter sense has led, eventually and inevitably, to what Everett Hughes has called the *moral* division of labour:

> 'An occupation consists, in part, of a successful claim of some people to a *licence* to carry out certain activities which others may not, and to do so in exchange for money, goods or services. Those who have

> such a licence will, if they have any sense of self-consciousness and solidarity, also claim a *mandate* to define what is proper conduct of others toward the matters concerned with their work. . . . All occupations – most of all those considered professions and perhaps those of the underworld – include as part of their very being a licence to deviate in some measure from common modes of behaviour. Professions also, perhaps more than other kinds of occupations, claim a legal, moral and intellectual mandate. . . . In such licences and mandates we have the prime manifestation of the *moral division* of labour; that is, of the processes by which differing moral functions are distributed among the members of society.'[9]

References to the existence of the 'moral' division of labour crop up in several of Everett Hughes' papers,[10] but is nowhere fully explicated. From the different contexts in which the phrase occurs, and from the kind of examples he cites, there seem to be two distinguishable bunches of meanings and connotations. The first is, nowadays, fairly commonplace, and has to do with the way in which the prevailing distribution of work in a particular society, community, or organisation can acquire a legitimacy of its own. Quite apart from the legitimacy which, in our kind of society, attaches to the division of labour on technically 'rational' grounds, work, whether it is done for a client or for an employer, is circumscribed by the law of contract. Questions of what is right and proper for a person engaged in some particular occupation to do is a matter to be judged, ultimately, by what might 'reasonably' be expected. The demarcation rules which apply to the division of labour between medical specialists, and between them and nurses, are just as hard fought over, though not so publicly, as the demarcation rules between welders and riveters, or between skilled machine-setters and semi-skilled machine operatives. The notion of a moral order, in this sense, which governs what Everett Hughes calls the 'drama' of work is familiar enough (once it is pointed out), but he goes further. The moral order governing the division of labour has a special indicator, which consists of the secret or 'guilty' knowledge appertaining to an occupation.

> 'The lawyer, the policeman, the physician, the scientist, the scholar, the diplomat, the private secretary, all of them must have licence to get – and, in some degree, to keep secret – some order of guilty knowledge.'[11]

Knowledge may be guilty in a number of different ways: most obviously, in that it is imparted confidentially, as in the priest's confessional or the doctor's surgery, or acquired through the licensed invasion of privacy, as with hotel servants, apartment-house porters, or secretaries; it may be guilty in that it is collusive or underhand, as with policemen and reporters and their sources of information in the underworld of crime and the backstage of politics; or it may be guilty in the sense of being dangerous, as it has proved in the case of physicists and biologists, or as it occasionally appears in the case of scholars who treat the political beliefs and religious or moral values prevalent in their own society as relative and contingent.

Not all occupations, of course, have any special licence to acquire or to harbour knowledge which is guilty in these obvious senses, but all do carry with them some kind of moral responsibility which is the exchange value of their entitlement to the job which they do as a licensed operator or an employee under contract. And it is this aspect of the moral order of work which involves the second and less obvious (though not necessarily more fundamental) bunch of meanings and connotations. It concerns the licence and mandate conferred on people who undertake the job of covering up or making good the mistakes of others, or do the dirty or rough work which has to be done so that other people can do their jobs.

> 'The comparative student of man's work learns about doctors by studying plumbers; and about prostitutes by studying psychiatrists. This is not to suggest any degree of similarity greater than chance expectation between the members of these pairs, but simply to indicate that the student starts with the assumption that all kinds of work belong in the same series . . . both the physician and the plumber do practice esoteric techniques for the benefit of people in distress. The psychiatrist and the prostitute must both take care not to become too personally involved with clients who come to them with rather intimate problems.'

> 'In a certain sense, we actually hire people to make our mistakes for us. The division of labour in society is not merely, as is often suggested, technical. It is also psychological and moral. We delegate certain things to other people, not merely because we cannot do them, but because we do not wish to run the risk of error. The guilt of failure would be too great.'[12]

Acting as the repository for the mistakes or the dirty work of others carries with it some measure of social responsibility, but also a kind of insurance for the people who do the work, in that the only people who, in one's own eyes, are accredited judges of the adequacy of one's performance are not those whose errors and omissions and leavings one attends to, but people doing the same kind of job. It is this which lies at the root of the *Leistungsbewusstsein*, the sense of a job properly done – which Hughes' students found prevailing among Chicago janitors as much as among physicians and cab-drivers – married to a sense that the job, whatever its prestige or rewards, was somehow as essential as any other (and perhaps more central than most) to the proper functioning of other people's lives, together with a sense, which brings us back to 'guilty knowledge', that the job gives one a privileged view of other people's lives and work which, if it were made public, could be more or less damaging.

The whole tendency of Hughes' writings is to depreciate or, at least, smudge over any rigid distinction between 'professional' work and other kinds of work, not so much by denying the special qualities which have been traditionally attached to professional work, but by pointing out that the same considerations apply to seemingly very different kinds of work. Indeed, one of the more immediate consequences of Hughes' work in the 1950s was the appearance of research papers which purported to reveal a general trend towards the 'professionalisation of everyone'. This kind of preoccupation has distracted attention from what is perhaps Hughes' main contribution, which is to stress the nature of the occupational system which prevails in society as a moral order, and the sense in which people who do a particular kind of work feel that their job, whatever it is, is done within an ordered distribution of work which carries with it some moral responsibilities, in return for which they acquire moral legitimation for the part they play in the social drama of work.

The technical and the moral aspects of the increasing division of labour are mutually reinforcing. The spread of technical specialisation in the BBC undoubtedly occurred more quickly, more effectively, and more completely because the simultaneous cultivation of the notion of professionalism throughout the Corporation provided a favourable climate in which it could grow. As soon as one particular specialism establishes its claim to professional standing, other people with jobs requiring a unique set of qualifications either obtained by education and training or derived from special qualities of sensibility, flair, intelligence, or verbal and social skills which have been refined, developed, and tested by experience are moved to make the same claim. And with the same professionalist notion of unique qualification for a particular kind of work goes the 'mandate to define what is proper conduct of others towards matters concerning their work'. This involves the disqualification of outsiders, which includes managers, not only from doing that kind of job themselves, but, effectively, from competence to evaluate performance.

The BBC is riddled with problems of the moral legitimacy attaching to different kinds of work. 'Only a specialist', as one man said in 1963, 'can judge the work of a specialist.' The claim has, of course, a rational basis – or, at least, a form of rationalisation. For the licence and the mandate which underwrites the moral division of labour is not something which can be claimed arbitrarily by the people who, at the moment, happen to be employed to do a certain kind of job. It has to be given recognition by others – by 'society'. This is especially true where the work itself, or the way in which it is done, may involve others ('society') in serious consequences; hence the very special licence and mandate, and the specific moral function, attached to medicine and the law. So the licence, the mandate, and the moral function is granted to professionals when the professionals, in turn, are seen to be able to institute and enforce a code of behaviour which relates to the needs of the client, as well as to the quality of the work.

> 'An organized profession rightly regards itself as a body placed in charge of an art or science and responsible for directing its use in the interests of society. These two obligations can be reconciled without difficulty if the true interests of society and of the individual are harmonious. A profession proceeds on the assumption that they are. When they seem to be in conflict it is usually because the individual does not know what is good for him. The client . . . is often ignorant. Authority passes to the professional.'[13]

So, below the surface meaning of the expertness one expects from a full-time worker, or practitioner, or a 'pro', as against an amateur, a part-timer, or a dabbler, there are quite explicit connotations of entitlement, of the licence and the mandate conferred on acknowledged members of a body of professionals; of criteria of professional competence which are claimed to be independent of any judgements by laymen, or clients, or the public at large; and, thirdly, a code of professional conduct which serves as a *quid pro quo* for that independence.

AGAINST THE IMAGE OF PUBLIC SERVICE

These arguments make more understandable what was, for me, the surprising absence, in so exceptionally articulate a working community, of discussion about the social purpose or the social consequences of broadcasting.

This may have been merely an aspect of what is supposedly a traditional British distaste for speculative discussion. Or possibly it derives from a perception of the comparative futility of the efforts made to trace direct causal connections between broadcasting and the conduct, attitudes, fears, or aspirations of the public, whether adult or child. It could, again, have sprung from a reluctance to disturb a complex of assumptions about the relationship of the BBC to its functions and to the public.

I am inclined to attach some importance to the last consideration. The lack of interest in the audience which was so evident can hardly be construed as a kind of schizoid withdrawal, which was the first construction I placed on it. Certainly, the functional relationship between the interests of groups within the BBC and their views of how the BBC should discharge its corporate task implies that the ideological systems so developed should be autonomous, and thus to some extent shielded from reality. Certainly, also, one encounters something of the 'insider' feeling characteristic of the cultural enclaves inhabited by the highly committed – such as professional musicians, scientific researchers, artists, and cult teenagers – although both the egalitarian principles within the enclave and the rejection of the totality of outsiders as 'square' lack the moral fervour of the archetypes.

There is a further general consideration. Occupations which exist to provide direct services to customers, an audience or a clientele require an organisation of effort or skill directed towards pleasing individuals. This carries with it a connotation of interest, attention or deference which, outside the context of employment for pay or fees, would imply that one had some special regard for them and for their well-being. Service occupations therefore tend to carry with them a countervailing, and ordinarily concealed, posture of invidious hostility. This 'latent reversed role' manifests itself at times when the public is not present but is under discussion: among servants, waiters and the occupants of those manifold positions which are needed to lubricate the passage of a public into, through and out of shops, aeroplanes, ships, trains and buses, hotels, restaurants and theatres. There are also the episodes of over-exigent demands for attention or deference, or some transgression by members of the public, which license retribution. More important, in the more highly esteemed reaches of the service occupations, there is the evidence of the traditionally rigorous and irrelevant disciplinary codes which used to prevail universally as a structure of institutional authority for patients in hospitals and pupils in schools, and have only recently begun to be displaced by the development of variant conventions. In the occupations which serve a large and absent public – journalism, advertising and films – the compensatory reaction against the service relationship appears to waver between a cultivated indifference and contemptuous dismissal. In 1963, this was evident among broadcasters, too. It was a successful television dramatist who pictured the 'typical television audience' as 'mum sitting in the best armchair drinking cocoa with a teenage son on the sofa trying to get his hand up his girl's skirts'. And a television audience of millions had, it seems, to be seen as 'moronic' by a distinguished radio producer.

It would be easy to multiply quotations voicing the same sentiments as these last, but it would also be absurd to suggest that they were representative of opinion within the Corporation. What is significant about them is that they could be uttered publicly by anyone at all inside the Corporation. That such remarks have been made is, I believe, partly because of the defensive, or retributive, posture I have mentioned, but is more directly the consequence of the incorporation of professionalism within a large complex organisation.

In the BBC, the relationship between broadcaster and public is enshrouded in a very large array of other relationships, each bearing some weight of commitment, and which are themselves arranged in a hierarchy – so that relationships with one's equals are usually of less consequence than the relationship with one's superior, and one's relationship with him of less consequence than any relationship one might have with his superior. The relationship between any individual specialist engaged in producing a programme and the public tends inevitably to become not so much obscured or extinguished as 'taken care of'. It is taken care of not simply by unloading the burden of relationship with the public on to superiors, but by the growth of certain institutional forms which empty it of personal involvement. It was possible to discern three such institutional forms within the Corporation: the limited, controlled, use of audience research to provide 'ratings' (audiences measured in millions) and a Response Index, a procedure which reduces awareness of the public to the safe dimensions of percentages; secondly, by the cult of professionalism in the special sense in which it is used inside the BBC; and, thirdly, by talk of 'a responsible attitude' in which could be discerned the ghostly relict of the public service idea.

The 'responsible attitude' seemed to manifest itself not so much in talk of ethical constraints as what seemed to me in some people a cloak of conventional unease:

> The fact is that if you are doing an hour's drama you are playing around with thousands of pounds of somebody's money – a lot of money. Again, the viewing figures: one producer was saying that on the night his show was being transmitted he was driving through a Cotswold village which seemed pretty unchanged from what it had been perhaps 200 years ago, but through all the front windows he could see a little blue screen, and it suddenly came home to him that these people – most of them – were watching something that he had conceived, in an office, in his own mind. The implications of this are considerable, I think.
>
> *Yes. They are always with you, presumably, in some form or other, though perhaps not in that concrete form.*
>
> They always *should* be with you.

This is, I suppose, the basis of the weight of responsibility which builds up as one approaches the time of recording or transmission?

> Yes, especially with live transmissions, when you know that it only needs just one person to go berserk for some 15 million people to be influenced in some way. . . . As Owen Reid said, if you show a hanging on a children's programme, the chances are that some of the children watching will have attempted to do the same, in imitation. This brings the responsibility home.

There seemed, in fact, no way of attaining any direct relationship with the audience which will be more significant, or even realistic, than the 'viewing figures' or driving past the front windows of Cotswold cottages. 'Responsibility', for the broadcaster, is institutional. It has had to be generalised, turned into a routine of thought and behaviour, and, outside the context of occasions such as these interviews, enclosed within the structure of the Corporation itself.

Responsibility, in this very general sense, was more readily and clearly articulated among engineers and others not directly concerned with programme production:

> In our organisation pressures are not commercial, but – yes, I think this is a fairly sensible term – 'public service conscience'. It is not a nice thing to say, it sounds a bit uppity, but if you do have a conscience the pressures in an organisation like this are tremendous.

Yet, even here, the 'responsible attitude' which bears on the relationship with the public at large has become subject to some ambiguity and manipulation. It can be dodged:

> The system in the organisation is such that you can either work very hard or you could live very happily – and it doesn't make an awful lot of difference either way to the immediate situation.

Among producers and directors, there seemed to be a feeling that 'responsibility' was somehow at odds with 'artistic integrity'; and that the 'programme ethos' which Stuart Hood mentions (p. 151) or the codes of practice laid down by the Board of Management, or the restraints traditionally exercised by heads of programme departments were a set of bureaucratic devices which it was smart, or wise, to outmanoeuvre. In 1963, one reaction to 'That was the Week that Was' was said to have been the relaxation of self-censorship over the themes and language of situation comedy series mounted by Light Entertainment:

> We've got a thing coming off now, a confidence trickster dressing up as a parson, and slipping into some Euston Road flop house.

> Well, this thing was billed for April 17th. We found that it's Good Friday, and we altered the date! But that's as far as we're prepared to go.

And, from another director in Light Entertainment:

> ... On my own programme, very often I have to do things which I know if I asked my boss, he'd say no. It would be right for my boss to say 'No, you mustn't do that'.

There is nothing inevitable about the decline from 'the public service idea' to 'a responsible attitude'. Given that the public service idea rendered the purpose of broadcasting a normative one – that broadcasters were concerned not so much with providing what the public would think informative, educational, or entertaining, but with using broadcasting deliberately to open up new areas of knowledge to the public, to widen and deepen its information about the contemporary world and Western culture, to enlarge its entertainment experience, and to fuse, so far as was possible, all three endeavours – there is little that any audience research could have added to the sensitivities with which people who write for a large public and speak to large audiences are ordinarily credited. Given the resources of social research and the money available for audience research during the fifties, when it grew to be what it has since remained, and given the increasing preoccupation of broadcasters with ratings, it is fairly safe to say that audience research, and the information it has produced, proved to be more of a barrier than a bridge between the broadcaster and his public.

Not so much a barrier, perhaps, as a barricade, behind which the 'professionals' shelter, and cultivate their own professionalism in a decent privacy, leaving the job (the 'dirty work') of managing the relationship between what they did and the listening, viewing, and paying public, and of fending off the more threatening mammoths and the more pestiferous mosquitoes in the surroundings, to be taken care of by 'the management'.

CRYPTOMICROCOSMOS

Of course, the basis of the reliance on professionalism as the guardian and measure of excellence lies in a second meaning conventionally attached to the word, which is of qualification by prolonged and specialised training. A telecommunications engineer is regarded as a professional in this sense, as much as a doctor or a lawyer, but so, apparently, is a man who has become a producer or director, after many years of experience in the theatre or in films – or in newspapers –

or as a floor manager or a production assistant in broadcasting. Because, the argument runs, the attestation of their professional fitness comes from their seniors and their peers in the profession, they can regard their standards, their competence, ethical code and values as independent of all 'amateurs' or 'laymen' – or, indeed, of the organisation they work for. According to Edward Epstein, this last claim was made explicitly by broadcasters and reporters employed by the National Broadcasting Company and other television networks in the United States:

> Even when it is recognized that network news does not in fact automatically mirror events but is the product of a decision-making process, network executives still deny that the news pictures are the product of the organization on the grounds that the individual newsmen involved in the process are all autonomous 'professionals'. And as professionals, it is argued, they make their decisions about news stories independent of the needs, expectations and hierarchy of the organization for which they work.[14]

It is this conception of professionalism as conferring a mandate of autonomous judgement which has made the mantle of professionalism so attractive – and which has created increasingly difficult problems for the Corporation. For the autonomy of the professional, which Epstein found claimed in NBC, which I found claimed, explicitly as well as implicitly, in 1963, and which has been publicly asserted more than once in recent years by broadcasters, is founded on the presumed existence not only of expertness founded on prolonged and specialised training, but of a code of behaviour such as supposedly exists in the classic professions, where the first consideration, according to one of the central articles of the professional code,[15] is the need of the client and the quality of the work.

This means the appraisal by the professional of what the needs of the client are, independently of his demands and wishes, and the appraisal of the service he gives by standards other than appreciation or reward by the client. Appreciation, or reputation, certainly does enter into the standards by which doctors and lawyers are measured, and even more certainly affects their reward. But these measures are mediated through colleagues in the profession. For the professional broadcaster, appreciation of the service he gives is mediated by the enquiries carried out by a department of the BBC – Audience Research – and the quality of his work is something which is judged by his seniors. Both directions of reference, to the client (i.e. the public) and to colleagues, therefore, are mediated through management and the system controlled by management.

Paradoxically, then, insistence on professionalism in the BBC seems to arise, at least in part, from the need to protect one's self from, or shelve consideration of, the unseen, unknown, audience, and from the judgements of higher management who – although often former 'professionals' themselves – are regarded as subject to other pressures and criteria, and whose 'professionalism' is in any case somewhat dated. Even in those output departments in which constant and open reference was made to audience figures and to R.I. (or A.R.) percentages, it was said with great firmness that what counted mostly was the judgement by fellow professionals of a programme's quality.

Yet it was also apparent – and frequently enough said – that producers hardly saw anything of each other. Two producers claimed they hadn't done more than exchange hellos with other producers for months – seven months, one said. Producers tend to isolate themselves, or to get isolated in their own productions:

> *One of the impressive things about watching a production going on is the special relationship which obtains between producer and cast, floor managers, and crew, and so on – a very difficult relationship, but all balanced on the isolation of the producer and the insecurity which necessarily comes from that. When the thing's in rehearsal, it seemed to me, he's going down a long slide –*
>
> Yes.
>
> *and he's got to end up at the bottom – safely, he hopes. He can't stop. The relaxation at the end, after the show, is very much a happy landing feeling. He's isolated because he's the steersman –*
>
> The isolation is the thing most producers are afraid of. They don't like it, they don't welcome it. That's why they stick so closely to the notion of the team. They're constantly referring to 'the team'.
>
> Particularly in this department, we're very much on our own.

Even in the studio, or rather, in the gallery above the studio and sealed off from it, the director is physically isolated. To retain control and the feeling of control, requires intense concentration:

> When you're directing and you sit in the gallery, you see twenty people, all of whom are expert – but incredibly slow. They seem to you to have a lot of inside knowledge, which you haven't got, but they seem at the same time not to be carrying out your instructions. Because from the point of view of a producer speaking into a microphone, to get twenty people to do the right thing at any one moment is inevitably a long process, and it seems utterly endless. The producer must have a tremendous amount of patience to get anything done at all. Occasionally the patience cracks.

The utter absorption of the director in his show – a commitment far more complete than I have encountered anywhere else – is the product of cumulative pressures. He may be, and often is, responsible for the original idea. The number of people involved, apart from performers, is larger than any other form of presentation requires. At the time of transmission he is responsible not for a film, which other people will market, or a performance which is now in the hands of the cast and the backstage workers, but for the output, at that time, of the BBC. More of the final product rests on his decisions than with other kinds of staged or filmed performance. And most important of all, his responsibility remains throughout the performance, whether it is recorded or transmitted live.

This absorption demands emotional reinforcement and expressive demonstration. No kind of detachment is really permissible; commitment has to be – and be seen to be – deep, sincere and binding, although surface cynicism, in the right circumstances and in the right company, enters in, as it does with other professionals whose occupational values have nevertheless to be central to their lives – scientists, priests, doctors. For directors, this aspect of professionalism develops naturally from the conventions of the theatre. In rehearsal, the twentieth repetition of a joke line or a comic sequence will be greeted with the same appreciative laughter by the other members of the cast and the other 'professionals' (director, stage manager, and aspirant juniors) as they gave at the first rehearsal. The director, especially, must respond. He must above all, it seems, 'believe in' his show.

> *What has struck me is that a director has got to feel that the show he is doing is really good, and that, moreover, he likes this kind of thing.*
>
> Yes, I think he must, even when he's offered an idea, and he takes it from this stage. It is rather like approaching a painting, for instance. One has to put as much of one's own personality into it as possible – but one has to rely on so many people around you. You have to work as a team.

Subsequent discussion, too long to reproduce here, made it clear that there did not exist an alternative professional attitude of dealing competently and expertly, even imaginatively, with a show that one did not regard as anything but unintelligent pop. Taking production responsibility, in these cases, would mean – if it were to be done *professionally* – remodelling the content and presentation so that it did represent one's own best, by any criterion.

The weight of commitments – of cast, studio crew, specialists, engineers and of the Corporation itself – which bear on the director is met by a total commitment on his side. Given not only the special unreality of theatrical or even film productions but the fact that the programmes broadcast in a single evening by radio and television all represent quite different orders or species of unreality, the director must immerse himself in the particular unreality in which his show exists, an immersion which demands involvement of a far more extreme kind than we accept under the ordinary dispensation of a 'willing suspension of disbelief'.

So the professional role of television or radio director requires him to insulate himself, for the duration of the rehearsal and production period, not only from the rest of his life's world but also from the worlds of other productions, from his own past efforts, and from those productions proceeding concurrently. He must match his production – 'A square show needs a square director', as one said – and, since this is not easy for people who live by being sophisticated, one must adjust one's perception of the outside world – including the public – so as to make it possible. So, if one is producing a show which I, as an outsider, suggest is very square indeed, the director must reply, as one did, 'But this is the squarest country in the world.'

Insulation applies to audiences too. The relationship with the audience has to be reduced to the simplest possible terms. I found it difficult to discover whether any kind of reaction from the outside world had been regarded as relevant or worth attention in the days of monopoly broadcasting. Since competition – between sound and television, between the BBC and commercial television, and between the three radio channels – had been instituted, a little more information about the response of audience had become admissible. But the information available – viewing or listening figures, and an Audience Response quotient or Reaction Index – applied only to the competitive situation itself.

Beyond the restricted use of such figures to measure the size of audience and the volume of applause, a use related exclusively to competition between rival broadcasters inside and outside the Corporation, there was, as one senior official commented, I think rightly, 'no evidence, to the people inside Television Centre, of people at the top of the Corporation knowing, or indeed caring, what the audience makes of the service it receives'.

Audience Research did not attract much attention from the Pilkington Committee. From the Beveridge Committee, however, the service received a good deal of criticism. This criticism still holds good. It does so, I believe, not because of any deficiency in the department itself, but because of the constraints put on its role within the Corporation, constraints noted by the Beveridge Committee (paras 234–5) and which called forth the comment 'To whom is the broadcaster responsible?

If it is only to his own conscience, the decision might better be described as irresponsible.'

What I have tried to suggest is that there are reasons for the constraints put on Audience Research and that these are not the irresponsibility, or arrogance, of broadcasters.[16] The pressure on those responsible for programmes is such that fuller or deeper analysis of audience reactions would amount to an intolerable strain.

Even the information contained in an R.I. or A.R. index may have to be rejected. The shock of a reported A.R. figure of 63 for a programme in a 1963 comedy series which had touched 75 was enough to disrupt the first hour or two of rehearsal of a subsequent production. Very little work was done. The atmosphere of dejection deepened with every new arrival. Clusters formed around the leading actors, the floor manager, and the assistant floor manager, with the producer circulating between them and the telephone.

'This,' it was explained to me, 'is what it's like on a morning when you've got a low audience figure.' For cast and production team, it was 'the figure'. Even after rehearsal began, the figure returned to the centre of the stage during waits: '63 – and I thought it was such a bloody good show.'

The whole gathering was, in fact, engaged in a more preoccupying task than rehearsal for the next show: the search for a reassuring explanation. It was found eventually in the concurrence of a sports film on the commercial network.

For a sociologist, it was rather like watching the whole practice of medicine being reduced to the use of the thermometer. But its significance lay not so much in the importance attached to a statistical index as in the lack of curiosity about its meaning, in the damage this particular return inflicted and in the way the damage was repaired. The clear objective throughout was to restore the safe enclosure of the autistic world within which they could sustain the complex system of commitment and belief their work called for.

The autistic world of commitment and belief which producers, programme departments, and broadcasting as a whole can create around itself is liable to be construed as complacency, as it was by the Beveridge Committee. It still is. It is a charge very easy to make and virtually impossible to refute. Yet to regard the apparent imperviousness to outside criticism shown by officials and broadcasters in the BBC as a sign of complacency seems ludicrously inappropriate; many of them are anxiously self-critical to the point of hypersensitivity. They are perpetually concerned with 'quality'. But within the context of broadcasting professionalism and the regular production of programmes, concern with quality means watching for the moment when new conventions degenerate into clichés, a fact which Brian

Winston[17] suggests can affect a whole approach to current affairs programmes.

> **** had all of the classic 'fourth estate' responses, the basis of which is the endless questioning of those in authority – that was what drove him. So he found Labour coming to power rather boring, and then the return of the Conservatives even more boring, because he felt he had been shying at those figures for so long by that time that he thought there wasn't much more that could be said.

Tony Essex, as reported by Nicholas Garnham,[18] sees the same trap recurrently opening up for the conventions governing documentary programmes:

> 'A good documentary needs a cause, always has. All the best documentaries which came out in the 1930s were about housing and unemployment and that sort of stuff; during the war – what a subject! – all those great pictures, the propaganda pictures. After that, the great social conscience started churning. You know, everyone started thinking of cripples, unmarried mothers, divorcees. All these are stale old things which we have looked at monthly. You know, "Look, what a marvellous old dying cancerous woman we've got for you this week; better still, folks, she has got a cataract." '

At a rather higher judgemental or 'editorial' level, the professional watch on quality is implicit in the watch for the moment when technical sophistication turns into needless clutter:

> 'Take the set of "Tonight", revived in the autumn of 1975. I mean this weird never-never land they come from, "Current Affairs Land", let's call it, has now assumed a sort of Grecian elegance which reverses ten years of electronic wizardry. It was quite simple; if you went into the gallery of Studio E in Lime Grove, they had actually got to the stage where it was possible to put so many electronic backings on any one camera's output that they had double monitors. I mean, it was just *the* most complex television studio in the country – and possibly in the world; I can't think of any one in New York as bad as that. So Bunce was right to say, "Forget about all that." '[19]

Thirdly, there are analogous, but more unmanageable challenges to the professional quest for 'quality' presented when the range of resources, which it is so exciting to explore and exploit in the earlier years of one's professional life, turn into imprisoning constraints:

> Institutional factors have a profound effect on the content of news and current affairs. For instance, I always used to think as

> I sat in the train going from Notting Hill Gate to Shepherd's Bush in the morning, 'But, dammit, I'm going to do something different. A small blow for freedom – I won't have ******** on talking about the economy. Right.' (My ambitions have always been extremely limited.) And I'd walk in and – Whah – and they'd say 'well, what about ****?', and I'd say '*No*!', and I'd go on to say that under no circumstances would we have him on the screen. And some shamefaced character would come up to me about half-past six and say 'Look, I've *tried* everything, and – he *is* at dinner, but – .' **** is a kind of television man; that's one of his lines. I mean, over NW1 tables, he is prepared to say, 'Look, I'm terribly sorry, I've just got to pop down to Lime Grove but I'll be back in an hour', and away he goes and does it.

Entry into this closed world, with its private enthusiasms and its new absolutes based on the shortest of critical perspectives, proved a disconcerting experience for newcomers used to the larger and slacker involvement of students or of writers and journalists, and led to some odd interpretations:

> There was one other thing which I did feel very uncomfortable about when I joined, and still do. I've been on two courses and each time there seemed to be an attempt being made by somebody to do a job of brainwashing. I don't think it was a conscious attempt. It was just that everything to a lot of the senior lecturers seemed to be for the best of all possible worlds. You were left with two uncomfortable thoughts. (*a*) Why it was necessary to try and brainwash like this; and (*b*) well, if everything is so grand, why aren't the programmes better? ********** was a case in point – the first lecture on this course, by a man who'd travelled all over the world, and had come to the conclusion that home was the best and that we had nothing to learn from anyone. This, constantly repeated during both courses, generally from administrators or from people fairly high up in the Corporation, left a sort of uncomfortable taste in the mouth.

These observations referred (by name, later) to heads of output departments ('administrators') who were regarded by producers as ruthlessly critical. 'Brainwashing' is an outrageously inappropriate word in this context. But the fierceness of the reaction of this particular newcomer to the BBC jogs one into awareness of the almost deliberate and certainly perpetual effort made to domesticate the world the Corporation inhabits.

Perspectives are drawn so that they terminate within the horizon of BBC control or influence; communication with audiences is reduced to the common *Gestalt* of a programme 'stream', a rating, and an R.I. figure; public issues are translated into methods of programme construction, moral problems into professional judgements.

To repeat – there is nothing peculiar to the BBC in the creation of a private world out of an occupational milieu. It is, in fact, a necessary corollary of becoming committed to a job and an organisation. But it is much more intense in the BBC. Withdrawal into a closed, isolated world of ideas, activity, involvement and resources has its most vivid manifestation, both actual and symbolic, in the studio production gallery. The elaborate provisions made to ensure that everything and everybody conceivably relevant to what is going on is available within the studio, and to exclude from the gallery everybody and everything not directly concerned in controlling what is happening in the studio – and the sheer necessity of these provisions for production to be achieved – afford a paradigm of the closed world which the people who work in the BBC have created for themselves.

BBC POLICY AND INTERNAL POLITICS

The BBC had not by any means turned its back on the Reithian ethos and purpose in the 1960s; many, indeed most, of its activities still faithfully reflected the traditional image. But there had been change, and it is change which is significant, as it is change of which we are most conscious. The breaking of the BBC monopoly had been achieved by political manoeuvres within one party, and however gamely the BBC strove to retain its reputation for political impartiality and detachment, it had been brought down from the heights of supra political, almost supranational, authority which it had enjoyed during the thirty years of broadcasting monopoly.

A consciously 'circulation-building' element entered into the handling of news, and comment on news; successful presentation was related more and more to exclusive, sometimes sensational, interviews and reporting. Many programmes appeared to make bids for popularity by disregarding the cautious or 'responsible' standards associated with the earlier days of monopoly. The hauteur which governed Corporation attitudes and behaviour towards commercial television at first gave way to a more or less open acknowledgement of rivalry on the same terms, a rivalry which admitted of the interchange or common employment of popular performers and producers and of the growth of a policy of short-term contracts – both of which tended to dilute any distinctively BBC style or approach, and reduce the public appreciation of differences of ethos and purpose between the Corporation and commercial television companies.

By 1960, the BBC had found itself compelled into a strategy which allowed for fighting on two fronts; the old certainty of purpose had gone; and the clear challenge and purpose had been replaced by a dilemma.

Concurrently with the slow, lingering 'dissolve' of the public service conception into the professionalism of the broadcaster, there have been increasing differences of opinion about the aims and purposes of radio and television broadcasting, about what was called programming policy. These differences were not new; what was new was that they came to serve as organising principles for dissentient factions. In radio, the Third Programme had come to be regarded as a flag nailed to the mast of a ship which the BBC had, effectively, deserted. This view was confirmed by what seemed the indecent haste with which the 'high culture' content promised for the second television channel was scaled down, as was said, to token offerings and BBC2 brought into the pursuit for audience ratings. More important, dispute about the proper interpretation of the concept of public service broadcasting, about the prescription laid down in the charter and the licence, about the aims which the Corporation should pursue, and the purpose of broadcasting programmes had become more prominent and to a visible extent, organised. Since then, the internal controversy has been increasing in range and volume. The borderlines between the dissentient groups have changed, as have the slogans, the vocabulary, and the beliefs expressed in them. The ideological debate – for that is what it is – has become assimilated, to some extent, with political controversy as it has developed in society at large. But for people inside the BBC, it remains firmly rooted in the 'internal politics' of the Corporation and of broadcasting generally. To some extent also, I believe, this process of assimilation with the general trend of the 'politicisation of everything' in Western societies has been compliant, rather than committed, unwitting rather than deliberate. In any case, it has not only gone hand in hand with the erosion of the 'public service' image among broadcasters and its replacement by the image of broadcasting 'professionalism', but has hastened it – inevitably so, because it is the function of ideologies to provide meaningful shape to experience when Burke's 'ancient opinions and rules of life' become irrelevant or obsolete.

Towards the beginning of this period of change, in 1963, three distinct views made themselves apparent.

For many people, the 'pragmatists', the three purposes of informing, educating and entertaining the public seemed to be quite distinct but nevertheless compatible because there was in fact an explicit and general public demand for all three things. This catholicity of outlook was not illogically related to the suspicions of the staff in Light Entertainment and in Schools Broadcasting, and of others who felt some affinity with them, that their contribution to the BBC's output was tolerated as an 'unfortunate necessity'. The slogan most frequently encountered among this group was 'a balanced programme' – i.e., a total output in which Light Entertainment programmes would have their 'rightful' share.

> There's some disquiet here because we see the top places in the Corporation all being filled by journalists. You see, when you had a few showmen up there, they'd take the view: 'I didn't like this but it's popular and – in the interests of a balanced programme – I'll put it in.' The journalists now will quite likely take the view that if they don't like a show and if it's not getting a very big audience, they can scrap it.

A 'balanced programme' policy, in fact, would have been regarded as an insurance policy. A pronouncement in favour of it would have quietened the unexpectedly widespread feelings of insecurity about the future which turned up in many of the 1963 interviews in Light Entertainment and in Schools Broadcasting. Thus:

> One has the feeling that the Corporation could well do without Light Entertainment. It has Light Entertainment because it has to – that although it did many good things even prior to the advent of commercial television, if they could do without us they would. That is the feeling. It's only very recently, when things became competitive, let's face it – that audiences are wanted to keep the Corporation alive – that they really acknowledge that they had to have Light Entertainment, and there was no way out of it. Although, of course, there's always the feeling that if you can develop the big audience puller with 'Your Life in Their Hands' then probably they'd junk it. They'd let Light Entertainment go.

And:

> You're here as groundbait. All right, so stick to your job as groundbait, and don't think of Light Entertainment being a viable television commodity in its own right.

And again:

> It's an unsafe world . . . If we're talking of allies – which is the point you made – I don't think there are any allies. I think they're a bunch of hostile critics.
> *Has this feeling of it being an unsafe world grown in the last year or so?*
> Yes, oh yes. Prior to Pilkington, there wasn't the feeling of quite so much insecurity as there's been since.

Obviously, there was no active, present fear that the Corporation would 'junk' Light Entertainment, or even that it wanted to, but there remained the uncertain feeling that Light Entertainment was there to act as 'groundbait' for the mass audience, that, first and last, its job was to attach the audience to the BBC channels, and that its existence depended on keeping mass audiences, in a way that other output departments' existence did not. There was, beyond this, an awareness that over the previous few years a critical ideological campaign has been fought and won in BBC television, the outcome of which had been to place Talks and Current Affairs (the 'journalists') in the centre of the programmers' picture of television, with Outside Broadcasts (which included sports) within the main frame. Both groups observed the same canons of live immediacy, of the television screen acting as reflector of the 'real world' of people, happenings, things and ideas – a world which is 'real' in that it is topical. Drama remained a datum of existence for television in its 'home cinema' function. Light Entertainment, equally, remained an 'unfortunate necessity', its marginal character inescapably perpetuated in the adjective tagged on to its very title.

The visible direction of these observations shows that the belief that BBC policy should be guided by the actual and actively expressed public demand for 'a balanced variety' of kinds of programme rested on apprehensions about the unwilling acceptance by 'The BBC' of the very existence of whole departments. The insecurity engendered by such apprehensions and the suspicion felt in such departments that they were victims of tacit criteria by which status or, at least, esteem within the Corporation were given gradings both found a rational basis in the sweeping successes of people from Talks and Current Affairs in gaining the dominant position in the Television Service, and the striking contrast of the shrinking of influence or representation of other kinds of production experience in the higher ranks.

As in other contexts, the goal of political conflict is to have the leaders of one or other party gain positions of power; thereafter, of course, they will administer in the interests of the community as a whole, and with strict justice and equity, but it is at this point of succession to positions of power that the political system and the careers system of organisations meet. The success of people from one section of the organisation rather than others must be seen as reflecting on the general level of ability and initiative in that section. The kind of talents and experience which that section requires and rewards is shown to be demonstrably relevant to the kind of talents and experience required by the organisation as a whole. The success of individual members from a section suggests that the cases it has argued have been well argued by them in the past; more particularly, that their view of the

Corporation's task and of the best way of discharging it has won over other views, so that the career victory is also an ideological victory. The structure of working relationships and functions in the section from which they came, and the jobs of people who operate within it, are less likely to be adversely affected than those in other sections by the changes instituted by the new men who have appeared from that section, have gained by its existing structure, and may perhaps have modelled it. While the experiences, expertise, and viewpoints the section now has in common with the man at the top may not be an unmixed advantage in the eyes of the members of the section, it seems to be so to others. And there is, lastly, the immediate benefit of the current of promotions set going by any displacement from the top positions in the section.

The outcome of competition for succession to senior posts in an organisation tends, therefore, to have repercussive effects throughout its membership, affecting far more people than the small group of contestants for the positions.

> *You used to have big names (from your side of things) around the Corporation at one time?*
>
> Oh well, you've got the journalists in now. When —— was here you felt you had the ear of the bosses. But now he's gone, and because —— [his successor], I suppose, is a BBC man, let's put it, from way back – he's probably looked upon as such by the top brass – we've become much more of a 'department' than we used to be, just another limb of the Corporation, and feeling just a bit more remote.
>
> *I see. So far from having your people fed up to the top of the BBC you're having BBC people fed into your top.*
>
> Yes. And I think this will probably go on. For instance, what future is there for a producer here? I'm personally quite interested in administrative jobs and have done them in the past . . . but I don't really reckon there's a great deal of opportunity, unless I managed to get the ear of somebody somewhere, to make the jump from production to administration. You see, and there's this feeling – as was definitely stated when —— [a former Director of Television] addressed us. One of the chaps said, 'You don't want to finish up with a lot of producers who are fifty-five or sixty' and the answer was 'That's quite right'. So you see immediately one feels a little more remote, and cut off and wondering about the future. . . .

It is this repercussive effect which links the legitimate self-interests of the members of a department or section in an organisation to the actual and possible changes which occur in the occupancy of the senior posts at the top.

Others saw the BBC as an institution with a specific and now inalienable historic part to play in the life of the nation. Whether this role had been deliberately chosen and achieved or was the consequence of social forces which had operated through historical circumstances, the BBC's relationship with the nation was now normative. In international or national crises, it had spoken in a real and important sense for the nation as well as to it. For the majority of people, the measure of the significance of any public issue was the weight the BBC attached to it. Moreover, while nobody was naive or presumptuous enough to see the BBC as prescribing some national code of morals, it was believed that the normative function which it undoubtedly had discharged for political attitudes attached also to its observance of standards of public morals, in entertainment principally, but also in comment and criticism; so the programmes it broadcast carried a special sanction in that they were what the BBC, the national broadcasting authority, saw as fit and proper to offer the nation.

For those who saw the proper role of the BBC in the life of the nation as exemplary, its civilising effects in cultural terms were something which should be matched in increasing the amount and the quality of information, and the level of sophistication among the public at large about social, economic and political issues and problems. True, the effect wrought by broadcasting was almost impossible to disentangle from the concurrent rise in the level of education, the increase in the proportion of people reading 'quality' (or 'up-market') newspapers, and perhaps most important of all, a qualitative shift in the extent to which national and international events impinged directly on individual welfare. But broadcasting had undoubtedly played a role, and could play an increasingly important one, in this particular long-term trend.

A third section of opinion seemed to regard any normative function, together with the Reithian adoption of a tutelary role, either as undesirably arrogant, or played out, or as imposing irrelevant constraints on the development of broadcasting forms so as to mirror contemporary events, society and culture swiftly and forcibly. There was also a recrudescence of the missionary role of the thirties, conceived this time out of what was seen as the abdication of the policy makers from their responsibility for maintaining the best traditions of public service broadcasting, and so aiding and abetting the anaesthetising of public opinion. It represented most clearly the stage reached by 1960 of the 'liberal dissolution' of that conception of public service which was moulded by Reith's generation. Their overriding concern was with the exploitation of the sheer immediacy of television so as to mirror society and acknowledged only two constraints – overwhelming pressure exerted on and through their superiors by outside organisations or articulate sections of the public, and 'programme ethos', a term which gained some currency as representing the individual's interpretation of his mandate, of his task, and of the constraints of what he imagined to be the state of public opinion relevant to his work.

A note written in 1970 by Antony Jay about the attitudes and aims of the 'Tonight' team during this period reveals, I think, rather precisely not only the prevailing mood of exhilaration in this group but the way in which that mood related directly to the feeling that the new men (and women) in Current Affairs had of breaking with the past, with tradition inside the BBC as well as outside it, a tradition which had clearly ceased to be viable as an institutional base on which they could build their own individual and joint endeavours, and was now an incubus of which they had a duty to rid the country and the BBC, both. For them, the dissolution of the Reithian ethos was much more a bonfire. Hence, even several years after, the inspirational tone of the account:

The 'Tonight' attitude to Britain

> We shared the feeling, especially Donald Baverstock, who as a naturally populist Welshman felt it most acutely, that there was an out-of-touch group of people running Britain and covering their failures with a cloak of government statements and PR half-truths and full-page prestige ads in *The Times*, and abetted by docile and amenable Fleet Street proprietors who were worried about their advertising, and that we had a duty to show the other side, the bad news about the shipyard order books, the faster growth of competitive economies, the consequences of underinvesting and overmanning and substituting 'made in Britain' on the label for the laborious analysis of export market requirements. This is a part of what is meant when *Tonight* is called 'irreverent'; we did not assume that the government knew what it was doing, that Whitehall knew what was wanted, or that anything could safely be left to the experts. This came chiefly from DB, and was very much the attitude and belief that gave a (slightly offensive) moral-crusading attitude to *Tonight* and made us all work far more passionately (and far longer hours) than we would have for simple programme success. We all believed passionately in the *idea* of the BBC, or *a* BBC, financed neither by the Treasury nor by the advertisers. This made us all the more contemptuous (arrogantly so, you could justly argue) of the way the BBC actually behaved, of its timid policies and its senior people and its weak compromises (Muggeridge being banned from the screen by Jacob), and we all had no doubts (then) about how much better

we could have done it. But we believed completely in the type of broadcasting freedom the system gave the nation. Did I tell you about Donald Baverstock turning the Charter upside down and asking 'What does it *not* stop us doing?' He found that we could have a Tory MP without 'balancing' him with a Labour MP in the opposite chair. That we could say 'Harrods' and not 'a Knightsbridge store', etc., etc. Like Luther, he was able to hack away generations of invention and interpretation by weak popes and worldly cardinals, and get back to the pure and simple gospel truths. I do not think there was anyone else in the BBC, not the Chairman or DG, except possibly Grace [Wyndham Goldie], who really understood what 'BBC policy' rested on in the way that Baverstock understood it.[20]

How far the whole system of control and consensus had separated out into a diversity of approaches which derived what coherence they had from the 'programme ethos' of professional broadcasters appears from the public statements made at that time by senior officials, acting as spokesmen of the Board of Governors and the Board of Management. In fact, the best statement of this viewpoint has been made not by any of these, but by a former Controller of Programmes, Television, Stuart Hood. He wrote, in 1967:

'The BBC functions on a system of devolution. A producer is given full powers in making a programme or series of programmes. On him rests the final judgment of what is right and seemly to present to his audience. His decisions may range over a wide field. They may concern a theme, a topic for discussion or debate; the choice of a film-clip; a dramatic situation; a camera-angle; the words of a song; a single word. If he is doubtful on any point he may refer his problem to his superior, who will either make a decision or refer the matter higher. The ultimate instance is the Director General, who – before giving his ruling – may consult with the producer himself or with senior members of the staff. Judgments are not based on written laws – although there is a code of practice governing violence in children's television or "that area of adult time when children are known to be viewing in substantial numbers". In part, they are based on precedent and tradition; but precedents can be ignored and traditions questioned and modified. What they are based on can best be described as a programme ethos – a general view of what is fitting and seemly, of what is admissible and not admissible, which is gradually absorbed by those persons involved in programme-making. It is intangible, undefined and baffling to newcomers and freelance producers or directors. One of the best definitions of it was provided by Sir Hugh Greene in an address delivered in Rome to the International Catholic Association for Radio and Television. One element in what he called "the in-grained code" was "the proper sensitivity of production staff to the world around them, so that they are concerned with a relationship to the audience which cannot exist if the language in which they are talking, and the assumptions they are making, seem to be too remote from the language and assumptions of the audience and of the times in which they are communicating". This formula is both liberal and flexible.'[21]

Stuart Hood's prescription, liberal and flexible as it may be, is nevertheless concerned with negative sanctions – with the exercise of censorship, rather than with a positive formulation of purpose or function. It accommodates the third view I have presented above, of 'broadcasting as a mirror of contemporary life', without underwriting it.

While I believe that the only injustice done in this account to these three views lies in its brevity, it should be said that they were in the first place my own inferences from interviews and conversations rather than summaries of statements explicitly made; the most explicit statements tended to be about opinions imputed to others which were in conflict with the stand which could be assumed to be the speaker's (i.e. 'That's the kind of thing I think they stand for, and if *they* are for it, I'm against it'). And there may well have been other views of the BBC's function, or purpose, or mission in society. All I have done is to present, in capsuled form, the three which made themselves evident to me.

As I have suggested, the emergence of different ideologies became overt in the increased diversity of 'slants', or forms of presentation and programme content characteristic of different output departments.

Individual programmes now have greater freedom. People think in terms of this or that programme rather than of the BBC as a whole. The amount of control exercised over them centrally has slightly diminished. Individual programmes have more autonomy.

This applies to matters of content – journalistic content, perhaps. Is there any other sense in which this greater freedom, or autonomy, is exercised?

Yes, I think in its attitude to its audience. This applies much more to television – a feeling not so much that a programme is only justified by the audience that it gets but that, bearing in mind the cost of the service, and the physical limitations of it, you have to think very very hard before you put on a programme that is only of interest, say, to one million as against six million. I think there is a difference between this and saying, 'This programme will bring in an audience of thirteen million and therefore we can charge a lot for the advertising.' I'm not sure, though, that the distinction is always made in that form. Sometimes the BBC attitude to justification by figures is just as blatant as the commercial companies. It can be very honest and very democratic, this feeling, but it can be used as a stick to beat everything that doesn't command a large audience.

The growth of the television service within the BBC, its success in the battle for audiences with commercial television, and the more recent emergence of a group of young and vigorous people into controlling positions within the service had all contributed to a greater autonomy in the administration of Television. The internal politics of this change are complicated, but nevertheless clear enough in the practical outcomes.

If you are right in saying that the BBC is becoming more 'plural' – culturally, administratively, and in terms of policy aims – than it was, obviously the resistance must come from the Administration, which is going to be much more comfortable with a monolithic Corporation than with a lot of groups who want to go their own sweet way.

I must say this had not occurred to me. It is very easy to talk isn't it, of 'The Administration' as an external body, without bothering to separate it into its various categories. Frankly, some sections of the Administration that one comes into contact with – you know perfectly well that they would never have anything to do with deciding the character of the output. But maybe, if one looks at it from the point of view of Television Centre, one certainly gets the impression that in one respect, that is in staffing and recruitment – and I think it is a very widely held impression – recruiting and staffing in Television is done far more according to the whim, or decision, of the heads than elsewhere. Appointments Boards, and things like that have less meaning in Television Centre than they do at Broadcasting House.

On the programme side?

Yes – on the programme side. I think it is felt that it is quite clear who will get the job because the man who runs the programme and his superiors have decided that they want him on the job. Now this may be a naked geographical thing. As you say, the Administration is at Broadcasting House. It is not there [at Television Centre].

The broad division of opinion about the way in which the Corporation should interpret the definition of its primary task which has been imposed on it as a public institution represents more than a natural but impotent interest in issues which had previously been for the governing body to settle – as indeed they still were. The debate was ideological, in the sense of the consonance between a coherent system of ideas and principles and the self-interests of a group of people. This is not to say either that the ideas themselves are thereby invalidated or suspect, or indeed that people are constrained to those opinions which will tend to their advantage. What they may do is to strengthen the particular attitudes and strategy which individuals regard as important for their present situation and their future hopes or chances in life. The kinds of views about policy expressed by individuals and which they impute to others are allied to their interests and their fears. They serve also to codify and rationalise courses of action which protect or advance their interests. But more importantly, they organise people's perceptions of the world which surrounds them and besets them, and, in Clifford Geertz's words 'make empirical claims about the condition and direction of society'.[22]

5 Press Freedom and Broadcasting Liberties

THE NATIONAL INTEREST AND THE PUBLIC GOOD

Before the war, Reith saw his public service broadcasting system acting 'as a dependable keeper of the nation's conscience', standing as 'an arbiter above the clamour of all political and social factions' and regarded as 'the paragon of impartiality, honesty and respectability'.[1] Politics excepted, he pursued his objective uncompromisingly and openly. He was able to do so, and to bring to bear what he called 'the brute force of monopoly' as his instrument because Government and influential public opinion supported his objectives, seeing them, as he did, as a means of promoting at least an appearance of national social and cultural integration in a country deeply divided but fearful of the destructive forces present, and gaining strength, in Britain and abroad.

The forties and fifties, however, did bring integration, and of a totally unprecedented kind. They seem now to have been a curious historical interlude, a social interregnum in which fundamental political differences and the whole structure of social and economic inequality seemed to be – through the overwhelming and shared experience of the war and, thereafter, the magic of technological progress – obsolescent. During the 1950s, the decline of political interest and consciousness in Western countries was a matter of common observation; and the decline affected all groups in the population. (Surveys in the U.S., for example, established that there was a *lower* level of interest in politics among the student population than among the population at large.) Politics came to be regarded as a matter of creating the appropriate technocratic structure, and of capable economic management; salvation lay in technological development.

In retrospect, the whole decade of the fifties seems characterised by an odd political anaesthesia. During the next decade, indeed, writers on the Left seemed to have thought of some malign process of 'de-politicisation' as having taken place. But at this present point in time, the truth seems nearer to what Paul Lazarsfeld and Robert Merton wrote, in a brief paper which is probably the most insightful analysis of the function of radio broadcasting extant, and which was published in 1948:

> 'With distinct variations in different regions and among different social strata, the outpourings of the media presumably enabled the twentieth-century American to "keep abreast of the world". Yet, it is suggested, this vast supply of communications may elicit only a superficial concern with the problems of society, and this superficiality often cloaks mass apathy.
>
> Exposure to this flood of information may serve to narcotise rather than to energise the average reader or listener. As an increasing amount of time is devoted to reading and listening, a decreasing share is available for organised action. The individual reads accounts of issues and problems and may even discuss alternative lines of action. But this rather intellectualised, rather remote connection with organised social action is not activated. The interested and informed citizen can congratulate himself on his lofty state of interest and information, and neglect to see that he has abstained from decision and action. In short, he takes his secondary contact with the world of political reality, his reading and listening and thinking, as a vicarious performance. He comes to mistake *knowing* about problems of the day for *doing* something about them. His social conscience remains spotlessly clean. He *is* concerned. He *is* informed. And he has all sorts of ideas as to what should be done. But, after he has got through his dinner and after he has listened to his favoured radio programmes and after he has read his second newspaper of the day, it is really time for bed.
>
> In this peculiar respect, mass communications may be included among the most respectable and efficient of social narcotics. They may be so fully effective as to keep the addict from recognising his own malady.
>
> That the mass media have lifted the level of information of large populations is evident. Yet, quite apart from intent, increasing dosages of mass communications may be inadvertently transforming the energies of men from active participation into passive knowledge.[2]

It is as well to remind ourselves, at this point, that in terms of programme expenditure, and audience size, the provision of entertainment is still broadcasting's primary role in the life of the nation. Again, this is not to suggest that the provision of entertainment excludes other roles, or that the other roles claimed for broadcasting exclude the provision of entertainment. But education, information, moral and cultural codes, are *carried* by entertainment. In this regard, the position remains as it was quite clearly perceived by the founding fathers of broadcasting in Britain and America, except that we have progressed beyond the 'groundbait' stage, when informative and educative programmes could be fitted into the interstices of mere (or 'light') entertainment, or interspersed with it. Nowadays, programmes of all kinds have to 'capture' their audience; if they do not, they are relegated to off-peak times, when most people are either at work or in bed.

It is the fact that broadcast entertainment and entertaining broadcasts capture immense audiences which has led to the presumptions about the pervasiveness and power of broadcasting common to almost all official and public utterances on the subject. The Pilkington Committee shared this traditional view: 'Unless and until there is unmistakable proof to the contrary, the presumption must be that television is and will be a main factor in influencing the values and moral standards of our society.' By 1973, Anthony Smith was prepared to go even further, in words strongly reminiscent of Vice-President Spiro Agnew:

> 'Broadcasting, in the process of rapid growth over half a century, has acquired a role of such magnitude that it (and its controllers) can steer the course of entire cultures; just as an economy can be manipulated today by a few who control the major offices in a few large corporations, so can a culture be oriented in certain directions by a tiny group of broadcasting impresarios whose main motive is the preservation of their own institutions intact rather then the actual "good" of the culture concerned.'[3]

Since the Pilkington Committee reported, the principal development has been for political attitudes and beliefs to have been added to moral standards and cultural systems as being subject to the power and pervasiveness of broadcasting.

The last ten years have seen the almost total reversal of the 'depoliticisation' trend of the 1950s. There has been what seems an almost compulsive drive to 'politicise' almost every aspect of human affairs, and a reawakening of political interest to the point of fervour in matters which had been the special preserve of institutionalised politics. This new trend has outrun the control and even the comprehension of professional politicians (and political scientists).

The imposed consensus of the thirties, the consciousness of national unity of the wartime years and the surface appearance of inevitable progress towards improved economic welfare and social equality had all dissipated by the mid-sixties. Conceivably, the country by then had recovered sufficient assurance and essential unity for people to acknowledge once again the existence of the divisions which had always been a familiar part of everyone's common experience and awareness as a citizen, and which had, moreover, though latent, persisted since the twenties. But, so far as broadcasting, broadcasting authorities, and broadcasters were concerned, dissensus of the kind which then revealed itself and has remained with us since was a shatteringly novel experience.

The interesting thing, from the present point of view, is that broadcasting was again regarded as playing something of a central role in this reanimation of political consciousness. This time, of course, broadcasting manifested itself not as a sedative or narcotic, but as a stimulant – at times, an hallucinatory drug.

This whole development has become so cliché-ridden that it is extremely difficult to describe, let alone explain, what has happened. It seems to be common ground that 'a dangerous gulf' has opened between leaders (i.e. politicians) and led (i.e. voters); that the consensus which has prevailed in Britain (seemingly from time immemorial) has broken up, and divisions which previously did not exist, or at least were unrevealed, had become obtrusively apparent; that trade unions, and the trade union movement, have become much more militant, both industrially and politically; that Scottish and Welsh nationalism, as well as Irish, within the United Kingdom, has gained enormously in strength; that re-politicisation, especially among the young, has led to extremism, both of the Left and the Right, with a consequent increase in the use of the vocabulary of Marxism and Fascism; that a new wave of feminism has emerged with much broader claims to equal rights; and that, finally, all these manifestations of 're-politicisation' are, for the most part, particularistic and have been quick to adopt the organisational structure, the tactics, and the armoury of pressure groups within the parliamentary system, and of dissident factions outside it.

INTO POLITICS

The sudden acceleration in the tempo of manifest changes in cultural and political life accompanied, and may well have encouraged the emergence of television as the principal regular source of news; and television news is a source of information very different in content and impact from newspaper news. In the United States, moreover, where the dominance of television news is much more striking, the expansion of news programmes to thirty and then, in some major cities, to ninety minutes is some indication of the increased weight accorded to information and news about the 'great' world as opposed to information about people's own 'small' world supplied by a mainly local press. The difference between the condition of the lives of 'them', of the named figures in the great world, and the anonymous 'us' of the small world became visible and audible to an precedented extent. 'Them' and 'us' had also taken on a new dimension. The former now made their appearance as the leading figures in a prearranged, often rehearsed and certainly staged performance. As against this, we were presented with the disordered, or embarrassed, or distraught, or – often enough – disfigured appearances of those of 'us' whom disaster, rioting, bombing, or the pavement interviewer in search of 'vox pop' thrust, unprepared, distracted, or dismembered in front of a random camera.

One obvious way in which the changed situation made itself felt is the implication of television organisations themselves, in Britain and elsewhere, in the political process itself, as one of the forces the nature, direction and control of which is inevitably a political concern. For, as the Select Committee on Nationalised Industries put it, the BBC and IBA have to be regarded as 'powerful institutions in their own right, whose whole style of decision making and action profoundly affects the community'.[4]

This must have been visible to people in controlling positions in the BBC no less than to members of Parliament and some sections of the public. At all events, there was a great change in attitude to the 'outside' world and to the BBC's relationships with it evident among officials in the upper reaches of the Corporation whom I interviewed in 1973 compared with the attitudes of their predecessors of ten years earlier. One rather obvious way this showed itself was the frequency with which memories of 'traumatic episodes' which had occurred in recent years came up in conversation. These were memories not only of dealing with powerful or vocal individuals or interest groups who had been outraged or affronted by what they regarded as partial or deliberately 'slanted' presentations of themselves, their conduct, or their opinions, in programmes which were regarded by producers and their seniors as 'good television' or 'responsible broadcasting'. They also remembered occasions when what seemed to the producers and themselves to be 'good television' turned out to be seen as prejudiced and offensive not just by the subjects of the programmes or by the all too predictable voices of public outrage but by disinterested others – of occasions when, in fact, the 'ingrained code' or the 'programme ethos' of the BBC had slipped.

What is more, some of the 'traumatic episodes' related to matters which would in earlier years have been regarded as exclusively internal affairs of policy or organisation. The reaction of most of the Board of Management and senior staff to what they regarded as a slap in the face – the appointment of Lord Hill, then Chairman of the Independent Television Authority, as Chairman of the Board of Governors of the BBC – was leaked generously to the press, which had something of a field day over the whole episode – to be renewed and refuelled by Kenneth Adam, who wrote up his own inside story for publication in the *Sunday Times* in four articles, the first appearing the day after he had retired from his appointment as Director, Television. The change of programming policy published in a pamphlet, 'Broadcasting in the Seventies', from 'Home', 'Light' and 'Third' to Radios 1, 2, 3, and 4 – a change planned by a 'Policy Group' made up of McKinsey consultants and senior BBC officials – provoked a public protest by a large number of programme staff. The peculiarly British form of the protest (a letter to *The Times* with scores of signatories) underlines the extent to which the BBC had, so to speak, 'gone public', with the BBC's own staff seeing it and themselves as implicated in essentially political processes affecting, and affected by, public opinion.

I don't think even at the time of 'Broadcasting in the Seventies' that the majority of people felt they were in danger of being cleared out.

Everybody talks about 'Broadcasting in the Seventies' as though it were some great trauma.

Oh, it was unbelievable!

Why the hell? Why do people call it 'traumatic'?

Because all sorts of settled patterns of relationships and aspects of behaviour were suddenly turned upside down. All sorts of things you thought you had the right to expect would continue were suddenly overturned. The organisation behaved – that's it, the organisation didn't behave in a benevolent way. This is almost the funny side of it, except that it did upset a lot of people. What people expected of the Corporation was that it would say, 'The time has come for a change. Let us organise change in a nice, humanitarian, concerned, considerate way – in the way that we've always tried to conduct our affairs in the past. Let us organise change in a co-operative way.' And it didn't. It turned round and said, 'This is the change – Bang!'

Really?

Well, that is certainly my impression.

I see. What you mean is that the 'trauma' was the result of a mere – well, not a mere, a major – tactical error. Hadn't McKinsey's told them about management style? – because McKinsey's were around then.

No, I think they may well have given them the nerve – maybe McKinsey had given them the nerve to do it that way.[5]

So, in accounting for the new attitude of people in the BBC I am myself inclined to give more weight to the alterations in the political and cultural climate than to the more obvious factors of passage of time and the turnover of incumbents of the top positions. There was in 1973 undoubtedly a greater sensitivity about the situation of the BBC than in the years after the Pilkington Report; there was also a new uncertainty that came, I believe, with the renewed consciousness of the BBC being involved in national politics instead of being a neutral, detached, almost aloof, observer.

> There has been a good deal of criticism of the BBC. I have yet to be convinced how representative it is.
>
> *It comes from a tiny body of people, but then that's how all criticism comes. If I get a bad review of something I've written, it's by one man. I don't know whether it's representative or not, but I have to take notice of it.*
>
> Well, you must then ask yourself whether these views are typical or shared by a large number of people. Now, in an inaccurate way, it seems to me that a lot of criticism has come from that part of society which is finding itself under the pressure of change and we keep on rubbing their noses in it. It's a bit like life becoming awkward for any individual – he tends to lash out. And I think that people lash out at us, as being one of the few things that they can see visibly there to grab hold of. But I'm not sure that you should accept as being valid the fact that all this criticism of the BBC is as widespread as people say it is.
>
> *I'm not suggesting that it's widespread. What I am suggesting is that the volume has grown.*
>
> Yes, I think that's true. It's inevitable. Enormous things have happened to this society.

Whether or not even the volume of criticism has grown was, in the view of other senior people, debatable. What all were agreed on was that it was neither better informed nor more accurate and significant than it had been. Nevertheless, what was manifest whenever this topic surfaced in the interviews was a self-critical consciousness, a sensitivity to the political and social situation of the BBC which was certainly not perceptible in 1963.

> Externally we face this huge problem that – to come back to the basic problem – we aren't liked. Here we are, an organisation that perhaps puts out more good and does more good and makes people more happy than anything else in the country and yet

basically if you ask people what they think of us, they will, in the first instance, respond with something unfavourable. Now this can be reduced, I know, to largely accidental factors and factors to do with politics and the way newspapers write about us – newspaper interests and so on – and other factors that are to do as much with society as with the BBC. And you can also pretty soon demonstrate that we are loved, on the other hand, because of the things we do and the programmes we do. Fundamentally I think we've got to open up this institution in a big way. We have been too closed. We've not admitted the extent of the dissent about us and dislike of us. We need to display our processes much more openly. Now that's only part of it and that's to do with our public image. The other aspect of that is to do with the sort of people who work for us. I believe, fundamentally, that we have no business being the sort of closed bureaucracy that we are, given the sort of business we're in.

Most observations of this kind had some explicit reference to the much increased salience of news and current affairs programmes in BBC output not so much for the total television audience but for that part of it which included the more powerful and the more vocal institutions and groups. It is also news and current affairs programmes which have attracted much the greater part of the attention accorded to broadcasting in the recent spate of criticism, informed and uninformed, expert and inexpert.

THE PRIDE AND TERROR OF BROADCASTING

While the consequences, both outside and inside the BBC, of the expansion of news and current affairs programmes, and of the increased importance attached to them, were not apparent until the late sixties, the new salience accorded to or won by them dates from ten years before. Anthony Smith, himself one of the people involved in the 'new wave' of that time, has given an insider's view of the creation of the 'powerful news and current affairs departments which are the pride and terror of broadcasting organisations and political establishments in the present time';

'They [Donald Baverstock in the BBC, Fred Friendly in the CBS] were among the individuals whose personal dynamism alone appeared to force their various parent organisations into a proper readiness to take the risks which enabled journalism to develop as a force within the world of broadcasting. The News departments of Television News ring with the legends of the Beowulfs of that time who simultaneously and with surprisingly little mutual inspiration fought a series of dragons whose presence had never been seriously challenged. They created news magazines where previously there had only been an announcer with a prepared bulletin or a sheaf of wire service tapes. They created the reporter with an individual style. They created traditions of hard-hitting interviewing, confrontation with authority, deeply researched investigations of national and international scandals. They forced the technology onwards to serve their creative ends; they put 35 mm. news film into the lumber room after some years of experimentation with "blown up" 16 mm. film. They forced the purchase of the "Eclaire" camera and the more sophisticated version of the traditional wartime Arriflex modified to silence its own operating noise. They thumped desks and terrified film editors, overturned the habits of generations. Laboratories were made to disgorge their film stock in hours instead of days. Rushes were no longer viewed by committees before technicians were allowed to start the process of editing. Reporters were taught to handle film crews and were made to shape their news reports around the film material available. The time-honoured perfectionism of the film world was jettisoned. Quite soon a film could be conceived, shot, developed, edited, its commentary written and the finished product transmitted within a day. Within the world of film-making and programme-making a revolution had been wrought, as great as the one which occurred in printed news when Caxton's converted wine press was set aside after many centuries and the rotary press was adopted. Technological and organisational changes followed in the wake of the idea of a new kind of broadcast news. The new magazine formats attracted huge audiences and built up powerful individual figures. At the same time it put broadcast news into the front line.'[6]

News and Current Affairs had already taken on their new lease of life by the end of 1959, when, as if to symbolise their rise to eminence, Hugh Greene, himself a former journalist, who had previously headed that group for some years, became Director General. Earlier in the same year, the BBC had covered its first General Election. More to the point, the new-style current affairs programmes had begun to win back audiences from Independent Television, a circumstance of strategic importance for the BBC. News and current affairs, which the new Director General combined organisationally in order that they would cooperate and interact operationally, remained split in Independent Television. The news was the responsibility of the Independent Television Authority itself. This left news-magazine, or current affairs, programmes to be mounted by the Independent Television Companies, and they were reluctant to spend money on this kind of expensive programme when there were manifestly easier and cheaper ways of keeping audiences entertained. The way in which the BBC scored has been recorded by Sir Geoffrey Cox, who was editor of Independent Television News for the first ten years of its life:

> 'I think it was a great pity that in 1957 Independent Television did not exploit the success and say to ITN, "You've got a superb operation here, widen it out into the news magazine field." Instead of that we were given a tiny and inadequate area to make "roving reports", and we had the bitter experience of seeing "Tonight" move in and make a major programme out of the same kind of programming that ITN had pioneered.'[7]

Whoever started it, and however it was started, there is no doubt that a new and highly successful television genre was created by Talks and Current Affairs around 1960. And Anthony Smith is right in suggesting that it was the speed with which filmed events could be screened, the entertaining collage of pictured news and goings-on editorially connected by the remarks of a personable and articulate man, which made it successful. It was no different from the mixture provided by most newspapers (which had moved decisively into the magazine field by that time), but for the viewer it was effortless, entertaining, put the news in a context which was both enlightening and comforting, and – perhaps most important of all – provided daily a grist for everyday conversation which only crises, sport, and big events had provided hitherto.

Like any other genre, however, it could not survive without growing; to stay alive, it had to invent, develop, expand, and for the first five or six years it did. 'That Was The Week That Was' came out of BBC Talks and Current Affairs (not Light Entertainment, where Ned Sherrin had started life as a producer). Later in the sixties, 'World in Action' took the lead, with a strong admixture of investigative journalism (or what passes for investigative journalism in television), moving, like many other programme series, into single-topic programmes and away from the collage format of the pioneer efforts. 'Man Alive', 'Horizon', and 'The Money Programme' have moved even farther into documentary treatments of contemporary issues and extended the ambit of Current Affairs into – for television – the exotic, 'minority-interest', areas of the performing arts, science, technology, business and industry.

The initial impact, then, spread, with repercussions evident in the new liveliness and frequency of documentaries and reportage. In sheer *coverage*, television during the sixties approached the range of the daily and Sunday press in news, current affairs and what can only be called 'magazine' items on which the press itself has been relying more and more over the past thirty years as the cost of news gathering has increased.

There have, of course, been failures and half-successes. 'Monitor' failed to develop, and died, as did 'Midweek'. 'Tonight' lived longer than most, but eventually lost its big audience. Even 'That Was The Week That Was' died – in what are still slightly mysterious circumstances. What is more puzzling is that the whole of current affairs output seems to have been losing its audience. Austin Mitchell's brief survey[8] includes the following figures:

	1967	*1969*	*1972*
	(*percentage of viewing figures – annual average*)		
'24 Hours' – 'Midweek'	12	8	4
'Panorama'	17	13	8
'This Week'	10	10	7
'World in Action'	15	14	13

It could, of course, be claimed that current affairs had been the victim of its own success: that the multiplication of programmes of this kind has spread the audience, as well as the coverage.

There are two other possible answers to this particular conundrum. First, television news has itself absorbed something of what the new style current affairs programmes had to offer (see below, p. 171-2, and Austin Mitchell's note):

> 'The extent to which audiences for news and current affairs do overlap is shown by estimates in 1967 and 1968 that between one-half and two-thirds of the audience of 24 Hours had seen the BBC bulletin, then at 8.50 p.m., and a further seventh had seen *News at Ten*. Clearly the first proportion would now be higher with the longer bulletin at nine. The preference for news programmes over current affairs is illustrated by the fact that when BBC panels are asked to rate the latter on a "not detailed enough/too detailed" dimension, opinion is very evenly divided; the only aspect, other than "gloomy", on which the audience is usually at all critical.')

This trend has followed the already established tendency in American television. In the United States the expansion of news features and, to an even greater extent, of what is called 'issue journalism', both of which form part of what is called 'current affairs' programmes here, was part and parcel of the sixty or ninety-minute 'Big News'.

Secondly, radio has also gained an audience for daytime and late evening current affairs programmes and talks, and it is possibly the success of radio in this kind of output which had reduced the size of audience for television current affairs programmes.

At all events, since television news has increased its share of audiences and of time, then, over the past fifteen years, broadcast news and current affairs together have prospered. They command bigger audiences and the proportion of broadcasting time allocated to them is bigger. They have certainly widened the range of information about current social, economic and political issues and problems on offer to the television audience; and since it now seems certain that most people get their news and information about public affairs mainly from television, and also believe that television news and information is less subject to bias than what they get from any other source, the whole development can be regarded as something of a success story for television.

DIVISIONS AND DIMENSIONS

All the same, news and current affairs programmes are only part of the output of the BBC. This means that there is a need to ensure that other broadcasting activities do not suffer, or are not put at risk, because of offence caused by the output of news and current affairs departments:

> I read about the anxiety that people outside the BBC feel. I suppose . . . that journalists are in fact the people who are going to affect the destiny of the BBC – because they are the people who come under attack.

The fears voiced by someone in the Drama Department are likely to be shared by his superiors. Naturally, apprehensions of this kind are unlikely to gain direct expression in the form of pressure exerted by other departments, or by controllers. But they may urge caution.

Keeping news and current affairs in a distinct organisational enclave of its own, directly responsible for policy and operations to the Director General, may therefore afford some measure of protection for News and Current Affairs Group within, as well as for, the BBC.

> The BBC is so big that people cling to their department in order to give themselves a sense of identity. . . . Also, television news worked in Alexandra Palace for years, and it's only since 1969 that they're down in Television Centre. We brought them down so that they could mix more with other people and solve this thing. Radio news used to be in the building over there, and now

> they're in this building. . . . It's gradually changing . . . It's very hard to break down, though.

Nevertheless, News and Current Affairs have developed sensitivities about the attitude of other departments. This, again, may serve to make overt pressure unnecessary, much as the BBC's sensitivities towards the powers that be make it unnecessary for them to exercise the controlling power they have.

> People in other parts of the Corporation wrongly think that news has more money than they have. We haven't. We have an adequate amount of money to do our job. We have a good deal less money than ITN have. People in Drama think that News and Current Affairs have more money than they have. It's not true. The money is, by and large, fairly spread out.

The sense of news and current affairs being in a special enclave is in some respects a consequence of the special relationship they themselves have with the outside world as part of the BBC, and especially with the more powerful establishments in the outside world. It is also an enclave with its own inner territorial divisions. They have been more or less publicly acknowledged since the time when Hugh Greene became head of the Group, with managerial as well as editorial responsibility for both kinds of output. This is how he wrote about it some years later:

> The news division I took over in 1958 had been the Kremlin of the BBC. In those days news was news and current affairs was current affairs and never the twain should meet. They had been living in watertight compartments for many years in an atmosphere of mutual distrust and even contempt. My job as I saw it was to weld together the news and current affairs elements in radio and television so that they could carry out their respective functions against a background of shared policy and journalistic assumptions. I had to create an atmosphere in which journalistic enterprise and talent could flourish without any loss of reliability. The BBC foreign correspondent or reporter had not been allowed to achieve a scoop. He had to share his exclusive stories with colleagues – particularly agency colleagues – or they could not be used by the BBC. To me as an old journalist the whole system was incredible. I changed it.[9]

The connotations of the Kremlin in this connection are a little obscure but news journalists were unfailingly quick to make quite clear the distinction between themselves, as somehow true professional journalists, and people who worked in current affairs. Any unguarded reference to current affairs editors or producers as 'journalists' would be picked up and corrected:

Earlier, when you talked about the 'journalists who were on top' [i.e. in 1963] I was quite astonished to hear the names you mentioned. Neither of these were journalists, not in my book. I'm an old newspaper man, and –

They were running journalistic-type programmes.

They were running journalistic-type programmes, but then, you see – You take 'Tonight'. Now 'Tonight' was – well, what would you equate it with? You certainly wouldn't equate it with any newspaper, nor would you equate it with any magazine.

Not colour supplements?

Well, possibly. Possibly. I suppose it's journalism of a sort.

By journalism, I didn't mean news reporting.

No. But I think the distinction is quite important. I accept that in that context they were journalists – or they were involved in a journalistic exercise. They were concerned in the entertainment side of it.

It could be argued that a large proportion of any newspaper, nowadays, is devoted to entertainment; journalists who can be entertaining command high fees or salaries in Fleet Street. But the significance of these remarks lies in the 'professional' distinction drawn between news and current affairs. There are ample materials to hand with which broadcast news journalists can raise or strengthen the walls of any Kremlin, or ghetto, within which they may want to withdraw; and it was senior managers and editors who were at most pains to do this:

I think you will find that there are news people in the BBC who themselves wish to define the news as a separate piece of output. Because within the confines of the news – and I think I probably agree with this view – within the BBC, there is a journalistic feeling that it is a good thing to draw the lines across the news. Because that is the area in which you are being absolutely different from any other programming. In other words, programmes are made by people having ideas and putting them into packages, and news is something which is motivated by events which are not originated, as it were, by the producers of the programme. They are, if you like, at the mercy of the events we are reporting, and, therefore, in order to maintain what they would regard as their own basic journalistic standards, they themselves within the BBC would like to feel that when the signature tune for the nine o'clock news comes on, that is actually different BBC output from a programme which has immediately preceded it. And when Robert Dougal says, 'And that's the way it is tonight', the thing that follows on is on a different basis altogether.

With demarcation principles of this sort applied to professional identities and to output, it was not difficult to substantiate the separation with evidence of incidents which demonstrate the different codes of professional conduct obtaining on both sides:

Anyhow, you were going to say something about this division between –

I don't like it one little bit. I think it is the root cause of all the weaknesses of both news and current affairs. . . . There is this endemic hostility between the two camps. You can have a news team chasing a story and you can have a current affairs team chasing exactly the same story, rubbing each other up the wrong way, rubbing whoever is giving that kind of story up the wrong way. That's only a petty example of this sort of problem. That's only at the lowest level.

What kind of instance would there be of that?

Well, I'll try and think of a specific one because I know I've had specific ones. One of the programmes that television news is responsible for is a programme called 'Westminster' which deals with the weekly round-up of the week in Parliament. For example, at the time – this is an untypical example, but it will do as an extreme – at the time of the 'Yesterday's Men' incident it was virtually impossible for us to work in the House of Commons because . . . the administration of the House of Commons, making decisions with a certain amount of discretion, if it was within their discretion to allow you entry to part of the House, they wouldn't, because relations were very bad. Because of the way the main producer had barged in and done all kinds of things he shouldn't be doing – the techniques that they use, because they very rarely have to go back to the people that they were involved with are fairly typical. I mean we are constantly having to use our sources again.

[At this point I remarked on one or two fairly notorious instances of the same kind of practice in social research – of studies made of organisations or communities, and published without any prior reporting back to the people who were principally concerned; these, I said, were known in the social research trade as 'smash and grab raids'.]

This is exactly the same kind of situation. Public officials or government departments – we all know that if they've been troubled by '——', you may as well give up. I mean, I've had specific examples of the Ministry saying, 'Well, we've put ourselves out for "——" for a whole day and they got it all wrong, and so we're not going to help you.' So that's at the lowest sort of petty level and there are far more important considerations and issues between news and current affairs. It seems to me that this is something that the Corporation has got to sort out.

There is, however, a sizeable obstacle in the way of sorting this difficulty out, one which points to another difference between broadcast news and newspapers. The editor of a newspaper is in control of the contents of the whole paper, and of every edition of it. In the BBC, while there is single managerial and editorial control of a kind, with the same man in 'policy control' over the whole output of news and current affairs, people in charge of each regular current affairs programme are editors in their own right, as are, to a lesser extent, the editors of each news programme; thus, continuing the same conversation:

But surely you have somebody whose job it is to do that?

No, I don't think so.

You have the Editor, News and Current Affairs.

It may be in his brief, theoretically, to do that, but he certainly doesn't. He's too high up to know that on a particular day, News, 'Nationwide' and 'Midweek' are all gunning for the same story. No, there's no sort of coordinated planning in that respect.

You mean to say that you could do this and not know it until you fell over each others' feet?

Oh, certainly. Now, I'm working on late night news . . . which is the nearest you have to an outlet for news feature items. If we're considering investigating a story in the morning for use that night, one of the considerations in the editor's mind is, 'Will "Nationwide" be doing it?' and if they are, then possibly we won't. But it's a very *ad hoc* sort of thing.

Doesn't he find out?

He might find out. For example, on these pyramid selling stories – you remember the M.P. who produced a report on pyramid sales? We were considering taking some specific examples cited in this report and using them to build the story of what the situation was, but we were warned off it because 'Nationwide' were doing it; they'd already done several items on pyramid selling before, so we knew they had a sort of general interest. So it has got to the point where we do ring up any of the current affairs programmes like 'Nationwide' or 'Midweek' and say, 'Are you doing such-and-such?'. But it can be a bit dangerous sometimes, because if they haven't thought of it, then you put it in their heads.

You see, there is a belief – I *know* there is a belief – among some people high up in the BBC that it's a good thing to have competition between news and current affairs. Now it may be, in some respects, but I am convinced that the harm it does is far worse than any beneficial effect. . . .

I must say I'd always thought there was some kind of person, or at least some machinery, for coordinating – editorially, that is.

Well, yes, I think you can say there is machinery for coordinating, if you mean that if it really comes to the crunch when two groups are competing for services, and there is some argument which has to be resolved within the Corporation [the Editor, News and Current Affairs] sorts it out. Every now and again there is a situation where he does have to give a ruling. But it's only these exceptional things that boil up to such a point that he has to step in. There isn't any ordinary, day-to-day, coordination that affects people on the ground, people who are doing a story.

Of course, rivalry between colleagues is the most commonplace of the facts of everyday life in organisations; within the BBC, rivalry presumably exists between individual producers and directors within the same department who compete to win approval and support for programme proposals, for a greater share of resources, and so on. But such rivalries are worked out in the interstices of time spent on the 'real' work of producing programmes. In News and Current Affairs they are part and parcel of work on the programmes themselves – indeed, an important element in a broadcast journalist's day. So some, at least, of the distinctiveness which marks off News and Current Affairs and its staff from the rest of the BBC is the incessant battling that goes on within the group, between different programme teams.

The fact that there are such rivalries contradicts the many assertions of a categorical distinction existing between news and current affairs, and between news 'journalists' and current affairs 'staff'. But the whole area is beset with contradictions. The same managers and editors who insisted on the distinction could also be at pains to point out how permeable the selfsame line of demarcation was:

I would have thought that current affairs now is crossing lanes with news far less frequently than it used to, simply because news

> is rather better than it was ten years ago in doing its job. . . . To take an example, '24 Hours' was a nightly programme which was continually responding to the news of the day. By 1972, '24 Hours' seemed to have no actual purpose because in the intervening years the news had caught up. News was doing a journalistic job on the day's news better than it had been, and a programme later in the evening which responded to the day and filled it in seemed to be less and less attractive. There was less and less left for it to do . . . the news had absorbed it.

Earlier in the same interview, the same man had defined the task of current affairs as 'responding' to the news. To have this kind of journalistic activity regarded as incorporated in the news itself, and properly so, is a mark of how far many broadcast news journalists had shifted from the essentially passive, 'mirror of society' role claimed for broadcast news a few years earlier, and which was still claimed by the most senior managers and editors.

But any telescoping of current affairs programmes with the news, at least at the 'responding to the news' end of their range, has been matched by extension at the other end of the range, at which current affairs merges with feature programmes. These shift in a somewhat mystifying way between providing information to explain the news, presenting the findings of investigations into situations which have been 'in the news' and composing a circumstantial exposé of corruption, of inhuman behaviour, of social injustice, or social disruption:

> One of the problems, certainly in Lime Grove [i.e., current affairs], and to some extent we see a little bit of it here, is of men who haven't any experience of the political world and Whitehall, and are making important programme judgements which are based on lack of knowledge and lack of experience. Therefore, as I see it, they're not making judgements, they're making assertions. And this has been the problem, taking journalism in the wider sense. I believe broadcasting – and it's not just broadcasting, it's the press, too – broadcasting journalism is moving away from the journalism of information to the journalism of assertion.

What has also been involved is a blurring of any distinction between 'information' journalism of the kind proper to current affairs and 'journalistic features' which deal freely in dramatic reconstruction. This development, too, has not gone unnoticed:

> I wouldn't dream of doing stuff that —— do in using actors. . . . I mean, the mixing of fact and fiction is one of the fundamental things we keep an eye open for. . . . it's absolutely dreadful,

particularly in current affairs – it's bad enough in historical things.

The problem for the television audience, however, is to follow, and allow for, this rather fine distinction between the 'instant history' of current affairs and recent history. The first 'World in Action' account of the Watergate break-in used actors in a dramatic reconstruction, but a staged reconstruction of the Poulson trial, on similar lines, for 'World in Action' was abandoned by Granada Television. Beyond – but only just beyond – the boundary of current affairs features,

> 'the BBC's "Grand Strategy" series in 1973 contained breathtaking examples of such misrepresentation: scenes of Polish cavalry attacking German tanks in 1939 taken from a 1940 German feature film; a Luftwaffe airstrike against London in 1940 in which American transports took part; a British aircraft carrier evacuating troops from Dunkirk.'[10]

THE FOURTH ESTATE

Naturally, there are qualifications to be made. In fairness, the achievements of the BBC – and of ITV – in this one regard, over the past fifteen years, have to be acknowledged. There is, though, another side to the picture, and the question has been raised more than once in recent years about whether this achievement, in itself, has really contributed to the public good. As television has become more familiar, so have the number and variety of its limitations as a principal medium for conveying news and information to the public: there are the political pressures and constitutional constraints which affect broadcasting organisations and not the press. There are technical constraints. There are limitations inherent in the amount of time it takes to convey information in speech as against print. There are deficiencies apparently inherent in television journalism and in the structure of conventions within which professional broadcasters operate. It is all these considerations which have raised the question of whether television news and current affairs programmes have been a blessing, albeit mixed, or a curse – a curse, ultimately, for the BBC as well as for its audience. For the incorporation of broadcast news and current affairs programmes – and of the broadcasting organisations responsible for them – into the traditional 'fourth estate' role of the press has seemingly confronted them with the perpetual and insoluble problem of steering a course between a policy of deliberate confrontation with Government and Parliament or of abdicating any claim to be independent of governmental control.

The dilemma is one the BBC, and other broadcasting authorities in this country, America, and elsewhere, share with their critics. Virtually all analyses and interpretations of their role in politically controversial affairs are beset with the ambiguity which follows from their being lumped with the press. This is partly because it is not easy to distinguish the improbable mixture of constitutional dependence and political independence in their relationship with Government and Parliament which broadcasting authorities have to try to make workable from the older, historic, freedom accorded to the press. It is also partly because broadcasting has assumed that it, too, can act as both reporter and critic of political events and utterances. Thirdly, and not least, it is because career paths in both broadcasting and the press are increasingly enclosed within the same occupational world.

There are essential differences, but it is impossible either to ignore the similarities and the ties between the two, or to deal with broadcasting without making clear the way in which the fourth estate role of the press, which has such overwhelming attractions for broadcast journalists, became established and was developed. For the special relationship which the press undoubtedly has with Parliament is the product of one special period of history, so far as Britain is concerned. The ambiguity, that is, may be regarded as written into the genetic code of newspapers, and they have some prescriptive right to retain it and to exploit it as they do; this is not to say that broadcasting cannot hope to emulate the press in this, but it is certainly not a right to which broadcasting authorities can lay equal claim.

The essential ambiguity in the political role of the press, a role broadcast journalism has seemingly tried to adopt, lies in the way it has claimed to serve as the mirror of events and the voice, the 'organ', of public opinion, and also to be seen (and occasionally claim to act) as the controller, regulator or even creator of events and public opinion.

The key, I believe, lies in the fact that there is another, much older, institution which claims to serve both as the mirror, the voice, the organ of public opinion, while claiming also to act – at times – as its controller, regulator and creator. It is Parliament. The Commons itself, after all, began life as the spokesman – and merely spokesman – of public opinion. The primary purpose of including representatives of propertied townsmen and propertied countrymen (the burgesses and knights of the shire) in the Model Parliament of 1295 and in subsequent Parliaments was 'to inform the crown about local conditions and help it to influence public opinion'.[11] This function seems to have been anterior certainly to any legislative powers and probably to any contributory legislative function which the Commons later, along with barons, churchmen and the King's counsellors, ministers and servants, were called upon to discharge. In fact, the earliest discernible functions of the House of Commons are much more those of what might be called a national public opinion panel than the supreme legislative body which it took Parliament five centuries to become. For Edward I, summoning representatives of the Commons to a parliament provided an effective instrument for consulting – and for influencing – public opinion. It was only when the voices of that public opinion became organised themselves, during the following century, that the Commons began to encroach on the legislative powers of the King and his council. But such power as the Commons acquired, then and later, rested on the validity of its claim to speak for the people – to be, in fact, public opinion made articulate. By the eighteenth century, the Commons not only claimed to be the voice of the people; constitutionally, in one distinguished lawyer's view, it *was* the people.[12] Applied to an age which extended from the Black Act of 1723 to the Combination Acts of 1799 and 1800, and beyond, to the Six Acts, a proposition which equates the Commons with the whole nation stands condemned as the most cynical of paradoxes. So it is. But it is a paradox which actions and events within the framework of the British political system worked, ultimately, to accommodate rather than emphasise, in much the same way as in the parallel case of the law.[13] The political role of the press evolved as it did during the eighteenth century largely *because* the practice of Parliament and the relationship of Parliament to the common people departed so grossly from the constitutional principles on which the authority and powers of Parliament were deemed to rest.

In a way, 1771, when the House of Commons abandoned the right to forbid its proceedings being reported and published is as crucial a date in the political and constitutional history of this country as 1295. Then, the King in Council – the supreme legislative, judicial and executive authority – sought to inform himself about the condition, needs, opinions and desires of his subjects by summoning representatives of the commons to his parliament. In 1771, Parliament, now itself the supreme legislative and executive authority, acknowledged the right of the common people at large to be informed about the needs, opinions and desires expressed in Parliament.

Sir James Macintosh is quoted by Aspinall as remarking, in 1803, on the great change which had taken place in the discussion of public affairs. 'The multiplication of newspapers has produced a gradual revolution in our Government by increasing the number of those who exercise some sort of judgment on public affairs.'[14] Aspinall also cites Brougham's considered assessment in 1831 of the importance of the press in the pre-Reform era. 'It alone rivalled the House of Commons, in that it was the only organ of public opinion capable of dictating to the Government, since nothing else could speak the sense of the people.'[15] This is the press in the full panoply of its classic Fourth

Estate role, and it is no historical accident that this particular term was coined to designate the political role of the press towards the end of the eighteenth century.

It was probably Burke who first used the term to signify the political power (a usurped and malignant power) of the press, and certainly Burke would have relished and exploited the full historical irony only partially evoked by the words, 'the fourth estate', when they first gained currency. For, during the years (1790–1820) when the unreformed Parliament assumed the political stance, the attitudes, the strategy and the legislative and administrative tactics of the absolutist *anciens régimes*, it was the press which took up the original role from which the third estate proper, the Commons, had apparently abdicated.

Parliamentary reports and political information formed an integral part of the staple of such news as was purveyed by the early newspapers. More important, in acting as the medium by which such information was disseminated, newspapers tended to take or to assume the stance of independence of political parties and the country's rulers. The very existence of newspapers and the nature of their contents presumed the existence of a public, political, opinion external to the small enclosed world of parliamentary politics. Further, the role they assumed was that not merely of carrying information but of articulating and expressing public opinion. In so far as they were successful – i.e., in so far as their sales grew, and their views were taken seriously by government ministers – they were not only the 'independent and responsible organs of public opinion' they claimed to be, but *organisers* of public opinion. That they were taken to be no less than this is plain from the amount of money spent by the Government in buying editors and journalists, founding its own newspapers and subsidising others, and harassing its critics.

Money was not the only weapon; there was a rapid succession of repressive measures. But, as in other cases, repeated legislation of this kind is an index of the strength, variety and frequency of the activities it is designed to suppress as much as of the anxiety and determination of the Government. There was plenty to be anxious about. In 1793,

> 'A convention met in Edinburgh where delegates from popular societies made preparations for secret meetings of delegates to deal with a foreign landing or resist government interference. For this three of the leaders . . . were transported. The response of the radicals was to issue appeals in 1794 for a further national convention. In doing so they obviously challenged the authority of parliament. However moderate their proposals for reform, they were, in proposing to meet on a national scale, claiming to be a rival body expressing the will of the people better than the house of commons.'[16]

Such conventions were difficult and expensive to organise, and rare even before they became illegal. Hence the importance of the radical press – pamphlets as well as newspapers – which not only were easier and less dangerous instruments for articulating and promoting opposition and protest than were meetings, but could themselves provide the occasion for regular, semi-clandestine, meetings, it being common practice for them to be read aloud in public houses and coffeehouses throughout the country. Even when the threat, real or imagined, of Jacobin revolution had passed, *Black Dwarf*, Cobbett's *Political Register* and other journals kept alive the movement for radical reform which the Opposition tacitly disowned for a whole generation after 1797, when the Whigs, having 'nailed their colours to the mast', in Trevelyan's phrase, with the forlorn gesture of a parliamentary motion for reform, 'proceeded to desert the ship'.

Around 1800 there was a clear line between the press which the opposition, both parliamentary and radical, regarded as a medium for expressing public opinion, and the press which the Government saw, and used, as a means of 'regulating' it; individual newspapers could be identified as lying on one side of the line or the other. This ceased to be true later in the century. While Lord Grey could write that 'newspapers could be divided into two classes: those which sought to mould public opinion, and those which took their tone from it', in either case, as he had good cause to know, newspapers chose which political side they wished to support. In 1830 there was scarcely one newspaper which found a good word to say for the Tories; ten years later most of them were against the Whigs.[17]

There were other changes. The 'people's press', which had flourished while it had been bullied in the courts and harried by punitive taxation, dwindled into extinction in the very years, from 1825 to 1861, when restrictions on size were removed, the tax on pamphlets repealed, advertisement duty reduced, and stamp duty and paper duty finally abolished. Those newspapers which became profitable eventually became financially independent of Treasury subsidies and party payments and shed their party ties. But the tradition of extra-parliamentary opposition which the people's press had established survived until the last decades of the century; the established dailies and weeklies, especially those in the North, found much of their material and their support in the multiplicity of movements which kept up the pressure on Parliament.[18]

It is the newspapers of the last three or four decades of the nineteenth century, the form and composition of which persists largely as a kind of folk memory, that provide the benchmark against which what happened later has been measured. For older people after the First World War – and for the politicians amongst them – the national press presented a deplorable contrast with the press they had known in their youth, of which descriptions like R. C. K. Ensor's, published in 1936, so poignantly reminded them:

> These penny dailies conformed very much to one character. Originally modelled on *The Times*, they catered distinctively for the upper and middle classes, and almost exclusively for the male reader. Though, as a rule, they earned comfortable profits, their ownership was not primarily commercial, and the newspaper world was about the last quarter in which any one then would have looked for a millionaire. Nearly all of them were family properties. Their controllers were usually well-educated middle-class people, cautious rather than ambitious, seeking no new worlds to conquer, valuing their papers chiefly for the political and social influence which accrued through them, and disposed in most instances to view the proper exercise of this influence very seriously as a sort of personal trust. On the contents side they were overwhelmingly political. They gave some space to business and religion, and some to racing and cricket; while for 'human interest' they relied on sensational law cases, and brought leaders of the bar and bench into a brighter limelight than ever before or since. But the staple was politics, especially speeches; and proceedings in parliament were reported and read all over the country at full length. The way in which the news-matter was handled would today be thought incredibly dull and matter-of-fact. Headlines were few and paragraphs long. But the reader was at least fairly given the facts, on which he could form his own judgment. Editorial opinion was more or less confined to the leading articles; which were written by the highest-paid men in the office, or occasionally (though always anonymous) by good writers outside. Propaganda was made by open argument; not, as in the twentieth century, by the doctoring of news.[19]

The slighting reference to the contemporary press is significant.

During the first half of the twentieth century, the alignment of the daily press, national and provincial, along political party lines became the rule. It was a development which came with both the growth and eventual dominance of mass-circulation newspapers and with the expansion of the ambit of parliamentary politics – and so of parties – far beyond any boundaries comprehended within the liberal idea of the state. The political ambitions of newspaper owners, or their boasts, are of little consequence[20] compared with the fact that newspapers, by the twenties, had begun to put their own construction on what constituted news, and firm constraints on the discussion of current political, economic and social affairs.

The power of the press barons which was claimed with such assurance in the 1920s, and acknowledged by Baldwin as such through the very fact of challenging it, has now gone, to be replaced by the authority of the balance sheet, which drives newspapers to compete not for numbers of readers but for the numbers of pounds their readers have to spend. Newspapers contend rather for influence over consumer expenditure than over public opinion; individual newspapers from time to time seek scandals to expose rather than causes to espouse; and the range of political opinion reflected in their columns is smaller than that covered by parliamentary parties themselves.

It is this which has driven the national press into the narrowly confined 'consensus' not only of opinion but on the agenda for discussion which they now display and which, as Hirsch and Gordon have argued, is based on a minority of the well-heeled professional and managerial middle classes:

> The picture that we suggest of the quality press is of a band of opinion occupying the broad centre of British politics from about half-way into the moderate left through to the edges of the extreme right; with individual papers occupying different and sometimes shifting positions within the band, and the band itself moving over time in response to events and political changes. But the most important characteristic of the consensus band lies not in the nuances of attitude taken on different items on the political agenda, but rather in the common agreement on that agenda itself – on the issues for discussion and the way in which they should be approached.[21]

The increasing concern about the press which has expressed itself in the setting up of three Royal Commissions since the war is centrally concerned with the shrinking of the number of national newspapers and the consequent shrinkage of the 'band of consensus' within which they operate. The quality newspapers may have survived, at a cost, but the mass circulation daily has certainly suffered, and this as a direct consequence of television, especially commercial television. Commercial television lives off the advertising money which would otherwise go to the mass-circulation popular newspapers, not to the quality newspapers. Since 1960, the *Daily Mirror*, *Daily Express* and *Daily Mail* have all lost a substantial proportion of their circulation; the *News Chronicle* died in 1961 and the *Daily Sketch* in 1970. The exception, the *Sun*, has almost four times the circulation of the *Daily Herald*, which it replaced in 1962, but has forfeited any pretence of representing public opinion.

The range of news presentation and opinion available to newspaper readers, radio listeners and television viewers (and most of us are all three) has narrowed much more over the past twenty years than is indicated by the decline in the number and range of newspapers. Moreover, this narrowing of range has not necessarily been towards any particular political, social or cultural mean (whatever this might signify in any of the three respects). So far as the representation of opinion among the public is concerned, 'minorities with high spending power find themselves excellently catered for. Minorities who have less find themselves neglected. There is no newspaper their money can buy.'[22]

It is television which has cut the readership of the mass circulation newspaper. More to the point, it has replaced it almost entirely as a source of news and information about political events and issues. Yet Hirsch and Gordon – and they are not alone in this – take it as self-evident that television journalism operates within the same 'consensus-band' as the quality newspapers.

FROM NEWS BULLETINS TO 'YESTERDAY'S MEN'

The BBC was founded at a time when the freedom of the press had begun to shed the absolute quality it once had, and 'freedom for what?' was becoming an increasingly pertinent question. Mass-circulation newspapers had long filled the vacuum left by the demise of the people's press. Along with popular weeklies, pulp fiction and children's comics, they had subverted the role of the printed word as an instrument of religious, cultural, social and political enlightenment. In a later view, indeed, they had become elements in, and supporters of, the institutional structure of established authority and of political and economic power which it had once been the primary task of the press, and its chief boast, to expose, discuss and criticise. In the 1920s and 1930s, the 'chief lieutenant of discontent', as Geoffrey Crowther has called it, was usually to be found thrusting a loud-hailer into the hands of the captain of dragoons.

The conception of 'public service broadcasting' which was formed during the twenties owes as much to the low esteem in which the popular press of the day was held as to Reith's missionary zeal and masterful ways. But the same combination of circumstances saw to it, not very surprisingly, that the new broadcasting service, be it as public-spirited as it might wish to be, occupied a very circumscribed and almost totally subordinate position, so far as broadcast talks with any bearing on matters of public controversy were concerned, to the press. Lord Riddell, at the very beginning of things, made it very clear to the Sykes Committee that, in the newspaper proprietors' view, the public was 'very well served by the Press', and that, while an evening summary of news might be broadcast (and this was only after lengthy and fairly acrimonious debate), the BBC would not in any sense 'provide its own news service'; and, for the first twenty years of broadcasting, it did not. What was broadcast was a 'news summary' (which was not to exceed thirty minutes), prefaced by the acknowledgement: 'Copyright news from Reuter, Press Association, Exchange Telegraph and Central News', all agencies which were owned by the newspapers. Added to this limitation was the control exercised by Government over 'controversial' broadcasts and expressions of opinion, a control exercised by successive Governments fairly strictly despite the liberality of clauses in the Crawford and Ullswater Reports recommending (or sometimes commending, as though it were established and familiar practice) editorial autonomy in the handling of broadcast news, talks and discussion programmes.[23]

But it would be utterly wrong to represent these early developments as thwarting the conscious purposes of any of the people at the head of the BBC in its formative years. Reith's speech at the dinner given at the end of 1926 (the year of the General Strike) to mark the winding up of the British Broadcasting Company gives his own priorities, and it is impossible to believe that he was being disingenuous in omitting any reference whatsoever to the part broadcasting could play – indeed, had played – in the political affairs of the country.[24] It is likely that, in dedicating 'the service of broadcasting to humanity in its fullest sense', he thought politics – party politics – of too slight importance, or too unworthy, to warrant inclusion. True, his first ambitions were political, but this was probably because he could see in himself, and hoped others would come to see, the 'Gladstone-Cromwell combination' the country needed so mightily.[25] Moreover, the fact that, before his BBC days, he offered his services first to the Labour Party and then, after too cool a response from J. R. Clynes, to the Chamberlain wing of the Unionist Party, shows how much he made his political judgements, such as they were, in the light of his own estimate of politicians and, rather more importantly, of what he took to be their estimate of him. His attachment was really to the Establishment rather than to any political ideas or party, the more so because he was not a birthright member.

These two sets of contemporary circumstances – the role, past and present, of the press and the particular situation, political, social and cultural, of the country at the time the BBC came into being – have to be borne in mind when considering the political role of broadcasting in the contemporary situation. And beyond these, there is a third circumstance which is of paramount importance, although it is usually ignored in most discussion of the politics of broadcasting. In the beginning, broadcasting was brought into existence to provide entertainment, free entertainment. Later on, broadcast entertainment served as a carrier for cultural improvement, as it did for advertising in America. Even now, the primary function of broadcasting, so far as its audiences are concerned, is to provide entertainment, and whatever else it provides depends very largely on its capacity to deliver enough, good enough and varied enough, entertainment.

This being said, it has next to be said that the political role of broadcasting was thrust on it by politicians – by Baldwin and other ministers after him in this country, and by Roosevelt, with his 'fireside chats', in America. The use of the press in this way and in similar ways by party spokesmen and election candidates, conceivable as it might have been in the eighteenth century, is inconceivable in the twentieth century. But heads of government in every country have the right to claim the use of broadcasting time for the purposes of government. Broadcasting in Britain, as in every other country, is controlled by government licence in a way that the press is not, and in most European countries is further subject to direct financial control by the government in a way that the press, at least in the West, is not. Even in America, where stations and networks are financially independent, broadcasting does not share the rights of the press which are guaranteed under the First Amendment. Broadcasting is a privilege, granted under licence by the Federal Government; station licences last three years, and in principle anybody is free to present evidence against renewal.

Such liberties as broadcasting authorities in this country and elsewhere have in the publication of news and in the discussion of public issues are due to three developments.

First, the political parties which constitute the Opposition managed, after some years of arguing the point in Parliament, to win the right to broadcast their own rejoinder to statements by Government ministers which could be construed as 'political'. This right was won earlier in Britain than in the United States. In America, however, it is subsumed under the more general provision for 'equal opportunity' which obliges all broadcasting stations to give broadcasting time so that views may be aired which are in opposition to those which have been featured in any programme. This is not an 'equal time' provision (though popularly supposed to be so) and does not apply to news broadcasts, but the provisions of the 'fairness doctrine' do apply in a very broad sense, and the Federal Communications Commission has frequently called stations or networks to account publicly for some items of news broadcast.

The second development is rather more complicated. The sheer speed and efficacy with which important information could be broadcast, as compared with being distributed in newspapers, gave broadcasting an advantage over the press which was not realised to the full until the late thirties. Then, in the gathering anxiety of the months between the Munich crisis and the outbreak of war in September 1939, the immediacy of broadcast news made the BBC the primary source of news. The next six years confirmed its leadership. In any case, all important news – i.e., news about the progress of the war – came from Government-controlled sources, so that, during the whole period of the war, the press and the BBC were, in this respect, on an equal footing; in other respects the BBC, especially after it began sending its own war correspondents to North Africa and, eventually, into Europe, became the leading, as well as the earliest, source of news. The circumstances which made for this supremacy ceased with the war, but nevertheless, some elements remained; the reputation the BBC had won in Europe for a closer approximation to 'objective' reporting than any other source of news, broadcast or printed, did as much as anything to establish a national reputation for BBC news as an honest and authoritative news service.

Authoritativeness became the overriding quality sought for news broadcast in television, too, after the television service was restarted. And the established practice of a news announcer reading the news 'over' a still photograph of Big Ben was designed to sustain that special quality; the equation of impersonality and formality with impartial authority is easy for a British audience to make.

Once again, it was the advent of Independent Television which brought about the big change. The legislation which brought Independent Television into being made the ITA solely responsible for Independent Television News. The ITA could claim, and was in fact bound to claim, to be as authoritative and impartial in its news service as the BBC, but, lacking the particular traditional authority which the BBC had acquired, it had to offer something different, new, and attractive. The ITA found it easily enough, and the BBC, perforce, followed suit. Competition brought 'viewability' into the news, and, almost immediately, formality and authoritativeness was transformed into something 'ludicrously ponderous and stuffy', as Robin Day called it:

> 'In 1975 it is scarcely possible to believe that the innovations described in this chapter could have been so revolutionary, and so stimulating in their effect on the BBC news. A recent series on BBC2 called "Inside the News" helped to explain why this was so. It included some old recordings of BBC news in the pre-ITN days. I had forgotten how ludicrously ponderous and stuffy they were. Indeed I found myself wondering whether ITN's original impact was not simply due to the fact that almost anything would have been a revolutionary improvement on the old BBC news. . . .

ITN newsfilm quickly developed a special character and quality. The aim was to get away from formal, carefully set-up situations as much as possible. None of us gave this approach to filming a name – but we all knew what was wanted. The TV critics called it "realistic", "true-to-life". The use of natural sound was a big element. Sound-recordists went with the cameraman, both often carrying their gear as they walked into rough unpredictable situations. They caught the atmosphere of a strike meeting, a riot, a disaster, in a way that silent film, even with added sound effects, could never do.'[26]

'Professionalism' had arrived.

The third development, always a possible corollary to the first, was inevitable once the second development had got under way. BBC Current Affairs programmes outflanked ITN to begin with, and BBC news went 'professional', in ITN's terms, too. With broadcast journalism at last coming into its own, there was a persistent effort by broadcasters to assume, or usurp, the traditional fourth estate role and the freedom of the press. This development has not been challenged too openly by Government, because Government has always stood to gain more than it lost by the chartered independence it writes into the licence to broadcast. It would find it embarrassing, after all, to exercise in public the rights of control it has, and in any case it would be open, in turn, to challenge by the Opposition if it did so. But the freedom so gained is almost entirely exercised within the limits of tolerance defined by the area of difference between Government and Opposition – i.e., between ministers and front bench, official, spokesmen of the Opposition's views.

Because of all three developments, there has undoubtedly been, over the fifty odd years of the BBC's life, a significant increase in the amount, the seriousness, and the range of criticism in broadcasts of the Government, and of the views and policies of political parties and of individual politicians. Much of this criticism has been secondhand, in that it is criticism which has already appeared in the press, and is either quoted by broadcasters or restated in broadcast programmes by politicians, journalists or representative spokesmen. But the liberties enjoyed by broadcasters have expanded beyond this; while, for instance, 'Yesterday's Men' did produce a very sizeable volume of criticism from politicians of different persuasions (and not merely from the Labour ex-Ministers who considered they had been lampooned by the programme), and while one or two heads of people held responsible for the broadcast did roll (in the direction of the BBC regions), the BBC did nevertheless survive, the licence fee was raised the following year, and nobody was dismissed, or even forced to resign. And it is safe to say that, ten years earlier, no one in the BBC would have thought such a programme even feasible. It is not that 'Yesterday's Men' may now be regarded as setting a precedent – anything but. The point is rather that the volume of hostile criticism which resulted is now available as a further guide to the limits within which criticism seems to be tolerable. And, since the mid-fifties, successive tests have tended to demonstrate that the limits are extensible. There is no grand, long-term, strategic purpose being pursued by the BBC in all this. It is something much more like a two-stage game of 'grandmother's steps' played, at one level, between the 'professionals' and the management and, at a second level, between the BBC and the political establishment, with advances at each level acting in a kind of ratchet effect on the other.

6 The Servant of Two Masters

When we reckon up the odds against it, the degree of independence in its handling of political news and controversies shown by the BBC and other broadcasting organisations is remarkable. American broadcasting networks and stations in fact exercise considerably more licence in their treatment of politics and politicians than in the treatment of sex, or obscene language, or, for that matter, what are called 'minority cultural interests'. The political licence enjoyed by American broadcasters probably owes as much to the decision of Congress to allow television broadcasts of committee and other proceedings as it does to the public-spirited endeavours of broadcasting organisations and their reporters; but, in turn, this decision by Congress stems from the continued recognition of the people as being the source of all power. In the United States, as the Foreign Editor of *The Times*, writing on this topic, has remarked, constitutionally 'the people are supreme, and their rights are fully protected by Congress. And because of their traditional distrust of government, and the confidence of the American press, the right to know has more than the force of law.'[1]

Yet even in America broadcasting systems and broadcasters have been much more diffident about their political role than have newspaper owners and journalists. No broadcasting authority has ever claimed to create or influence public opinion, or even to be its voice, or 'organ'. What they did claim, and the claim was made with astonishing unanimity, was to 'reflect' – to act as a mirror to society and to events. This was the dominant view of television's role in Lime Grove around 1960, when Hugh Greene's 'young lions' were winning back audiences from ITV with their new-style current affairs programmes. The same view surfaced frequently in America later in the 1960s, when the questioning of broadcasting's role first began. R. D. Kasmire, a vice-president of NBC, said, 'There is no doubt that television is, to a large degree, a mirror of society. It is also a mirror of public attitudes and preferences.' The president of CBS, Frank Stanton, claimed that 'What the media do is to hold up a mirror to society and to try to report it as faithfully as possible.' David Brinkley, in a CBS 'news special', remarked, 'What television did in the sixties was to show the American people to the American people . . . it did show the people places and things they had not seen before. Some they liked, and some they didn't. It was not that television produced or created any of it.'[2]

Closely allied to this claim is the belief that news events are generated by what is, for those whose job it is to collect and present news items, essentially a random process. 'Newspapers and news programmes could almost be said to be random reactions to random events. Again and again the main reason they turn out as they do is accident: accidents of a kind which recur so frequently as to defeat statistical examination.'[3]

Both versions – collective presentations – of the principles which govern news broadcasts by people at or near the top of broadcasting organisations are slogans (the news as mirror of events; the news as random response to random events) which in effect repudiate any responsibility for *what* is broadcast as news; the only admitted responsibility is for *how* news is broadcast, and even this kind of responsibility is limited to those aspects which can be judged according to technical or professional criteria.

The statements of Kasmire and Stanton to Congressional committees give some clue to what it's all about. Obviously, the reiteration of either creed is a good defence, perhaps the best, against the interminable charge of bias which comes from interested parties. However, public criticism of this kind does not worry any broadcasting organisation very much; charges of bias from one side can almost always be countered by quoting similar charges from the opposite side. What is far more important is that the principle behind the slogans is the best defence against any attempt by Government – or even any particular wish by Government – to exert the controls it undoubtedly has. For, as the Estimates Committee so uncompromisingly, and correctly, put it in 1969:

> 'The powers of the Government over the BBC are theoretically absolute. . . . The most important of these powers is the direct control the Government possesses over the income of the BBC through prescribing the amount of the licence fee.'[4]

It is the existence in perpetuity of this kind of control which makes so categorical a difference between the freedom of the press and such liberties as the BBC has taken in its handling of political matters. Any political liberty the BBC has taken and won – and it has won a good deal – is a liberty licensed by Government.

Moreover, since the liberties accumulated by the BBC in political reporting and comment are owing largely to the fact that the Parliamentary Opposition (as potentially the party, or parties, of government) has insisted on the right to have its own views represented in the content of news and current affairs programmes and reflected in the manner in which these programmes are presented, this in itself puts limits to which controversy and opposition may be carried. It was all put quite neatly and explicitly by one official:

> What chiefly protects the independence of the BBC – which is what we were really talking about, of course – is the two-party system, and the fear that something disagreeable done by one party when it's in power would lead to the Opposition, when it was in power, doing something even more disagreeable. It's as though the independence of the BBC was maintained by mutual agreement between the two, because of the common interest they have in the kind of neutrality, objectivity or impartiality of the BBC as such.

Political parties also have a common interest in confining liberties of this kind to themselves, which can mean confining them to the presentation of each 'official' party line, which is in turn designed to appeal to the largest possible number of actual and potential supporters of the Party.

Broadcasters therefore have to be sensitive to the limit of tolerance of views and points of view allowed them within the brackets of established, Government-Opposition debate. It is this sensitivity which works to define the editorial standpoint of broadcast news and current affairs. Political pressure there is, inevitably, but the absolute powers of Government are never applied (except at times of 'national emergency') simply because they are unnecessary:

> Wherever you go in the world, broadcasting organisations depend in the end on Government for finance of one sort or another. We depend upon the majority in the House of Commons to increase the licence fee, in the end. Also, politicians, I think rightly – well, I'm not sure how rightly, it's less important than it was – feel that broadcasting reaches so many people and is also monopolistic, by and large, and therefore it should not be in the hold of one political party or another. It should be in the middle. Alternatively, different sorts of government think it ought to be totally in the hold of the political party that the Government is; which is why you have broadcasting in many countries run by the Minister of Information. But in our sort of society, they feel it should be in the middle, and while we have this dependence on politicians for finance (though we are better placed than a lot) and while we have, more importantly – because this happens in the States as well – dependence on government's for a licence to operate, it's reasonable that governments should give these licences to operate on behalf of the whole community. Because broadcasting is so big and broadcasting, especially news and

> current affairs, is a very sensitive area for politicians, all broadcasting organisations have [somebody responsible for the whole of news and current affairs output] working for the Director General, and the Director General keeps a close eye on it. Because if things went badly wrong it could hurt him considerably.

So, while the BBC, apart from its earliest years, and during wartime, has not been the voice of Government,[5] it has had to speak in ways acceptable, ultimately, to the political Establishment.

THE POLITICS OF ACCOMMODATION

Changes in the power structure of Britain (or, more precisely, the redistribution of rights and privileges within British society) are brought about and translated into established fact in ways which can be broadly classified into two: parliamentary and extra-parliamentary political processes.

By itself, the parliamentary process is lengthy, tedious and often fruitless. Mediated, as it now is, by the institutionalised processes of party politics, Parliament, if left to itself (i.e. shielded or safe from outside pressure, as it was, for the most part, during the inter-war years) follows a single principle: inertia. But, though Parliament is not in any statistical (i.e. J. S. Mill) sense representative of the people, it 'represents' the people.

However, changes in the structure of society are either implemented or ratified through the Parliamentary process. Simply, the law must be changed. Parliament does this, eventually, by responding to 'pressures from without',[6] although its response is not necessarily adequate, direct, correct, or even positive. It does so most obviously and formally at election times, but this response, again, is mediated by the machinery of party politics. At all other times, Parliament is made aware of 'pressure from without' by four main means:

1. Influence and persuasion exerted by sectional interests and pressure groups.
2. Public opinion as manifested in public utterances, spoken or written, mass meetings, demonstrations and petitions.
3. Action which focuses attention on grievances or demands through attacks on property, through riots, through assassination.
4. Action designed to enforce change either through the organised disruption of civil life or by revolution.

Extra-parliamentary political action has taken all four forms in this country, as in others. Historically, the English and Irish, and to a lesser extent, Scots and Welsh, have been no more docile politically than the people of any other country. The major difference, in the past, has been the greater responsiveness of the parliamentary process to pressure from without. Even during the nineteenth century, it was the first two forms of pressure which gained the real successes, but how far this was so because these two forms had gained a legitimacy which they did not have elsewhere, or because they were recognised for what they were – the milder manifestations of pressure which could easily range into the more violent forms; how far the breadth and intensity of the first two kinds of manifestations allowed parliamentary politicians to assess the strength of the pressure; or how far these modes of manifestation of pressure ('public opinion') had become recognised and institutionalised as modes of political action, it is impossible to say.

But during the past decade or so, things have changed, and what seems to have changed is that the first two modes of expression of 'pressure from without' have become much less effective.

There are three reasons for this:

(*a*) Increasingly, from the 1930s on, the economic and political order prevailing in Britain has been affected by external factors so that the parliamentary system has had to respond to them, as well as to pressures from without which come from society. (Before a generation or so ago, these pressures were largely mediated by diplomacy or war; over the last generation they have become increasingly manifold, complex, and unmanageable, so far as Parliament itself is concerned.)
(*b*) The diminution of British power and prestige which has gone along with the increase in extra-national pressure, has diminished the sovereign power of Parliament, or its ability to use it, and made for a corresponding increase in the power of the Government, which has to act as the mediator. Both factors have combined to reduce the effective and the apparent force of the first two modes of exerting pressure on Parliament from without.
(*c*) There has been a reduction in the number of different means by which public opinion can be made manifest, together with – an almost inevitable consequence – firmer and more comprehensive control over the remaining means of articulating public opinion by professionals: by professional journalists and professional broadcasters and by professional surveyors of public opinion.

This brings us to the point made by the title of this chapter. The two masters of the title are the national interest and the public good. And whereas the BBC saw its purpose for the first thirty years of its history in serving the public good, it has to be accepted that for the last twenty years it has turned away to the pursuit of what it conceived to be professional excellence, and in so doing has come to accept that the national interest (as construed in Parliament) must be served, if only as the price to be paid for devotion to professionalism.

The politics of broadcasting are the politics of accommodation. The accommodation arrived at between the national interest and the professionalism of broadcasting is, of course, mediated by the Government of the day and the existing management of the two broadcasting organisations. While it may need perpetual vigilance and a readiness on both sides to mend fences when one side breaks them, the accommodation between Government and the BBC does, in fact, work. Almost certainly it works because the BBC goes to great lengths to inform itself about Parliamentary matters and about the attitudes, and shifts of attitudes, among politicians which concern broadcasting in general, and the BBC in particular:

Of course, the Director General is involved directly [in Parliamentary contacts], *I know. Is this mainly run-of-the-mill, or not?*

There are two central directors now concerned in this area. There is the Chief Assistant to the Director General, whose business is partly editorial control, on behalf of the D.G., partly the handling of what one might call 'operational relationships' with the front benches. So that questions about party political broadcasts and election broadcasts and this sort of thing come his way. Again, if the Opposition Chief Whip or Government Chief Whip wishes to communicate something to the BBC – and vice versa – in a confidential, but formal, fashion, then he is the chap. So he's got a concern here. This office has a concern more in the P.R. sense, meaning by that to ensure that they know how to make their views known, if they want to, and to provide them with opportunities for doing so – as well as keeping them in the picture of what we're up to. So, we have a variety of social occasions on which we entertain M.P.s here; we try to choose people who are particularly interested in broadcasting, or particularly influential in some area, or whatever. We make a major effort at each year's Party Conferences – we have parties, entertain them to dinner and this sort of thing. There's a good deal of to-ing and fro-ing of this sort. . . .

Does that extend to, say, trade unions, the C.B.I. and that sort of thing as well, or is that somebody else's cup of tea?

No, that area – take the unions – falls partly to me, partly to the Director of Personnel – he's obviously in touch with them throughout the year – there's an annual party for these senior union people. . . .

There are some doubts about the wisdom of the Corporation's cultivation of the Parliamentary connection – perhaps to the neglect of others:

> I think perhaps that the various causes of dissatisfaction, resentment, or what-have-you with the BBC aren't nearly as simply and straightforwardly to do with M.P.s as the BBC imagines. Have you noticed how unbelievably sensitive we are to anything M.P.s say?

The accommodation between Parliament and the BBC, nevertheless, is more tolerant and perhaps more relaxed than anything which obtains abroad; and, over the decades, it seems to have been regarded increasingly as something both sides wish to maintain and improve on – in spite of upsets like 'Yesterday's Men', in spite of Lord Hill's appointment as Chairman, in spite, too, of what Lord Hill called 'Mr Wilson's Suspicions' (see p. 232). This is because, at bottom, national interest and broadcasting professionalism have proved to be not incompatible. There is nothing mysterious about this. They need each other.

The terms of the relationship between Government and the BBC are implicit in the creation of the BBC as if not the first, then the model, of the score or so of 'quasi-autonomous non-governmental organisations' which now populate the public sector. These organisations form the instrument of the cooptation not only of resources but of purposes to the promotion of the national interest as construed by Government; they are a special breed of organisations peculiar to the present stage of development of industrial society. Quasi-autonomous non-governmental organisations, the BBC among them, are constructed so as to absolve Government of direct responsibility for a whole discrete set of activities while at the same time acting, when need be, in conformity with Government purposes and at all times so as not to embarrass or obstruct Government. By way of ensuring this, Government keeps hold of one or other essential instrument of control – over prices, fares, or other sources of revenue, or over capital investment – but the essence of the arrangement is that, except in exceptional circumstances, the exercise of governmental control is a matter of negotiation, not of ministerial instruction. In this situation, the fundamental purpose of any organisation – which is to survive, and to survive on the best possible terms – prescribes a strategy which reflects, or even replicates, the negotiated quasi-autonomy in which its existence is grounded. Hence

> The concept of the national interest for which the Governors stand as trustees is one that belongs essentially to the middle ground.[7]

The professionalism of television journalists is attuned to the constraints imposed by the technical apparatus of television, its cumbrousness and cost, and by the set of conventions governing the way they relate to news events and topics and to their audience. Both sets of constraints are mediated through the organisation, and there are many ways in which the television journalist (like broadcasters in general) has to be much more of an organisation man than most journalists. For the special relationship which exists between the BBC, as a quasi-autonomous non-governmental organisation, and the Government is reflected in the relationship between the professional broadcaster – reporter, presenter, editor, producer – and the senior management of the BBC. Producers especially have to act in constant awareness of the enclosure of their own professionalism within the framework of organisational constraints and prescriptions. A producer is inescapably both a professional creator of programmes and – as an internal official memorandum has put it – 'an official delegated to supervise broadcasting policies', for the whole output of one BBC channel at the time his programme is broadcast is, so far as the BBC is concerned, his responsibility.

EYES, RAVENOUS AND HALF-SHUT; MIRRORS, UGLY AND IN CORNERS; THE MANUFACTURE OF BAD NEWS FROM NOWHERE; ETC. ETC.

Every occupational milieu has generalising conceptions about its proper purposes, its position in society, its worthwhileness, and about the possible trade-offs it offers between achievement and reward. The conceptions which are in good currency at any one time may change in value. In the world of broadcasting, the biggest change in the conception of the role of broadcasting between 1963 and 1973 was the discrediting of the idea of broadcasting as a mirror, the true task of which was to represent society 'as it is'. By 1973 there prevailed a much more heavily qualified, or deprecatory, or sophisticated, or suspicious attitude. This new attitude was present not only among critics, whether of the right or the left, informed or uninformed, but also among broadcasters. It reached the level of open, reasonably authoritative, publication in this country after 1968 with the appearance of books like *The New Priesthood* and *Demonstrations and Communications*, and in the United States with the utterances of Nicholas Johnson, a member of the Federal Communications Commission as well as with the full-scale attack delivered by Vice-President Agnew, a man of very different political and ethical complexion, in his Iowa speech in 1969, which cause such widespread consternation among broadcasters and newspapermen.

Charges of political bias have been for so long a fact of broadcasting life for the BBC, and are so easily, and routinely, met by pointing to the fairly even distribution of the allegations between representatives of both left and right political opinion that they can be shrugged off. What was new about the criticisms now being made was that the causes of bias were said to be intrinsic to the technical apparatus, the organisational structure, and the professional conventions of broadcast news and current affairs. Inevitably, criticism has focused on television because of its larger audience, because its 'impact' is presumed to be greater than that of radio or newspapers, and also because it is, for a large proportion of the population, either the sole source of information about political events and controversial issues, or the most authoritative source.

If one forgoes any attempt to catalogue all the arguments, testimony and evidence, or to assess their force and weight, it is relatively easy to present the nature and the range of the factors involved, which have very little to do with political bias, but focus on the exigencies and the limitations which affect television news and current affairs programmes, the special purposes television serves, and the special ordering of television 'news values'.

TECHNICAL CONSTRAINTS

First, there are the constraints imposed on the content of television news which are sheerly technical. When a 'newsworthy' event occurs out of doors, the state of the light almost always presents difficulties:

> 'The extent of the scene, the size of the crowd, is hidden. This is why there was a slightly disproportionate emphasis on fires in the television coverage of such disturbances as the one at Cleveland in July 1968. Besides being a powerful symbol of pillage and ruin, a fire is its own source of light.'[8]

Technical advances reduce these disadvantages almost yearly. But a camera crew and a reporter have to get to the scene, the equipment has to be set up, the story photographed; afterwards, the film has to be sent to the studios, processed, and edited to 'fit the story line', and made ready for narration before transmission. All this takes time. Ordinarily, therefore, it is only possible to film a news event if it leaves photographable debris or survivors – or if it is known about some hours beforehand:

> 'Television can do very little with events of which it has no foreknowledge; although the clumsiness of its equipment diminishes every year, television can still be the slowest newsgatherer to get to work.'[9]

ORGANISATIONAL CONTROLS

Organisational control over broadcasting output is exerted in four ways: first, through the occasional publication (usually for BBC staff only) of official policy statements, such as those on 'Taste and Standards' and on 'Principles and Practice in Documentary Programmes'; it is safe to assume that these have force only as statements which can be referred to when there are matters of dispute to resolve, or of control by superiors to affirm. What is drummed into producers is that if there is any doubt in their minds about a topic, or viewpoint, or film sequence, or contributor they must refer up to their chief editor, or head of department. 'The wrath of the Corporation in its varied human manifestations', runs a memorandum from the Managing Director, Television, 'is particularly reserved for those who fail to refer.' But referral upwards, although it is used to resolve a producer's doubts – especially when standards of taste or political values seem to be changing rather fast – has symbolic rather than operational significance. Anthony Smith, after insisting on 'the enormous individual leeway which every producer in British broadcasting is allowed', is equally insistent on the way in which the organisational control implicit in the procedure is made effective operationally:

> '. . . Clearly the pressure on a man who is free to make decisions in his own way is much greater than that on the man who merely does as he is told. The greater the collective responsibility, the greater the sense of pressure, on each unit. . . . In practice the BBC works more or less exactly as it says it does: there is a system of referral upwards of difficult decisions (those, quite simply, are decisions which when taken are likely to produce a public row) and there is a system of meetings at various levels at which judgments are formed and shared. There is seldom any doubt about what the man above you thinks on any important issue. You can therefore avoid referring upwards by deciding them in a way which you know he would approve of; only if the decision is worth arguing do you refer. . . .'[10]

Smith then points to two 'important characteristics' of the system. In the first place, 'the producer feels that he is making his own decisions, and indeed is doing so'. The other characteristic concerns the way in which the relationship between the producer and his superiors reflects the relationship between the BBC and the powers that be outside: 'the staff of a broadcasting organisation, and here I am not referring simply to the British examples, turn the external needs of the organisation into their own philosophies.'[11]

Thirdly, the selection of broadcasting staff and their promotion is also a sanctioning process which reinforces the standards and requirements which the organisation implicitly, as well as explicitly, wants observed. Again, whatever sanctions there might in principle be, they are hardly ever invoked; operationally, they are incorporated in the career system.

Lastly, there are the presenters – the familiar faces and voices of broadcasting who, as announcers and 'continuity men' in the early days, then as news-readers, and finally as television 'personalities' in their own right, incorporate the BBC's 'collective personality', and, as such, exert the most direct and insistent control over both producers and 'lay' contributors to programmes.[12]

THE GRAMMAR AND THE RHETORIC OF BROADCAST JOURNALISM

The combination of the technical limitations on filming and the overriding need, nevertheless, for pictures produces a further set of special limitations. As one news reporter remarked:

> Basically, television is just film, that's all it is. You know, if you've got a story, to write it the way you should do for television, you've got to twist it to fit in with the film, you see.

And, from another reporter:

> Reporting on a newspaper, you only work in words. That's all you have to think about, whereas in television they're about the least – well, not the least – they occupy so little of one's time, relatively, getting the script right for television news.
>
> *What do you have to get right for television news?*
>
> There's such an enormous number of logistic problems. I'm thinking not so much of working in the newsroom, but I've done a lot of work on the road, as sort of news features producer, doing five- or ten-minute films, sometimes longer, and it's always a question of finding the right material to film, getting at a story for film that you know exists. . . . It's putting it on film that's the problem, always.

Because of the extreme difficulty, apart from exceptional or lucky circumstances, of having the foreknowledge necessary for filming a news event, the most common use of film is of meetings, demonstrations, public ceremonies, and 'the news source of last resort, the airport statement'.[13] Conferences and conventions have become as indispensable to television as they are to political parties.

What is involved here is not so much a constraint or limitation as a deflection of purpose – a bias. It is not so much that the content of news programmes may be arranged so as to give more time and emphasis to filmed action and people as that individual news items – stories – are composed in terms of the available pictures. This is evident in the contrast between the wholly different parts played by interviews in newspaper reporting and television reporting:

> On a newspaper one can go around and talk to a lot of people – sometimes officially, revealing who they are, sometimes not, and the answers one picks up can all be put into the one case. If you're a television reporter any conversations that you might have are virtually useless unless they lead you on to an interviewee who's prepared to be filmed.

The concentration of effort on obtaining a good interview has been remarked on more than once as giving, or reflecting, a special slant of broadcast news journalism away from reporting and towards dramaturgy. In line with the same urge towards action and actuality, news editors cut in film of on-the-spot reporters standing in the street and delivering their story to a camera. At least, the setting in which they are being filmed adds information – which may reduce the number of words, and the amount of time, the story needs – but it also adds authenticity. This is a legitimate enough use of the dramatic convention which associates action and scene. But beyond this, there is a whole stock of conventions which are used for the same purposes of brevity and authenticity. There is, in fact, a rhetoric of television journalism. A speaker has

> 'to transmit to the audience the conviction that such behaviour is taking place in a coherent, credible world, and is socially authentic. . . . Rhetorical conventions rely on what Aristotle, in *The Rhetoric*, called "the very body and substance of persuasion", the use of the *enthymeme* to play on the spectators' share in a "stockpile of attitudes, of expectations, of scruples and conventions, of truisms and commonplaces".'[14]

Introducing the notion of rhetorical and 'authenticating' conventions[15] into the discussion of broadcast journalism perhaps makes it possible to capture some sense of the broadcaster's predicament. The conventions change – or evolve:

> *Some years ago there was an article in* The Listener *which said that news, more or less, creates itself . . . there was a suggestion – and it was no more than a suggestion – that a newsman's job was to do no more than act as – oh, midwife to events, bringing events to the screen. Now, I think, news people are prepared to accord themselves a much more positive role. Would you agree that there has been a change?*

Well, yes, there has been a change, but I find it very hard to define. I wouldn't accept the way you put it. I think journalism, essentially, is having some sort of intuitive feeling of what people are interested in. In that sense, it's very much a craft. And if it's changed in the last ten years, it's because there's been some kind of public change in its response. But the thing which ten years ago would have had everybody talking in the buses and tubes in the morning doesn't make them talk tomorrow morning.

Yes. Obviously, the focus of interest does change, but what I'm talking about is much more the attitude of newsmen to their own job. This is what I think has changed.

I think newsmen are probably much more conscious now than they were ten years ago, even, of public suspicion of what they're actually about, which is a very good thing.

Yes, that would have been my guess.

This manifests itself in lots of ways. The sort of television programme you were doing [in current affairs] ten years ago – the sort of crude confrontation of views, etc. – if you put it on now, there'd be total apathy about that sort of programming. Unless you presented it in a different sort of way. Because we do do confrontations, but to do it as we might have done it ten years ago, with the roll of drums. . . .

What you're saying is that between you and the public there exists some indefinable but nevertheless very real set of conventions about what constitutes interesting stuff –

And what is acceptable, and what's credible –

Yes, And this is very much the same kind of thing as obtains in the theatre. There are conventions in drama which are carried –

A very good analogy!

It strikes me that this goes on in newspapers and television news, too. . . . With a newspaper like the Guardian *you do by golly know when they get out of touch and their conventions start becoming hollow.* The Times *found that out, and they haven't really discovered, or rediscovered . . .*

Well, in a sense, we are running away from a collision with the world of Monty Python, which, in a way, comes very very close.

The notion of there being a 'grammar' of television production is commonplace enough in the BBC, and, on occasion, discussion of 'grammatical rules', widened so as to touch on the rhetoric of broadcasting – the conventions which apply to the manner in which a television producer tries to capture and hold his audience:

In 1963, when I could wander round Television Centre, there was a lot of discussion of 'That Was The Week That Was'. A lot of people were agin it. Some of the arguments used took the line that it was an 'unprofessional' job, in that they didn't mind at all showing the cables, other cameras, and so on.

Yes, this was a typical example of what was called – a stupid phrase – 'brutal' television. It was the cult phrase at the time. And it was quite an important moment in time. In a way, it was a kind of tearing-up of the technical safety rules accompanied by a tearing-up of the ethical rules. It was a risk-taking, jolting kind of epoch, whatever the rights and wrongs were. We had, I suppose, gone as far as we could on the old, safe, rules, and something else had to be found.

What you're saying is something very important, I think. Let me see if I've got it wrong. That is, there comes a time when the whole business of broadcast television becomes institutionalised to the point where people are afraid of its becoming a routine, in terms of the techniques of production. Now, if you've got bright, young, people coming in – and you did have very bright people coming in then – they just refuse to do a routine job. They've got to make an impression, so they do it in terms of breaking the rules – breaking the grammatical rules – of production. Because it's nice to break the rules if you can get away with it. Fine, it wakes people up, as you said. But there may be a spillover effect in that they're not the only rules they break; they also break codes or rules in other areas, like thumbing your nose at politicians, institutions – all kinds of sacred cows around the British scene. You also start thumbing your nose at sexual mores and other moral rules, too.

What all this suggests is that although the ordinary interpretation of all this is that the BBC is reflecting changes in society, and doing no more than that – which, after all, was said to be its job – it may be something more, something which is equally familiar though not so easily or publicly discussed. This is that change often occurs 'for the sake of change'. This occurs just as much in technology as elsewhere. One innovates for the sake of innovation, i.e., because otherwise you're going to relapse into a stable, miasmic, situation in which nobody takes the slightest notice, and television really does become wallpaper. The way you stop television becoming wallpaper is to break the rules – technically, professionally, and break the rules in other respects, too – intellectual, moral, cultural.

Is this going too far?

No, I don't think it is.

THE CORPORATE IDEA

Working within a set of conventions is an imperative, not an optional element in broadcast journalism. The news – and comment on the news – has to be constructed in terms of a set of assumptions about the 'stockpile of attitudes, of expectations, . . . truisms and commonplaces' which the journalist believes is held in common by the audience he addresses. But it is not for him, alone, to arrive at such assumptions:

I think there is a sense in which the BBC is still very much a private world.

Yes, I agree. This does sometimes strike us in the newsroom. The terms in which we would put it are these – we would say that we've been broadcasting to the people along the corridor [i.e., to editorial and managerial superiors] not to the people who are listening. You know – one has followed their policy, done the sort of thing that we know will please them, and we haven't really thought about the listener, about what is the best way to tell the listener.

But how can you, if you don't really know the listener? Have you any information about the listener?

Quite. Yes, this is true. I haven't talked much about it, but it would be nice to know more about the sort of people who are listening. We're given sort of morale-boosting figures of the audience. I don't pay much attention to them. It would be far more interesting to know the *sort* of people who are listening. Then we could make assumptions about how much they are likely to know of the news, how much background we have to fill in for them, how regularly they listen.

In the end, if information of this kind about one's audience is impossible to obtain, as it is, one has to rely on the 'collective representations' of colleagues and, especially, of one's superiors. A third broadcast journalist with whom this same matter of conventions was broached had had a good deal of newspaper experience.

Now, let's say I'm sitting at a desk copy-tasting. In a newspaper, as you know, a copy-taster's job is to . . . make the first initial rough judgement about what is newsworthy and what is not. . . . Now when you're making a judgement and a piece of paper comes in front of you – I can only talk about the way I make judgements, but I suspect that other people operate in the same way – which is about some incident, some personality, the first big gate that it is pushed through, the first rough mesh, has to be whether it interests you. . . . There are several other gates to go through. There is one having to do with whether it's legal or not . . . but you also force it through a sort of gate which is your appraisal of how people who are your superiors will react to it. It may be for instance – oh, say Mozart. I read a piece of paper that says it's just been discovered that there are twenty-eight more piano concertos of Mozart; they've been found somewhere in manuscript. Now it may be that this interests me a great deal, but maybe if I work for the *Dail Mirror*, I think that it will not interest them very much . . . and I put it on the spike – it's not something which is enclosed in the area of what my superiors will find of interest in the paper. What is happening is because of your idea of your superiors, and your corporate idea of what your audience wants and is interested in. . . . So your judgement is first what interests you and secondly what interests your superiors, and these two together are going through another judgement which is a corporate idea of what your readers want . . . I put the superiors first because when a person who is junior goes to work in any organisation, although he's part of that organisation himself, he also feels that his superiors have a better grasp, through longer experience. They are the controllers of what the corporate idea of the paper is.

Inevitably, the search for a currency of news values valid for a broadcasting audience ends in 'the corporate idea', mediated by superiors:

You see, in newspapers, and in television and radio, and I think films and plays as well, anyone who is at the producing end – and I mean that in its widest sense – has a relationship with an audience, be it one person or five million . . . I would have thought that the output of television . . . probably reflects much more the people who work in television than it does of who the audiences really are. . . .

People in the theatre are visible, you see them from the stage, you get direct reaction from them. Even cinema chains get to know something of their audience. With the BBC, it seems to me, there is a certain set of conventions which are visibly present (though almost impossible to specify) in programmes, from news to comedies. These can't be conventions

> *developed between the audience and the people doing the programmes. So there is a natural inference that they are developed within the BBC. What I'm interested in is how they've developed. . . .*
>
> I believe it's partly a product of the sort of people who work here, and it's their collective background that is one of the largest factors in (determining) the type and quality of programmes which are produced. I equally believe that the BBC tends to be self-selective.

One product of the kind of conventions developed in this closed world of news values and story angles, inevitably, is what the Glasgow Media Project group called 'media stereotypes'. In dealing with 'factual news' about, for instance, the troubles of the car industry early in 1975, the television news journalists slipped easily into the set of 'attitudes and expectations, truisms and commonplaces' current not among their audience (of whom they knew no more than did anyone else in Britain) but among colleagues in the BBC, in ITN, and in the newspaper world. By the mid-seventies, that is, television news had become indeed a mirror, at least mentally, but a mirror reflecting not society at large, but the *Weltanschauung* – the vision of society – held by television journalists. For the presuppositions which go to make the accounting frame for news stories can only be assimilated by television journalists from other journalists. There is no other source.

Hence the charge that journalists of all kinds dealt with the 1968 Grosvenor Square demonstration in terms of an already composed, 'manufactured', consensus about student violence,[16] hence also the charge of television journalist bias against trade unions made by the Glasgow study team, a charge based on analysis of telerecordings of six months of television news broadcasts by the BBC and ITN:

> 'Our analysis goes beyond saying merely that the television news "favour" certain individuals and institutions by giving them more time and status. Such criticisms are crude. The nature of our analysis is deeper than this: in the end it relates to the picture of society in general and industrial society in particular, that television news constructs. This at its most damaging includes, as in these case studies, the laying of blame for society's industrial and economic problems at the door of the workforce. This is done in the face of contradictory evidence which, when it appears, is either ignored, smothered, or at worst, is treated as if it supports the inferential frameworks utilised by the producers of news. It is by these strategies and techniques, encased in the overall structure of the news bulletins, that we have endeavoured in this volume to reveal, that the ideology of "neutral" news achieves its credibility on the screen.'[17]

What the Glasgow Media Group argues is not just that the news is biased but that news stories are necessarily *accounts* of news events, and that, in *accounting for* the news (which is done by implication, as well as explicitly) there is a predilection for 'inferential frameworks' which support accounts favourable to established authority in politics, in industry and in society at large. While this may be true (and the Glasgow group can produce a formidable body of evidence in the form of telerecordings of news bulletins), the distortion arises, I believe, not from 'media stereotypes' of trade unionists and car workers (along with stereotypes of 'the City', 'Whitehall', 'university students', and others) but from a coherent set of attitudes, expectations, truisms and commonplaces which television journalists must impute to their audience order to communicate with it.

'Bias' implies conscious design, intention. The problem would be much simpler if it were simply a matter of accounting for bias. Rather, it is something which arises from the rhetorical circumstances involved in speaking to audiences rather than writing for readers. A newspaper page, or a whole newspaper, can be scanned before any item is read. Broadcast news, even single items within 'the news' have no context of this kind, do not allow the listener or viewer to arrange his own selection, his own sequence. This 'de-contextualising' of the news, the brevity of each item, and the varying visual impact make the continuity provided by a news presenter and the editor a human necessity. And it is the continuity, the 're-contextualising', which drives the broadcaster to resort to the imputation to the audience of the corporate idea of its stockpile of common assumptions and beliefs. It is this which governs the syntactic and semantic links which provide 'continuity'.

THE ADVERSARY STANCE

To have to combine brevity and convincingness means that the responsible news editors and broadcasters, aiming at impartiality, must often be content with safety – i.e., with ensuring that, at the very least, they do not offend the most powerful outside interests – which must always, for British broadcasting authorities, be parliamentary parties.

The BBC, like the IBA, is forbidden to 'editorialise' – i.e., to voice opinions about controversial issues, take sides, to favour one interpretation of politically significant events rather than others. This means that editorial control, which does exist in broadcasting, is exercised almost entirely negatively; it consists of instructions about what must not be broadcast. It means also that in attempting to be neutral, news broadcasters must also be persuaded that their function is passive – that they are mere receptors of news items generated by the 'outside' world, selecting those items to be broadcast in terms of 'outside' criteria. The people responsible for broadcast news, that is, have inevitably to adopt an uncompromising, unshakeable, 'mirror of society' view of the task of purveying news:

> I regard it as my job to make sure that I can say to people, whether in news bulletins or in current affairs programmes, 'Look, this is happening in your country, and we think you ought to know about it – and think about it, you know, at the most serious level.' If things are happening in the country that the country doesn't like, they tend to blame me – when what they ought to be doing is doing something about it.

What the 'something' is that should be done about it is not, unfortunately, always clear. The likely consequence of repeated news stories and feature programmes of happenings and circumstances the country doesn't like is a mounting frustration, and a political alienation not only from the Government of the day but from Parliament, parliamentary politics, and the administrative structure.

> 'The constant emphasis on societies' sores by television feature journalists, with little or no attempt to seek out the root causes or to discuss the ways by which the sore might be removed, may even be dangerous. It may contribute to the alienation felt by the victims of societies' inadequacies and imperfections. They can be forgiven for sharing in the assumption apparently made by many feature journalists that a sore easily highlighted should be a sore easily removed.'[18]

While television news and journalism is not necessarily trusted by all the people all the time, it seems to be trusted rather more than government, and it is this which presents a mounting problem for government, and for politicians generally. For of all the powers which have been credited to broadcasting the most important is its ability to arouse suspicion and to feed suspicion. During the sixties, 'That Was The Week That Was' and other programmes made entertaining use of innuendo and parody, especially when they dealt with politicians and politics; their appeal, their audience-catching properties, lay in the 'send-up' rather than in satire. (Satire is essentially a rather serious affair, requiring a great deal more intellectual effort from the audience as well as from writer and performer.) Politically, the end-result was the development of a massive cultivated disrespect, shared between broadcasters and audience, first for politicians and their antics, but then, inevitably, for political institutions. One senior official put it more forcibly, arguing that there was bred in this corner of the BBC, in the early sixties, a 'lack of interest and possibly even contempt' for political institutions, and for 'the process of actually giving information', which may have been no more than mildly harmful then, but quite possibly led to the 'traumatic experience' of 'Yesterday's Men'.

Few people in Britain, it could be argued, have ever had what could be called respect for political institutions; this is one reason for the otherwise rather odd fact that we still have Kings and Queens (and the traditional working-class view of them is hardly one of respect). But it does seem the case that television journalism conveys the impression, which has sometimes surfaced to conscious formulation, as Antony Jay's remarks, quoted earlier on pp. 162–3, reveal, of a long-run adversary strategy directed against the whole political and administrative governance of the country. It fastens on 'the snags and drawbacks in any proposed new policy. It normally communicates these more effectively than the policy as a whole or, indeed, the overall problems to be solved.'[19]

It is not, of course, a strategy intentionally planned and consciously executed. It is a particular attitude, or demeanour, or stance.

There are good reasons, to do with lack of time, the relatively cumbrous technical apparatus, and the conventions of television journalism, why what is bad news in newspapers seems worse on television, why television journalism lends itself much more easily to the snags and drawbacks than to the rationale of policies and the complexities of the problems they are meant to solve. But there are also good reasons why the adversary stance should accord with, perhaps ultimately spring from, the constraints of the special constitutional and political framework, within which broadcasting organisations, and the journalists they employ, have to operate.

BEATING THE CLOCK

Constraints of time seem to be more strict, and more immediately apparent, than any other; certainly, it is the constraint of which producers seem most conscious. There is, it seems, too often simply not time enough for adequate interpretations of actions and events, or reactions to them, to be aired. This particular constraint goes beyond the sheer limitation imposed by the comparatively small number of words which can be used, which in news and current affairs programmes together amount to a fraction of the verbal content of any daily newspaper.

Philip Whitehead, who once worked in the BBC on 'Gallery' and 'Panorama', seems to have regarded this as the major constraint on current affairs programmes:

I think the most serious compromise always is the tyranny of the slot and the timescale. I am talking now simply as somebody who produces a twenty-seven minute political programme every week. It is impossible for me, in the present set up of ITV and the network, to go to people and say, 'I cannot deploy this argument and these facts and these pictures in twenty-seven minutes, I could do it in thirty-nine.' And they say 'No dice, old boy. You go away and make two programmes out of it if you want to.' But I then say to them, 'I can't do that, because it's a dense mass of facts, information and reasoning. It has to float all together. . . .' So I think the worst compromise sometimes is clipping all your material down below the point of maximum comprehensibility.[20]

'VIEWABILITY'

There are other constraints: the news, or any other programme, must be seen and heard at one sitting; it cannot be re-read, or skipped (which is why television advertising is so much more obtrusive and therefore more profitable than newspaper advertising); the significance of any item cannot be indicated beforehand by size of headline or column space. Yet because television news and current affairs programmes convey action, movement, facial expression and demeanour, scenes and actors, as well as verbal messages, they seem *more* complete, *more* satisfactory than any account provided by newspapers. 'Viewability' is easily construed as reliability because any intervention by broadcasters is largely invisible, and because the dramatic intensity of film and video recording carries conviction and guarantees authenticity in ways which words cannot. And the constant striving for 'viewability' sets its own traps:

'*The average audiences are simply not aware to what extent things inevitably have to be rigged, and so on. Does that worry you?*'

'Yes, it does. Television is the only profession in which the word "cheat" is an inseparable part of the vocabulary. I think it's alarming that so often, in order to preserve a smooth visual flow and in order to recreate an assumed sequence of events or to prepare a visual montage which approximates to an idea, you do dishonest things.'[21]

Words like 'cheat' and 'dishonest', which no outsider would dare to use, are a response to the pressure on television journalists to 'find the right material to film' when there is nothing to film. Because 'viewability' is so supreme a trump card in the hands of television, journalists often feel it has to be played, regardless of the rules of the journalistic game, and sometimes when it is inappropriate to the particular hand of cards being played:

> Instant coverage – natural disasters, of course, are simple enough, but that's only part of the stuff of news. It's all these reports we have to cover, a report about handicapped children, for example, or whatever. All these things are very badly done, by and large.

Sometimes, too, the demand for 'viewability' has meant the omission of information altogether. For there is the 'sad fact', as Whale calls it, that it simply is not possible to *illustrate* the ideas in which television journalism must deal. 'The vital details of a rent bill are not made clearer by little drawings of houses. Economics defy pictures altogether.'[22] John Grist, then Head of BBC Current Affairs Group, despaired, at the 1970 Leicester Conference, of ever making local government 'newsworthy' in television terms.

The limitations under discussion here come partly from the constraints of time and the technical equipment involved, but principally from the overriding demand for easily understood stories which will hold viewers' attention, combined with the broadcasters' awareness of the sheer size and the heterogeneity of the television audience. Uniformity in content and treatment – or the 'trivialising' which the Pilkington Committee complained of – lies in the way broadcasters perceive their audience, or, rather, of the impossibility, as they see it, of their addressing sensibly or sensitively a multitude whose ages, intelligence and knowledgeability remain completely unknown to them. John Whale's observations on the insuperable difficulties in the way of explaining the power of Chicago's Mayor Daly to a television audience watching what was happening at the 1968 Democratic Convention tells one, in fact, more about television news reporters and editors than about television viewers:

> 'Television viewers were never given more than a cursory explanation of why the mayor of a provincial city was able to rule not only his own region but a national political convention with an iron fist. They could not have been: the structure of patronage was too complex, too abstract, too private to be set out on television. There was nothing to photograph.'[23]

Five years later, there was Watergate and the Watergate cover-up – far more complex, more 'abstract', and still more private, but nevertheless set out in extraordinary detail in all its complexity, and on television.

Whatever sparked it off, the Watergate affair turned into national and then international news because of the investigative journalism exploits of newspapermen. But, in its later phases, of constitutional crisis and what might be called the 'Selling-out of the President', it was television from which the public drew its information, not only in the United States, but by reflection in this country and elsewhere abroad. And the whole Watergate episode puts a sizeable question mark behind John Whale's final comment:

> 'As a reporter of politics, television is obliged by natural and artificial forces to focus on pictures more than ideas, the abnormal more than the normal, people more than issues, idiosyncracy more than character, conflict more than synthesis, what the rulers want to show more than what the ruled want to see. This has nothing to do with managerial avarice or journalistic myopia: these are the given facts.'[24]

The trouble is that the 'given facts', the datum line of what television journalists and editors regard as fit to broadcast, change. Broadcasters, it is evident from Anthony Smith's remarks (see above pp. 162–3), like to see themselves as central and entrepreneurial figures in any changes made in the public's acceptance of what constitutes news. But, time and again over the past fifty years, they seem to have been the sheep as often as they have been the shepherd, to have acted in anxious defence of the constraints whose removal they later celebrated,[25] and consistently to have paid much more regard to a consensually predetermined view of what constituted news (translated as 'journalistic instinct' or 'flair') than from any articulate set of principles or code of practice.

John Whale ends his book, *The Half-Shut Eye*, by remarking that 'mass literacy has promised a slow advance towards an educated electorate, which would have some hope of taking reasonably well-based decisions. That advance will not be sustained by an electorate which looks principally to television for its news.' A mildly optimistic conclusion follows:

> 'This prospect becomes less menacing as soon as it is acknowledged. If television has gaps in its equipment, so have all other methods of reporting. Television assumes its proper place in a political system the moment voters at large realise that there is more to know than they should learn from television itself.'[26]

Yet his answer is embarrassingly weakened by the words with which he prefaces the problem: 'There is by now not much serious argument left about whether it is a good thing to promote social harmony, or rebuild the slums or keep down inflation, or avoid foreign military involvement. The argument is about how, not whether. It is about the how of these questions that people must vote.'

But if television has become the main source of news and information and if, as now seems certain, people also believe that television news and information is less subject to bias than news from any other source, how is the electorate to reach the 'how' of solving the problem of putting television in its 'proper place'? There can be only one answer: if television is the main source of news and information, and if it is regarded as a more reliable source of news than any other, then any solution to the problem must come from television journalists and the organisations which employ them.

Kumar[27] notes the adversary stance which is so habitual to the current affairs style, and suggests, too, that this is related to the need to play up its quasi-autonomy. This it does, he goes on, by acting as *tertium gaudens* to the conflicting groups whose differences it fuels; but this is to misconstrue the point. There are, after all, limitations to this kind of role for an organisation like the BBC, limitations which are in fact noted by the same writer at another point, where he remarks that this kind of strategy stops well short of 'making the BBC an "oppositional force" in society', which would clearly have the effect of pushing 'the organisation in a suicidal direction'. But he is entirely right in pointing to the *professional* necessity for the broadcaster of playing up insistently his non-partisan stance through the adoption of a quizzical, sceptical, cynical or downright contumacious attitude to everybody who presents himself – or is presented – as partisan.

The adversary stance which comes in so handy for the professional broadcaster is not just the easy identification of the professional non-partisan stance with playing the part of ' "us" as "the unrepresented", "the consumers", "the suffering public", the victims of planners and public servants of all kinds, as well as large industrialists, selfish trade unions, property speculators and the like'.[28] This accords well with the vague populism which comes readily – naturally – to the broadcast journalist, but it is, at bottom, best understood as a reaction against the very restraints imposed on broadcasters by the accommodation reached between their professionalism and the national interest, mediated through the Corporation and Parliament. It is this which underlies and accounts for the anti-establishment posture of the 'Tonight' programme which Antony Jay remarked on and which spread to other programmes and set the tone for so much of current affairs; much the same attitude seems to have developed quite independently in America. It spread not only because success bred imitation but because it gained acceptance as a price which could be exacted for that accommodation.

There are other prices which have to be paid. One is the diffuse suspicion of politics and political institutions which some people in the BBC have noted and deplored. Another is to be found in the rhetoric of television – and radio – news, which is embedded in the corporate idea of the set of assumptions and attitudes supposed to be in good currency among the public, but which derives ultimately from established ideas held by broadcasting organisations to be in conformity with the national interest.

A third is the product of all the others: the collusion thus forged with both the Establishment and the 'silent (and invisible, perhaps imaginary) majority' against 'pressure from without' in any of its forms, against any disturbance of the peace.

Broadcast journalism, it seems, has become not so much a new priesthood as a new constabulary.

7 Managing the BBC

THE INDUSTRIALISATION OF THE BBC

The biggest difference between the interviews I had in 1973 and those of 1963 was in the more widespread, more specific, and more intense disgruntlement displayed with superiors and with what was called 'the management' than anything I had encountered in 1963. The very fact the talk was of 'managers' and 'the management system' rather than of 'senior officials' and 'central administration' or 'Broadcasting House' was striking enough. Senior officials too were, without exception, apt to explain and discuss the machinery of management, as against describing 'the kind of administrative problems' they faced, which had been the currency of interviews with them in 1963.

During the interval the Corporation had carried through a sizeable reorganisation, which makes the salience of management matters not altogether surprising. Yet the reorganisation was by no means unprecedented. It was the fourth in the space of forty years. What was novel about it was that the idea of reconstruction had been prompted largely by the need for a corporate strategy directed towards improving and maintaining cost-effectiveness; previous reorganisations had been concerned almost solely with attempts to improve the terms of the trade-off between administration and output – between control by the Broadcasting House administrators and the licence and mandate claimed by broadcasters. This was a factor this time too, even though it was masked by, or mixed with, the need for more complete and more rigorous financial control. Also, Lord Hill succeeded as Chairman late in 1967 at the time a number of changes were imminent at the very top of the BBC. Kenneth Adam, the Director of Television, and Sir Francis McLean, Director of Engineering, retired in 1968. The Director of Radio, Frank Gillard, was due to retire in 1969, and the Director of Administration, J. A. Arkell, soon after. And the Director General himself resigned, not unexpectedly after Lord Hill's arrival, in 1969. By 1971 the Board of Management consisted of entirely different people from the Board of 1968.

But this last element really counted only in that it provided an opportune time; for that matter, the reconstruction of the relationship between programme departments and central administration – a perennial problem – was no more necessary then than previously, although perennial problems do tend to become more irksome as the years pass, and so wholesale a change in the composition of the Board of Management might not recur. The decisive factor, however, was the need to overhaul the system of financial control so as to cope with the recurrent threat of financial crisis which seemed all the worse because it was unprecedented. Of almost equal importance was the need to demonstrate to the outside world (particularly to Government) that the Corporation was making a determined effort to manage its activities efficiently.

The management structure that was eventually built up in the 1970s was, in fact, designed almost entirely as an instrument for devising, administering, and monitoring corporate strategy in much the same terms – and, of course, with the same ends in view – as are familiar in the administration of large industrial and business corporations. The changes that this brought about are rather more profound than appear from a recital of the overt organisational changes themselves: a change in title for the heads of Television, Radio and External Services from Director to Managing Director; overall responsibility for the entire budget for broadcasting, including studio engineering and broadcasting services, in all three directorates to be vested in the Managing Director; engineering operations and maintenance staff in Television, Radio and External Services made subordinate to the three Managing Directors; all proposals for individual broadcast programmes to be presented with detailed estimates of the costs involved, internal to the BBC as well as external. Also to ensure that, in television particularly, actual costs, as against forecast costs, were kept within bounds, and to allow also for necessary adjustments for new and unforeseen circumstances or improvidence, a television management information service was developed. This took some years to get under way, but, like similar systems in other organisations, was to be based on computer-stored data, collected from budgeted proposals, when they had been accepted, and from cost-generating sections and activities in Television and in other parts of the Corporation (e.g. Engineering and Personnel).

In the interviews, the generic change between 1963 and 1973 was discernible early on in the use of the words 'industry' and 'industrial' in connection with the BBC of the seventies in ways which would have been unthinkable in 1963. There was also a change in mood, in style, conveyed in the use of 'working for the BBC' as against 'working in the BBC'. But changes of this kind are intangible, and of very little significance, detached from the changes in structure, in procedure and in emphasis from which such talk derives. One instance of changes in emphasis and procedure which provoked some discussion about 'industrialisation' shows how sensible in management terms such changes could be, and also gives a hint of what changes in approach to their jobs and in their working procedure could demand of producers and other programme staff:

> Radio has achieved a great deal in this field [studio usage] by applying what I call O and M [Organisation and Methods] techniques – looking at some of the old Spanish customs, such as booking a studio for four hours and only booking the orchestra for three. Again, the climate has been very favourable; the new Radio management has been very willing to accept changes and, indeed, to enforce them. The old cry was, 'Oh, but you have to adjust your studio bookings to the availability of artists. You can't ask so-and-so to come on Tuesday; he prefers to work on Thursday.' We said, 'Well, the question is, does he prefer to work? Because if he prefers to work, he will work on Tuesday. And if we go to him and, instead of saying "What day would you like to work?" we say "We have booked a studio on Tuesday, we do hope you'll be able to come. If you can't manage it, what a pity. We shall have to get somebody else for the 5th." ' They find they can – except one or two top stars, and, O.K., we bend things for them. But we start off with efficient allocation of studios, *then* we depart from it if necessary, so as to accommodate the awkwards – instead of starting with the awkwards and trying to fit the rest round them.
>
> This has been accepted by the performers very readily – and, indeed, by producers in the matter of studio bookings in Radio. Ever since Savoy Hill, a producer would decide he would like to do his show on Friday, or he rang studio bookings and said, 'I want such and such a studio on Friday', and they said, 'Yes sir.' And the result, of course, was that in every week and in every quarter you got terrible peak loading, because, oddly enough, most producers like to work towards the end of the week and record their shows on Thursday or Friday; Monday and Tuesday were waste land. Towards the end of the quarter, or towards holiday time you'd get them saying, 'Quick, get some programmes recorded before we go on holiday.' Peak loading again, and, correspondingly, empty studios after. So we said, 'Let's start from the other end. We know what the quarter's output is going to be, we can translate that into studio time required, let's see if we can fit that time into our studios efficiently.' Then, instead of waiting until the producer wakes up and says, 'Oh my God, I've got a programme next week – I need a studio', as soon as we give him an assignment, we say, 'We want you to do a series of six

> programmes on egg-boiling, or whatever, and we have allocated studio so-and-so on every Tuesday for the next six weeks to you.' Ninety-five per cent will say, 'Thank you very much, that's fine. I don't have to worry about booking a studio, it's there already. Lovely.' The odd five per cent will say, 'Oh, I don't like that studio', or, 'Please could I do it on Wednesday?'

This simple turnaround in the studio bookings procedure meant that

> We were able to give up these expensive rented outside studios and put the money back into programmes. In two years we gave up four outside studios. Producers still had all the studio time they needed and money went back into the kitty.

But it also meant that whereas, in the past, producers and programme departments had called the tune and service departments had tried to meet their demands – 'because they'd accepted this, they'd never questioned it because they'd always done it this way' – now, the programme controllers said, in effect, to programme departments,

> *We've got to use these resources that we have – and they're damned expensive – as economically as we can. Given what we've got, this is the best way to do it. Now fit, if you possibly can, what your requirements are into this pattern – which, by and large, represents a reasonably productive balance.'*

> Indeed, you see . . . we could sustain our output and, indeed increase it . . . not only within the existing studios, but in fewer studios.

A review of the ways in which the BBC changed between 1963 and 1973, then, follows a chronological sequence, which is also causal, of financial pressures – reorganisation – consequential changes – repercussions. But, in order to make clear what the changes were, and to provide some background against which the consequential changes, anticipated and unanticipated, may be discussed, we have to begin with some account of the organisational set-up as it was before the 1969 reorganisation.

A SEGMENTED ORGANISATION

In 1963, the Corporation was organised, under its Board of Governors and its Director General, into five Directorates, or Divisions: Sound Broadcasting, Television Broadcasting, External Broadcasting, Engineering, and Administration. Outside the Directorates there were two groups. One comprised the secretariat, Audience Research, publications, advertising and public relations; these were handled by the Chief Assistant to the Director General, who served with the five Directors on the Board of Management. The departments dealing with News and Current Affairs for both Sound and Television Broadcasting were also outside the Divisional structure, being directly subordinate to the Director General.

External Broadcasting was something of a separate entity, financed as it was (and is) by a direct Treasury grant, and with the languages in which it is to broadcast and the length of hours for each service prescribed by the Government. This Division apart, the Corporation was divided into the two programme broadcasting divisions on the one hand, and Engineering and Administration on the other. These two latter divisions provided 'services' for Sound and Television Broadcasting, but also had a sizeable number of residual activities which were operationally and organisationally distinct.

For Engineering Division, these residual activities were (1) Research; (2) Designs (i.e. development); (3) Equipment (i.e. production of equipment not purchased from manufacturers or contracted out); (4) Planning and Installation (mainly concerned with the specification of new requirements for studios, for the provision of technical equipment, and the layout of new buildings); (5) Buildings; (6) Civil Engineering; and (7) the Operation and Maintenance of transmitters and lines. All these activities stayed within Engineering Division after the reorganisation.

The technical side of broadcasting, and the maintenance of all the equipment in studios and control rooms was the concern of three Operations and Maintenance departments which were 'under' the Director of Engineering but 'responsible for day-to-day working' to the Directors of Sound, Television and External Broadcasting.

This was one of the solutions adopted within the Corporation for the problem of fitting service or functional relationships into the hierarchic structure of line management. A rather different solution was adopted in the case of the other non-broadcasting division. Administrative Division was divided similarly between a group of residual activities dealt with wholly within the Division (Legal Affairs, Catering, Buying, Organisation and Methods, Staff Grading, Training, and Appointments) and finance and personnel matters, which were handled, along with accommodation and office services, by administrative officers who held appointments within the other four Divisions but worked closely with headquarters departments under senior officials responsible for finance and accounts, personnel administration, accommodation and office services throughout the Corporation.

The two solutions apply, of course, to vastly different functions, although in principle there is little to choose between the intimacy and complexity of administrative relationships between broadcasting divisions and head office on the one hand and the need to relate the technical apparatus of broadcasting production to networks of lines and transmitters on the other. The numbers involved are also different. Engineering Division employed over 4400, of whom about 2740 were monthly-paid staff. Over 60 per cent of the Division, and 71 per cent of monthly staff, were engaged in the operations and maintenance departments of the three broadcasting divisions; indeed, 44 per cent of monthly staff of Engineering Division were employed in Television alone. Against this, the total number of administrative staff employed in the other four divisions amounted to about 450, of whom 220 were monthly-paid – about 36 per cent of the combined total of 606 monthly staff employed in the Division.

In other respects, lines of authority led towards Broadcasting House. The Regions, television as well as sound, were included in the Sound Broadcasting Directorate. So was Schools Broadcasting, although this meant less in operational terms, since Schools Broadcasting (Television) was located in Television Centre.

Manifestly, the Corporation found it difficult to develop an organisational structure in which the lines of authority coincided with operational responsibilities. This is much more than a simple matter of the balance of centralised authority as against departmental autonomy, although there was, as usual, a tendency to translate organisational problems into these terms, which represent, as usual, the political opposition of superior and subordinate groups more than true alternative arrangements of a management structure which in either case remains hierarchical.

The situation was further obscured by the adoption, in a somewhat extreme form, of the widespread assumption that 'administration' or 'management' is separable from the operating activities of an organisation. This notion has obvious attractions for the large complex bureaucracies with which so much professional work is carried out. It appears to offer the possibility of a secure supporting organisational context for the professional, who can then be left to devote himself wholly to his specialism, freed from more mundane concerns and anxieties. American universities and English hospitals are perhaps the most extreme examples of this – of administration as a managerial crêche for professional workers. The attractions are diminished somewhat when it becomes apparent – in the same universities and hospitals – that power is shed along with the mundane concerns and anxieties. Thereafter, the relation between administration and specialist departments tends at best to be uneasy, and all too often to deteriorate into unending campaigns of attrition.

By 1963, the Corporation had a long tradition of protecting its 'creative workers' from the responsibilities and preoccupations of administration, dating from the reorganisation of 1933 (the year of Sir John Reith's darker reflections on the greater efficiency of dictatorships), when the Corporation was split into two, the 'creative side' and the 'administrative side'. The principle of relieving producers and programme staff of all managerial responsibilities was pushed to extremes. Programme administration and engineering, as well as office administration and staff matters were put under a Controller of Administration, Programmes, while talks, information (i.e. public relations) and the editorial side of publications were all grouped under a Controller of Programmes and insulated from administrative burdens and responsibilities. Later in the 1930s and in the early war years, the organisation tree grew more branches, but the division between administrative and broadcast production remained.

After the interregnum under the Ministry of Information, a wholesale reform was carried through directed towards the decentralisation of administration. This meant the creation of over a dozen departments, each reporting to the Director General, in place of the administrative hierarchy of the 1930s, and the shifting of responsibilities for programme administration and some staff administration on to the Output departments, the Regions, and Engineering.

A settlement of sorts was achieved between the polar opposites of the 1930s and the war years by the creation of the post-war system of directorates in 1948. Administration Division was trimmed and altered later, it lost publicity and publications management as conferring 'overmuch power' when Hugh Greene was promoted from Director of Administration to Director General, but the pattern remained much the same until 1969.

The wide swoops between opposite principles of organisational construction, and the eventual solution in 'compromise' provoke a variety of comments, but in the present context it is sufficient to point to a history of extreme sensitivity about the extent and the manner of administrative control over broadcasting. The advent of television and its eventual dominance of broadcasting – realised by 1960 – made things even more difficult.

Thus, not in spite of, but because of the very fact of, the principle by which Administration was supposed to permeate the whole of the Corporation, the BBC of the sixties was a highly segmented organisation, with some individuals striving to create, or to defend, their own 'baronies' (powerful heads of departments or of sections are inevitably called 'barons' in the BBC, as elsewhere), and the less secure seeking protection from the Director General's 'young lions'. The segmentation of the BBC was clearly visible to some officials, and there is some hint also, in one observation, of the seigneurial structure to which it gave rise:

> The Corporation has a very strong sense of vertical organisation, and absolutely none at all of horizontal. The only horizontal bridge across the Corporation is the Board of Management. There's nothing below it. . . . I think it's proved a very grave weakness, myself, but perhaps this is looking at it too much from and administrative point of view. . . . It means this terrible business that if you don't get consensus at your own level, if there's any disagreement at all, the thing has to go right to the very top.

Even minor problems represented potentially explosive issues between Directorates, with Administration mainly involved, either directly or indirectly. Inevitably, therefore (given the increasingly stronger voice of Television, and the renewal of the operational hegemony of Engineering which the development of television brought with it), the authoritarianism characteristic of Administration in the thirties had, by 1963, faded into a chronic diffidence and tentativeness. Universal deference was paid to the image of the producer as responsible for the 'real job' of the Corporation, as the creative person, as the worker at 'the coal face'; administration was accorded a subsidiary, banausic, role – even by administrators. This engendered a hesitant, almost guilty, approach to the whole problem of management which was apparent in a number of contexts. The kind of hesitancy and self-doubt involved showed itself clearly in one discussion about television producers with a member of Staff Administration in Broadcasting House:

> How far people should 'get away with it' – play on their personalities to get away with it? I just don't know. Can you acknowledge in questions of management that some people get away with it more than others? Isn't 'playing personality' a good thing anyway, in this particular environment?
>
> *This is a very difficult one, because what counts so much is not their getting away with it, and doing a good job of work eventually, but the repercussions among (a) those people who would love to 'get away with it' in the same way but can't, or feel you can't have two people doing it, and (b) the people who have the feeling that they're being exploited but who just can't say 'no' – who can't be the ones who say 'The hell with it, – I'm finishing at ten-thirty', or whenever it is – although the one T.O.M. who did in fact say that a few weeks ago is a hero . . .*
>
> Yes, yes. He's done an enormous amount of good!
>
> *This is surely symptomatic of the unexpressed resentment which had been*

growing beforehand and now could be discharged on this particular outside producer.

If the end-product is successful – and I don't mean in terms of audience-rating – it's very different from when you've been putting up with all this and the end-product is very mediocre. . . . This is an awfully difficult problem, really, because you can't put in local managers here, there and everywhere. You try to boost up your senior lighting supervisor, your senior engineer, your senior make-up, and senior wardrobe, but they're all obviously limited in area, and it's really only the producer who is in overall charge. And who is to stop the producer at that moment? That is the real difficulty, isn't it? However much local management you put in, you're never really going to deal with that. . . . And they're very diverse people. You can get a producer who's marvellous at getting a wonderful performance out of his artists but who's hopeless at dealing with technicians.

I imagine you can.

Well, one hears of producers who can produce blood out of a stone, and the most magnificent performance will come over the screen, but only at the expense of a lot of wear and tear and nervous energy. Should you tie these people down with regulations, stop them going on for eight hours rehearsal without a meal break, and so on? Are you right to do this? Mightn't you be stopping the flow of creative genius at the most creative moment?

I wonder people don't get rather cynical about the 'creative genius' in the Corporation.

Well, don't you think that in a sense everybody who joins the Corporation has a sneaking desire really to be a producer, you know, and therefore will put up with it? Everybody, I suspect, is sneakingly wanting to get nearer and nearer to programmes. And, I think, too, that one is always frightened, in Administration, of stopping something.

To see production as 'the coal face', to be occupied with the precise arrangement of the organisational environment of the producer so as to 'optimise his working conditions', to seek to relieve him of managerial chores and routine business so as to allow his creative impulses free play without endangering the structure of the Corporation, to watch so anxiously for signs of failing powers and to strike a balance between established members of staff and short-term producers and technicians which will 'maintain vitality' and not endanger commitment to the job – all this bespeaks a sedulously developed protective regard for the situation of producers and an involvement in fostering their highly valued personal qualities which calls out, humanly speaking, for some defensive or self-assertive reflect. So the self-effacing, supportive, even cossetting demeanour of administrators towards programme staff very often carried with it some compensatory mannerisms and a slightly adult-child tone in observations about them or, more firmly, in a manipulative, organising attitude. With this there went what can only be described as a strong esprit de corps among administrators. Each attitude was, in fact, complementary to the other.

Central administration at that time clearly performed functions – public relations, financial control, the determination of personnel policy, negotiations about pay and conditions of service, training, legal matters, purchasing – which it is possible to regard as matters which must be dealt with centrally because of the need either for uniformity and economy or for control by the head of the Corporation or the Board of Management. The arguments for such an arrangement would apply in almost any concern, public or private, of similar size. But in such cases the substance of any discussion would be the balance of effective decision-making and financial responsibility between the centrally organised administrative structure and the operating sections. In the Corporation, financial control was in the hands of Administration Division and was exercised by administrative officers, situated in the Divisions and in major centres of operations. The financial responsibility directly borne by engineering branches or by output departments seemed to be minimal. I found it somewhat surprising to attend a meeting at which the outcome of negotiations with a theatrical performers' association was being reported and, to find that the consequences for individual programmes and producers were being spelled out in simplified terms to people who were 'entirely responsible', perhaps every fortnight, for productions which might cost between six and ten thousand pounds.

Staff Administration operated the 'personnel function', in much the same comprehensive way, through Establishment Officers. But beyond these two main functions, and certain ancillary affairs such as office accommodation and buying, Establishment Officers were inevitably involved, because of the seniority of their rank, in most decisions affecting the policy of divisions. This was to a large extent an inheritance from the past, but the presence of senior administrative officials with their own 'direct line' to Broadcasting House was a constant invitation to unload any uncomfortable problems which could be labelled 'administrative' on to them. Even in small sections of the Corporation, Administrative Assistants had sizeable managerial responsibilities which necessarily involved them in the general direction of departments.

The scope of their responsibilities, as one man put it in 1963:

> bred a kind of philosophy in the BBC which is possibly damaging. There grew up a kind of idea that the head of an output department was a highly creative chap with great talent and great gifts, but he didn't want to be bothered certainly with administration and possibly a bit with the more routine side of the people. There's been a tendency when something difficult has happened to say, 'Go and solve it' to the A.A. And they've come to look after a great many things that people occupied with programme problems shouldn't be interrupted by.

Outside Administration Division, the emphasis was on divisiveness. Interests in promoting the prestige of one's specialism relative to others, and to so raising one's grade, and improving the material return for one's work, reinforced the tendency to endow specialist occupations with professionalism, a tendency encouraged by superiors so as to provide the organisation with an unearned increment of dedication.

The proliferation of professional and quasi-professional specialisms went with a markedly status-conscious attitude, and in places with a gruelling competition to gain the edge over others in technical qualification, or in expertise, or in flair, or in artistic insight.

> There's a lot of Engineering snobbery about [i.e. directed at] Technical Operations. They complain that Tech. Ops. people have only worked in the Corporation's time, so to speak, while an engineer has had to spend his own time on training to get where he is. And they work it off in different ways. You get a cameraman complaining about a viewfinder, and an engineer will come along with a test card and get – you know – perfect image and so on. Well, it isn't the same as looking through the thing day in and day out and knowing there's something wrong. But you'll never get them to agree.

There were other ways of playing the unending game of prestige-poker. A man might be warned against raising a subject in an inter-departmental committee because there were differences of opinion about it in the department 'and it wouldn't do to wash dirty linen in front of other departments'. By contrast, successful representation of one's own department or section at such a committee earned departmental approval.

> You can win battles with your mental superiors merely by playing your cards right. . . . The very fact that you've explored a new area which they've overlooked completely throws them, and in this void you can then trample through with your main argument and win. This has happened on a number of occasions. This sort of thing gets you the reputation of being a bit of a rebel, but it also

> does you a lot of good with your immediate superiors and those in charge of your whole division. 'Here,' they say, 'is a man who goes in and wins battles against —— department.'

Where the opportunities for doing battle were absent, competition took the negative form of withdrawal and exclusiveness.

> The BBC is desperately departmentalised. It's incredible how watertight these departments are. I've been in the Corporation for seven or eight years; I haven't been asked my opinion – either because I have a knowledge of this special kind of programme, or because I happen to be a scientist – more than a dozen times. They would much rather ring up somebody outside. There's very little consultation across, and if you do it yourself, people act slightly surprised. If I were doing a programme on, say, psychic research, and I rang up somebody who'd done something on these lines two or three years ago, they'd want to know in the first place why I wanted to know. Why them?
>
> *They'd think you were poaching?*
>
> Yes.

The immediate objectives of competition shuttled between those of simple trade-rivalry and status-gaining activity:

> *Is there any question you thought I might have raised and haven't?*
>
> Cooperation between different departments of the BBC – strikingly lacking – as between, let's say, Current Affairs departments. An absence of any interplay at all. In fact, positive rivalry, and a tendency to play down the contribution of others. . . .
>
> *Rivalry? In what terms?*
>
> I'm talking about cooperation between, say producers on 'Tonight' and 'Today', between 'Panorama' and 'Ten O'Clock'. . . . It is – horrifying. To some extent, if you persevere . . . For example, we quite often have to ring up 'Ten O'Clock', or 'Panorama', and after a time, just because they get used to you doing this, they're quite cooperative. Of course the classic example of non-cooperation is always 'Tonight'. You can't get anything out of them – but *nothing*, no matter what the reason. They just haven't got the time to do anything for you. So offhand.

Inter-departmental rivalry has a direct appeal to management, because it seems to import the classic merits of competition into the organisation. By relating the goals and activities prescribed for discrete sections of the enterprise to this central system of values and belief, personal involvement can be promoted at little cost of thought or effort. Secondly, it eases the task of senior management by converting it, in large measure, from that of strategic planner to one of referee or arbiter. At the same time, it relieves management of the onus of keeping the organisation informed about its total situation; responsibility for initiating plans and formulating choices can be shifted down, together with the hazards of failure; authority is reinforced by the aloof, non-committal, role of court of appeal.

FINANCIAL PRESSURES

All in all, then, the 1969 reorganisation had to deal with the unending problems of providing for administrative control and coordination and of providing and promoting harmony and a reasonably unitary (though not unchanging) consciousness of purpose without at the same time provoking resentment or suffocating initiative – of how to build authority into the system without a return to the authoritarianism of the earlier generation, and of how to support individual enterprise and imaginativeness without endangering the existence of the BBC by creating dangerous hostilities outside it and debilitating conflicts within it. One senior official spoke of how keenly aware he had become of 'the almost insuperable barriers which obtained, with engineers and programme staff, headquarters and regions taking on the roles of Jews and Samaritans, and administrators classed by everyone as lepers'. What was needed, he thought, was some quite fundamental change, so that people could begin to see their overriding attachment to the common sense and validity of ideas and plans jointly arrived at, rather than an overriding attachment to Engineering Division, Administration Division, and so on.

There was, at least in the minds of the people most responsible, no incompatibility between a successful solution to the chronic administrative problem and the introduction of stronger and more accurate financial controls; indeed, they could be seen to be logically connected. As against this, the element of increasing financial pressure made what was seen as the administrative problem so much more intractable; even the most sensible and civilised people tend to turn nasty when 'organisational reconstruction' comes to be seen as a way of clearing the path for axemen from the accountant's office.

The rising costs and the inflation which combined to make life so unpleasant for the BBC after 1960 faced management with problems which were not only unprecedented for the BBC, but unique to it. For all previous broadcasting developments had been financed without direct recourse to the Government for increased licence fees. During the 1930s, the BBC had developed and put into operation its experimental television service, and created its Empire Broadcasting Service and Foreign Service out of its own licence-fee income – and this in spite of the fact that licence-fee revenue was raided to the extent of 25 per cent by the Treasury. The post-war national television service, also, was financed out of licence-fee revenue. BBC2 was initiated in the same way during the early sixties. But all subsequent developments were directed towards *improving* broadcasting services. This has never been, in the eyes of any Government, a very acceptable argument for raising the licence fee, especially when the increased fee has to be paid by everybody for many years when the improvement is available only to certain favoured areas.[1]

So as to put the accumulating financial pressure which preceded the reorganisation more in reasonable perspective, it will be better to present the broad outline of the BBC's financial situation from 1960–1 up to 1974–5. (Reorganisation dates from 1968–9, but it has to be remembered that this was also the year which ended the period of large-scale expenditure on BBC2 and on colour.)

In simplest terms, the picture is this: in 1960–1 the total operating costs of BBC Television and Radio services (i.e., excluding External Services) amounted to £30½ million. By 1974–5 they had risen to five times as much: £153 million. And whereas in 1960–1 licence fees had amounted to £1 for radio and £4 for television (with £1 of that going to the Treasury in the form of 'excise duty'), in 1974–5 the combined television and radio licence fee cost £7, with £5 extra payable for the seven million licence holders who had colour television receivers. Moreover, the BBC ended the financial year 1974–5 with a deficit of £17 million, by far the biggest in its history, and licence fees were raised immediately thereafter to £8 and £18.

During the fifteen years there had been major extensions and technical improvements to the service: a second television channel; colour, 625-line transmission; local radio and UHF transmission, all of which required sizeable capital expenditure and increased staff. Even these extensions and refinements hardly seem to warrant a fivefold increase in expenditure within fifteen years. But, of course, the 'broad picture' presented by these two figures is grossly distorted by inflation. To present the picture rather more accurately, a second set of figures is needed, showing expenditure in each year at constant (1960) prices.

Rendered into 1960 prices, annual expenditure rose at a rather more moderate pace – doubling, it is true, in the first ten years, but showing a distinct levelling-off after that. During the sixties, most of the extra money was for Television. The start of BBC2 in April 1964 is largely responsible for an increase in revenue expenditure on television in 1963–4 of £5m. over the year before (21 per cent increase over 1962–3), and of a further increase of £7m. in the following year (25 per cent increase over 1963–4). The annual increases in expenditure which marked the advent of colour from 1966 onwards were less considerable in percentage terms, but were of the same order of magnitude at current prices (i.e. £5m. in 1966–7 and £7m. in 1967–8).

Growth in expenditure in each set of terms (current prices and constant 1960 prices) is shown in Figures 1 and 2 on p. 226 and p. 227.

At the same time, the Corporation had to cope with greatly increased capital expenditure, which rose from £2.7m. in 1960–1 to £8.3m. in 1964–5 and £10.3m. in 1964–5, which was equivalent to one fifth of revenue expenditure on operating the services. Colour brought a further access of expenditure on capital equipment a few years later; it stayed at over £11m. from 1967 to 1971. Capital expenditure is inevitably determined by decisions which commit the Corporation to expenditure for several years ahead; the change from 405 lines to 625 lines as the standard for television and the development of UHF transmission, as well as the earlier development of BBC2 and colour, have all involved programmes of capital expenditure lasting upwards of ten years.[2] Building construction, as well as transmitters and equipment, come within the responsibilities of the Engineering Directorate. The £11m. capital expenditure in 1967–8, 1968–9, and 1969–70[3] (as compared with the £67m., £75m., and £81m. operating expenditure on domestic television and radio services during the same years) is, on the face of it, something of which the Directors of Television and Radio had to be informed, rather than something they could 'control', other than as members of the Board of Management.

In like manner, there is little direct control the Directors of Television and Radio can exert over the biggest items of expenditure in their operating budgets – fees to performers and artists, and wages and salaries. Naturally, it is for them to set limits on the crude numbers of staff employed in different sections of their directorates, but, given that negotiating agreements with the unions concerning performers' fees, manning, and pay and conditions, are the affair of Personnel Division, the increased costs which almost invariably arise from a new settlement (or a regrading exercise) are completely beyond the Managing Directors' control. As one senior official said:

> Even when you've said to a programme controller, a network controller, that is your budget, this is what you're going to spend, and he has then allocated it to specific programmes, we can do something at the centre which will wreck that budget fairly considerably. You see, in round terms, our staff costs are 50 per cent of expenditure both in television and in radio. Contracts, which again is artists, copyright, performing rights, and so on, is

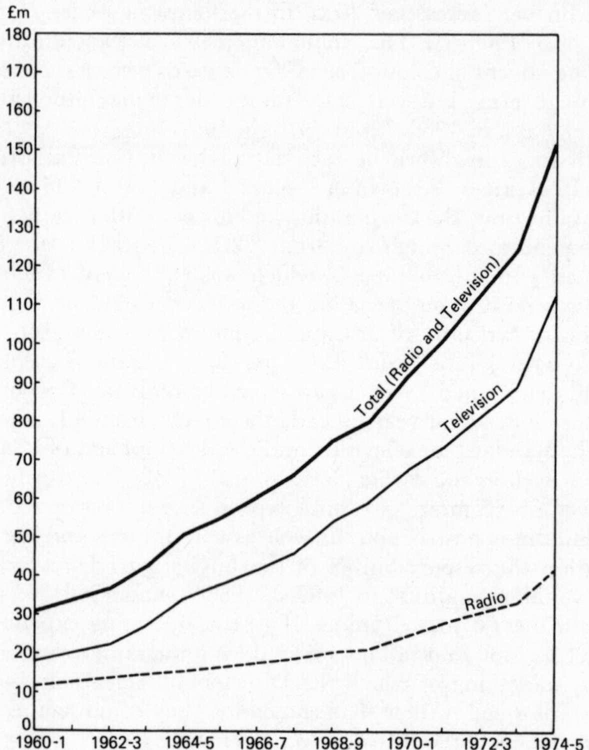

FIG. 1 Growth in Revenue Expenditure at Current Prices, 1960–1 to 1974–5

> about another 30 per cent. Now both these factors are controlled by [Personnel] Directorate,[4] so that ******* can go along to the Performing Rights Society, or we can go in front of a Tribunal, and lose the case, and another million quid's got to be found. And there's nothing the television service or radio service can do about it, except fork it out. Similarly, we may have industrial trouble – and I think, in fairness, this applies much more to television than radio. A programme will be all buttoned up, and suddenly an O.B. crew will say 'Sorry, but we're not going – unless something else happens.' Again, that can muck up your budget.

Artists' fees and the like form, as a matter of fact, a decreasing proportion of operating expenditure, falling gradually from the peak reached in 1964–5, the year BBC2 started, when they accounted for 36 per cent of television operating costs, to 31 per cent in 1972–3, and 29 per cent in 1974–5.

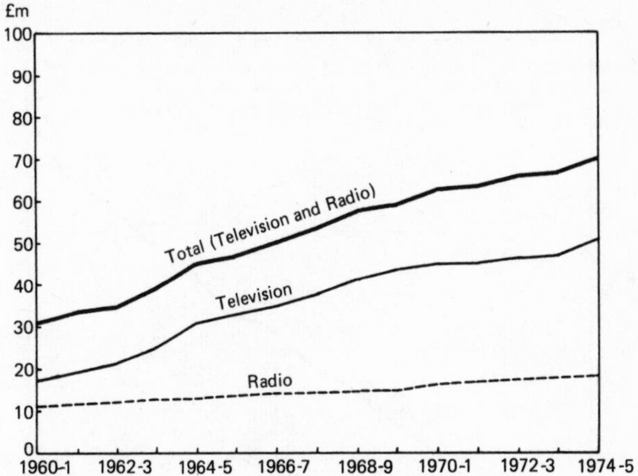

FIG. 2 Growth in Revenue Expenditure at 1960 Prices, 1960–1 to 1974–5

On the other hand, staff costs have risen. 'Production and other staff costs' chargeable to television rose from £8m. in 1960–1, or 45 per cent of television operating expenditure, to £43m. in 1972–3, or 53 per cent of operating expenditure (and continued to rise thereafter to £64m. in 1974–5, when they represented 58 per cent of television operating expenditure).

The picture, especially during the seventies, is one of staff costs growing faster and faster and of expenditure on performers, performing rights, and the like levelling off and – in real money terms – actually declining in the later years. Capital expenditure has also been reduced, relatively speaking, although this is understandable and appropriate, after the big outlays on developing BBC2, 625-line transmission, colour, and UHF during the sixties.

Increased staff costs are to some extent, of course, the consequence of a larger number of staff. Between March 1960 and March 1975, full-time staff numbers grew from 15,886 to 24,779, an increase of 56 per cent. (The increase between 1963 and 1973, the period with which we are principally concerned, was 33 per cent.) The biggest increases in staff occurred in the first half of the sixties, however, and it is since 1965, by which time 6000 had been added to the 1960 total, that staff costs have risen as steeply as they have (Figure 3, p. 228). The reason, of course, lies in pay increases, and these increases have been the result of a relative increase in the numbers of specialist engineers and production staff, of competition for qualified staff with independent television (although the biggest pay increases which can be ascribed to this factor

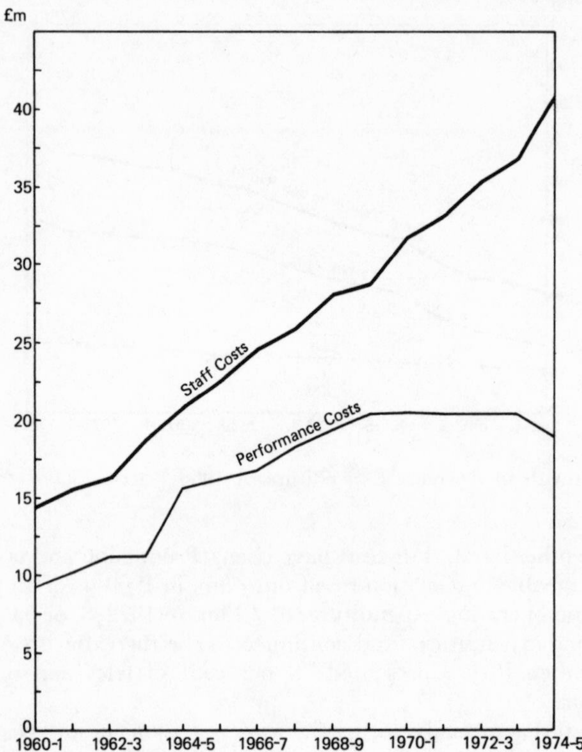

FIG. 3 Salaries and Wages of Staff, and Costs of Fees for Artists, Performers, and Copyright, 1960–1 to 1974–5, at 1960 prices

had already occurred in the late fifties) and, of course, trade union pressure. At all events, an admittedly crude but nevertheless telling indication of the part played by increased pay as against increased numbers of staff is given in Figure 4 on p. 229 which shows that – ignoring the small and fairly constant numbers of part-time staff – the average labour costs (wages and salaries, employer's contributions to national insurance and pensions) per member of staff rose from £854 a year in 1960–1 to £3679 a year in 1974–5 (or £1682 at 1960 prices).

It is not unreasonable to conclude that the strongest of the financial pressures on the BBC between 1960 and 1975 was the almost continuously accelerating rate of increase in staff costs, the larger element in which is not larger numbers but higher pay. It is also reasonable to infer from this that the pressure of rising staff costs has forced the BBC to economise on artists, performers, performing rights, royalties and the

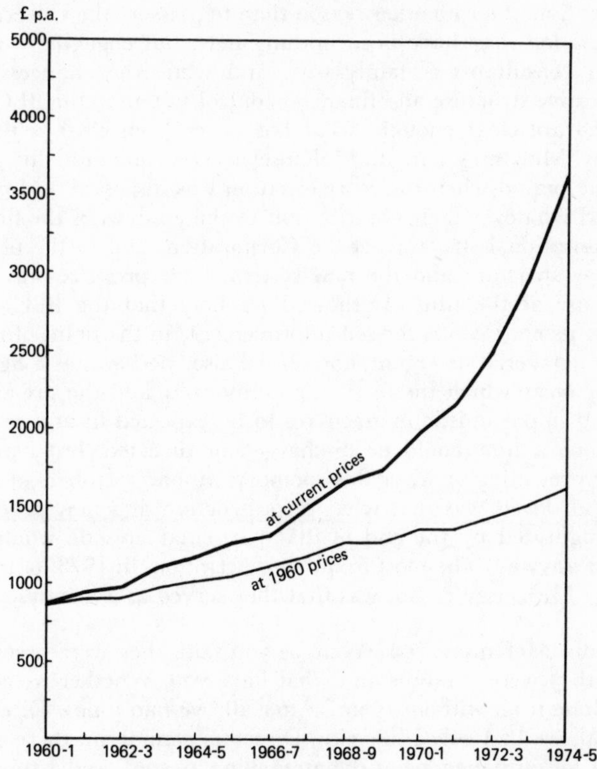

FIG. 4 Labour Costs per Full-time Member of Staff, 1960–1 to 1974–5

other basic costs of *performance*, as against broadcast *production*. Self-evident as I believe these conclusions to be, the facts they are drawn from are of course obscured by inflation,[5] the effects of which were far more obvious and serious, so far as the actual exigencies of budgeting were concerned. The BBC was bound to allow for inflation at the rate forecast by the Treasury, which was much less than it proved to be, and there was little to be done about its effects other than asking yet again for increases in the licence fee, despite the troubles which attended its appeal for an increase in 1968.

THE 'MCKINSEY REORGANISATION'

By the late sixties, the financial pressures were serious enough to warrant some serious examination of the system of financial control and of administration, if for no other reason than to reassure the Government. Reorganisation may have been nothing new, but engaging a firm of industrial consultants certainly was; and while the changes in the administrative structure and financial control system of the BBC made since 1968 are clear enough, what has never been clear is the part played by McKinsey's in it. McKinsey's were undoubtedly present during the period when the reorganisation was discussed and decided upon, and whatever their contribution to the analysis of the financial and organisational structure of the Corporation, and to the planning of the new structure and the new system, their presence was of undoubted use at the time. It showed publicly that the BBC was in earnest in its endeavours for self-improvement, to the point of using a popular managerial detergent, and served also, perhaps, as a lightning conductor on to which the fears, the animosities, and the pre-emptive strikes and opportunistic manoeuvres to be expected in any organisation at such a time could be discharged or diverted. But four years later, the prevailing view, or folk memory, among members of staff at virtually all levels was that what reconstruction and new procedures were inaugurated by the end of that particular episode would have happened anyway. The most frequent description, in 1973, of the part played by McKinsey & Co. was that they served as a 'catalyst'.

> What did McKinseys' do? Well, as you said, they were precipitants; they were catalysts and what have you. Whether we could have done it all without them? After all, we had a new Director General, we had new Managing Directors coming in, there was quite a lot of management dynamic lying around, and I think it quite possible we could have done it without them. We would certainly have avoided these gross errors of judgement which led us into so much public trouble.

The whole episode remains somewhat mysterious, as the House of Commons Estimates Committee found. At the time the Committee reported, in 1968, the McKinsey investigation was still under way, but nevertheless, the Committee felt able to make a few fairly sceptical comments:

> 'The BBC commissioned this inquiry in April 1968, and the former Director General admitted that, in deciding to take this step, they had been influenced not only by a desire for self-improvement, but also by a regard for public relations; they had thought "that it would strengthen the BBC's case, that it would do away with . . . a misleading impression given in the press that the BBC is over-administered and wasteful." '[6]

The Committee went on to express some astonishment, as well it might, that despite this declaration of intent, the BBC had never imparted any of McKinsey's findings either to the public or to any government department. In view of the Committee's reactions, and the fact that the BBC has remained just as silent ever since, it seems that, after the first announcement was made, what benefit in terms of publicity the 'public relations exercise' afforded was gained, for the most part, by McKinsey & Co.

The only published account of the genesis of the reorganisation and of the decision to involve McKinsey & Co. is by Lord Hill, who gives a characteristically uncomplicated account in his 'broadcasting memoirs'. He entered on his chairmanship of the BBC on 1 September 1967; both his appointment and his entry into his Chairmanship met with what he called 'initial hostility' in a chapter which ends by labelling the conduct of 'some people at the top' of the BBC as petty and childish. The account of why, and how, he initiated the reorganisation follows immediately after these words: there is just a hint that the sequence is more than chronological. At all events, 'soon after' the first meeting of the Board of Governors to be chaired by him, which was late in September 1967, there was 'a telephone call from the Postmaster General, who told me that Ministers had been considering the BBC's finances'. Apparently the Postmaster General was very frank:

> There were Ministers, he said, who felt that the BBC was extravagant, that there was surplus fat in its finances, and who, in any case, were unfavourable to any suggestion that the licence-fee should be increased. Some Ministers favoured reference of the licence-fee to the Prices and Incomes Board. No decision had been reached and the Prime Minister had asked that I should immediately begin a personal and comprehensive study of the BBC's finances, including the possibility of further economies and alternative ways of raising any money needed, reporting thereon. No decision on the licence-fee was to be reached until this report had been considered.
>
> I told the Board of Governors of this invitation at the next meeting, adding that I had agreed to comply with the request.[7]

The reference to increasing the licence fee is important; the BBC had just put in the latest of three requests in as many years for an increase in the licence fee. This must have been a danger signal as visible to the BBC as to anyone. In the old days, the radio licence fee had remained unchanged at ten shillings for twenty-four years. In 1946 it was raised to £1, and the new licence for 'combined T.V. and radio', at £2, introduced. This combined licence fee was raised to £3 in 1954, where it stayed for almost ten years. In 1963 the BBC was given the full amount of £4 for the combined licence fee (the Treasury had imposed an 'excise duty' of £1 in 1957). It was raised again in August 1965 to £5, with the 'radio only' licence going up to 25 shillings.

Even so, increases in licence-fee income barely kept up with the increases in operating costs. Revenue expenditure rose by 80 per cent during the five years before 1968, the period when the costs of the new television channel, of broadcasting all television in colour, of paying for satellite communication, and of the increased elaboration of television productions all made themselves felt in quick succession. Appeals to the Government for the raising of the licence fee became more frequent and more urgent. The third rise had been asked for before Lord Hill joined the BBC.

In 1968, moreover, relationships with the Government, always uneasy during the 1960s, were made particularly difficult, according to Lord Hill, by the susceptibilities of the Government Ministers. Early in the year, 'A comedian on one of our programmes had used a phrase once used about Lyndon Johnson about Harold Wilson. It was, "If his lips are moving, he's lying." A few days later the same joke was repeated on another programme.'[8] The response of the Prime Minister was to 'seek legal advice' and to demand a public apology.

This was followed by an attack on the Post Office in another programme which 'unfortunately for the BBC . . . contained inaccuracies, not the least of which was a statement that the Postmaster General was a junior Minister of State'.[9] Not surprisingly, around this time, Lord Hill reports that he had to tell the Governors that 'we had heard through the Post Office that the atmosphere in relation to the licence fee had never been worse, or the prospects of a favourable decision dimmer'.[10] He is, in his book, careful to deny that there was any connection between the Prime Minister's 'clear dislike' for the BBC and the licence-fee difficulty, but the interleaving of both accounts in a chapter headed 'Mr Wilson's Suspicions' carried its own evidence of the meaning Lord Hill wants to convey.

The need to campaign almost incessantly for raises in the licence fee – which, even when they were granted, were greeted regularly by the Chairman and by the Director General as 'too little and too late' – added yet one more requirement: publicity. To carry sufficient weight in its appeal to the Government for the licence fee to be raised, and to overcome the increased resistance with which the appeal was being met, the BBC had to counter, and if possible, forestall, charges, or even suspicions or questions, about extravagance – a fairly easy point to score against an organisation so involved – too involved, in some people's view – in providing entertainment, and in any case implicated at so many points with the entertainment industry, which in most regards and for most people is a fairly easy target for charges of extravagance.

If the BBC was to make the necessary fuss about its financial tribulations, it had to make doubly sure that it could deal quickly and firmly with the charge that it was wasteful.

It was these last considerations which persuaded the Board of Governors and the Board of Management to call in the help of an outside agency, which might possibly be helpful in carrying through the reorganisation, but would certainly be very useful as a demonstration of its determination and good faith to the outside world, especially to Government and to Treasury officials.

Whatever mysteries surround the involvement, or contribution, of McKinsey and Co., the strategy which emerged in 1969–70 was clear. The BBC was reorganised along lines which by the 1960s were conventional, even traditional, in large industrial organisations. Television, Radio and External Services were reconstructed as 'product divisions'. In essence, the new system handed the financial responsibility for operating and capital expenditure to the three heads of Television, Radio and External Services, henceforth to be known as Managing Directors instead of Directors.

Under the new arrangement, all expenditure – operating, overhead, and capital; studio engineering and services, as well as artists' fees and other direct production costs – was henceforth charged to Television Division or Radio Division (as it had been for the past twenty years in the case of External Services). Much more to the point was the fact that each individual programme was to be produced within the limits of an estimated budget which included the cost of all 'in-house' services and overheads as well as the staff costs, performers' fees, and the cost of materials for design, setting and wardrobe, which were all that had been budgeted for previously.

Other organisational consequences followed the same 'corporate strategy' conventions. The most important of these affected Engineering and Finance. Having adopted the convenient fiction[11] of charging 'line management' (i.e. producers and directors) with total financial responsibility for the programmes they produced, it was thought logical, and proper, to incorporate all engineering staff engaged in programme production in television and radio within the Television and Radio Divisions, rather than have them continue as members of a separate Engineering Division.

Engineering had been, from the very beginning, the largest and most expensive division of the five which had formed the Board of Management. In 1967, for example, there were 5398 staff in Engineering Division as against 8855 production and programme services staff in Television, Radio and External Services combined. Before the 'McKinsey reorganisation' cameramen and lighting supervisors in television, and studio and sound engineers in all three services, were all part of the

Engineering Division, as was also a large section of the sizeable numbers of people engaged in maintenance and other services.

Again, before 1968, Finance had been one of the seven groups or departments under the Director of Administration; thereafter there was a Director of Finance on the Board of Management, alongside the three Managing Directors and the Directors of Engineering, Public Affairs, and Personnel.

Just how radical these changes were, in terms of accountability, it is difficult to say. BBC accounts had always shown a clear enough distinction between Radio and Television. External Services, separately financed by the Foreign Office as they were, had had to be accounted for separately. Even the revenue expenditure of Administration Division and both revenue and capital expenditure of Engineering Division, organisationally separate as they were, were charged, in the published accounts, to the three programme divisions.

The declared purpose of the changes, however, was to improve the system of financial accountability within divisions. Each programme proposal by an individual producer had to be accompanied by a statement of costs which included 'overheads' (charges for staff time, equipment, studios and resources contributed by service departments within the Corporation) as well as performers' fees, operating staff costs, supplies and services specific to the programme's requirements. By this means it was hoped that financial responsibility, and accountability, would be delegated downwards to the point at which costs were actually generated – i.e., to the producers and directors of broadcast programmes.

The arrangement is, in fact, rather more complicated than this very common description of the new system suggests. Programme proposals ('offers') are indeed formulated by producers and directors and examined formally at 'offers meetings' (two each year), but the offers meetings are merely episodes in the annual planning cycle.

THE PLANNING CYCLE

The account of the planning cycle procedure in Television which follows is a composite of the descriptions given by three people at Controller level; i.e., it uses their words but they have been composed in a single sequence.

> The theory, and, by and large, the practice is that you have an annual production planning cycle, which is something you must have if you're trying to plan within finite resources, and if you want to give the advance notice to programme and service departments that they need, in order to have scripts ready, book

artists and disperse their staff in a sensible way over the year. What happens is that the two Network Controllers [of BBC1 and BBC2] will spend a good deal of time during the summer thinking about the general shape of the current year's programmes, its emphasis, content, audience reaction, and, as far as they can, the general run of public opinion. They will make some tentative decision, and then talk to their Planning Group. Head of Planning can be regarded as a Chief of Staff; the Planning Group work to the Network Controllers and give them detailed as well as general advice on transmission and production possibilities. They'll say that they are thinking of making this and that change during the coming year, and how that works out in logistical and financial terms. And the planning group may say, 'Well, you do realise, don't you, that if you have a lot more drama on film, you'll need a lot more servicing, and if you want more sport, you'll need more Outside Broadcast units, and you can't produce these in a flash.' – I'm giving the obvious examples. In the end, some indication of what is thought can be afforded, in terms of both money and resources of staff and equipment, is worked out. At that stage, they have some broad notions of the strategy they want to follow. It's never radically new; it starts out from the situation of the current year, the year before that, and so on. You can't make big or sudden changes, largely because of the resources and the people you have, and partly because of the sheer organisational problems involved. The *status quo* has to be a decisive factor; the last time there was a blank sheet of paper around was when BBC2 started and, let's face it, BBC2 started disastrously, and a whole major change had to be made. If you want to bring about changes in a schedule, which is really the heart of the thing, obviously, finance is the key factor, and not just sheer money, but the resources available, not only resources of studios and filming, but resources in human terms. Ideas are plentiful – that isn't really a problem. There are certain inevitable changes, the ones that are fixed because of dates coming along – a general election, or the Olympic Games. The much more difficult ones are those that we think desirable and those that might come about as a sort of groundswell. Of course, there's always the safe way of saying, 'Well, this is how it worked last year, boys, we'll do it again.' It needs an enormous effort of will to make the kind of changes which will make the schedule look totally different. After all, we are now [in the spring of 1973] working on the '74–75 season in some ways. So it can take two years to bring about real, visible, changes – and, of course, there are always people feeling we ought to play safe. In addition, there are the landmarks in the schedule which are untouchable, and the news is obviously one; it took eighteen months to two years to change the news from 8.50, where it used to be, to 9 o'clock, because the schedule had to be rebuilt that way. It sounds easy, I know, but it's a pretty complicated operation. Anyway, these are the things we'd leave alone. There is no blank sheet of paper. One puts the news down first; you put in 'Panorama'; you put Plays down; feature films here and 'Omnibus' there. By the time those landmarks are in the schedule, you've used quite a bit. *But* these are only strands – outlines of strands; say three comedy strands, three drama strands, two feature films, 'Play for Today', 'Omnibus', the news, 'Panorama', late night current affairs and early evening current affairs. By that time the skeleton outline is there. Then, to put flesh to that, it is up to the heads of output departments to say which drama series and so forth might be possible, and so on. So, while the outline may look familiar when all the switching has been carried out, the ingredients can be very very different. They then have a series of offers meetings with the head of each programme group or department in turn – Features, Talks, Drama, Light Entertainment, Music, and so on. Offers meetings are a fairly formal ritual that one goes through twice a year. Of course, there is a routine meeting with all the group heads every week, and the plan is discussed over the weeks, obviously. The offers meeting is a ritual because planning is in, finance is in, and lots of paperwork is done in advance to make sure that we can do it in financial and resource terms and that we can fit it all into the schedules. They are tiring meetings, actually; thank God they're only twice a year – they used to be four times a year. The time scale that we work on is much longer now than it was, and it's a very difficult thing to get used to.

Of course, there have been meetings throughout the year in anticipation of this occasion, but this is a formal affair at which these heads of output departments come up with what can best be described as 'costed ideas' – proposals for programmes, single or serial, with a pretty full indication of content, style, performers, writers, and a detailed schedule of the resources each programme requires, and the cost of each item.

From these meetings stem a sense of decisions which are communicated to the department which put up the offers, decisions like 'Yes, I like that', 'No, I don't like that', 'I like that, but we can't afford it', 'I quite like that, but let's wait and see', 'That depends on your getting such and such an artist' and so on. The logistical effects of all these decisions are fed into the computer which spews out successive loads which all the engineering and supply departments then look at in terms of their people and their capacity. So, by the end of the year, we have a range of possibilities, with services saying, perhaps, 'Well, that's fine as far as filming is concerned, but, for God's sake don't expect us to recruit twenty fully qualified make-up supervisors in three months' – to put it in extreme terms. Gradually, during December, January, February, with much argument and give-and-take, the thing is smoothed out, a plan is worked out which is both financially viable, can be done with the resources we've got, and will give the channel controllers the transmission pattern they want. That's the system, and it gives us a fairly defined schedule for a year, though the end of the year is much more mushy than the beginning or the middle. It's never perfect, of course, when it emerges; there are all sorts of hiccups and snags which happen as the pattern developing out of the offers meeting gets firmer and firmer, but there is no formal acceptance by the Managing Director of the annual plan, he will not accept it, until he gets a statement from his chief accountant, his director of programmes, his chief engineer and his whole management group that this thing's a goer. He relies on them to get the thing right. They can come to him for a policy decision, but in terms of practicalities, and practical difficulties, they've damn well got to get it right, within the total resources of every kind available, human and financial. The process is of course easier some years than others. Last year (1972–3), it so happened, it was comparatively easy. This year, it so happens, it's very difficult, because money's tight. The extra money we've had coming in from colour licences and elsewhere is eaten up in rising costs, because the people who provide raw film stock, who make our scenery, they don't stand still; payments to our own staff don't stand still, nor to artists, so it's financially very tight. And it's very tight in terms of facilities, because there's a natural tendency on the part of producers and designers to press the limits, to find new ways, more complex ways – more beautiful ways – of doing things.

This composite account of the planning procedure (which holds good, in very general terms, for radio as well as for television except that resources are much less of a problem) has been set down at length in order to demonstrate as conclusively as possible how orthodox and commonsensical it is – given one particular context, given one particular point of view. That context is industry; the particular point of view is that of production management. The word 'industrialisation' itself, as I have said, unthinkable ten years earlier, occurred in several of the 1973 interviews.

The nature and extent of the climatic change becomes a little clearer in the immediate sequel, in the same interview, to the last few sentences of the composite account, in which the speaker referred to the natural desire of programme staff to 'press the limits' of television production. At that point in the interview, I put in,

But not more economical ways, ever?

The rejoinder to this remark makes clear, I believe, just how far BBC management in the 1970s had moved from BBC administration as it had been in the 1960s and earlier:

> They are under a permanent instruction to look for more economical ways of doing things, but the tendency is for scripts to call for more – more scenery, more filming. If you are to resist this pressure, which of course you must – not because it's a bad thing; it's very good that ideas should be fermenting, and for people to want to do more, differently, and better – but because they drive you towards more costs, more complexity.
> And there is increasingly – what's the best way to put this? – I don't think this is just my personal opinion, although I do feel it – there is pressure from the staff, both directly and through their unions, to want to be more and more involved in decision-making. This is combined with a feeling that television has been going for a long time, we have rivals elsewhere, we're a great, continuous running industry, many people look on it more as a job of work than they did before, and there is less and less inclination on the part of more and more people to work enormous hours with great enthusiasm and with limited rewards. There is more insistence – and I'm not saying it's improper insistence – on having the 'right' number of people associated with a programme. So there is therefore a general tendency for things to be more expensive than they were.

The planning cycle is the crucially important feature of the three new elements in the contemporary situation of the BBC, elements which are in fact connected in logical and chronological sequence, and in which the 'McKinsey Reorganisation' of 1969 figures at most as a gesture, a landmark. They all emanate from, or were initiated by, the financial pressures which began to mount during the 1960s, and continued into the 1970s; they are, first, the development of a corporate strategy designed not so much to control those pressures (inflation proved uncontrollable) as to devise some means of surviving the contrary pressures of increased costs and of increased demand from the programme departments for more elaborate and more expensive productions; secondly, the development of a planning system which converted conventional programme planning into continuous production lines ('strands') which could be predicted in terms of production costs and were governable in terms of meeting the expectations of the outside world – the public and government – from which revenue came; and, thirdly, the construction of a management system which could operate the planning system and monitor costs and content of broadcast productions, and which could assume legitimate command of output departments because it was manned by people who claimed the same professional identity and interests as producers themselves.

UNDER NEW MANAGEMENT

By 1973, there were 37 people at Controller level and above, including the ten members of the Board of Management. Of these 37 only two had been among the people of the same rank who constituted the senior administration in 1963. In particular, the membership of the Board of Management was entirely changed – as, indeed, was the Board of Governors. This meant, among other things, that there was an understandable tendency for the same senior officials to emphasise the part which the top management had played in the changes which had occurred during the past ten years and, also, perhaps, to make much of the changes themselves: The 'obvious changes', for one Controller, were the change in Director General, and the five or six years of Lord Hill – 'a change in leadership, clearly'. Another Controller – in radio this time – thought that what changes had occurred were 'much more to do with the fact that a different kind of person has got into the management of things'.

No one was brash enough to say, or even hint, that 'what changes had occurred' were clearly for the better, but, equally naturally, it is to be presumed that they saw the changes which had been carried through by the existing top management, or had brought them to the top, as necessary, or at least a considerable improvement on what had obtained previously.

This view came out most clearly in one interview with a Controller:

> I've been given this job because I've had a variety of other jobs and because I'm a certain kind of chap. I happen to think I'm right for the job, and one of the qualifications for the job is that I think I have a view of society and what it needs – and I think I've got the sort of mind that leads me to listen to evidence. God knows, I may not do it properly, but at least I try to do it that way. I don't think I've got an *instinctive* sense; you know, one trusts one's instincts to a certain extent, but there is a view of a

Controller as a guy who just knows with his fingertips what society wants, and does it, because what he wants must be what society wants. I certainly don't feel this way. You've got to listen, judge, and assess – and a large part of my time goes in persuading producers that what they're trying to sell me as broadcasting ideas are too narrow, too insensitive in relation to what, really, we ought to be broadcasting. And I think I'm speaking for society there.

How the hell can you be so confident about speaking for society?

Well, I'm not. I just think it's my job, that's all –

What you're doing, really, is trusting the system that brought you where you are.

Well, if one's to have any self-confidence I suppose one has to. Equally, I believe the system does make other mistakes. But I can't believe the system has been wrong putting me here . . . I'd describe my functions as essentially being an agent of change. If I were only to do the part of the job which consists of keeping things going, I would only be occupied ten per cent of my time – an exaggeration, perhaps, but what I'm really here for is to redirect, to energise change.

And the sanction for that is that the system has put you there. Which is a nice little circular argument, isn't it? As in my own case, you trust the system because it put the right person in the right place – it's a terribly self-defeating thing. I suppose one has to. The question is whether that view is shared down below.

More generally, people on top trusted the system that had brought them there because of one special characteristic they all shared. Outside the specialist Directorates of Engineering, Finance and Personnel, all 37 people at Controller level and above had had experience of broadcast production. This had never been the case before, at any time in the Corporation's history. It seemed as if to celebrate the jubilee of public service broadcasting the BBC had overturned the dispensation which had prevailed since the days of Controller of Administration Carpendale; at long last, in the eyes of top management Output was clearly on top and no longer on tap. While this latest – and greatest – change was credited to Sir Hugh Greene, it had been completed and consolidated since his departure.

Planning the development of broadcast services every five years ahead, and the annual planning cycle itself are certainly central features of the new management set-up, but only in that they show that corporate planning, in fairly conventional terms, features as an important task for top management. It always was, of course, but under the new system both exercises are part of every year's work, and are intended to serve as the framework within which programmes are to be devised, produced and broadcast. Forward planning used to be almost a by-product of the very considerable amount of work put in by task forces assembled by the Director General to prepare evidence for successive broadcasting committees. The very first long-term plan, one for ten years, I was told, was worked out at the behest of the Beveridge Committee. Planning broadcasting schedules for the coming season was the affair of 'programme controllers', who seemed to have worked, at least to a large extent, on the basis of a ranking of priorities which emerged from their own preferences and from continual discussion with heads of departments and even individual producers.

By the early seventies, both long-term planning and the annual planning cycle were done on a routine annual basis, and according to a regular pattern. 'Top management', thereafter, can be said to carry a specific reference to those individuals directly involved in corporate planning, i.e., the Board of Management, Controllers of Programmes, Network Controllers, and the members of the television Development Committee. The key figures in top management, therefore, are the Managing Directors, who are both members of the Board of Management and also in charge of planning, operations and finance in Television and in Radio.

It is probably the formalising of the powers of the heads of Television and Radio, along with the transfer to their directorates of all engineering staff concerned with broadcast production (as against transmission) which accounts for the constant use by top management of the term 'decentralisation' and 'delegation' to describe the changes which the reorganisation had brought about. These changes could, in fact, be interpreted as making for greater control centrally, if 'the centre' is taken to mean the Managing Directors, who are also members of the Board. Indeed, it was so interpreted by production staff. The ambiguity involved here shows up clearly in this passage from an interview with a senior member of the Finance Division:

> We regard the great breakthrough as the first part of the decentralisation of the Finance Division and the setting up of the new Managing Directorates.
>
> *This was because of, or followed on, McKinsey? Was it 'because of'?*
>
> This was one of the McKinsey recommendations, certainly, to separate Finance from the Director of Administration. There is a

Director of Personnel, now, and there is a Director of Finance.

That arrangement, if I may say so, was mad, anyway.

Having the Director of Administration looking after finance?

And Personnel, both.

Well, we'd agree with you, of course, but these were the facts of life for many a long decade. Anyhow, this was the first stage of our decentralisation. We are intending to decentralise further by making the Chief Accountant [in each Directorate] not only responsible for the management information and the budgeting, as he is at the moment, but he will also take over the financial accounting function, which again, had been centralised, and in effect, making all his own payments and this kind of thing. Again, we feel that by decentralising further, at this stage, he will become much more identified with the efficiency of the accounting operation, through tightening up bad routine flows of paperwork – of invoices coming in and not being passed – this is the Chief Accountant, Television. If there are any glaring instances of very bad work being performed by people – from a systems flow point of view – he is now far better able to bring influence to bear, through his Managing Director, than the Central Finance Division ever was, because it had to be done through third parties. It always comes back to the same point, that the Chief Accountant is regarded as a member of the production team and is in a better way to get things done. . . .

There is also a great interest being shown by the management of Television and Radio in the various costs of strands, of series, and of individual programmes – in a way that is very much more than it was, in comparison, ten years ago. . . . .

That really is revolutionary!

Well, I think it's worked extremely well. But, as I said, the big psychological barrier was overcome by the Accountant being attached to his Managing Director rather than to head office. . . . The structural changes are even bigger than purely in the accounting field. I mean, for example, the Managing Director has the whole of the Operations people working for him as well. I mean, he's running his own factory. This is what it is.

The gravitational pull of the managerial system made itself felt in other ways than through the operation of the planning cycle and financial control. 'Decentralisation' – i.e., from the old 'Director of Administration' to the new Managing Directors – also obtained in personnel matters:

> *Administration Assistants were very much the fingertips of Administration Division.*
>
> Well, they've now got a very big personnel group inside Television, and it would deal with almost all their day-to-day problems, unless they run into industrial relations [difficulties] – in which case they will come to us, because they are running into something of a Corporation-wide aspect. Or else it's a general grading issue, or a pay and conditions of service one, in which case they've got no scope for mucking around with it, and they've got to come to us. But the sort of problem which you are postulating [i.e., 'bad communication' – see pp. 256-60] would come to me only if it was raised formally by a union. If that case was raised formally by the union, I would probably say, 'Well, look, you really must talk to Television about this' – or if it got a lot of head of steam in a particular area, which then came off into underground press and then hit the national press, otherwise, I wouldn't expect to interfere. I would anyway be doing no more than preaching to the head of Personnel and the Managing Director, 'You must communicate. You must get your groups to tell their people what's happening, on this that and the other.' If they say, 'Nuts to you, I'm running this my own way, and I'm happy with it', then I've got no real right to intervene.

In fact, Managing Directors acted as head of a small 'top management' group in each Managing Directorate, constituting the Managing Director's Committee, but also closely involved in all aspects of corporate planning, financial control, and programme planning affecting the Directorate. The inner core of this group consists of the Controllers of the Networks (i.e., BBC1 and BBC2 in Television, and Radio 1 and 2, Radio 3 and Radio 4) with the Director of Programmes as the Managing Director's lieutenant. ('One rather simple way of putting it is that the Director of Programmes does everything the Managing Director of Radio doesn't want to do.') Formally, the Director of Programmes is responsible to the Managing Director for the content and standards of broadcasting in the networks; he is also head of Establishment, which means

> responsible for the staff of the Directorate, in the sense that I have to approve the establishments of the different departments, and I have to approve the annual reports, gradings, bonuses – that sort

> of thing. And I very much interpret my job to mean that I am basically concerned with ensuring the good morale of the staff, that they have the means whereby programmes are made, that the networks are carrying out the policies laid down for them, and that the standards are of the kind that the Board of Governors require.

This last, monitoring, function is discharged differently in the two Managing Directorates, although in neither case is there any formal procedure. In 1972–3, the average daily output of Radio, Network, Regional, and Local, was 261 hours, and, in the absence of any special monitoring service, it is clearly out of the question for top management, individually or collectively, to vet anything more than the tiniest fraction of this output. In Radio, it is Network Controllers who see themselves as in 'editorial command' of the output of their networks.

> My predecessor was essentially a working producer and departmental head. He was rather different from some of the people who preceded him in this kind of job. He *saw himself* as the editor of the network. I rode in on his departure in an ideal position to take this a stage further. I *behaved* as the editor of the network. The other Network Controllers have done the same. . . . I think that temperamentally we work in that sort of way. It has far more to do with the personality of the people concerned than with any organisational changes as such. We all want to be editors. We think that the function of being an editor is to talk at first hand with producers. To be very frank with producers about the merits and demerits of their programmes, both before the event and after the event has, I think, created an atmosphere of frankness, candour, and perhaps liveliness, which was previously lacking. As far as I'm concerned, this is a funny mixture of authoritarianism and non-authoritarianism. I mean, I operate on the principle that I will push my views and my vision of what the network should be like as hard as it can be pushed. And that means literally what it says – as hard as it can be pushed: that's to say until my force meets an immovable object. And what I always say to producers about their programme ideas is, 'If I don't like your idea, I shall say so. If you persist in a rotten idea, I shall refuse it and I'll refuse it again. But if, in the end, you go on making the case for an idea that I'm just not convinced about, in the end, if you persist long enough, I will give in. Because, in the end, producers are the people who make programmes, not Controllers. I shall just let you have your head and then we'll see what comes of it and we'll criticise it afterwards.' So that in a sense, it's a mixture of

authoritarianism and permissiveness. I think that's much more to do with the change in atmosphere than anything else.

In fact, of course, management 'style', which is what was being described in terms of the 'funny mixture' of authoritarianism and permissiveness, is indissociable from the structure of management; at the very least, the style has to be consistent with the structure. Although a good deal was made of the fact that three out of the five men in the top management of Radio were 'from Television', the outstanding feature of the management of Radio was that, since the reorganisation, all five people had been allocated adjacent rooms along a corridor. They saw a great deal more of each other than of individual departmental heads or producers. Further, the 'funny mixture' varied from authoritarianism to permissiveness for different departments; it was not applied in the same proportion to all.

It varies very much from department to department. Obviously, I can't, in effect, be the editor of the entire network – 120 hours a week, and heaven knows how many departments. To take two extremes, —— Department has a very efficient head indeed. He knows his job. He runs a very tight department – everything from accountancy to booking is all very well done indeed, and in the nature of things, with 12–15 hours a week coming out, I simply couldn't effectively control the output of that department. So that all I do there is to lay down what slots should be filled, discuss the broad policy for the slots, and pick out examples of where I think things are going either exceptionally well or exceptionally badly. That's minimal control.

Maximum control comes in a department like —— or —— where the output is much smaller, maybe it's four or five hours a week of original material. None of it is banded in strips across the week, so that it all remains hand-tailored stuff and has to be separately recorded. Every single idea is raised at a fortnightly meeting, which I chair, and is talked out and everything is reviewed after the event. That's maximum control. Everything has to go literally through my editorial hands. The other departments vary in various grades between these two extremes. Light Entertainment is a halfway house, in that everything is in 'strips'. The sheer quantity of Light Entertainment is far too great for me to control, but the fact that the programmes are invariably bought in 6-, 13-, or 26-week series means that it is quite easy, while not listening to all of them, to sample a pilot or sample a first one and therefore to exercise an effective running commentary on the quality.

In Television, control was exercised differently. Output was smaller – under 21 hours daily from the two channels and from Regions, as against Radio's 261 – which meant that a higher proportion could be seen by top management. On the other hand, the sheer complexity of television meant that control had to be much more than 'editorial', which presumably refers almost wholly to the sheer verbal content of a broadcast. To give some indication of the difference, one Managing Director guessed that whereas in Television the proportion of producers and directors to other programme staff, technical and studio, was probably 2:25, in Radio it was 2:3. Monitoring output was done in a weekly meeting convened by the Director of Programmes and attended by the Managing Director, the two Network Controllers, and all heads of groups and departments. In Television, the 'editorial' aspect of the Radio Network Controller's job was diffused (and de-fused) in a regular meeting of critical, lively, sometimes heated, discussion of programmes from every department by department heads themselves; nevertheless, the managerialist implication of monitoring output was apparent even in Television, through the presence at those meetings not only of the Director of Programmes, whose meeting it was, but of the Network Controllers *and* the Managing Director. This made it, in reality, just as 'authoritarian' as the practice of the Network Controller in Radio of 'everything literally' going through his hands, and of the fortnightly meeting, with him as chairman, which reviewed all ideas for programmes and in which 'everything is reviewed after the event'. In that instance, the meeting was between himself and the producers in one department. The Television Weekly Programme Review was regarded as a valuable meeting, which, in addition to providing a forum for critical discussion of programmes from each department by all heads of department, was also said, by some, to be 'therapeutic':

> It's a good meeting – actually, it's the best, because it does represent a very clear, critical *professional* view, than which you can go no further, as it were, in professional terms – this programme was good, bad or indifferent for the following reasons. Or it represents the recording [i.e., in the minutes] of good work done which other people have missed. Or it represents the outpourings of departmental violence which, in tribal terms, as it were, needs to be released.
>
> *Well, these are two questions arising from that. By what possible criteria do you decide that programmes are good, or bad, or indifferent? – or is this an impossible question?*
>
> Well, yes. I think it probably is, actually. I could write a book on it. I suppose, but . . . I mean, we know –. No, we don't always

agree, but if it's a very good programme – this is about the quality of the work, actually – if the work is good, at that meeting you'll find 99 per cent of people saying, 'That was a marvellous programme.' There's a kind of movement of the bowels, you know – 'By God, what a marvellous thing to have been participating in.' Equally, if a programme is rank bad, there's no point in wasting any time on it. I mean, two voices will say that this was a programme which was disastrously badly done, and nobody demurs; you know that somehow the universal judgement is in terms of damnation. The middle, of course, is where people disagree. We disagree very violently over all kinds of things. But the polarities are quite clear. . . .

The other question is about this expression of hostility. Do you think it's therapeutic?

No.

Is it interesting for you, because you are sitting on top of it all, and you feel you ought to know?

No. I don't have to – because if they go on slighting each other – Damn it all, I see the memos coming in – there are copies all over the place – and if you see the sniping after a while getting out of hand, particularly when a head of group in a static situation may have under him a simmering individual or group of people whom he is personally deeply worried about and something may happen to cause them to be stirred up, therefore it reacts on him and he reacts on the rest. I think, on the whole, bringing it out into the open is therapeutic, yes. Oh, it can cause bloody great explosions also, but I think on the whole in an organisation like this if you try and paper it over you must have trouble, you get bad work. That's the worst thing of all. In the end you get programmes which are not good enough.

Apart from using different procedures for monitoring output in Television and in Radio, a Controller of Programmes acts as the *alter ego* of the Managing Director, with Network Controllers (three in Radio, two in Television) working out their annual or half-yearly schedules within the framework allowed by precedent and major forthcoming events, and also by the technical, financial and manpower resources available. However the different top management functions may be divided amongst these five, or four, people, though, the arrangement is a very considerable departure from what used to prevail. Reminiscing about his earlier days in television, one Controller said,

> It was certainly the case that 'baron' is the word we used in Television. It was certainly the case that the departments were very strong – certainly the heads of departments did behave like barons and there was warfare between them. There is no doubt, for instance, that Features and Current Affairs wouldn't talk to each other, any telephone conversation or other communication between them would be conducted in the most hostile, suspicious, and cautious way. Any attempt at liaison imposed on them would be resisted, suspected and – well, it was out-and-out warfare between them. Similarly, when they went to the royal court, as it were, the attitude they adopted was that they 'held the land', and were the source of all power, and that the court had to treat and negotiate with them, and be dependent on their favour.

As against this, the new system shifted power and authority into the hands of top management in both Television and Radio. The change was more apparent to the Network Controllers in Radio, partly because more 'barons' survived in Television than in Radio, partly because of the direct involvements of heads of departments in the Weekly Programme Review meetings, and partly because of the reconstitution of Radio 3 and Radio 4. The ability to change planning schedules for future broadcasting was seen as something only the Network Controller could do; this makes him preoccupied with change, and, inevitably, as the most appropriate person to envisage and institute changes:

> [In the past] the planning function and the editorial function were so handled [see pp. 47–51] that predominance was given to the planning function. Editorially, that was tied to a situation where no change was envisaged. The moment you began thinking of change – of doing away with this department because its function no longer existed, and creating that department because they ought to be concerned with a different kind of broadcasting – the moment you look at the talks I've put into Current Affairs, for example, and decide that instead of the straight talk, or the talks magazine, or the news bulletin – instead of that you had a sequence and you began reshaping your departments – the emphasis, almost inevitably, editorially, moves over to that of the Network Controller.

When I questioned the 'almost inevitably', the answer was that a head of department 'tends to be conservative', because he is 'more concerned with the wellbeing of his department than with broadcasting as a whole. He's concerned with securing employment for the members of his staff, and with ensuring that what he was doing last year he is going to do next year as well.'

Under the new regime, therefore, not only had there been a shift of power and responsibility to Managing Directors and their immediate subordinates, the controllers and chief engineers and chief accountants, there had also been some surrender of the 'baronial' powers of heads of departments to the top management – 'inevitably' because of the need to change network schedules in Radio, 'inevitably' because of the constraints on finance and resources in Television. Heads of department, now, were much more 'men in the middle' – the all-purpose word 'interface' was used to describe their position. Their attendance at the Weekly Programme Review and at 'offers meetings' meant that their most important encounters with top management occurred in contexts in which they competed with each other for applause or approval in front of top management. In addition, they had become, to a large extent, agents of the economic and efficient use of money and resources:

> The producer's task is very simple. It's to make what he considers the best possible programme in the best possible way. Somebody did say that in the BBC the producer is king, but he's a monarch whose powers are constitutionally limited, which is very true. The producer must go for perfection, regardless of resources, regardless of cost. It is the task of management, his own departmental management as well as top management, to say, 'Well, yes, we know it would be a better programme if you took six months and used five film crews, and we realise we are thwarting your artistic freedom but, chum, you are going to have to make your programme in three weeks with one film crew.' Again, if Television management accepts the professional advice of Head of Drama Group – this is the way I'd see it as a constitutional issue – say he says 'If you want better drama, we've got to have more film facilities, and we can cut down on electronics', then, over a period of years, this can be done and should be done. Because, in my picture of the BBC, the ultimate professional is the head of department.

One other feature of top management which distinguishes them, and the posts they occupy, from the rest of the Corporation is that the 'appointments board' procedure which obtains for all other posts is abrogated in their case. This is one feature which has not changed. In 1973, I was told that there are boards for appointments up to and at Assistant Controller, although at that level they are 'invited' boards – i.e., composed with the agreement and approval of the top management of the Directorate. 'Above this, the Board of Management decides. For example, there is this Controllership of Staff Training and

Appointments now falling vacant, and I'm not sure that a board wouldn't be better than the Board of Management decision about this.'[12]

Since the Corporation is a career system as well as other things, the men who have reached the highest positions represent a kind of show-case of the characteristics of success. If intellectual capacity, technical information, local experience of the resources available and managerial skill in the ways in which they may be employed to the best effect are the main criteria of success, there are none the less other considerations which are, in the Corporation as elsewhere, taken into account. Indeed, it was argued in 1965, these extraneous considerations carried more weight when many senior appointments were made. While the Appointment Board System, it is said, imposed its own discipline on selection procedures, in that all considerations other than those related to choosing 'the best man for the job' are ruled out –

> very senior appointments are not made with the same discipline as those which come under the Appointments Boards system. If you are a member of an Appointments Board, you cannot exclude the possibility of somebody else on the Board coming out with exactly the opposite opinion. You are under the discipline of controversy. Again, every time somebody says, 'If only we take Candidate A and promote him then that means I can promote B in that department and that will mean he will cease to quarrel with C, because he'll no longer be dealing with him', there's always a chance that there'll be somebody else there, because it's part of the job, to say, 'Look I'm sorry, I realise it's desperately important to you as Head of Department, but it's totally irrelevant to the Board.'
>
> But with senior appointments which are not conducted by a Board, but by somebody saying, or agreeing with somebody else, that this is the best man to put in, not only are you not subjected to this discipline, but you can follow all your inclinations over these extraneous things. Such as – you don't, as a Board has to, have to try and determine who is the best candidate. With your senior appointments it's always possible to have appointments of convenience, very understandable convenience, but not necessarily the best man. He's not forced on you. That's always a difficulty about top appointments – there's every inducement to think up these other points.

As the balance of power shifts at the top of the Corporation, or of its divisions as the need to redress the balance alters, and as policy considerations themselves alter over time and call for different arrays of talent and kinds of commitment, so the line alters between relevant and extraneous considerations, and their relative importance shifts. Yet, over time, the people occupying the top thirty or so positions may be taken – indeed, must be taken – as the preferred models of effective performance, conduct and demeanour thrown up by the perception, by the Board of Management, of the Corporation's needs. This basic assumption of the career system is carried into the basic assumptions of the generality of staff about preferred behaviour which will lead to their own success.

There are also other assumptions which have the appearance of insurance against, or reassurance about, failure, assumptions which have to be generated within an organisation for any career system to operate. These assumptions about the values implicit in the system are, like the others, grounded in, or at least related to, observable facts or behaviour. For instance, in Engineering, professional and career commitments presented themselves as a dilemma, if not more strongly, then to far more people than in programme departments. Ascent of the career ladder tended to mean, for most people, losing touch with the technical expertise on which their image of themselves as 'professionals' is founded. With the high premium placed on professionalism in the Division, as elsewhere in the BBC, there was an inescapable feeling that as people ascended the ladder of power, responsibility, and reward, they lost the authority which comes from superior professional skills and knowledge. The special emphasis on monitoring the performance of juniors which marked this Division made for plenty of occasions which called for display of this kind of authority, and which therefore engendered a good deal of insecurity – covered up, as is usually the case, by exploiting the authority of superior rank.

Involvement in the organisation is developed, therefore, through the operation of the career system itself, which serves to demonstrate both the degree and the direction of dedication which are the prerequisites of success and, at the same time, the qualifications, the social skills and the qualities of character which personify the ethos of the Corporation.

8 Management Structure and Organisational Process

THE NEW MANAGERIALISM

The BBC's long tradition of 'protecting its creative workers' from the preoccupations and responsibilities of administration had, by the sixties, become a central feature of organisational doctrine, to the point of administrative officials claiming to 'tread rather warily' in dealing with producers and programme staff:

> One is always frightened, in Administration, of stopping something. You know, we preach the gospel, that we're only here to help – blah blah blah – but this is true. Therefore people tread rather warily.

And, from another senior administrator in 1963:

> We do have in the BBC a deep suspicion of so-called pure administration. It's a dirty word. I think personally that this is very healthy. After all, the BBC exists to put out programmes and the people putting out programmes are in the front line and all that sort of thing, and they have to have more consideration than anybody else. The rest of the chaps are there to help them in one way or another.

As a matter of historical fact, Administration had always been distinguished from Output (producing programmes) and had always been on top rather than on tap from the very beginning. It was only during the latter years of the war and the pressure of circumstances, and of new men, that Administration assumed an eminence that was first grey rather than black, and later tended to fade still further into embarrassed diffidence.

The reorganisation which began in 1968 seemingly reversed that tradition. But there is an alternative view. The apotheosis of programme makers, and even broadcasters, into administrators could be seen as in reality re-establishing the administration – now so very decisively 'the management' – into an ascendancy comparable to what had existed in the days of Carpendale and Dawnay. Such an interpretation would make sense of an otherwise curious feature of the recital of the many changes identified for me, by people who had been in the Corporation for the previous ten years, as occurring during the sixties and early seventies. This was the ending of the 'cycle of ascendancy'.

One of the striking characteristics of the BBC in 1963 was the conflict of interest between different departments and sections, a conflict which was associated with different interpretations of the function of broadcasting and of the way the BBC should discharge it see (Chapter 4, pp. 144–54). I found traces of this in 1973, but they would almost certainly have been invisible had I not remembered the earlier situation, and looked for them. There were rivalries, but they did not carry the 'ideological' element they had ten years earlier. This 'end of ideology' phenomenon, so patently contrary to the general tendency in society at large for ideological commitments to flourish so abundantly and obtrusively, was rather disconcerting. After a week or so, however, a number of interviews had made it clear that what had happened was that the axis of confrontation, the bones of contention, had changed.

The view from Controller level seemed to indicate that the competition between the 'balanced programme' advocates, the 'mirror of society' journalists, and the neo-Reithians had indeed died down.

> When you were here ten years ago, the journalists [Talks and Current Affairs] were in charge. . . . These things go in a circle. As you know, there was a time when O.B. Group were the masters – the boys who were really in charge were Outside Broadcasts Group. It then moved quite a bit to Drama – I mean when Sidney Newman came in and made 'The Wednesday Play' what it was, etc., Drama took quite a hold. I wouldn't like to say which side is on top at the moment. It's certainly moved from Drama.

When I came to interview people lower down the organisational hierarchy, the question of who was 'on top' – in the sense of ideological dominance – was soon answered.

It was management.

Whereas in the early sixties what had assumed prime importance was that BBC purposes and policies should be constructed so as at least to support and if possible give prominence to the kind of output one's own department existed to produce, and to aid the advancement of the kind of people who produced that output, by 1973 the lines of confrontation seemed to be horizontal – between the 'professionals' and the 'managers', who were no less the agents of the new managerialism for being ex-professionals.

'Confrontation' is, of course, too positive and precise a term for the kind of statements made to me. In the case of the ideologies of 1963, the evidence for their existence lay not so much in the affirmation of beliefs as in the attribution of rival or opposing beliefs to others who were usually unspecified and often clearly unknown. In 1973, the same kind of attribution was made about the managers, who, although they were certainly specified, were equally certainly unknown:

> I know that Paul Fox is Controller of BBC1 and I know that Robin Scott is Controller of BBC2. I do actually know what he looks like; I don't know what Fox looks like. . . . ***** has a bias towards sport and current affairs and he's not really much in favour of drama. It seems to me that if he's interested in drama at all, it's the soap opera variety – which we despise.
>
> *How did you get hold of this idea?*
>
> Well, it's a sort of folklore . . .

And again:

> The things that money is allocated for are very bad projects that seem to be what the top brass think the people want, as opposed to being good ideas that people produce, [to which] they say, 'Yes, that's a very good idea, let's do it! . . . It's like marketing. I worked for an advertising agency, and there was one man who used to sit and dream up what shape to turn the dough into that would sell most.

What matters about such beliefs is not whether they are true or false but how strongly and how widely they are held. It is out of the question to determine this from fifty or sixty interviews, half of them, in any case, with the 'top brass' themselves. But the fact is that they surfaced frequently, and spontaneously, in the interviews I had, and this is at least *prima facie* evidence of their prevalence and strength. Usually, of course, bias, opposition to 'good ideas', and so forth were all attributed to 'the management' or to 'the system', and not to individuals – certainly not, in any other instance, to an individual the speaker claimed not to know. At the same time it was held, after the question had been raised, that the interpretation being advanced was 'very widely held at my level'.

It also became apparent that a sizeable number of people in positions either immediately or some distance below the top saw the changes as neither necessary or beneficial. Even if the occasional displays of anti-establishmentarianism were discounted, it became increasingly clear with succeeding interviews that there was a much stronger sense of managerial control than had obtained in 1963. This sense was just as prevalent among the controlling managers themselves, but carried, so to speak, the opposite valency.

One straightforward way of showing how this impression gained on me is to reproduce some passages from an interview, fairly early in the 1973 series, with one of the people on the programme side whom I had talked with ten years before.

> *Mostly, in the interviews so far, I have followed the obvious line, that is, to ask people how has the BBC changed in the last ten years. I've had three kinds of stories. The first one is that there's been a new generation of people coming in. You always get this in an organisation. Change always seems to be the product of new people.*
>
> *The second one is the 'McKinsey reorganisation' which of course people say was not due to McKinsey's at all but merely coincided with it, except that the people running the financial side now, who are very different from what used to be, say that the McKinsey reorganisation, the creation of the manager-directorships and the infusion of the whole management organisation, therefore, with a knowledge, an awareness and a responsibility for everything that was going on, made a very big change. It's made for a realignment, for example, between the Output side, as it used to be called, and the 'bureaucracy'; they are now welded together. There may be something in what they say.*
>
> *Then there's the third thing (which may well be something I am feeding in and then having it being said back): the feeling that the BBC like the rest of the country, has gone through a very long post-war phase, from which it's now coming out. The fifties and most of the sixties were spent in living with the feeling of being a nation which has been very hard hit, but is coasting along fairly happily, though. Ten years ago, there was a lot of criticism of the way things were being run in politics, and of institutions of different kinds, the BBC included. The critical reaction itself was quite interesting.*
>
> *It was 'satire'. You took a mickey, but you didn't do anything about it. Now the atmosphere has changed and for me that spells an improvement. People think there is quite a lot wrong and are now prepared to do something about it. The something may be quite mad, or silly, or wrong-headed, but I think that now there is much more a feeling that it's time we got things under control. And this accounts for a whole range of things that are happening which cause a great deal of discomfort to people here in the BBC as well as elsewhere.*

My respondent's reaction to this was that the 'new people' at the top of the BBC were more ruthless (because more career-minded) than ever, and that 'McKinsey had given them the nerve' to 'behave the way they did'. All of which prompted me to say, towards the end of the interview, after hearing an account of the 'traumatic episode' of 'Broadcasting in the '70s' (see p. 160):

> *You've changed, you know. Ten years ago, in response to talk about 'they'*

you would have said – in fact, you did *say, when we were talking about the administration, and I have a record of it – 'It's all very well to talk about "The Administration" as though it were some sort of monolithic set-up but you really have to think of what part you're talking about.' I thought it was a very good statement. I know it brought me up short. But now you talk about 'they'.*

Yes, I do. Which is odd, considering that I know a number of 'them'. With one of them, whom I know particularly well, I have to think about him as a 'person-person' person, whom I know, rather than as an administrator; I don't altogether recognise him as an administrator, whether I disagree with what he does or not as an administrator. This is curious. I was wondering about this the other day. I noticed (I don't just think this is part of the conditions of work which I now enjoy) a distinct tendency on my part to be slightly paranoid about the organisation.

We are presented, then, with a situation in which intelligent, sensitive and hard-working people, as this man was, can speak of feeling 'slightly paranoid' about the BBC management, and hard-working and committed, although perhaps less sensible and sensitive, people can talk about 'the very bad projects that seem to be what the top brass think people want'. At the same time, senior officials could congratulate themselves on the much better control the management now had, and on the new legitimacy and acceptability which management had acquired now that it was composed almost wholly of people who had had experience of programme production, a fact which was cited often enough as demonstrable validation of the authority and acceptability of the new top management.

What seems to have happened, then, is that having, between 1963 and 1973, entered a totally changed financial situation, the Director General, with the Board of Management and the senior officials immediately subordinate to them, all backed – or prompted – by the Board of Governors, responded by carrying through a reorganisation of the administrative structure designed to give it more direct financial control, and, in consequence, more direct overall operational control, but in the process lost touch with, and the confidence of, sizeable sections of the staff.

Some sense of this last consequence was, in fact, present among senior officials:

You're up against a communications blockage. Now I'm very worried about communication. Heads of departments, however able themselves, are extremely busy. They don't find it difficult to do their job, to communicate their own ideas and to see their own

> people and to see that their own programmes are on budget and delivered on time, which are the two salient factors in programmes, but they seem to find it very difficult to pass on information about the BBC generally, or about the television service or radio service. . . . I don't think they are good at passing on what they could pass on with advantage.

Disquiet about 'communication' is, of course, a familiar variant of the classic self-confidence trick played by management. The most common form it takes is for all problems to reveal themselves to managers as located, or originating, 'on the shop floor', or at some other subordinate level, but talk of 'failure in communications' serves as a way of interpreting opposition, or misunderstanding or distrust as an impersonal 'problem' in its own right – i.e., as a defective piece of organisational apparatus quite separate from their own conduct, and having nothing to do with the other, more pressing, problems which – at least in 1973 – were only partially and dimly visible to management itself. This is not to say that the proper communication of information is either a trivial concern or is easily provided for. It is simply that 'communication problems' are more often than not symptomatic of structural faults in management, or defects in organisational processes. In the BBC, 'communication problems' seemed to be in large part the consequence of the overriding preoccupation of the management system with monitoring.

All organisations are cooperative systems assembled out of the usable attributes of people. Individuals enter into a contractual undertaking to contribute in specified ways to the achievement of the ends specified by the organisation. While the individual's engagement as a resource affects his conduct and demeanour and self-conception, the organisation, on its side, is also shaped by the contractual engagement – or by the way that engagement is normally interpreted by management. Commitment, at the contractual engagement level, requires supervision. Management has to see, in fact, that contractual undertakings are discharged, and that the resources employed and paid for are being used in its service.

In the early days of this study I became convinced that it was the supervisory part of management which dominated the Corporation. The notion of monitoring as a central managerial concern was a recurrent theme in conversation. According to one account, the function of the Board of Management itself was 'to monitor the work of the Corporation in general'. Another interview contained a lengthy discussion of 'the monitoring system' (under that name), dramatised by reference to a 'top man' who 'tore you apart' if any detail was wrong, or if he turned to an aspect of the situation at issue on which the subordinates before him were uninformed.

Further acquaintance with the Corporation suggested that these reactions were untypical. Nevertheless, monitoring does bulk large in the management system of some sections of the Corporation, especially engineering. Moreover, there are features of management as a whole which have the appearance of corollaries or incidental aspects of a system dominated by the principle of monitoring the performance of subordinates. The Weekly Programme Review in Television is clearly part of such a system.

By monitoring, I mean a strict and critical examination of one's juniors' work which either has to be passed up to one's superiors, or is visible to people outside the section. Obviously, this is a quite essential management task. If, however, this serves as the normal pattern of working relationships between seniors and their juniors, there is a tendency for much effort, and some anxiety, to be put into ensuring that all particulars which might conceivably be relevant are in fact presented, or immediately presentable. There is, of course, a long and esteemed tradition that meticulous precision in this regard is the foundation of sound administration, and that to question its necessity is to point towards the pit of organisational chaos. But it is questionable, even in the most stable of bureaucratic dispensations. In principle, interaction between superior and subordinate should be a two-way affair; the enthusiastic pursuit of perfection in monitoring subordinates may arouse the feeling that nothing less should govern the issue of decisions and pronouncements to them, which means that information affecting the jobs and prospects of sizeable numbers of people may be held up until every question has been settled and every nuance of interpretation and possible misinterpretation has been argued out – leaving subordinates to feed on leaks and rumours.

At all events, there are consequences flowing from the central place in the role of management occupied by monitoring, which, although not by any means peculiar to the BBC, seem to some of its members to bear heavily on its capacity to act quickly and effectively.

Producers, for example, accept the administrative good sense of the head of department's insisting that ideas for programmes be developed fully in a written submission with a detailed exposition of the form of programme, the cast and, eventually, a programme budget estimate, but they contrast this with the liberation of discussion which rescued them from their isolation. 'Nobody can sit in an office between four walls and think up ideas for programmes. At least I can't. Ideas have got to bounce – bounce off other people.' Discussion with superiors succeeded where departmental meetings did not, partly because 'there are fewer people to ridicule you'.

In Engineering, it was said, the need to know everything about the details of a proposal or a problem affected not only the man concerned with presenting them but other people at different levels and in different parts of the division, who might have to know about details which could be referred to them. So, when any document or proposal was going up, not only did the people concerned in presenting it have to know all about it but people 'right across the board' spent a good deal of effort in briefing themselves, in finding out every aspect of the technicalities of a situation which might be referred to them if a blow-up occurred.

Weighty communication of this kind between lower and higher levels generates of itself a heavy load of work. Secondly, it tends to inhibit communication apart from what is absolutely essential. One found quite senior people saying, 'Isn't it really terrible to put something up which is turned down? You go away thinking "what do they think of me?", and they must be thinking too, what I think of them.' So it was not surprising to find that 'putting things up' was seen by many people as a hazardous, arduous, nerve-racking enterprise. ('This', I was told, 'is really the iniquitous part of the organisation.') It was this, I believe, which made for all the barriers to communication up and down the system, the existence of which was deplored so often at management conferences. Thirdly, a secondary system has been developed in the more competitive areas of the Corporation – an unofficial system of communication. Quite specific bits of organisation machinery are involved in this. There are white conspiracies to cover up all kinds of under-cover dodges. A lot was said to depend on the personal contacts one had with other divisions and departments. The real use of committees was also said by some to lie in their usefulness in providing an informal network of personal acquaintance.

Management at the level of supervising performance in terms of contractual engagement is a control system. In the BBC, there is a traditional tendency towards a rather positive control, expressed not in crude or simple authoritarian ways, but through insistence on high standards and the monitoring of performance. If one takes a strictly practical view of this, it is fairly clear that management, if it insists too much, errs on the right side. Reliability, in terms of the technical side of the service, and the BBC's proficiency in terms of broadcasting itself, is only possible if insistence on the best possible performance permeates the whole organisation. There are, however, prices to be paid for pressing this aspect of management so hard. They show themselves here and there in slowness, in an expensive use of managerial time and effort, and in the absolute loss of some of the contribution which junior managers – and producers – have to offer.

The price paid also shows itself in frictional losses and distortions of information as it passes down the system, when top management, as one put it, 'discover, when talking to junior people, that they either do not know what I myself have communicated to their seniors, or have a seriously distorted view of it – to the point of mythology'. This is, of course, a failure of communication – but it may also point to something rather more seriously, and permanently, wrong with the organisation.

THE EXPROPRIATION OF COMMITMENT

'My job', said one senior official of Administration Division in 1963, 'is to encourage attitudes which will pull out of the staff more than you could justify getting out of them by any of the usual criteria which exist in say the business world.' Further, 'what you have in mind when setting conditions of service is to set them so as to get the best out of people. This is an increment you don't pay for, and because of that, it's invaluable. Management is really entitled to so much but what we have to do is to stimulate people into giving all they're capable of.'

Almost any manager would subscribe to such sentiments. They are echoed in public pronouncements on the education and selection of managers, and are implicit in the talk of leadership which is part of the currency of 'business psychology'. What is unusual about the statement is the clear perception it reveals of the distinction between two kinds of commitment – engagement and involvement, or dedication – and the task of management as expanding the latter, and using it. Whether commitment of this latter kind, of dedication, is something which personnel managers can create is doubtful; but it is perceptible when it exists, and management can seek to preserve and even foster it. In the BBC of the early sixties, many, perhaps most, individuals, especially in programme departments, programme services, and engineering seemed ready to devote themselves to ends and to values which were consistent with those of public service broadcasting without being necessarily derived from the BBC as it was, or identified with it, but they were values and ends – as the man I have quoted saw – which a formal contractual undertaking cannot contain or provide for. Neither was the consistency which did obtain, however incomplete, the consequence of some happy accident. The answer, I believe, lies in the fact that the ends and values of the BBC itself were, albeit only in part, and to few people's complete satisfaction, the product of the personal values of the people working in it through which the BBC's ends and purposes, so far as they were identifiable as those of the BBC, were deployed and attained. In fact, in the BBC of the time, one encountered a formidable hierarchy of ends to which individuals dedicated their occupational selves and to which they brought their whole intellectual and intuitive faculties.

The central matter of human organisation lies at this point, where deeply-felt concern in the attainment of best results merges into the elements of organisational requirements. For the specialisms which technological development has introduced into society have created involvement out of the demands they make on ingenuity and skill; operating a television camera or a lighting panel, designing costumes or acting as studio engineer, have grown their own vocational interest and appeal. So that in so far as organisation is a *process* through which individuals are enabled to produce – i.e., make what they do available to others, to socialise their work – organisation is an essential instrument for the accomplishment of their individual ends and values. As against this, in so far as organisation is a *structure* which allocates individuals to specific parts of the total task which the organisation exists to perform, organisation is the scriptwriter of roles to which individuals find they become morally committed.

The oscillation of the whole system between process and structure reveals itself most clearly when committed individuals find themselves baulked of the inner, immaterial, rewards to which their own performance entitled them. Such occasions reveal the fact, and the nature, of organisation as a process by which the collaboration of others is necessary for the realisation of one's own work, *and* of organisational structure as the manufacturer of commitment:

> The producer was never giving the operators time to rehearse and build the thing up into a proper performance. When they eventually came to do the telerecording, half the stuff had been unrehearsed and they couldn't remember what to do properly. Then they'd get terribly exasperated because they'd say, 'Look at the recording – it's lousy; and it wasn't really our fault. It looks as if we didn't do this pan properly, or this move properly, but we never rehearsed it.'
>
> *I suppose what the producer is looking for, inevitably, is the same kind of emotional identification with his production as he gets from his cast.*
>
> He's looking for this, and in fact he gets it. . . .

And again:

> You only get an emotional kick out of a production when it begins to work. A lighting supervisor can really get a tremendous thrill out of something really beautifully lit. He thinks 'Did I really do this? Isn't it marvellous?' . . . But, as you see, you can spend hours and hours and hours gradually building this up, and you can get a tremendous amount of frustration if the producer is always changing things. You're saying, 'I know there's a light

> in the corner there. I wish he'd come to that shot so that I can just see what happens.' You never come to it, and just as he's going to come to it, he decides on something else.

With all its manifold failings, the pre-McKinsey administrative structure reflected and provided for the complementarity between organisational structure and organisational process, and thus recognised the division between contractual engagement and personal involvement.

Programme services had always been within Television Division; what the reorganisation did was to move all technical operators (cameramen, sound and vision engineers, studio engineers) and maintenance engineers in Television Centre into a parallel location within the management structure. In any case, and at all times, the structure of managerial authority was quite separate from the organisation of a production team or, within that, of a studio crew. These are assembled from the individuals available in the programme services and technical operations departments from whom the contributions necessary for any production are requested. Once constituted, the crew has its own organisation. People from Programme Services merely 'work to' the producer. Allocations of staff from programme services are made according to planned schedules worked out by the management of each department. One account of how this is done was given by a designer who had, by 1973, spent ten years in the department.

> *How many people are in the design department – roughly?*
>
> Roughly, I think we've got about eighty designers and sixty assistants, but I may have got that wrong. I'm speaking of scenery design – which is us. In addition, there's Costume, Make-up, Graphics and Design Services – which includes Visual Effects, Scenic Artists, Scenic Projection. All of us together form Design Group. The entire Group comes under C.H., and each department is run by its own head. In our case, S.B. [Head of Television Design Department] is, I suppose, responsible for the day-to-day running of the department, and how we do our jobs.
>
> *There are two jobs, then, one supervising the department in the ordinary sense, the other to do with programming the work, allocating people to different jobs and so on. Does he manage both?*
>
> No. It varies with different departments, but the way it works with us is that we have what is called a design manager's office, which is run by H.S. [Scenic Design Manager]. H.S., in conjunction with S.B., is responsible for allocating the programmes to the individual designer. The way this is done is that a certain

proportion of programmes is allocated on the basis of directors or producers requesting individual designers, as far as this can be accommodated. To a certain extent – though this isn't possible in so large a department – individual designers' wishes may be taken into account.

How do you do this?

For example, someone like F.T., who is my senior designer, a very expert and experienced drama designer – loves drama design, has always worked in drama, and isn't necessarily interested in Light Entertainment design – it's reasonably easy to make sure that she has the sort of design she's interested in. It isn't always possible, because there's an enormous range of work to do across the board. For example, myself, I like a whole range of programmes, which I don't always get. . . . Perhaps one would like a greater variety, but it isn't always possible. . . . One knows one is here to service the requirements of the programmes as they come up.

Ten years ago this used to be fiddled – in the nicest possible way, of course – by designers and camera crews and so on, when the show finished, making sure that the producer, if they liked him, would earmark them. This was done, and done quite successfully. Has that kind of thing gone by the board, now?

To a great extent, it has.

So, while the increased complexity of television production demanded a greater involvement of designers along with other members of each production team, the exigencies of the economic scheduling and use of resources, as articulated by and through the management structure, tended to make working relationships less durable, voluntary and personal, more *ad hoc*, temporary, and dependent on formal procedures. At the same time, the sheer richness of the working environment and the opportunities it afforded for each specialist to develop and to demonstrate his own talents proved overwhelmingly attractive:

Television gives you a very detailed eye and it sharpens your faculties in all sorts of other areas. Why I choose to work for the BBC is not to do with it being a public service corporation, it is to do with the fact that if I'm going to work in television I want to work in a place where the most interesting work is done. I'm not interested, basically, in the fact that I could earn more money with one of the ITV companies. Each ITV company is feeding the network with a range of programmes, but here we're doing one hell of a lot, which means that, as a designer working in a department like this, your chances of doing interesting and stimulating work are very much greater – at least, that's my personal feeling – than when I'm working with a smaller company.

Still, even though working at the BBC offered so much, 'If it was an ideal world for me, I'd spend six months of the year working for the BBC and six months back in the theatre because I think one regenerates the other. Of the two types of design work the theatre is much freer, much more flexible.' So the individual 'project' – the organising principle behind what this woman was investing in her different commitments – is allied to her 'professional' career more than to her role in television production, and far more than to the BBC as a public service broadcasting organisation. Building up understanding and the requisite level of tolerance and tact – assessing the relative competence of the people one was dealing with, and trying and testing out the whole language of communication – of words, gestures, demeanour, and also of all the signs which have to be read to ensure that questions and requests are really understood, and that the answers and responses one got were really appropriate – all these things now have either to be worked out afresh for almost every production, or left to 'the language of bits of papers and forms'. And what is supremely characteristic of the world of broadcasting, especially television, is that the success of a production depends almost entirely on the effectiveness with which working relationships are developed among the whole production and studio team, not just from the director downwards.

Yet, because of the need to allocate time and resources economically, working relationships in a production team, i.e., between all those engaged in making a television programme, had become impersonally 'functional' rather than personal. That is to say, designers, production assistants, cameramen, wardrobe designers, floor managers and so on who worked with each other during one production might well have the same kind of working relationships with the others that they would have in subsequent or previous productions, but the man or woman doing each of these jobs might well be different. Working relationships had become 'de-personalised':

Working here is so full of all the incredible evils you get from working in a big organisation – you know, the terrible thing of no direct communication, everything in the language of bits of paper and forms. You can't go to Joe Bloggs on the floor and say, 'Look, Joe, this is what the show is all about, this is what I'm after, this is the effect I want', you know?

You know what happens in a small organisation? You may go to Joe Bloggs directly, and then he says, 'Well, you bloody well can't have it!'

Yes! [Laughs] This is why I work at the BBC. I feel that working in television as a designer I get a chance of doing more interesting work than I would with another, commercial, employer.

That's very interesting. It means that the emphasis has changed. This squares with what I have heard in other connections with other people. It's very much a world of professionals who work in the BBC because it's a good place to work in for their own thing – not because it's some superb public institution.

Programme services generally, and not merely the design department, had grown between 1963 and 1973, but whereas the advent of colour, the increase in hours of television broadcast (from 4663 hours in 1962–3 to 10,532 in 1972–3), and the greater complexity of productions had enlarged their contribution and made heavier demands on them, the part each played in programme production remained fairly constant. It is among the people whose work was in the studio itself that the full consequences are revealed of the multiplication of demands for reconciling technical possibilities and programme ideas. Reorganisation acknowledged this by shifting all studio engineering staff – lighting and sound engineers, cameramen, studio engineers, and so forth – out of Engineering division to within the widened authority of the Head of Television – now 'Managing Director'.

The technical changes both enhanced the technical contribution of engineering staff *and* demanded greater integration of them with the people involved in producing programmes. All this is best conveyed in the words of a studio engineer who went to some lengths to explain the changes to me; using his words is the more appropriate because, in fact, his explanation – which lasted most of an afternoon – was prompted by a remark of mine, early on, which made it clear that I assumed that the work of the studio engineer was much the same as it had been in 1963: 'a matter of controlling the interface between what is going on in the studio and the central control room'. He set out to correct this obsolete notion.

Apart from any other considerations, the task of lining up cameras and controlling what is coming out of the studio and being passed to Central Control had become 'much more of a team effort':

It is really since the advent of colour that you tend to work more as an actual team; for instance, it is now found beneficial to work in very close liaison with other departments – make-up, costume, lighting – and also to know what the technical limitations of your equipment are. And you have got to make people aware of the technical limitations. For instance, costume. There are certain colours, certain hues, which cannot be seen by present-day colour cameras, and these are mostly in the reds and certain of the blue/greens. Some of these colours can be incorrectly analysed. What can happen is that the costume person can come up and say, 'Why is that costume coming up blue when it is in fact mauve?'

We then have to explain that the reason is that the camera can't see the red content of that particular costume; this is one of the unfortunate side-effects of a colour camera as it stands at the moment, the red tube doesn't see certain reds – the eye sees them, the tube doesn't. [The colour cameras then in use discriminated between man-made dyes and natural dyes; natural dyes often occupy a broader band of the spectrum than artificial dyes.] There is of course a later generation of colour tubes which will in fact analyse these things and you will get exactly the colour, rather than the colour minus red, which can happen at the moment, and can be very off-putting!

So – to come back to the point – since the advent of colour, you are working in very much closer liaison with the production team. I think you might have found perhaps in the monochrome days, when you conducted a similar interview at that time, that studio engineering was rather divorced from programme material, rather more than now, anyway. For instance, we have one lighting engineer who in the past has been working on quite a number of costume drama programmes, and he tends to prefer a sort of candle-light effect on his pictures, which means special treatment for the pictures. Now we can provide that special treatment by adjusting the colour balance in the colour cameras to suit his particular requirements.

I see. And you do all this beforehand, so that it's all lined-up?

That's right. We have a line-up which we adhere to, and this is carried out on the equipment before the start of every rehearsal. We have a camera line-up, subjecting the camera to a black and white chart, the theory being that if you get an immaculate black and white chart out, then the optics within the camera are adjusted, so that when you now point the camera at the normal colour picture, you will get correct colour analysis. This is all done, fundamentally, by lining up your camera on what is called a grey scale; you then adjust the colour balance from the camera so that you maintain a completely neutral black and white.

So there you are. But when you finish that part of the line-up, that's not the end of it, because unfortunately, analysis *between* cameras does vary very slightly, and there are subtle differences.

> Also, the camera does not see subtle changes in a white; the eye is very much more critical when it is looking at flesh tones. Consequently, we employ a colour girl. They are usually actresses. The object here is for the girl, after the initial line-up of the cameras, to sit in front of all the cameras that are all now pointing at her, and you then carry out very subtle adjustments to the colour balancing of the picture to get the flesh tones absolutely identical.

The most obvious consequence of the advent of colour is that rather more technical staff are required than before and that the equipment is more complex. But implicit within these changes is the manifest need for closer understanding between engineers handling different parts of equipment and for mutual understanding of needs, possibilities, constraints and opportunities between them and costume, design, make-up and other services.

Increased technical complexity at this level has clearly made working relationships between all the different specialists represented in the studio more manifold, more varied, and more important for the proper discharge of each individual job. The whole operation is, obviously, much more costly, too.

It is this increase in complexity, I believe, which underlies the almost universal and strongly held belief among staff that the BBC has, during the last ten years, grown enormously in size – has grown, in fact, to the point at which it is 'too big'. I found this repeated comment made in the interviews I conducted in 1973 rather puzzling. In 1963, the Corporation employed 17,930 people, full-time. Just under half of these were engineers, production editorial staff, and staff 'employed in supporting and administrative services'. The rest were secretarial, clerical, manual and catering staff. In 1973 the numbers employed had gone up to more than 23,000. A rise of the order of 28 per cent is certainly fairly sizeable, but spread over ten years hardly seems to warrant the belief that expansion over the ten years had been so rapid and so great (it works out at an average of just over 2 per cent per year) as to render the BBC unmanageably large.

If one turns to the ten years previous to 1963, one finds that numbers grew from 11,686 in 1953. This represents an increase over the ten years of 54 per cent, and nobody, in 1963, seemed to think that the BBC had grown 'too big'.

Even at the point at which the work of studio engineers occurs in a television production, it is still possible to see the growth of complexity as enlarging their task, as bringing them into closer working relationships with programme services, and thus, perhaps, as requiring greater involvement. Yet, like designers, they began and ended their part in production at much the same points as before. When one comes to the studio crew itself, however, the changes were more far-reaching.

> It's a most complicated story, but I can make it brief, though I'll oversimplify it. In the old days we used to have camera crews. You had the dolly-pusher plus the cameraman on Camera No. 1, the same for Camera No. 2, and so on, then the racks engineers [i.e., for manipulating overhead lighting etc.], the chap in the microphone booth, the vision-mixer. So there were twenty or thirty in that particular studio crew. That crew had a gaffer – that's what he actually was – he was called T.O.M., Technical Operations Manager, but the best name was gaffer; he was the boss of the camera [studio] crew. If you were director, you would talk to the gaffer, and if the gaffer thought you were driving 'em too hard, he told you.
>
> Now, as we moved into colour – it had begun to happen before we moved into colour, but the movement into colour enormously intensified this – the specialisation demanded of the gaffer became greater and greater, because, to start with, colour meant far more complicated lighting – and to this was added, by the way, tape [i.e., video recordings]. It meant that if you were going to set up something in the studio, what with colour and tape, chaps like me, directing, wished to have the gaffer at a planning meeting on a Thursday and then to see him again on a Friday afternoon, before going into the studios on, say, Monday, Tuesday and Wednesday. Well, it was agreed; this was a rational demand, but what it meant was that the gaffer, as he had been known up to that time, was no longer a viable chap: you were dividing him into at least two, for a start, and they were both becoming specialists. What's more, they were both becoming specialists who were wanted by the production team not simply on the days on which they were in the studios, but on other days, beforehand. In consequence, there gradually came into being here a whole set-up where you had studio crews – we still have nineteen of them here – who work on all sorts of shift systems, and they will go into a studio and they are at the disposal of the director for the morning, or the day, or for four days, or whatever it is. They come under heads – technical heads – but those technical heads are no longer chaps who are with them all the time – they can't be, you see. This has made an extremely difficult administrative problem of command. I mean, it really has become very difficult to handle studio crews. . . . It's so complicated, it gets insane.

While the increased complexity of television called for more involvement, more commitment to the overall task of producing a programme from the studio crew of technicians and craftsmen, rather than to the pursuit of excellence in one's own special techniques, as was more the case with programme services and studio engineering, management was at the same time developing new modes of control, developing new organisational structures, and creating new means of specifying contractual engagements which required due performance of individual tasks. Early in the seventies, a series of agreements with trade unions were worked out to ensure that directors and crews occupying studios did turn out a minimum amount of finished work, specified in minutes of programme time, for each day, or half-day, they spent in studios. This accentuated the difference, already significant, between working in studios and filming on location, providing additional incentives for directors and technicians to prefer filming programmes to recording them in studios.

When I was here ten years ago, you would find people in these office jobs who would say, 'O.K. I get more money, I can get home in the evenings and so on, that's fine, but it's a hell of a job. You might just as well be working in a cheese factory up here.' 'The best job in the world', I was told by one of them, who had wanted promotion, had got it, and hated it, really, 'the best job in the world is on the studio floor.' That feeling was pretty general. You'd find people who were at the top of Technical Operations – in Engineering Division, then – who obviously felt that – O.K., they were paid more, they had their own office, but really they were second-class citizens. Now, I feel, that's changed. It's not that the people on the studio floor are the second-class citizens, but the management system is really running things now. It really is a system, controls coming in, and costing, which everybody swears by in top management but may, for all I know, be the same kind of nonsense it is in industry, a bit of numbers ritual. . . . Here, it seems to me, you're boxed in, and there is this awareness – not of always being in more or less the same workplace, though you do get a factory-like feeling there sometime – but of this enormous, elaborate, machinery of offices and management all the time. You don't get the same sort of liberated feeling. In the old days, I'd have thought, you did get this liberated feeling as soon as you went into the studio – 'Now we're on the job, and we're all in it together' – and there was a good deal of give and take. . . . The world of film takes you out and still does produce this atmosphere which you described. By and large, I'd have thought that with your productivity agreement there's a good deal of intrusion by this whole apparatus of management into the studios. Studios have become infested with it. Is that true?

Yes, it is.

But one area that hasn't become infected – is filming on location?

> We [film operatives] operate in much the same way as in studios. We have a crew incorporated with a unit – cameraman, lighting, sound, etc. The basic difference is that *I know* all the people on a far more personal basis because I've been away with them on location; I know them by their first names, I know their characters and temperament. But also, I think there's a more light-hearted air about filming – more jocular.

Involvement in the sense in which it used to obtain for studio crews, still obtains; however, in the studios involvement nowadays tends to represent involvement in one's technical specialism. For a film cameraman, working outside, on location, meant something much more:

> I don't think our skills are particularly technical. I wouldn't call myself a technician. I call myself a programme maker. I mean, the sort of skills we bring to the job are artistic more than anything else.

At the same time, explicit control by management was becoming much more distinct from the working organisation established in a studio crew and production team – more distant, and more obtrusive.

> The BBC is now a large institution which has a market and is therefore looking for resources. The corollary of this is that it looks at its staff, whether they are on long-term or short-term contract, or whatever, as resources. This is precisely one of the problems. Because you're a resource, this alters the relationship between you and the people above you; if you're a resource, you're buyable and you're sellable and therefore you're expendable. And perhaps, knowing that is how you are viewed and is how you may be used, it creates this feeling . . . of people being used as objects, which now really seems to be quite considerable.

One way in which management controls, of the kind which became so popular after reorganisation, made themselves obtrusive to staff in production, programme services and technical operations departments was, inevitably, in what seems to them to be the entirely capricious ways in which expenditure was budgeted for and permitted or disallowed. One man was 'shocked at the prodigal way money was thrown around', and cited what he thought of as a classic instance of extravagance:

> I could be more specific about this. One Current Affairs programme was away over budget, flew down all its people from a far-flung empire to London, and put them all into an hotel – to tell them that they were short of money and everyone would have to tighten belts! But that's only one example of it.

A classic instance, perhaps, but not so much of extravagance – the same sort of incident could be quoted in almost any organisation of comparable size – as of the way in which cross-purposes can be generated between management structure and organisational process, which, in broadcasting, represent different kinds of commitment linked in different systems of relationships between different people.

Members of studio crews and film crews were prepared to reel off catalogues of examples of wastefulness, needless expenditure, irresponsibility and downright theft, contrasting this with what struck them as the penny-pinching procedures applied by the accountants to their own legitimate claims:

> . . . a motor-car kept all day, when someone should have told the driver to go after the first shot, but they forgot. So this Rolls-Royce – and driver – costs them a great deal of money. Now I put an expense in. When I come home I put '15p – telephone call home'. It's crossed out – 'No, we don't pay for that.' You see? On one side squandering; on the other side they worry about pence.
>
> *It happens in every organisation I know. It may, though, be more crucial here because you're dealing in the ephemeral. But the ephemeral, people think, ought to be cheap. You don't have ephemeral Rolls-Royces – if you have a Rolls-Royce, it really means something. With ordinary people, if they have a Rolls – for a wedding, or a funeral – which is the only damn time you do – you hire it by the hour. You don't worry about that too much, but you don't forget and leave it hanging about. There's a general commonsensical feeling about it.*
>
> There just seems to be no idea of waste.

Keeping a watchful eye for extravagance and waste is not a significant item in the code of professionalism; it is for management. And the cult of professionalism, as the designer quoted earlier showed, has been fostered by the growth of management controls. One consequence of scheduling time and resources to ensure their economical use is that technical specialists find working relationships with other specialists more problematical, more effortful, and subject to more formalities and thus find greater satisfaction in devoting themselves to their own specialist interests or to improving their own competence – and this despite the demand for closer and more immediate working relationships with others which increased complexity has brought. The organising principle which the professional follows is his professional future rather than the success of the whole production team's task or, beyond that, of the BBC or, ultimately, of 'some public service broadcasting idea'.

The biggest change in the BBC between 1963 and 1973 was not, I believe, the reconstruction of top management, the institution of stricter financial budgeting and surveillance, the increase of the powers of Managing Directors and the Controllers under them, or the depletion of the 'baronial' powers of heads of group and heads of department, nor was it increase in size, or increased union militancy or the appearance of a 'radical underground'. What did make the difference was the breakdown of the ordinary institutions of social interaction between the variety of people engaged in programme production – i.e., the unanticipated consequences of those changes, which did more to alter the internal working of the organisation than the intentional changes effected by management.

There is in most workplaces an extraordinarily large and diverse number of modes of social exchange, interaction and conversational conduct, all of them carrying some of the moral weight of institutions or of conventions. It is these which subtend work relationships – which make them, in fact, 'workable'. This necessary foundation for the kind of work the BBC existed to carry out had, in 1963, been brought to an exceptionally high pitch of refinement. They are not to be thought of, I should emphasise, as an appropriate, tributary, response to an efficient structure of management control, or even as some voluntaristic system of action called forth by the manifest need for organisational processes. They are rather the preconditions of the effective operation of this kind of organisation – the fabric of relationships through which both structure and processes have to work. The remainder of this chapter deals with some aspects of this fabric of social interaction, by way of illustration, and with its significance to individuals and to the organisation. It was this fabric which, by 1973, (or so it seemed to me) had been seriously eroded by the development, to a large extent complementary, of managerialism and professionalism in the intervening years.

THE COMMON INTERESTS OF COMMON RESOURCES

While the distinction between ourselves as total persons and ourselves as human resources may become concrete only at revelatory crises of competition for appointment or preference, or in moments of self-doubt or introspection, it remains alive, though latent, in our persistent efforts to improve our chances for betterment when the time comes. These efforts may be made individually or in combination. Since what counts for the organisation is the individual's contribution as a resource, it is manifestly often appropriate to argue the claims of the resource itself to more attention and higher rewards. In doing so, we find ourselves promoting in an organised way the interest of those who share some or all of the elements of the resource with which we are identified – with our particular skill, or job, or more generally with our educational qualifications or our knowledge of life or the organisation, with youth and energy or with experience and *savoir faire*, with research results or with teaching experience, with technical know-how or with creative flair.

The BBC is a highly segmented organisation. This is clear enough to some of its members, especially those who find themselves in departments or production teams contending with other departments who are regarded, and regard themselves, as inevitable or traditional rivals. It is not, of course, the product or even the by-product of some system inaugurated by management protocol, and so something which can be reformed by the issue of a new manual of instructions. So the new management system, while it has brought integration to top management, has not altered the segmentary character of the social order which is an intrinsic part of the BBC's organisation which has developed over time, and which persists at all levels below the very highest.

Any complex organisation must, by definition, divide its total task according to a recognised division of labour among a number of individuals and groups of individuals. Each section of the total task ordinarily requires to be treated as a whole job, to which individuals may often devote themselves regardless of the totality into which it fits, or of the other fractional tasks being performed elsewhere in the organisation. But for many reasons, which I have tried to set out in previous chapters, such commitments are not bounded by the task itself, and have consequences for the individual which extend far beyond work performance. They also have consequences for the organisation. The structural divisions of an organisation – between functionally different sections, between managers and staff – may serve as frontiers between conflicting groups. Such conflict need not, of course, appear in any dramatic form. It makes itself felt as a series of more or less difficult episodes and situations. Any manager, working according to any system of management, must impose some constraints on the way in which his staff do their jobs and conduct themselves in the organisation, and these constraints inevitably arouse some resentment, often even when they are understood and accepted. Again, people find that superiors, or subordinates, have misconstrued remarks or pronouncements, and feel annoyed or frustrated. Managers find deep and horrid meanings being read into notices, and staff find their unthinking reactions, or their banter, being treated as revealing fundamental attitudes. Managers and staff resent being caught unawares by new moves. Everybody can suspect from time to time that he is undervalued, or believe that his best effort has gone unacknowledged. Ultimately, feelings of dissatisfaction or insecurity are projected, by what seems to be an unfailing psychological process, on to other people's ignorance, stupidity, obstructiveness, hostility, or personal inadequacy.

All these experiences are endemic in any organisation; they are the frictions generated by a less than perfect competence in dealing with others. What matters organisationally is when the frictions themselves are aligned with structural divisions – between departments, between management and staff, and between categories of staff. In this case, structural division of the organisation, the functional and technical differences between people's jobs, the relevant technology itself, and the differences in rank, power and rewards which therefore obtain, present people with a system which they themselves must organise in their favour, or lose out.

> But you know generally what the level of everybody is. All the lighting supervisors know pretty accurately what the grade is of the floor manager of what the grade of a designer is. Because they regard themselves as of equal status with these people, at least. Now they therefore, I think, keep a very close eye on the relativities. 'Am I slightly higher or slightly lower than Jones?' is what's in the uppermost of your mind rather than the absolute amount of money. 'Can it be presented that my job is in fact more important than Jones' job?' In the end – 'Can you formulate it into a scheme which the union could make into a claim?'

Commitment to alliances with colleagues is an extension of the basic engagement of the individual to the concern. It reinforces the definition of the individual as resource. Commitment to the organisation, since it is as a resource, carries with it the implication of commitment to one section in rivalry with others; individuals are thus both co-operating members in the common enterprise of the concern and members of rival groups in competition with each other for a greater share of the benefits available. One account by a manager in Technical Operations, Television, in 1963, gives a somewhat different account from that supplied by a senior manager in Television ten years later (see p. 268), and fills in some of the episodes omitted in his professedly 'oversimplified' review of the factors which provoked the series of changes in the organisation of studio crews:

> Once again we go back to history. Originally you had the senior maintenance engineer in the studios. He was in charge of everything, including the maintenance. We then had a split between maintenance and operations and this man became Technical Operations Manager, also in charge of everything. You then began to find that he wasn't an expert on lighting; lighting people were always rather specialised. You had therefore to increase the status of the lighting man, and for a long period the

> Technical Operations Manager and the Lighting Supervisor were the same grade, and worked as a partnership.
> Now the Sound Supervisor remained part of the crew, and very submerged. For the last couple of years sound has become more and more important. This is another sidelight on politics. When I say it became more important, the physical evidence of this was that producers began to say, 'Ought we not to get Studio Managers in from sound broadcasting, where they really understand sound, instead of these silly people who came from Technical Operations?' So what we did was to say, 'Well, we must increase the status and expertise of the Sound Supervisor and we'll start off by increasing the number of Sound Supervisors and allowing them to go to outside rehearsals and planning meetings.' This once again reduced the status of the Technical Operations Manager, who no longer had to do anything with sound. So you get a troika: Technical Operations Manager, Lighting Supervisor, Sound Supervisor, all going to [producers'] planning meetings. The Lighting Supervisor deals with most of the vision side, Sound Supervisor deals with most of the sound side. What's the Technical Operations Manager to do, query? Only the oddments which the other two haven't dealt with. Wouldn't it be better for the other two to deal with the lot? This is the state we've reached now. Still, we agree that a third man is needed. In practice the producer needs somebody sitting at his right hand to whom he can turn when Bloggs fails to do what he should have done. So what we're doing is saying that the Lighting Supervisor becomes an overall vision supervisor, with an assistant. The assistant sits beside the producer and finds out what goes on in case the senior man is busy on the floor dealing with the lighting.

Exit, therefore – although, as it proved, only for a brief period – the Technical Operations Manager.

The label 'engagement' has been applied to contractual commitment. It applies, to begin with, to the undertaking into which the individual enters to contribute in specified ways to the achievement of ends specified by the concern. But there are consequential undertakings which the individual may enter into with other contributors so as to enhance the value of the resource they and he contribute. So, while the basis of trade union claims is the labour-value of the contribution of all members to a concern, this can in many cases best be done by advancing the claim of one set of people as against others, especially in large concerns like the BBC, where rivalry between groups tends to be organised and given institutional form.

For the unstable and complex system of organisational purposes to be realised and pursued by individuals and groups, there has to be a superstructure of involvement, or dedication, added to the contractual engagement which binds people to a concern. Because involvement, in this sense, means the assumption by the individual of aspirations, values, and purposes which are private to him, as well as implicit in the ends and functions of the organisation, involvement is personal, autonomous and, except in special circumstances, distinct from attachment to the organisation as it presents itself to him. In the last few pages we have been examining the way in which such involvement, while in general consistent with organisational ends, may yet generate rivalries which are not in accordance with the purposes and effectiveness of the organisation, in the same way as the contractual form of commitment carries with it consequential engagements to sections and grades, and so provides a foundation for internal politics.

Nevertheless, despite its apparent independence of organisational needs and requirements, the involvement which is so essential an element in the contribution required of the individual is still rooted firmly in the simple business relationship with the concern in which membership itself is founded. This is best demonstrated by reference to television producers, whose involvement and professionalism carries the highest value. For, in this case, there are alternative basic business relationships between the individual and the Corporation. One can either be established as a permanent member of staff, or be engaged on contract for a few years. The very existence of the alternative has interesting implications.

The advent of short-term contracts in television is, in some ways, yet another symptom of the changed social situation of the Corporation. Television broke the BBC monopoly in broadcasting in more ways than one. The craftsmanship of promotion, or the conventions, the dramaturgic skills, the machinery and the design resources of stage and films all became more immediately relevant to broadcast production. As television developed, a little of the traffic began to move the other way.

Producing or contributing to television programmes is interesting in its own right, the medium offers its own problems, challenges and opportunities, it is no longer a freak. Nevertheless, BBC Television, although a very special part of the world of journalism, cinema, theatre and entertainment, is perceived very much as part of it, not only by performers, but by producers and editors and their aides.

This breaching of the occupational and cultural barriers has been acknowledged concretely by a new kind of business relationship between the Corporation and staff in programme departments. In Fleet Street, and especially the theatre, in films and in the entertainment industry, work is traditionally insecure, unpredictable in its rewards, or, at best, subject to specific contract for a limited period. In the Corporation work is traditionally secure, established, and – virtually, if not contractually – for life. But the Corporation now offers a proportion of short-term contracts for producers and other professional and technical staff.

This has all the appearance of a sensible, indeed, a necessary, shift of policy. It introduces a useful flexibility into the difficult task of recruiting suitable people for the crucially important function of producing television shows. But the two kinds of engagement appear to encourage the belief that there are two quite different kinds of people whose personalities, or expectations, or ambitions square with each kind of contract. Interviews with producers under either kind of contract, moreover, give almost the impression of a package of values and beliefs which are associated with the two types of engagement.

First, a television producer on the established staff:

> *What brought you into the BBC?*
>
> I wanted to continue working in the entertainment industry, I wanted a higher salary and more security than I thought the theatre offered me – by this time I was married, with two children, and a third on the way – and I think it's true to say that almost everyone in the entertainment industry wants to work in the BBC at some stage or another in their careers.
>
> *What do you think they do want this for? One can see that 'a good steady job' is attractive – is there anything beyond this?*
>
> Oh yes. Basically, the entertainment industry is run by thugs, and there's a general feeling that the BBC isn't – that it's a civilised organisation. And this is perfectly true. It enables someone who wants to do something creative to do it without feeling that the pressure of profit motives is going to disturb everything he wants to do. . . . I'd think there's a certain prestige . . . to say to people I work for the BBC carries something – some weight. It carries weight even with one's bank manager.

No other kind of employment in the entertainment industry offers anything like comparable advantages; every producer, whether established or on short-term contract, was well aware of them, and they counted overwhelmingly with most.

There are some important qualifications and corollaries to be made, but for the present it is sufficient to point out that what is under discussion is a kind of social contract between producers and the Corporation which extends well beyond the business contract and the monetary considerations which undoubtedly do cement people to their jobs in the Corporation, and which do bulk large in discussions – because they are the only considerations which can usefully be discussed, and because in turn, they can be changed arbitrarily and effectively.

Nevertheless, it is this social contract, with all its implications, which some people reject, not the settled income.

> If you've got something else to hang on to – if you've got another life – if you've been meeting writers and artists, as I have, a different world altogether – so much the better, because it gives you something to set against the BBC.
>
> *What does this mean, exactly? Does it mean that you don't really want to commit yourself to an organisation?*
>
> No, I don't. It's a personal opinion, but the idea of being on long-term contract, signing away maybe ten, twelve, twenty years of my life, is complete anathema. –

The very existence of short-term contracts gives established posts the appearance of lifelong unbreakable, indentured service.

> I would never want to work for the Corporation except on short-term contract. But I'm not married, and maybe that's a lot to do with it.
>
> *Yes, though not every marriage leads to a semi-detached house and a car.*
>
> But I think marriage, to a bachelor, does.

Marriage to the BBC meant, in this case, having to settle permanently in London, only four weeks off a year, a wholehearted commitment to television, to name only the more obvious drawbacks.

The producers I have quoted were a year or two on each side of thirty. One can presume that they were either actually or potentially valuable members of their department. One can more certainly presume that each was aware of the existence, and of the benefits, of the other kind of relationship. Neither really conceived the choice as between security and constraint on the one hand, and insecurity and freedom on the other.

Each kind of reaction, each set of valuations, is in fact a crystallisation of beliefs around the two kinds of contract offered by the Corporation. Both reactions were feasible because both relationships are possible; a decision one way or the other precipitates and forms the values attached to them – or rather, attracts and organises them into a coherent confession of beliefs. The upshot is two alternative arrangements of commitment, and ultimately, two sets of life-chances and careers, one institutionalised in terms defined by the Corporation and its activities, the other in terms of the traditions of the independent professional artist, writer and actor.

THE CONDITIONS OF ENGAGEMENT AS A HUMAN RESOURCE

Unavoidably, in all the talk of a BBC type, of dominant models of conduct, of age-grading, and commitment, there is conveyed an impression of individuals being moulded into conformity with certain patterns of personality and conduct which are somehow determined by the Corporation. The half-truth here is more misleading than most. What is missing is the perspective provided by the notion of entelechy. The behaviour we have been discussing is a small coherent range of forms of conduct organised out of people's potentialities, which are not infinite, perhaps, but are wider in range than what is observable in the actual behaviour of members of the Corporation. In fact, the truth, as against the half-truth, of the matter lies not in mapping a structural matrix in which conduct and personality are formed, but in seeing how people learn to guide their conduct into the distinctive forms people in the Corporation present to the observer.

The ambiguity present in the concept of commitment is fundamental. The total membership of a concern represents the human resources assembled in achieving its ends. But also, of course, the total membership of a concern *is* the concern; the ends it exists to serve can only be posited, let alone realised, in so far as they represent obligations, undertakings, or purposes which may be discharged by the individual and corporate efforts of the people who constitute the concern. In either sense, as system of resources or system of ends, the concern is ordered into a hierarchy. Resources are exploited and administered through a hierarchy of controls, which is also one of commitments. The hierarchy itself therefore assumes a dual character, displaying in one guise the human resources and their exploitation, and in the other the ends which each individual sets out to serve.

So, in the first place, a man gets a job in a concern because of his utility as a resource (proved or potential) of physical strength, manual dexterity, technical information or skill, business experience, creative ability, and so forth. The search by management for the right constellation of skills and interests leads to a very precise articulation of requirements, even in the case of adolescents, who, besides adequate performance in school leaving examinations, have to fit a human specification:

> Now we've trained the recruitment people to realise that a technical operator has got to be interested in the arts, photography – it would be nice if he could play the guitar, had joined his local drama group, or had learned to make 16mm. films in his spare time. . . . You need a man who is basically going to fit in with a theatrical career, as it were, the sort of man who in other circumstances might become studio manager or even possibly an actor – though, ah, this is going a bit far, because an actor's often highly untechnical.

However, such specifications inevitably become current knowledge among the sections of the population which contain potential recruits, and the search for the right constellation of talents and interests finds its answer in the individual aspirant's collection of testimonials to the presence of such interests and talents in himself:

> I set out to fit my university life to what I saw were the kinds of things the BBC looked for. I knew they wanted the kind of man who'd been Secretary of the Union, produced shows for the dramatic society, and edited the student newspaper, or at least written for it. So in my last years I ticked each of them off. . . .

For most of one's working life the distinction between oneself as a resource and oneself as a 'whole person' can remain concealed; the functionary who limits his conduct and demeanour to the strict requirements of his task is a fearsome or comic automaton. But for all of us there are times when the distinction between assessment of ourselves, by employers or their agents, as containers of usable faculties and information, and their fellowship with us in common humanity, becomes disconcertingly apparent: when we present ourselves as candidates for appointments; or when promotion vacancies occur; or when we ask for resources or backing for enterprises identified with ourselves. It is at these times that the expressive aspect of our personality – our persona – receives an almost cosmetic treatment; we proffer only the more relevant qualifications and the more congenial qualities, and mask those sentiments, beliefs, or biographical episodes which may be inconsistent with or, at best, irrelevant, to the requirements for use of oneself made explicit by the employers or regarded as implicit.

This is not a matter of simple duplicity; it would be less worthy of attention as a social phenomenon and more easily controlled if it were. What is involved is the adaptation of behaviour to the forms most approved and rewarded by the organisation – the easiest, most rational, and commonest thing in the world. It accords with the acquisition of technical and educational qualifications which will do similar service. However, it does happen that where a high premium is placed on success, and where there is accordingly an unusually strong urge to develop a socially and technically impressive front, a visible division may appear between the impression one conveys to arbiters and sponsors and that which one's fellows and subordinates see.

All conduct has an expressive aspect, and all individuals endeavour, more or less deliberately, more or less persistently, to control the impressions this is likely to arouse in others. Most individuals assume more than one front, and there are occasions when their acquaintances familiar with one will have opportunities to see another, and to infer the purposes for which it is assumed; children are often disconcerted by such occasions when their parents are involved; adults are sometimes critical of others in whom they observe such changes:

> You mustn't get so used to producing people that this colours your whole attitude to people, being the big lord, you know . . . I think it shows far more when they're dealing with canteen staff, or someone who's only come to sweep the floor, because they're people they've no need to impress – one's attitude to them then should be as to people as such, and not to people in some special position. But it's then you can see that below a certain level, people don't matter. They don't think this consciously, but it sort of happens.
>
> *Oh, I see what you mean – they treat such people with a certain amount of disregard. Oh, but this is very usual stuff, very human. . . .*

There is also suspicion of those whose capacity for dramatically effective self-presentation carries a particular front into inappropriate situations.

> . . . *I thought you meant the other thing, which is insidious, that they get so much to enjoy their skills in manipulating people that they employ them on everybody within sight.*
>
> This is the other side of the thing. Yes, I'm sure this is true, and it's very unpleasant.

Reasonably sophisticated people are themselves conscious at times of the falsities into which commitment to the contemporary ethos of their occupational world leads them. It forms a favourite theme in the fictional genre created out of the occupational world of advertising agencies and newspapers by Sunday novelists. But the experience is real enough, is an inescapable danger of exposure to the demands of organisational 'civilisation', and is felt as a constraint, or as a distorting pressure.

The generalised pressures exerted by the organisation on the individual seem to be experienced in two different ways. Some objectify the experience, and see themselves as somehow at odds with 'the system':

> I'm one of those people who started with the Corporation when he left school, who left school during the war, who didn't have a good education – I had a so-called technical education. . . . I joined this Division and stayed in it throughout. And really I'm not really qualified to judge the Corporation. . . . And this worries me a great deal.
>
> *Oh, does it?*
>
> Yes. It always has.
>
> *Why?*

> Because I often think that some of the feelings I have about the Corporation – feelings . . . [long pause] . . . feeling rather ineffective, I suppose, ineffective against the system . . . Whether this is a function of any – of being in a large organisation, or of the BBC kind of organisation. . . . One sees this not as people but as a vague thing.

The other formulation is a concern about an occupational self which has been developed out of personal resources assembled and groomed to accord with the organisation's requirements. There is a fear lest this occupational self take over, and affect the impression which is conveyed to others in any context whatsoever:

> There's one thing I've always felt, and that is, whatever job you're doing, not to let that job shape you as a person. I mean, for example, someone who doesn't know you're a teacher, he can go away and say 'he's a teacher'. Do you know what I mean?
>
> *I do indeed.*
>
> Any job is going to develop certain sides of you. . . . Academics get over-academic. . . .
>
> *What are the other things you have to be aware of not being?*
>
> This sounds too much like preaching. . . .
>
> *Yes, but you have to be aware of these things if you are to avoid them.*
>
> Exactly. I can't put this at all to be just, because on the whole my impression of the BBC is favourable. . . . You have to be terribly well up on the done and the not-done – but even to say that isn't true . . . I didn't feel that people were studying me to see whether I was the right kind of chap, but this is my fear, that one has to be the right sort of chap.
>
> *You're afraid you do measure up?*
>
> Well, I suppose, in a sense, I might. What I'm trying to say in all this – is that there's a danger the BBC wants people to be the chaps they like, who'll fit into certain patterns. You can be intellectually way-out, but at the same time you must have the right sort of accent and the right approach, and if you've got a northern accent, you must have something else to compensate.

The final aspect of the dualism arising from the contractual engagement to the concern, then, is one involving the conscious development of different selves. Perception of the kind of qualities and skills the sponsors of their careers seem to look for encourages the development of a front which is occupationally presentable. ('Looking knowledgeable is terribly important in the studios', one senior engineer said, and truly – non-technical people have to rely on people who look reliable.) Offsetting this is an 'ordinary', 'integral', above all 'fuller' self, essentially non-occupational and non-competing, which is formed almost consciously by way of refuge or disclaimer.

This partitioning of the self, like the strategic manipulation of one's occupational experience and conduct in the pursuit of advancement, and like the membership of different social groupings distinct in age, behaviour style, and so on, must be set in the context of the self-awareness apparent in all the quoted interviews, and which is indeed an essential element in the capacities we develop to carry off a multiplicity of social commitments. There is, in all behaviour, a sense in which we observe our actions and our participation. Often enough latent, the sense springs into the forefront of consciousness when we are faced with a 'first occasion', a situation new to us but familiar to the others present, or when the most desperate search for a prescription for a line of conduct fails. It is at these times that an 'Is this really me?' question obtrudes itself, and sometimes absurdly, sometimes painfully, divorces us from reality.

The sensation of unreality, of a world of social existence which is seen as a total artefact and also to be devoid of meaning, is a common enough experience, although it is usually transient, outside pathological states. Short of this, however, the consciousness of the artificiality of one's own conduct and demeanour seems to be more acute among people whose social roles are newly developed, not fully 'institutionalised', in the sense that the exchange value of all the kinds of behaviour appropriate to the role on all occasions is not unquestionably established. The BBC is full of uncertainties of this kind. Sensitivity about commitments, about the partitioning of the self, and about the absorption of the self into the different systems which make up the occupational milieu of broadcasting, seems to derive from an endemic uncertainty about the rules of the particular game one is playing, or whether the rules are recognised by other players, or about the object of the game. This sensitivity, which is so familiar an element of the experience of members of therapeutic and training groups during their first sessions, expresses itself in the emergence into consciousness of the inner observer. To observe oneself in this way is to detach oneself from full participation, to dissociate an essential part of oneself from the business in hand.

It is in this sense that the Corporation remains, for many people – perhaps the majority of those I met in 1963 and in 1973 – an unreal world. More than elsewhere, 'commitment' to one's job, to one's career, colleagues and even to oneself is visibly bracketed in quotation marks, is self-conscious – an 'act'. The difference, however, is one of degree, and rests on the novelty and insecurity – the insufficient establishment in society – of the principal roles available in broadcasting, and, finally, on the still questioned role of broadcasting itself.

SOCIAL INTERACTION, SKILLED AND UNSKILLED

It is in the television studio that the distinction between contractual engagement and personal commitment is most obvious, and when the contrast between supervising contractual engagement and creating personal commitment is most vivid. Monitoring the work of individuals in contractual engagement terms is, in fact, largely the task of supervisors and managers not present in the studio. Creating personal commitment – involvement – is the director's affair.

The television director, in organising a production, is faced with an *ad hoc*, heterogeneous, assemblage of individuals and groups. While they acknowledge his authority so far as the direction of their contracted work is concerned, he has none over the definition of their functions, powers, or responsibilities. Yet the success of a production depends largely on his success in persuading them not merely to act, to operate cameras, to design sets, to plan a lighting plot, in ways which will fit in with the scheme of production, but to exploit their special capacities to the full in the interests of the programme, and in the development, expansion, improvement of his ideas. He has to generate as full an involvement in the success of the production as possible, and an equal commitment to himself as the leader of the whole organisation. To do this, many producers seemed to work up an odd, fictive, style of authority, something we can perhaps best call pseudo-charisma.

The development of involvement is critically important at the early stage of planning meetings and first meetings with cast, and it is at this point that the producer exercises to the full what social skills he has so as to fabricate the temporary bonds of commitment. Pseudo-charisma, in this context, denotes the finished explication of one or the other recognised models of theatrical demeanour and conduct – 'camp' or 'butch' – together with effective devices to achieve empathy – jokes, host display, and a curiously common feature, a Cockney, or even a Liverpool, accent. All these appurtenances of a producer's appropriate persona are almost consciously donned at the commencement of a planning meeting or a rehearsal; there is an observable moment of bracing. Significantly, there is room for only one such performance in any setting; when a planning meeting for a production was interrupted by the executive producer of the series, liveliness and temperamental quality at once transferred to him, the director assuming a rather flat, businesslike tone.

Outside the special relationship between directors and the leading members of the production team and studio crew, work relationships between senior people and the staff under them are both more durable and less susceptible to natural or assumed styles of command.

Even in the most rigorously ordered system of management and supervision, many of the items which enter into the definition of jobs, and the way they are to be done, are worked out by a common consent arrived at by work groups in the face of precedent, of the demands of the job as acknowledged by them, and of direct instructions or requests delivered by their superiors. 'Work norms', if the phrase may be used in this connection, thus represent a shifting balance of feasible demands for time and effort, a balance which has limits of oscillation and a 'true level'. Subordinates, no less than superiors, have to be perceptive about the balance and the limits. As Mason Haire once remarked: 'How late is late? The answer to this question is not to be found in the rule book, but in the superior. Late is when the boss thinks it is late. Is he the kind of man who thinks 8.00 is the time, and 8.01 is late? Does he think that 8.15 is all right occasionally if it is not a regular thing? Does he think that everyone should be allowed a five-minute grace after 8.00 but after that they are late?'

But in the case of studio crews, involvement is not something which can be elicited by the demeanour or style of conduct of a manager or supervisor; often enough, there is no direct working relationship, as there is between director and cast, and between director and leading members of the studio crew. What does operate is a tacit code of behaviour which was assumed to be known to every member of the crew. The correct reading of the balance of demands and obligations which are regarded as appropriate for any particular occasion requires immersion in the prevailing codes, and universal, though unspoken acknowledgement of their rightness. There is involvement, but it is a compliant involvement. The ability to appraise the correct balance without explicit appeal or order is essential. To make an explicit rule about lateness, for example, indicates ignorance of the importance of the system of consent or an outright betrayal of it.

> I remember some years back, when I was in the studios this was, we used to have one chap who was always turning up late. . . . It was always this one man. Well, eventually it was decided that something had to be done, so everybody was told that they had to show up on time at 10. Well, there was a lot of cribbing about this, but the people who created most – as you'd expect, really – were just the people who nearly always turned up fifteen minutes early. . . . If we went by rules rather than by conscience, the Corporation would lose out. But this can only come from being brought up in the atmosphere of the Corporation.

With so much dependent on the ability of superiors to perceive the boundary between explicit specification of the needs of a particular job and tacit recognition that the engineering specialists or technical operators or designers or production assistants working under them see these needs as written into their roles, people acting as superiors have to rely on their own ability to read the extent to which behaviour and demeanour complies with requirements. This must mean that they look for compliance with their own view of the requirements of the work situation – with their own appraisal of 'conscience' and 'atmosphere'.

> You get youngsters falling into traps – not understanding the way things go in this place. The biggest trap I suppose is the mateyness. Some youngsters get deceived by this, youngsters with no real discipline. I had one of them in here only recently. We had a very interesting conversation, really – because after a time we got to talking quite openly. He said he saw no reason why his opinions about things outside work weren't just as worth saying as his boss's. I said there's lots of opinions I have which I don't parade in front of my bosses. After all, I said, people fifteen or twenty years older are entitled to some deference. . . . He was one of the chaps – you know – he kept looking out of the window when I was talking to him. I took him up on this – he said he'd always done that at school – used to play with his pencil, look miles away, while the teacher was speaking. Then they'd jump on him with a question and he'd always know the answer – make them furious!

Outside the fairly prescribed boundaries within which specific instructions are given, therefore, jobs have to be carried out in compliance with the needs of the particular situation, in compliance with one's superior's reading of those needs, and, what is more, in compliance with some code of deferent behaviour which indicates to that superior that his reading is accepted.

Optimally, a superior's reading of the requirements of the situation allows for discussion of them and of ways of meeting them. But this is not always so, and the tact on which the system of compliance rests is replaced by a positive demand for obedience. Again, this is behaviour which implicitly distinguished commitment to one's specialist task from commitment to the organisation as it is.

'Wearing one's rank' seemed to run so much counter to the obvious egalitarianism of manner which prevails in many aspects of the Corporation's world that I had some difficulty in accepting it as a substantial element in management. That this is so, that 'doing things my way' can be insisted on as a matter not of the argued rationale of a situation but of superior rank, was maintained by people in very different parts of the Corporation.

Do people wear their rank? There are said to be occasions when a junior having some mild – or serious, for that matter – difference of opinion about the way a thing should be framed, can be told: 'Look I'm two grades above you, or one grade, I'm senior man here, and we'll do it the way I want it.' When I first heard this, I thought this was probably a peculiar situation – untypical. Would you agree?

I haven't come across it in exactly that way.

Nobody above you . . . ?

But the situation exists. Definitely. Even half a grade. You know, 'I'm in charge of this part of the organisation, and I want it done this way. We may have discussed it beforehand, but this is what's got to be.' This is no exception.

So far, what is under discussion is the devolution through the management hierarchy of the Corporation's authority to direct the effort of individuals under contractual engagement to it. But commitment at this level is not enough in the Corporation, where management is everywhere conscious of the need to involve people in their work over and above the measure of their contractual engagement.

There's no feeling that you have to carry people with you, whatever the cost?

This varies from situation to situation, and person to person. I'd say it goes with the organised part of the labour force, when chaps are very very sensitive, and very delicately treated. There are many occasions when people have to be 'carried' with you in this way. I'd say there was an equal number of occasions – more often when dealing with individuals or small numbers of fairly closely graded people, that you get the senior person finishing things by saying 'It's got to be done my way, and now you will support my policy', and not only that, I'm conscious on certain occasions when I'm one of the people having this kind of thing imposed upon me, of it not being satisfactory just that you concede this point, that the senior, confronted with a conflicting view has the right to make the decision, and I, as a loyal member of the staff, will support it. This is not enough. You have to subjugate your own opinions completely, and accept that this is the right way to do it. – As far as that. And there's a feeling of antagonism there if you don't.

The pressures on senior people to act in this fashion were said to arise from the insecurity attached to lower – or lowered – technical competence among older people and to the compelling need to maintain or raise the department's 'professional' standing. There were also said to be a few personal tragedies occasioned by lapses from professional standards, enough to make this a matter of constant preoccupation which would lead to an over-anxious dominance of subordinates' activities. While it may be true, and it is a familiar aspect of higher rank in large organisations, that compelling subordinates to swear their faith in the rightness of decision is evidence of doubt about their rightness, it may also be seen as an attempt to escape from the loneliness, and the onus, of command which (hierarchic) forms of management thrust on people, into shared responsibility.

ORGANISATIONAL PROCESSES WITHIN MANAGEMENT

Below top management, the Corporation is divided into directorates, divisions, groups and departments, and these are further subdivided as one nears working level. All divisions of this kind, following normal organisational practice, are in accordance with the technical division of labour among the BBC's total resources, complicated only by the need to disperse some specialisms throughout the whole structure and some also among a number of different locations within the London area as well as in the regions.

At working level, however, organisational requirements are quite different from the normal requirements of managerial control. Operations and planning in almost all aspects of the ultimate task of producing programmes and broadcasting them calls for combinations of people from many different branches and levels of the whole structure. And above the operational level of production teams and studio crews, and of the attendant film and telerecording editing staff, maintenance engineers, carpenters, scenery painters, and the rest, there has to be a system by which such combinations can be planned for and agreed between the managements of the sections in which the individual members of staff are, for managerial purposes, located.

It is the complementary nature of the structure of managerial control and operational coordination which makes organisational processes in the Corporation so different in character from what obtains in manufacturing industry and, for that matter, in most service industries. In these, operations can themselves be distributed among sections of the whole structure, and their coordination handled for the most part (although by no means entirely) by the same management structure which exists for control purposes. There is in the BBC, however, a balance to be maintained between managerial structure and organisational process which is far more important, and difficult, than it is in most organisations, where both can be accommodated within the same system – i.e., the management structure. For organisational effectiveness in the BBC is a function more of the proper working of organisational processes as against management structure than it usually is. Indeed, the history of the past twenty years suggests that the BBC has been at its best when the network of working relationships through which organisational processes are given effect was much more apparent in operational practice than was the structure of management control – factious and friction-laden though that network was, awkward and bothersome though it may have seemed to top management, demanding and complicated though it may have proved for those directly involved.

All organisations are in practice segmented, in that rivalries and friction of all kinds between individuals and groups tend to be aligned in conformity with the structural divisions of the management system. The BBC seems to be more so than most; and its principal problems of organisation over the years seem to spring from the divisiveness inherent in the structural divisions which any conventional system of management imposes, but which, in the Corporation, are so reinforced by segmentation as seriously to hamper the equally important processes of organisation. I have in this chapter been concerned to illustrate the ways in which the articulation of the Corporation into grades and into departments and sections, all according to conventional principles of management, also creates social groups divided from each other by conflicting interests, values, sentiments and expectations.

The reinforcement of structural divisions, or, rather, their conversion from a convenient classification and ordering into separate precincts, each with its own preoccupations, interests, values, sentiments and expectations, is the way in which segmentation manifests itself in organisational terms. When we have regard to the way in which it operates in any one context, and to the way in which segmentation arises out of the separate commitments of the individual, the consequences relate to what presents itself as a 'breakdown in communications', as protracted bargaining and negotiation instead of an expected accommodation, or to arriving at awkward or less than optimal decisions. For the individual concerned in making arrangements with 'opposite numbers', or representing his section or department at a committee meeting, will have with him a variety of commitments which may, and often do, prevent his wholehearted implication in the task of working towards the best outcome along with his fellow committee members, or of arriving at the best joint decision. In practice, the considerations and the arguments appropriate to any operational problem are never isolable from their implications for other situations in which the individual is involved because of the interests of his department, or his career, or his other commitments.

Yet all this is in itself part of the context in which organisational processes occur. There runs through the network of cooperation and subordination a set of tacit assumptions about the limits which individuals will set to their acceptance of considerations or arguments which obtain for other people in situations demanding decision or action. This set of tacit assumptions is in fact the 'legitimacy' of the operational process – a legitimacy quite different from the rationality which, for Max Weber, underwrites the legitimacy of bureaucratic organisation.

So, while the segmented character of the BBC's organisation may be no worse than in any other organisation, the consequences may be more serious. At all events, in 1963, long before the 'McKinsey reorganisation' started to build up the management structure into something so obtrusive and dominant, there prevailed a dense network of working relationships and alliances for use in the conduct of organisational processes.[1] This fabric of relationships, governed by their own distinct conventions of interaction, can be regarded as the outcome of the involvement of individuals – of that 'invaluable increment you don't pay for'. Of course, working cooperation among the members of production teams and *ad hoc* work groups is something expected and provided for by management, but cooperation of the kind needed in the BBC was achieved only because of the commitment of individuals to the ultimate task of producing and broadcasting programmes – as distinct from their commitments to their own specialism, to their career, and over and above their contractual engagement as resources. As it was, the fabric of relationships and of conventions by which those relationships were sustained was constantly liable to be disrupted by rivalries or suppressed by the onset of segmentation – the tendency for the structural divisions prescribed by the management system to be defended as territorial boundaries; it was also, even before the 1968 reorganisation, liable to be overridden or extinguished by managerial changes.

The system of personal interaction which subtended operational relationships below top management was always, therefore, fragile. Inevitably, it was eroded over the years by the growth of trade unionism and the response of management to it, and by the industrialisation of the BBC subsequently, which put an end to the accommodation between staff and management which grew up in place of the consensus of Reith's day. The unimpeded growth of managerialism reduced it still further.

Organisational processes above the level of operations, mainly concerned with planning and integration, tend to be much more arranged, and more visible in a variety of devices which are common to most organisations but clearly had more depending on them in the Corporation than elsewhere. Indeed, the perennial tendency towards segmentation below the level of top management sharpened the need for an apparatus of social arrangements for working out the practicability of action and decisions, and for establishing their legitimacy. In order to work at all, and certainly to maintain the close coordination required for programme production, the working organisation had to override all the actual and potential barriers to cooperation. This was achieved by the development of a collegial network through which there operated a carefully maintained system of mutual understanding wholly peculiar to the Corporation.

The Director General who remarked that the issue of an instruction on the Corporation was a signal not for action but for discussion (an anecdote recounted by several people with a good deal of relish) gave only half the truth. An instruction appeared as an incident in a continuous process of discussion; the process ended not in an instruction but in an agreement.

Viewed from below, the process looked like this:

> When you're at the bottom, you always have an immediate boss who isn't doing a lot of things you think he ought to do, and then when you get to be that boss, your next immediate boss isn't doing a whole lot of things you think he ought to. When you get to my level, you come to realise that there isn't a boss in the BBC. The BBC consists of these committees. No individual will literally commit himself on something of importance. He does it through a committee. . . . I don't mean this in any nasty sense, it's just the way the BBC works. I wouldn't hesitate to pin a ruling on something if I thought it was within my competence, but there are a tremendous number of things on which one feels one ought to take advice.

This does not give the whole truth either, but it provides a clue to the principles on which much of the Corporation's organisation, as against management, used to rest.

The basic principle was that of accommodation – of management by consent. Agreed decisions which were to be taken account of in formal terms by management proceeded out of this by means of four bits of consultative procedure:

1. Formal committees, which serve two purposes. Information could be disseminated through them not only to people and groups whom the source believed to be involved, but to people and groups who might conceivably be involved and had established the right to know. And committees are ritual acknowledgement of the participation, cooperation and involvement of each committee member (and of the departmental group he represented) in the field of activities which is

the committee's concern; equally, of course, membership is a symbolic act of involvement in the task the committee has been constituted to deal with.

2. Working parties, which were commissioned for *ad hoc* purposes to do with formulating proposals and making plans. In doing so, they carried out the important job of searching for all the information relevant to their task and of informing the functionaries relevant to it. Formal procedures are much less important than in committees, and very close working relationships are the rule. These groups, of which the production planning meeting is a useful instance, were forcing grounds of accommodation; other working relationships grew naturally out of acquaintanceships formed in working parties and meetings.

3. Working consultation, falling somewhere in between committee work and working parties, but depending for its effectiveness on the existence of both. Consultation ('the tremendous number of things on which one feels one ought to take advice') was directed towards the formulation of decisions of any consequence whatever to other people, in the secure knowledge that they were in conformity with the general attitudes, values and technical competence prevailing in the Corporation, especially at one's own level. The procedure contributes to, and derives from, the Corporation's own forms of etiquette, and from the convention of strict demarcation of professional-specialist jobs. It is also, at all times, a form of insurance, for the individual concerned as well as for the organisation; it therefore exacts a premium in the expenditure of time and in the creation of complications over and above strictly operational requirements. 'Referral upwards' (see p. 151 and p. 195) falls into this category.

4. Insurance against making mistakes could, in some instances, extend to taking out insurance against having to bear the onus of decisions by demanding 'accommodation'. For to stand on the authority of superior rank or greater experience or expert knowledge and so exact agreement with one's interpretation of a situation as well as compliance with the decision arising from it also produces accommodation, and at least the show of management by consent.

The constant immersion of the individual manager in a milieu in which decisions emerge from the interplay of shifting and regrouping representatives of different functions had generated in almost everyone I met a very great sensitivity to the prevailing attitudes on problems confronting him, and a reliance on this sensitivity and on his continuing contact with others.

If, however, we consider the accommodation system alone, there are some consequential observations which can be made:

(*a*) A premium is put on social skills as certainly essential and sometimes the most important component of managerial aptitude.

(*b*) Any individual who was or thought he was out of tune with the consensus of management at large could either accept frustration, which many did, or carry out his own preferred line of action in secret, which some did, or rebel, which very few did. Rebels were regarded with some admiration, and were thought to be headed for success.

(*c*) A collusive counter-system could be built up by rebels as a way of getting things done quickly without interference. ('Some of the people on top here just don't know what is happening.') It was, however, more than an informal system supplementing the formal machinery of communication, and decision-making. It operated in opposition to the formal structure; rules had to be broken, instructions and decisions ignored ('On my own programme, very often, I have to do things which I know, if I asked my boss, he'd say "No". It would be right for my boss to say, "No, you mustn't do that." ') It was a counter-system – 'Some people two or three levels higher up than me would murder me if they knew what was happening.' Despite this, it is reasonable to suppose that people on top did have some suspicion, sometimes, of the kind of things that were happening. So there were two systems which to some extent worked against each other. People whose position and powers depended on the operation of the formal structure tried to suppress the counter-system, and occasionally succeeded, and people whose effectiveness and speed of action depended on being able to use the counter-system proceeded to outflank these moves as soon as possible.

(*d*) A bold man might use awareness of the importance attached to agreement and accommodation, and the dependence of management on them to push through his own preferred line of action, or to further his own interests, relying on the desire of his colleagues to maintain the collegial system at all costs.

(*e*) Lastly, the system could operate to isolate an unwanted member. Often an explanatory label was attached: 'ageing staff', or 'extinct volcano'. It may be that the organised exclusion of certain members of the Corporation from the 'accommodation system' originated in their proven incapacity, but there is always a case for exploring the connection further; the paralysing apprehension of the conspiracy around one which is the mark of paranoia is not always an illusion.

THE BBC AS UNFINISHED BUSINESS

The personal identity of a man and the social purposes to which he lends himself are intimately connected, yet separate. What was very apparent in the interviews, and what indeed appears in many of the passages quoted, is that people can observe themselves in situations which require them to employ their intelligence, skill and knowledge to the full, can feel an 'I' which remains critical and detached from engagements and commitments. So, at the end of a chapter which deals so much with the ways in which social selves are the creature of organisations, it is necessary to disown explicitly the customary connotation of a luckless humanity sliding into some neo-Freudian martyrdom of alienation, 'other-directedness' or organisation-mindedness. In so far as the organisation of society, and the articulation of our lives according to its structure, have changed, it is in the direction of complexity and explicitness. This calls for more consciousness of self and of society – for a more sophisticated conduct of life. If, as Socrates said, the unexamined life is not worth living, human existence is, perhaps in this one respect at least, gaining a little in value.

I have posited the existence of a mediate self between personal identity and the social activities in which we are engaged, which I have called a social identity. This is the sense of self which arises in social experience and is also the acting self which we can observe 'from inside'. In many of the quoted passages from interviews there is a clear implication of detachment not only from the roles which are being acted out but from the self which is being, or has been, formed in order to act out the roles effectively, a detachment familiar to everyone at times which divests the situation and one's presence and actions in it of reality.

This stretching of the elastic connection between personal identity (the 'I' of George Herbert Mead) and the social identity (the 'me') becomes evident in periods when people are learning the institutional rules of the game in a new role in an unfamiliar setting. The perceptiveness and self-awareness of newcomers to the BBC is characteristic of novitiate itself, although their ability to discuss the experience, even to regard it as a matter for words, derives from other attributes. The same disjunction, reaching to the point at which it emerges not only into conscious consideration, but into matters for 'unselfconscious' discussion in interview was perceptible in older people confronted with career dilemmas. At this point in life, too, the individual sees the role he has worked into his social identity as an object, stands back from it and compares what he has made of it and what it has made of him with the identity which another role, and its attendant advantages, could provide.

Yet there is, throughout the Corporation, an awareness of a separation between personal and social identity, a sense of being 'on', which is not present, or does not obtrude itself on the observer, in industrial or commercial milieux, or in the civil service – or in the academic world, for that matter. It comes, I believe, from the same general source as it does in the more episodic cases of novitiate and secession – an awareness of one's social identity as an artefact. This time, however, the factitious quality, being an enduring characteristic, is obviously intrinsic to the whole situation.

The Corporation as a whole, that is, and the roles which are enclosed within it, manifest in a continuous fashion the factitive character which elsewhere attached to situations and behaviour when their institutional form becomes obtrusive – at times of entry into and departure from institutional structures. The Corporation, in short, is not yet altogether an institution, not yet fully institutionalised. This fact of existence suggests itself as the reason for the continuing debate inside as well as outside the BBC concerning its objectives and purposes, its social, cultural and political role. Not only the character, the interpretation of its tasks, and the assessment of its influence but its place in society are still unsettled issues:

> There is great scepticism in certain circles about giving the public what it wants, yet to be fair there are those people who work in Radio 1, which exists by definition to give the public what it wants, who are determined to do precisely this. They are chaps who regard the capturing of a significant section of the audience as their justification in life, and when you say to them, as I said on Wednesday, that mere head-counting is not something the BBC should be totally preoccupied with, if it is a fact that 45 per cent of our listening is to Radio 1 – and this is the case – haven't we a duty to ensure that those 45 per cent have something other than continuous pop music? And they're uneasy about that kind of move.
>
> I mention this simply as a counter-balance to the other argument one hears which comes from concern about the role of the BBC and the extent to which it has in some ways fallen short of what it has achieved in the past.
>
> *It seems to you then the BBC has now become confused itself about the distinction (which may have changed) between a public service for the public good and a public service for keeping people happy, which might be seen as in the national interest?*
>
> Oh, I'm sure it's confused. The issue was much simpler to understand when there was no competition, and total monopoly. Then it was possible to have splendid ideas about the role of a broadcasting organisation and the ways it was intended to serve society. But as soon as competition came about, there was an

immediate realisation that ultimately the politicians were masters. . . .

Even now, a good fifty years after its foundation, the BBC is still at some stage anterior to full social acceptance and identity, still short of the completely institutionalised form in which it can lapse into unself-conscious performance of a familiar role. Hence, the internal politics of the BBC, and the endeavours to find a management structure appropriate to its organisational needs, relate to far more fundamental, and interesting, issues than those which divide a business concern, a government department, or a university. They are the politics and the constitutional and administrative problems of a newly founded state rather than of an established nation.

For more than fifty years, the BBC has been exposed almost incessantly both to applause, and to attack, to unthinking support and to uninformed criticism, to self-interested cossetting and to hostile suspicions from Government and Opposition, to appropriation by the cultural establishment and to disparagement by Old Tory and New Left. And, every ten years or so, it has had to face arraignment by heavyweight committees of inquiry which, in effect, put the BBC on trial for its life, or for possible dissection. It seems to me that the BBC has been driven by all this into assuming a place in the established order of things British as a kind of protective disguise. It has behaved as though born in impregnable, centuries-old, tradition; its history has been made to appear as one of unqualified and continuous success, to be a record of expansion rather than evolution, of the acquisition of new territories of activity rather than of development and change.

The BBC is even now, I believe, comparatively immature and unformed. Misguided and intolerant though he may have been, Reith's conception of broadcasting as a public service, of a BBC imbued with a sense of mission, of the people who worked in it as a community dedicated to the public good was, I believe, wholly appropriate. It is also the only conception which makes political and economic sense, perhaps especially in the present situation of this country. It is also the only conception which has a hope of superseding the miscellany of values and purposes compounded of individual commitments to professionalism, to careers, to managerial efficiency, to saving money or making money, which are the prevailing currency. Potentially the BBC still represents an enormously effective agency of political, cultural and social enlightenment.

If this potential is to be realised, its liberties extended and established, its morale restored, some means have to be found of freeing it from its client relationship to Government; above all, it has to be delivered from the paralysing threat contained in a licence which measures out its life-expectancy in ten-year doses. Public criticism and surveillance by Parliamentary Committee are safeguards enough, if Parliament were more durably the agency of the country's will it has so infrequently shown itself to be. The radical reform which will deliver the BBC from imprisonment in competition, within and without, for ratings, and from incorporation in the world of industry and business can only come from within the BBC.

BELFAST PUBLIC LIBRARIES

Notes

Preface

1. Tom Burns and G. M. Stalker, *The Management of Innovation* (Tavistock Press, 2nd edition, 1966) pp. 12–14.
2. For lengthier accounts, and defences of this procedure, see A. W. Gouldner, *Patterns of Industrial Democracy* (Glencoe: Free Press, 1954) pp. 248–50 and 256–60; and Tom Burns, 'The Comparative Study of Organisations', in V. Vroom (ed.), *Methods of Organisational Research* (University of Pittsburgh Press, 1967) pp. 154–5.
3. Paul F. Lazarsfeld, 'The Role of Criticism in the Management of Mass Media', *Journalism Quarterly*, Vol. 25 (1948), reprinted in *Qualitative Analysis* (Allyn & Bacon, 1972) p. 123.
4. Max Weber, 'Parliament and Government in a Reconstructed Germany', trans. and published as Appendix II in Max Weber, *Economy and Society*, edited by Guenther Roth and Claus Wittich (Bedminster Press, 1968) pp. 1417–19.

Chapter 1

1. P. P. Eckersley, who ran the programmes broadcast from Writtle, wrote (in 1923):

   'Many declare that if it had not been for Writtle, and the interest that Writtle stimulated, broadcasting would never have come to England.

   'While I, as a worker at Writtle, and one who was responsible for the artistic and the technical side of the transmission, am much flattered by the suggestion, I am still unconvinced.

   'Broadcasting came about because those interested came over from the States and pointed out what vast sums of money were being made there, what interest broadcasting was creating, and how England had got left behind. This, I think, was the great stimulant – American broadcasting.' (*Captain Eckersley Explains: a Reply to his Numerous Correspondents*, p. 2, quoted by R. H. Coase in *British Broadcasting* (Longman, for the London School of Economics, 1950) p. 8.)
2. Erik Barnouw, *A Tower in Babel: The History of Broadcasting in the United States to 1933* (Oxford U.P., 1966) p. 59.

3. Barnouw, op. cit, p. 60.
4. Ibid., p. 115.
5. Except for Government broadcasts of weather and crop reports, which were broadcast on 485 metres. These were relayed by local commercial stations which shifted for them to 485 metres and then back to their own wavelength 'across the dial, urging their listeners to tag along' (Barnouw, p. 92).
6. The Postmaster General (then F. G. Kellaway) referred to 'the chaos brought about by the unregulated erection of transmitting stations' in the Commons debate on the Post Office role in May 1922.
7. Appendix C, *Broadcasting Committee Report, 1923* (Sykes Committee) (Cmd. 1951) pp. 44–5.
8. Sykes Committee Report, para. 16.
9. *Imperial Wireless Telegraphy Committee Report*, 1924 (Cmd. 2060) p. 26.
10. Andrew Boyle, *Only the Wind Will Listen* (Hutchinson, 1972) p. 127.
11. P. P. Eckersley *The Power behind the Microphone* (Scientific Book Club, 1942) p. 53.
12. The three signatories were Attlee, the only member of the Labour Party on the Ullswater Committee, Clement Davies, one of the two Liberals (but himself, then, a National Liberal) and Lord Elton (a National Labour peer).
13. *Report of the Broadcasting Committee, 1935* (Cmd. 5091, 1936) p. 51.
14. The ratio is substantially different now, with the operating costs of television costing 20 times as much, per broadcast hour, as radio, and with the very considerable inroads on the British market made by Japanese, German and other foreign-made receivers. The latest estimate for the proportion of expenditure on broadcasting as against reception is one half. (P.E.P. Broadsheet no. 520, July 1970, 'The Economics of Television'.)
15. See articles by Sir H. Norman, Chairman of the Wireless Sub-Committee of the Imperial Communications Committee in *The Times*, 8 and 9 May 1922. The report of the Sub-Committee was not published, but its recommendations were said, by the Postmaster General, to have been adopted. (R. H. Coase, *British Broadcasting* (Longmans Green, for the London School of Economics, 1950) pp. 10–11.)
16. See James O'Connor, *The Fiscal Crisis of the State*, St. Martin's Press, 1973.
17. *Report of the Broadcasting Committee, 1935* (Ullswater Report) Cmnd. 5091, 1936.
18. *Second Report from the Select Committee on Nationalised Industries* Session 1971–2 (Sub-Committee B) House of Commons Paper 465, 1972.
19. K. Adam, 'Fifty Years of Fireside Elections', *The Listener*, 14 February 1972 (Vol. 91, p. 208).
20. 'The Question of Ulster' – a lengthy discussion programme broadcast on 5 January, 1972 on the rights and wrongs of the troubles in Northern Ireland; the Home Secretary (Reginald Maudling), who was consulted beforehand, thought the broadcast would do more harm than good, and urged that it should not be broadcast. (After the Post Office became a public corporation, on 1 October, 1969, the Home Secretary became the Minister responsible for broadcasting.) Maudling refrained from exercising

any ministerial authority; the Director General, backed by the Board of Governors, decided that the programme be broadcast.

21. 'Yesterday's Men' – a Current Affairs feature broadcast on 17 June, 1971, a year after the Labour Party which had been in office for six years was defeated in the 1970 General Election. The programme was publicly attacked by the Labour ex-Ministers interviewed for the programme as 'shallow and trivial' and, moreover, 'grotesquely and indecently different' from the programme which they had been led to believe would be framed around the recorded interviews with them. One of them, Richard Crossman, wrote, in a full-length article on the programme in the *New Statesman* (of which he was then editor), 'The effect was achieved first by the deliberate fraud by which politicians were persuaded to take part and, secondly, by the even greater fraud by which fragments were snipped out of the interviews they gave and juxtaposed in order to convey a false impression of what they had meant and even of what they had actually said.'

    The BBC Board of Governors instituted an enquiry almost immediately and published a report in *The Listener* (15 July, 1971) which dealt with the charges and claimed that almost all of them had been refuted. This did little more than provoke further criticism of the BBC, as well as the programme.

    A detailed account of the whole episode is given by Michael Tracey in 'Yesterday's Men – A Case Study in Political Communication', in J. Curran, M. Gurevitch and J. Woollacott, *Mass Communication and Society* (Arnold, 1977) pp. 249–269.
22. Robin Day, 'Troubled Reflections of a T.V. Journalist', *Encounter*, May 1970, p. 88. Mr Day took what might be thought a more reasonable line – and what was, in the circumstances, assuredly a more accommodating one – in his evidence to the Select Committee on Broadcasting of Proceedings in the House of Commons in 1966, when he said, as his second argument for televising Parliament: 'In particular, television viewers would be able to see parliamentary leaders being questioned and challenged by those elected to do so on the floor of the House and not *merely* [my emphasis] by television journalists in studio interviews.' (*First Report from the Select Committee on Broadcasting, etc., of Proceedings in the House of Commons*, 1966, Minutes of Evidence, p. 62.)
23. J. Blumler, 'The Media and the Election', *New Society*, 7 March 1974 (Vol. 27, p. 572).
24. Sir William Mitchell-Thomson (Postmaster General), *Hansard*, 14 July 1926, Vol. 198, cols 4466–8.
25. J. C. W. Reith, *Into the Wind* (Hodder & Stoughton, 1949) p. 108.
26. Boyle, op. cit., p. 199.
27. *Beatrice Webb's Diaries, 1924–1932*, ed. Margaret Cole (Longman, 1956) pp. 91–2.
28. Asa Briggs, *The History of Broadcasting in the United Kingdom* (Oxford University Press): Vol. 2, *The Golden Age of Wireless* (1965) (p. 141).
29. Ibid. Here Briggs lists this extension of the ban to publications as one of the 'minor' points of difference between the Ullswater Report and the Govern-

ment White Paper, adding 'in fact, publications always had been treated in this way' (p. 511).

30. Boyle, op. cit., p. 287.
31. Boyle, op. cit., p. 289.
32. Boyle, op. cit., p. 268.
33. Asa Briggs, *The History of Broadcasting in the United Kingdom* Vol. 3, *The War of Words* (O.U.P., 1970) p. 6.
34. Briggs, op. cit., Vol. 2, p. 632.
35. *Report of the Broadcasting Committee 1949* (Beveridge Committee), Cmnd. 8116, 1951.
36. Boyle, op. cit., p. 224.
37. Reith, *Into the Wind*, (Hodder and Stoughton, 1949) p. 127.
38. The 'Whitley document' was never published but is quoted in full in Lord Simon's report on his own spell as Chairman, *The BBC From Within*, (Gollancz, 1953) pp. 46–7, and reprinted in Anthony Smith, *British Broadcasting* (David & Charles, 1974) pp. 60–1.
39. Tom Burns, 'The Sociology of Industry', in A. T. Welford (ed.), *Society* (Routledge & Kegan Paul, 1961).
40. Briggs, op. cit., Vol. 2, p. 135 (quoting *Into the Wind*, p. 300).
41. BBC Internal Memorandum No. 233, 29 August 1933 (quoted Briggs, Vol. 2, p. 445).
42. Boyle, op. cit., pp. 256–7.
43. Briggs, op. cit., Vol. 2, p. 446.
44. Reith's Talk to the Staff Training School, 2 October 1936; quoted Briggs, op. cit., Vol. 2, p. 436.
45. Memorandum of 13 November 1936, quoted Briggs, Vol. 2, p. 123.
46. Reith, *Into the Wind*, p. 88 (quoted Lord Simon, *The BBC From Within*, Gollancz, 1953 (pp. 49–50).
47. *Report of the Committee on Broadcasting, 1960* (Pilkington Committee), Cmnd. 1753, 1962.
48. Simon remarked that there were one or two exceptions. Waldman, Head of Light Entertainment at the time, was one.

    'He hated the jungle atmosphere of commercial television and the absurd power of the sponsors, but was bowled over by the intoxicating discovery that the Americans accepted as perfectly natural that television was entertainment. He wrote a boldly indignant report, pointing out that to the Americans British TV was small, dull, slow, poor, starved and amateurish.' (Peter Black, *The Mirror in the Corner* (Hutchinson, 1972) pp. 23–4.)
49. Anthony Smith, 'Internal Pressures in Broadcasting', *New Outlook*, 1972, No. 4, p. 4.

Chapter 2

1. Pilkington Committee Report, op. cit.
2. D. McQuail, *Towards a Sociology of Mass Communications* (Collier-Macmillan, 1969) p. 49.

3. Kurt Lang and G. E. Lang, *Politics and Television* (Quadrangle Books, 1968) p. 305.
4. A. Aspinall, *Politics and the Press, 1780–1850* (Home & Van Thal, 1949) p. 1.
5. Asa Briggs, *The History of Broadcasting in the United Kingdom*, Vol. 1, *The Birth of Broadcasting* (O.U.P. 1961) p. 239; p. 238.
6. Hilda Matheson, *Broadcasting* (Butterworth, Home University Library, 1933) p. 17.
7. James Bryce, *The American Commonwealth* (Macmillan, second edition, 1910) Vol. 2, p. 840.
8. See A. Aspinall, *Politics and the Press 1780–1830* (Home & Van Thal, 1949).
9. First published 1972; Penguin Books, 1974, p. 277.
10. 'What the proprietorship of these papers is aiming at is power without responsibility – the prerogative of the harlot throughout the ages.' (The remark is said to have been fed to him by Rudyard Kipling, Baldwin's brother-in-law.)
11. 'A single man, Sir Thomas Beecham, did more for British music than was done by the massed battalions of the BBC.' (A. J. P. Taylor, *English History 1914–1945*, (O.U.P., 1965) p. 234.)
12. 'Beveridge rejected the BBC's argument that its past achievement entitled it to be preserved unaltered, rejected its claim that only a monopoly could have high standards and social purpose, agreed that the BBC was too big, too metropolitan, too powerful. . . . He asked how the monopoly of broadcasting could be prevented from developing the faults of complacency, injustice, favouritism and want of initiative. . . . But after all this he came down solidly in favour of monopoly and the continued prohibition of advertising.' (Peter Black, op. cit., p. 34.)
13. Gerald Beadle, *Television: a Critical Review* (Allen & Unwin, 1963) pp. 77–8.
14. 'Ratings' of this and similar kinds are based on the product of two estimates, based on small samples of the total viewing audience and on the amount of time they spent in watching television (or, in the case of ITV measurements, the total time the television set is left switched on).
15. Peter Black, *The Mirror in the Corner*, p. 111.
16. Gerald Cock, quoted in Beadle, op. cit., p. 41.
17. Robert Silvey, *Who's Listening?* (Allen & Unwin, 1974) p. 192.
18. 'Ronnie Waldman' [the Department's Head in the early fifties] 'had to fight that mysterious, unattributable body of BBC opinion which recognised that light entertainment had to exist but regretted the necessity, and were just as likely to feel shame at its successes as pride. ("Do you mean you have a Head of Heavy Entertainment?", a puzzled American asked Waldman.') Peter Black, op. cit., p. 23.
19. Huw Wheldon, 'Competition in Television', an address given at a joint meeting of the Faculty of Designers for Industry and the Royal Society of Arts, 1971.
20. B. C. Roberts *et al.*, *Reluctant Militants* (Heinemann, 1972).
21. *Royal Commission on Trade Unions and Employers' Associations*, (H.M.S.O., 1966) Minutes of Evidence, No. 36, DATA.
22. 'It was apparent from our survey data that technicians themselves were

aware of a growing "graduate barrier" blocking their access to the technologist career ladder.' (B. C. Roberts *et al.*, op. cit., p. 251.) They add, in a footnote, that 'there was a tendency for this to hold good in general management as well'.

23. See T. Burns, preface to second edition, Tom Burns and G. M. Stalker, *The Management of Innovation* (Tavistock, 1966) pp. xvii–xxi.
24. R. Dahrendorf, 'Recent Changes in the Class Structure of European Societies', in *Daedalus* Vol. 93, 1964.
25. See A. Briggs, Vol. 2, pp. 472–4.
26. Ibid., p. 466.
27. Ibid., p. 514.
28. Beveridge Committee Report, para. 469.
29. Ibid., BBC evidence, quoted para. 472.
30. Ibid., Recommendation 93, p. 199.
31. See Tom Burns and G. M. Stalker, *The Management of Innovation* (Tavistock, 1961) chs. 5 and 6, and Tom Burns, 'On the Plurality of Social Systems', in Burns (ed.), *Industrial Man* (Penguin, 1969).

Chapter 3

1. Robert E. Park, *On Social Control and Collective Behaviour* (ed. Ralph H. Turner) (Univ. of Chicago Press, 1967) p. 67.
2. E. P. Thompson, 'The Moral Economy of the English Crowd in the Eighteenth Century', *Past and Present* No. 50 (1971), pp. 76–136.
3. N. E. Long, 'The Local Community as an Ecology of Games', *American Journal of Sociology*, Vol. LXIV (1958) pp. 251–61.
4. J. Doulton and D. Hay, *Managerial and Professional Staff Grading* (Allen & Unwin, 1962).
5. Technical Operations Manager ('T.O.M.'), often called 'gaffer'; usually a promoted cameraman or lighting supervisor. Now entitled Technical Manager I ('T.M. One)'. I have retained the older title T.O.M. throughout.
6. See Tom Burns, 'Preface to the Second Edition', in Tom Burns and G. M. Stalker, *The Management of Innovation* (Tavistock, 1966) pp. xii–xiii.

Chapter 4

1. R.I. = 'Reaction Index', a composite indicator of audience appreciation of individual programmes made up by the Audience Research Department from data compiled from questionnaires returned by the BBC's Listeners' Panel of just over 2000 people. It is slightly more complicated index than the earlier A.R. ('Audience Response') figure which it replaced.
2. In a Royal Society of Arts lecture, reported in *The Listener*, 17 January 1974, p. 81.
3. Charles Curran, *Code or Conscience?* (BBC Publications, 1970).
4. Everett C. Hughes, 'Work and Self', in J. H. Rohrer and Muzafer Sherif (eds.), *Social Psychology at the Crossroads* (Harper & Row, 1951); repr. in Hughes, *The Sociological Eye* (Aldine Atherton, 1971) p. 340.

5. W. J. Reader, *Professional Man: the Rise of the Professional Classes in Nineteenth Century England* (Weidenfeld & Nicolson, 1966).
6. I.e., the reorganisation of the management structure initiated in 1968–9 with McKinsey & Co. employed as management consultants (see Chapter 7).
7. Adam Smith, *The Wealth of Nations* (1776); ed. E. Cannan (Modern Library, 1937) p. 3.
8. Ibid., p. 7.
9. Everett C. Hughes, *Men and their Work* (Free Press, 1958) pp. 78, 79, 79–80.
10. E.g. 'Good People and Dirty Work'; 'The Study of Occupations'; 'Social Role and the Division of Labour'; 'Mistakes at Work'; 'Work and Self', all reprinted in Everett C. Hughes, *The Sociological Eye* (Aldine Atherton, 1971).
11. E. C. Hughes, 'The Study of Occupations', in R. K. Merton, Broom and Cottrell, *Sociology Today* (Basic Books, 1959), repr. in *The Sociological Eye*, pp. 288–9.
12. E. C. Hughes, 'Mistakes at Work', *Canadian Journal of Economics and Political Science*, Vol. XVII, 1951, repr. in *The Sociological Eye*, p. 316.
13. T. H. Marshall, 'The Recent History of Professionalism in Relation to Social Structure and Social Policy', *Canadian Journal of Economics and Political Science*, Vol. V, 1939, pp. 327–9. Repr. in T. H. Marshall, *Citizenship and Social Class* (C.U.P., 1950).
14. E. J. Epstein, *News from Nowhere* (Random House, 1973) p. 25.
15. See, e.g., A. M. Carr-Saunders and P. A. Wilson, *The Professions* (O.U.P., 1933); T. H. Marshall, op. cit.
16. The situation is not, therefore, one which can be met by a Public Representation Service, as the Beveridge Committee recommended.
17. In a seminar given in the University of Edinburgh, November 1975.
18. Joan Bakewell and Nicholas Garnham, *The New Priesthood* (Allen Lane, 1970) pp. 186–7.
19. Brian Winston, ibid.
20. Antony Jay (personal communication).
21. Stuart Hood, *A Survey of Television* (Heinemann, 1967) pp. 49–50.
22. C. Geertz 'Ideology as a Cultural System', in *The Interpretation of Cultures* (Hutchinson, 1975) p. 232.

Chapter 5

1. Andrew Boyle, op. cit., p. 239.
2. Paul F. Lazarsfeld and Robert K. Merton, 'Mass Communication, Popular Taste, and Organised Social Action', in L. Bryson (ed.), *The Communication of Ideas*, (Harper and Bros., 1948) pp. 106–7.
3. Anthony Smith, *The Shadow in the Cave* (Allen & Unwin, 1973), Preface.
4. *Second Report from the Select Committee on Nationalised Industries* (H. of C. Paper 465), 1972.
5. A full account of the 'Broadcasting in the Seventies' episode was given by the Director General, Sir Charles Curran, in a lecture to the Royal Town

Planning Institute in February 1974, under the title, 'Planning and Consent: The Technocrat's Dilemma'.

6. Anthony Smith, op. cit., pp. 78–92.
7. Sir Geoffrey Cox, in J. Bakewell and N. Garnham, *The New Priesthood*, p. 145.
8. A. Mitchell, 'The Decline of Current Aftairs Television', *Political Quarterly*, Vol. 44, 1973, pp. 127–36.
9. Hugh C. Greene, *The Third Floor Front* (Bodley Head, 1969) pp. 126–7.
10. Jerome Kuehl, *New Society*, 10 July 1975.
11. G. Lapsley, editorial note, in F. W. Maitland, *Selected Essays*, (C.U.P., 1936) pp. 3–5.
12. James Bryce, *The American Commonwealth*, (Macmillan, 3rd ed., 1914) pp. 35–6.
13. See E. P. Thompson, *Whigs and Hunters* (Allen Lane, 1975) p. 269.
14. A. Aspinall, *Politics and the Press, 1780–1850*, op. cit., p. 1.
15. Ibid., p. 3.
16. Steven Watson, *The Reign of George III, 1760–1830* (O.U.P., 1960) p. 350.
17. Aspinall, op. cit., p. 381.
18. See P. Hollis (ed.), *Pressures from Without* (Arnold, 1974).
19. R. C. K. Ensor, *England, 1870–1914* (O.U.P., 1936) p. 144.
20. It seems fairly certain that Rothermere's claim that he could make, and keep, Bonar Law Prime Minister had very little substance to it. In the election in which 'the power of the press' was exercised most directly and blatantly – in 1923, when the *Daily Mail* published the 'Zinoviev letter' – the Labour Party, against which the forgery had been directed, increased its vote by a million. Empire Free Trade, the policy Beaverbrook invented in order to have one to champion, quickly became a dead letter – indeed, A. J. P. Taylor suggests that 'perhaps it was ruined by the support of the press lords' (*English History, 1914–1938* (O.U.P., 1965) p. 283), a remarkable historical verdict on what was, in the same writer's view, 'a great attempt' made 'for the first and last time . . . to change party leadership and party policy by a battery in the columns of the popular press'. (Ibid., p. 282).
21. Fred Hirsch and David Gordon, *Newspaper Money* (Hutchinson, 1975) p. 19.
22. Ibid., p. 12.
23. Reith recorded in his diary the way in which Committee recommendations turned out, after they had been 'adopted' by Government, to mean something quite different: '11 November, 1926. I cannot express my opinion on the way that the Post Office has treated us; they have been unfair, arbitrary and positively dishonest. . . . The constitution [of the new Corporation] was to be enlarged to admit of more scope and more autonomy, but none of these has materialised. I think the P.M.G. and Murray [Secretary to the Post Office] have behaved in a very caddish way.' (*The Reith Diaries*, ed. C. Stuart (Collins, 1975) pp. 141–2).
24. See Boyle, op. cit., pp. 213–14.
25. *The Reith Diaries*, p. 81.
26. Robin Day, *Day by Day* (Kimber, 1975) p. 184.

Chapter 6

1. Louis Heren, 'All Journalists are American', *Journalism Studies Review*, Vol. 1, 1976, p. 6.
2. Edward J. Epstein, *News from Nowhere*, op. cit., p. 10.
3. John Whale, quoted by Charles Curran in 'Researcher/Broadcaster Cooperation: Problems and Possibilities', in J. D. Halloran and H. Gurevitch, *Broadcaster/Researcher Cooperation in Mass Communication Research* (Centre for Mass Communication Research, 1971) p. 43.
4. *Third Report from the Estimates Committee*, Session 1968–9, *The British Broadcasting Corporation*, House of Commons Paper 387, 1969, paras. 10 & 11.
5. Although there have been critics who have declared that it is the voice of Government:

   'Today, the BBC holds – in the field of art, intellect and politics – the power once held by the Court. It has become the main indirect organ of government, all the more potent because its influence is indirect.' R. S. Lambert, *Ariel and all his Quality – An Impression of the BBC from Within* (Gollancz, 1940) p. 317.
6. See Patricia Hollis (ed.), *Pressures from Without* (Arnold, 1974).
7. *Taste and Standards in BBC Programmes* (BBC, 1973) p. 11.
8. John Whale, *The Half-Shut Eye* (Macmillan, 1969) p. 30.
9. Ibid., p. 33.
10. Anthony Smith, 'Internal Pressures in Broadcasting', *New Outlook*, 1972, No. 4, pp. 4–5.
11. Ibid., p. 5.
12. Krishan Kumar, 'Holding the Middle Ground; the Public and the Professional Broadcaster' *Sociology* Vol. 9, 1975, p. 75 & p. 74.
13. Whale, op. cit. He adds, 'It is a particularly British love. Journalists in few other countries are so assiduous in questioning politicians when they are at their least clear-headed. Few airports in the world have space deliberately set aside for the purpose. . . . At Heathrow, in different parts of the airport, there are three specially equipped studios.' (p. 34)
14. Elizabeth Burns, *Theatricality* (Longmans, 1972) p. 32.
15. Ibid., ch. 4, 'Conventions of Performance'.
16. J. D. Halloran, P. Elliott and G. Murdock, *Communications and Demonstrations* (Penguin 1970).
17. Glasgow University Media Group, *Bad News* (Routledge & Kegan Paul, 1976) pp. 267–8.
18. John Birt, 'Can Television News Break the Understanding Barrier?' *The Times*, 28 February, 1975.
19. John Birt, loc. cit.
20. Philip Whitehead, interviewed by Nicholas Garnham, in J. Bakewell and N. Garnham, *The New Priesthood*, op. cit., p. 173.
21. Ibid.
22. Whale, op. cit., p. 25.
23. Ibid., p. 12.
24. Whale, op. cit., p. 203.
25. Cf. Andrew Boyle's remark concerning the handling of news by the BBC

during the years preceding the outbreak of war in 1939. Controllers as well as producers tended to act on the wise prescription: 'better safe than sorry'. (*Only the Wind will Listen*, p. 290.)

26. Whale, op. cit., pp. 203–4.
27. K. Kumar, op. cit., p. 162.
28. Ibid., p. 85.

Chapter 7

1. Between 1962 and 1965, television operating costs rose from just over £20m. to £35m., and the licence fee from £4 (with £3 payable to the BBC) to £5. Most of the extra money was for BBC2, which was available only to viewers in the south-east of England and to some in the Midlands (*BBC Handbook 1965*, p. 110). By the beginning of 1969, when the TV licence (black and white) was raised to £6, 24 per cent of people in the U.K. were still unable to receive BBC2 (*BBC Handbook 1969*, p. 119). Transmission in colour was confined, during the sixties, to BBC2.
2. According to the Crawford Committee Report, 1974, the UHF service which is capable of providing 625-line transmission for four television channels, will cost the BBC £4m. a year until 1980, when Phase I of the transmitter building programme will be completed. Phase I will provide 98.5 per cent of the population with UHF 625-line service; to extend the same service to the rest of the population would cost – presumably at 1974 prices – a further £17m.
3. At constant prices, of course, this represents a substantial decline in capital expenditure. Even the £14m. spent in 1974–5 represents a further decline, in terms of real money.
4. The Programme Contracts section is located in Personnel Division 'for convenience', but is not in fact 'controlled' by it. In negotiating fresh terms, Programme Contracts naturally keep the Managing Directors of the programme divisions informed, and will be briefed by them. The outcome of negotiations, nevertheless, usually increases programme costs beyond the original estimate.
5. By mid-1975, the purchasing power of the 1960 pound had fallen to 36p. According to conventional reckoning, this is equivalent to 176 per cent inflation over the fifteen years. The inflation rate was, of course, accelerating over the whole of the period, reaching 21 per cent during the financial year 1974–5.
6. *Third Report from the Estimates Committee, 1968–69, British Broadcasting Corporation*, H. of C. paper 387, 1969, paras. 20–22.
7. Lord Hill, *Behind the Screen* (Sidgwick & Jackson, 1974) p. 82.
8. Ibid., p. 99.
9. Lord Hill, op. cit., p. 101.
10. Ibid. p. 84.
11. This is not to say that BBC practice is especially eccentric, when compared with what obtains elsewhere. All accounting procedures involve fictions of varying convenience and inconvenience.

12. Nowadays, appointments at this level, I am assured, are made by the Board of Governors.

Chapter 8

1. I ought to make it clear that the reference here is to something which has been a commonplace of empirical observation, in organisational studies, for at least forty years. Unfortunately, the term 'informal organisation' (in contrast to the formal organisation of management) invented for it by Chester Barnard led to its being confused with the 'informal organisation' of the Hawthorne studies. For a good twenty years after the publication of *Management and the Worker*, Roethlisberger and Dickson's notion of the informal organisation of workers on the shop floor served as a receptacle for observations about the behaviour, the relationships, the sentiments and beliefs, the commitments and self-identifications of workers which were taken to be irrelevant to the formal organisation or incompatible with it and with its purposes. In Chester Barnard's rendering, informal organisation appears as an essential adjunct to formal organisation, in that it facilitates 'the communication of intangible facts, opinions, suggestions, suspicions, that cannot pass through formal channels without raising issues calling for a decision, without dissipating dignity and objective authority, and without overloading executive position.' (*The Functions of the Executive*, Harvard University Press, 1938.)

   Barnard comes closest to the formulation I have sought to arrive at and, what is more, emphasises the affinity of the informal organisation of commitment – which he calls 'loyalty' – which, he says, is 'the most important single contribution required of the executive'. Even so, he misses what I have treated as of central importance: the fact that essential organisational processes involving actual operations and work are grounded in the person-to-person relationships formed by people at work, and as such constitute the necessary counterpart and complement to the control system maintained by the management structure.

Index

accommodation (political, etc.), 191–3, 209, 291–3
accountants, 128
Adam, Kenneth, 159, 211, 299
administration (Administration Division), x, xiv, 23–5, 43, 98–9, 109–10, 148, 153, 211, 214–23, 252, 260
Administration, Director of, x, xiv, 241–2
administrative assistants, 220–1, 243
age-grades, 103–4, 106
Agnew, Spiro, 157, 193
Annan, Lord, 33
annual interviews, 117, 121
Appointments Boards (appointments system), 73–4, 91, 97–8, 114–21, 249–250
arbitration, 92–3
Arkell, J. A., 211
Aspinall, A., 39, 175, 177, 301, 305
Association of Broadcasting Staff (ABS), 65–7, 89–90, 91–3, 96
Association of Cinematograph and Allied Technicians (ACAT – later ACTT), 61, 64–6
attachments scheme, 117
Attlee, Clement, 10, 18, 299
audience (relationship to), 132–4, 136–7, 141, 143, 149, 152, 156, 162, 165, 200, 240, 295
audience research, 134, 136–7, 141, 215
Audience Response (A.R.), *see* Reaction Index (R.I.)

Bakewell, Joan, 193, 304, 306
balanced programme, 47–8, 145–7, 253
Baldwin, Stanley, 14, 15, 20, 39, 179, 181, 302
Barnard, Chester I., 307
Barnouw, E., 3, 4, 298–9
barons, 217, 248–9, 272
Baverstock, Donald, 124, 150–1, 162
'BBC manner', ix, xiii
'BBC type', xiii, 27, 44–5, 99
Beadle, Gerald, 52, 53, 302
Beaverbrook, Lord, 39
Beecham, Sir Thomas, 302
Benn, A. W., 13
Beveridge Committee, 21–2, 28, 29–30, 32–3, 46, 60–2, 141, 301, 304
Birt, John, 204–5, 306
Black Peter, 32, 301, 302
Blumler, Jay, 14–15, 300
boardmanship, 115–21
Boyle, Andrew, 8, 18–19, 25–6, 299, 300, 301, 304, 305, 306
Briggs, Asa, 18, 20, 22–4, 25–6, 36, 60, 300, 301, 302, 303
Brinkley, David, 186
British Broadcasting Company, 1, 6, 8, 22, 27, 28, 29
Broadcasting House, 22, 79–82, 92, 153, 211
Broadcasting in the Seventies, 160, 255, 304
broadcasting liberties, 187–8
Bryce, Lord, 38, 175, 302, 305
budgetary control, 225–6, 270
bureaucracy, 42, 45–6, 73, 162
Burke, Edmund, 145, 176
Burns, Elizabeth, 197–8, 306
Burns, Tom, xi, xii, 298, 301, 303
Bush House, 88
butch, 104

cadres, 57–9
Cambridge, 98–9
camp, 104
capital expenditure, 225, 227
career system, careerism, ix, x, 97–8, 107–8, 112–21, 251
Carpendale, C. A., 21, 23, 24, 240, 252
Chamberlain, Neville, 14, 20
Charter, 28, 29, 30, 40, 60
Churchill, Winston, 13, 14, 16, 17

cinema (films), 37–8, 42, 64, 126, 136
Clarendon, Lord, 21–2, 29
Coase, R. H., 11, 298, 299
Cock, Gerald, 53, 302
Collins, Norman, 52
Columbia Broadcasting System (CBS), 5, 162, 186
commitment (*see also* contractual engagement, involvement), xi, 26, 67, 106–8, 139, 260, 273, 279, 283, 290
Committee on Broadcasting Coverage (Crawford Committee) (1974), 307
communication, 74, 243, 256–60
competition (with Independent Television), 43, 51, 53, 55–6, 140, 144, 297
compliant involvement, 285–6
Confederation of British Industry (CBI), 191
consensus, 26, 42–3, 218, 223
contingent, 58
contractual engagement, 108, 112–12, 257–9, 270, 273–5, 278, 282
Control Board, 23–4
conventions, 37, 122, 140–1, 193, 197–9, 201, 205
corporate strategy, 223, 233, 241
Cox, Sir Geoffrey, 164, 305
Crawford Committee (1926), 15, 16, 22, 28, 29, 33, 40, 181
Crossman, Richard, 300
Crowther, Geoffrey, 180
Curran, Sir Charles, vii, xvii, 125, 303, 304, 305
Current Affairs, 46, 50, 64, 103, 142, 146, 150, 162–7, 169–72, 188–209, 215, 248, 253–4, 270

Dahrendorf, R., 59, 303
Davies, Clement, 299
Dawnay, Alan, 24–5, 252
Day, Robin, 14, 183–4, 300, 305
'de-contextualising', 203
dedication, *see* involvement
Department of Employment, Arbitration Conciliation and Advisory Service, 93–4
designers, 261, 265, 267
Dickson, W. J., 308
Dienstklasse, 59
Director General, xvii, 18, 22–6, 28–9, 31, 123, 125, 151, 163, 199, 214, 217, 239–40, 256, 291
Director General, Chief Assistant to, xiv, 215
directors, *see* producers
dirty work, 130, 136
division of labour (social, technical, moral), 126–32
Doulton, J., 87, 303
Drama, 147, 166–7

Ealing Studios, 79
Eckersley, P. P., 3, 9, 298, 299
Editor, News and Current Affairs, 170
Electrical and Musical Industries Ltd (E.M.I.), 10
Electrical Trades Union, 65–7
Elton, Lord, 299
Empire Broadcasting Service, 224
Engineering, Engineering Division (Operations and Maintenance), x, xiv, 44, 91–2, 95, 100, 108–9, 115, 121, 127, 212, 215–16, 218, 223, 232–4, 240, 251, 258–9, 269
Ensor, R.C.K., 178, 305
Epstein, Edward J., 137, 304, 306
Equity, 61
Essex, Tony, 142
establishment officers, 95
Estimates Committee (1968–9), 230–1, 306, 307
ethos, 27, 43, 86–7, 99, 107, 144, 251
European Service, 224
External Services, 19, 34, 46, 215, 224, 234

failure system, 115–17
Features, 172
Federal Radio Commission (later, Federal Communications Commission), 5, 182, 193
film crews, 271
finance, 7, 9–11, 19, 46, 182, 214, 223–34, 237–8, 240–1
floor managers, 82, 104
Foreign Office, 18, 34
fourth estate, 175–6
Friendly, Fred, 162

Galbraith, J. K., 58
Garnham, Nicholas, 142, 193, 304, 306
Geertz, Clifford, 154, 304
General Strike, 14, 16–17, 181
Gillard, Frank, 211
Glasgow University Media Group, 202, 306
Goldie, Grace, W., 151
Gordon, David, 177–80, 305

Gouldner, A. W., 298
Government, 8, 10–21, 72, 155, 169, 173, 183–5, 187–92, 204, 223, 230–1, 296
Governors, Board of, 14–16, 21–2, 27–33, 73, 124, 159, 189, 214, 231–3, 239, 256, 300, 308
grading, 67, 78–97, 106, 112, 121, 215, 221, 274
grammar of broadcasting, 197–9
Greene, Sir Hugh C., 151, 163, 167, 186, 211, 240, 305
Grist, John, 207
guilty knowledge, 129–31
Gurevitch, H., 306

Haley, Sir William, 53
Halloran, James, *et al.*, 306
Hay, D., 87, 303
Heren, Louis, 306
Hill, Lord, 33, 159, 192, 211, 231–2, 239, 307
Hirsch, Fred, 179–80, 305
Hollis, Patricia, 305, 306
Hood, Stuart, 123–4, 135, 151–2, 304
Hughes, Everett, C., 125–9, 304
human resources, 106, 112–13
humours, 104

ideologies, 133, 145–8, 152–4, 253–4
Imperial Wireless Telegraphy (Donald) Committee, 8, 299
Independent Television, 15, 43, 47, 51–6, 63–4, 66, 122, 141, 144, 153, 159, 163–4, 173, 183, 186, 203, 206, 263
Independent Television News (ITN), 164, 167, 183–4
industrial relations, 56–77, 89–94, 238
industrialisation of the BBC, 212–13, 237, 269
inflation, 223–4, 238, 307
informal organisation, 308
institutionalisation, 97, 122, 142–3, 198, 278, 283, 295
internal politics, xi, 76, 144–54, 274
involvement (dedication), 67, 108–10, 144, 260–1, 273, 275–6, 285

Jacob, Sir Ian, 49, 53
Jay, Antony, 150, 205, 209, 304
job evaluation, 87, 95–7
Johnson, Nicholas, 193
journalists, 137, 146, 148, 163, 165, 167–8, 172–4, 193–209

Kasmire, R. D., 186–7
Kellaway, F. G., 299
Kensington House, 79
Kipling, Rudyard, 302
Kuehl, Jerome, 305
Kumar, Krishan, 209, 306, 307

Lambert, R. S., 306
Lang, Kurt, and G. E., 35, 302
Lapsley, G., 305
Law, A. Bonar, 39, 305
Lazarsfeld, Paul F., xv, xvi, 155–6, 298, 304
licence, 28, 40, 182
licence and mandate, 129, 131–2, 137–8
licence fee, 7, 10, 19, 20, 53, 184, 187, 223–5, 231, 306
Light Entertainment, x, 46, 54, 135–6, 145–8, 245, 301
lighting supervisors, 80, 89–90, 262, 274–5
Lime Grove, 79, 102–3, 172, 186
local community, 85–7
Long, Norton E., 85–6
loyalty, 60, 106

MacDonald, Ramsay, 16, 20, 22
Maclean, Sir F., 211
management, management structure, 69, 73, 86–7, 92, 98–9, 111–12, 131, 136–8, 185, 211–12, 219, 240, 261, 271
Management, Board of, xvii, 29 32, 73, 76, 211–12, 218, 220, 232, 239, 241, 249–51, 256–7
management control, 219, 245–6, 248, 256, 269–72
management information service, 212
management style, 245
managerialism, 68, 106, 126, 143, 252–60, 272–3
Managing Directors, 212
Marconi Company, 1, 3, 4, 6–9
Marshall, T. H., 304
Matheson, Hilda, 37, 302
Maudling, Reginald, 299
McKinsey & Co. ('McKinsey reorganisation'), 94, 127, 160, 211, 214, 229–234, 238, 241, 255, 290, 304
McQuail, Denis, 35, 301
Mead, George Herbert, 293
Merton, Robert K., 155–6, 304
Mill, J. S., 189
mirror of society, 149–52, 172, 186, 193, 197, 204, 253

mistakes at work, 130
Mitchell, Austen, 165, 305
Mitchell-Thomson, Sir W., 15–16, 27, 28, 300
monitoring, 243–6, 258–9
moral order, 84–6, 126, 130–2, 199
Musicians' Union, 61

naming, 101–2
National Association of Theatrical, Television and Kine Employees (NATTKE), 63, 66
National Broadcasting Company (NBC), 5, 137, 186
national interest, 190, 192
National Union of Journalists, 61, 65–6
news, 14–15, 18, 19, 34, 46, 144, 155–210, 215
newspaper press, 8, 9, 37–40, 42, 136, 149–50, 155–6, 158–9, 162, 164–5, 168, 174–83, 198, 201
Norman, Sir Harry, 11, 299
Norman, Ronald, 20

O'Connor, James, 11, 299
offers meetings, 234–6
Ogilvie, F., 46
Opposition, 14, 177, 182, 184, 187–8, 296
organisation process, 111, 261, 271–2, 284, 288–93
Output, 48–50
Outside Broadcasts, 147
Oxford, 98–9

Park, Robert, E., 84, 303
Parliament, 11–18, 34, 40, 159, 169, 173–5, 187–9, 191–2, 209, 297
patronat, 58–9
performance costs, 225–9, 237
personal grades, 90–1, 96
Personnel Division, 88, 95, 212, 220, 240–241
Pilkington Committee, 30, 33, 34, 35, 40, 42, 48, 53, 122, 141, 146, 157, 161, 207, 301
planning, *see* programme planning
planning cycle, 234–8, 240, 247
political parties, 13–14, 17, 34, 37, 182, 187
politicisation, 145, 157–8
Post Office, 2, 6, 7, 8–10, 13, 20
Postmaster General, 4, 8, 12, 15, 16, 20, 22, 25, 27, 40, 231–2, 299
Poulson trial, 173
power of broadcasting, 17, 34–5, 188, 194
press, *see* newspaper press
press, freedom of the, 39, 187
'pressure from without', 189–90, 210
producers (also directors), 80, 100, 104–105, 110, 128, 135, 139–40, 148, 213–214, 218–20, 244, 249, 258, 277–8
producers' assistants, 80, 87
production team, 81, 264–5, 271
professionalism, professionals, xi, 76, 97–9, 106–8, 110–11, 122–32, 134, 136–41, 143, 145, 173, 184–5, 190–1, 209, 215, 221, 246, 253, 264, 271–2
programme budget estimates, 212, 232, 234
programme ethos, 150–2, 159
programme planning (planning, scheduling), 49–50, 56, 234–8
pseudo-charisma, 284
public opinion, 176–7, 186, 190
public service broadcasting, 9–10, 11, 19, 35–7, 40–1, 43, 62, 108–11, 122, 125–6, 135–6, 145, 149, 155, 180, 260, 263, 295
Pym, W. St J., 60

quasi-autonomous non-governmental organisations (Quangos), 192–3
'Question of Ulster', 14, 299, 300

radical underground, 71, 272
Radio Corporation of America (RCA), 3–5, 7
ratings, 52–3, 134, 136, 152, 165, 219, 302
Reaction Index (R.I.), Audience Response (A.R.), 134, 138, 140–1, 303
Reader, W. J., 126, 304
rebels, 221–2
're-contextualising' 203
referral-up, 151, 195
Reith, Sir J. C. W., 1, 14, 16–26, 26–7, 36, 37, 40, 42, 60, 63, 79, 96, 126, 144, 149, 155, 180–1, 217, 296, 300, 305
relativities, 95–6
responsibility, 134–5, 144, 159, 193
revenue expenditure, 224–7, 231–2
rhetoric of broadcasting, 197–9, 203, 209
Riddell, Lord, 180
rivalry, 48–51, 148, 170, 222, 289, 297
Roberts, B. C., 56, 59, 302
Roethlisberger, F. J., 308
role-reversal, 133, 220

Roosevelt, Franklin, D., 4, 182
Rothermere, Lord, 39, 305
Royal Commission on the Press (1947–1949), 39
Royal Commission on Trade Unions and Employers' Associations (Donovan Commission) (1966), 59, 302

satire, 204, 255
scheduling, *see* programme planning
Schools Broadcasting, x, xiv, 82, 145–146, 216
segmentation, 107, 217, 221–3, 273
Select Committee on Broadcasting etc., of Proceedings in the House of Commons (1966), 300
Select Committee on Nationalised Industries (1972), 13, 159, 299, 304
Selsdon Committee on Television (1935), 10
Selsdon, Lord, *see* Mitchell-Thomson
short-term contracts, 144, 276–8
'shorts agreement', 64
Simmel, Georg, 41
Simon, Lord, 28, 30–2, 301
Silvey, R , 302
size, 68–9, 264
Smith, Adam, 128, 304
Smith, Anthony, 32, 157, 162, 164, 195, 208, 301, 304, 305
Snowdon, Mrs, 29
social distance, 101–3
social drama of work, 131
social interaction, 284–90
social networks, 81–4
social self, 280–3, 293–5
social status, 100
sound supervisors, 89, 275
specialisation, 58, 106, 131
square, 100
Staff Administration, 23–4, 220
Staff Association, 60–5
staff costs, 227–8, 237
staff numbers, 21, 22–3, 46, 267
Stalker, G. M., 298
Stanton, Frank, 186–7
state, 35, 40
strike, 91–4
studio crew, 81–2, 100, 104–5, 264–5, 269–71
studio engineers, 265–7
studio gallery, 80, 144
studios, 80, 104–5, 213–14
success system, 115–17
Supply, 48–50
Swann, Sir Michael, 33, 124
Sykes Committee (Broadcasting Committee, 1923), 5, 7, 35, 110, 299

Talks, 100, 147, 164, 253
Taylor, A. J. P., 39, 42, 302, 305
Technical Operations Manager (T.O.M., later Technical Manager, T.M.1), 80–3, 89–90, 127, 219, 268, 274–5, 303
Television Centre, 74, 79–82, 88, 91, 99, 107, 152, 166, 198
theatre, 104, 128, 139
Thompson, E. P., 84, 303
Tracey, Michael, 300
trade unions, 17, 56–70, 89–95, 191, 269, 272, 275
trivialisation, 40, 53

Ullswater Committee (Broadcasting Committee, 1935), 10, 11–13, 20–1, 25, 33, 60, 181, 299, 300
United States, 2, 3–6, 8, 37, 41, 57, 181, 186–8, 193, 207–9

Variety Artistes Federation, 61
vision-mixer, 80

wage-drift, 91
Waldman, R., 301, 302
Watergate, 173, 207–8
Watson, Steven, 305
Webb, Beatrice, 17, 300
Weber, Max, xvi, 74, 298
Weekly Programme Review, 74, 123, 246, 258
Whale, John, 194, 207–8, 306, 307
Wheldon, Huw, 55, 302
white-collar unions, 56–60, 95, 126
Whitehead, Philip, 205–6, 306
'Whitley Document', 21–2, 301
Whitley, John, 20, 22, 29
Whitley, Oliver J., vii, ix, x, xiv, xv, xvi, 13
Wilson, Harold, 192, 232
Winston, Brian, 141–2
wireless exchange stations, 10–11
working community, 86–8

'Yesterday's Men', 14, 33, 169, 184–5, 192, 205, 300